W9-CXT-646

THE REFORMATION AND THE
TOWNS IN ENGLAND

THE REFORMATION AND THE TOWNS IN ENGLAND

Politics and Political Culture, c.1540–1640

ROBERT TITTLER

Professor of History
Concordia University, Montreal

CLARENDON PRESS · OXFORD

1998

Oxford University Press, Great Clarendon Street, Oxford OX2 6DP
Oxford New York
Athens Auckland Bangkok Bogota Bombay Buenos Aires
Calcutta Cape Town Dar es Salaam Delhi Florence Hong Kong Istanbul
Karachi Kuala Lumpur Madras Madrid Melbourne Mexico City
Nairobi Paris Singapore Taipei Tokyo Toronto Warsaw
and associated companies in
Berlin Ibadan

Oxford is a registered trade mark of Oxford University Press

Published in the United States
by Oxford University Press Inc., New York

British Library Cataloguing in Publication Data
Data available

Library of Congress Cataloging in Publication Data
Tittler, Robert.
The Reformation and the towns in England : politics and political
culture, c.1540–1640 / Robert Tittler.
p. cm.
Includes bibliographical references.
1. Great Britain—Politics and government—1485–1603. 2. Great Britain—
Politics and government—1603–1649. 3. City and town life—England—
History—16th century. 4. City and town life—England—History—17th century.
5. Political culture—England—History—16th century. 6. Political culture—
England—History—17th century. 7. Cities and towns—England—
History—16th century. 8. Cities and towns—England—History—
17th century. 9. Reformation—England. I. Title.
DA315.T58 1998
942.05—dc21 97–47540
ISBN 0–19–820718–2

1 3 5 7 9 10 8 6 4 2

Typeset by Jayvee, Trivandrum, India
Printed in Great Britain
on acid free paper by
Biddles Ltd., Guildford and King's Lynn

ACKNOWLEDGEMENTS

This book reflects an interest in Early Modern English provincial towns dating back to the mid-1970s, and it draws upon research undertaken ever since that time. Though from time to time I have stopped to explore particular points (some of which are reconsidered here) and to discuss some of them in print, this is as comprehensive a summary of my adventures with the subject as I expect to produce.

Carried out, as it must be in my case, mostly from across the Atlantic, long research on any phase of British History requires steady funding. Research on local history, with its requisite labours in local archives, requires yet more. Even BritRail passes (and cheese sandwiches from the buffet trolley) and a captive's tour of the Lesser Bed and Breakfast Establishments of the Realm add up over time. This book could not possibly have been written without the generous support of several agencies. The US National Endowment of the Humanities provided a 'Travel to Collections Grant' in the spring of 1990 and a Research Fellowship to support a term's sabbatical in 1991. The Social Science and Humanities Research Council of Canada provided a Research Fellowship for the period 1991–4, and the American Philosophical Society provided a grant in 1995 which allowed me to take up a Visiting Fellowship at Clare Hall, Cambridge University, in Easter Term of that year. Concordia University's General Research Fund contributed to other expenses along the way. I am very thankful to all these patrons.

I do not work well or happily in isolation, and I am thus heavily indebted to those who have allowed me to try out versions of chapters on their seminars or colloquia outside of Montreal and Quebec. These kind and patient people include Daniel Woolf at Dalhousie; Mark Kishlansky at Harvard; Patrick Collinson, Keith Wrightson, and Tim Stretton at Cambridge; Caroline Barron, Vanessa Harding, David Ormrod, Negley Harte, and Professor the Earl Russell at the Institute of Historical Research in London; Alexandra Johnston and Sally-Beth MacLean at Records of Early English Drama and Joseph Black of University College, all three in the University of Toronto; and Ian Archer of Oxford (and of the pre-Modern Towns Group).

I have refrained from burdening anyone with the whole manuscript, but a number of worthy friends, fine scholars all, have given generously of their time and learning in reading parts, helping me reflect on ideas, and responding to specific questions. Though I alone remain responsible for everything written hereafter (and though I have not always listened to good advice), this would undoubtedly have been a far lesser book without the help of Patrick Collinson, David Dean, Kit French, Paul Griffiths, Dale Hoak, Alexandra Johnston, Norman Jones, Sally-Beth MacLean, Ben McRee, Shannon McSheffrey, James Moore, Catherine Patterson, Susan Reynolds, Michael Schoenfeldt, Gary Shaw, Malcolm Smuts, Tim Stretton, Joe Ward, Joanna Woodall, Daniel Woolf, and Keith Wrightson. I am grateful to them all.

I am delighted to acknowledge the research assistance of Michael Berlin, Marilyn Livingstone, Graham Dawson, Tanya Blumel, and Janis Housez. Stephen Porter, Ronald Rudin, and Michael MacCarthy-Morrogh have provided important encouragement at crucial stages.

I am pleased to thank the publishers and journals which have kindly published essays which I have drawn on extensively in this book. Parts of Chapters 5 and 8 have appeared in 'The Incorporation of Boroughs, 1540–1558', *History*, 62/204 (Feb. 1977), 24–42. Parts of Chapter 12 have appeared in ' "Seats of Honor, Seats of Power": The Symbolism of Public Seating in the English Urban Community, c.1560–1620', *Albion*, 24/2 (Summer 1992), 205–23; in 'Political Culture and the Built Environment in the English Country Town', in D. C. Hoak (ed.), *Tudor Political Culture* (Cambridge, 1995), 133–56; and in Robert Tittler, *Architecture and Power: The Town Hall and the English Urban Community, 1500–1640* (Oxford, 1991). Parts of Chapter 13 have appeared in 'Reformation, Civic Culture and Collective Memory in English Provincial Towns', *Urban History*, 24/3 (Dec. 1997), 283–300.

Parts of this book have been written at the Institute for Historical Research at London University (my academic 'home away from home' since 1968), at Fellowship House of the London Goodenough Trust (my residential 'home away from home'), and at Clare Hall, Cambridge (which is not like home at all but, in some ways, even better!). The bulk of it has been completed in Montreal with the resources of the Concordia Library. The staffs of many libraries and archives have been helpful over the years, but that at the Institute of Historical Research (especially Donald Munro and Clyve Jones)

and Concordia's Vanier Library (especially Judy Appleby, Luigina Vileno, Diana Maharaj, Ursula Hakien, Chris Bober, Marvin Orbach, and Wendy Knechtel) have been exceptionally professional, competent, and courteous. I also thank Raoul Antelme of Clare Hall for untangling the mysteries of the house computer system.

Most important, it is not everyone who can work an eight-hour day followed by a three-hour choir rehearsal and still have patience to hear about the vagaries of spousal research on pre-industrial English towns. My wife, Anne, has been my mainstay in all sorts of ways, most of them having nothing to do with academe.

R.T.

Montreal, Canada
March 1997

TABLE OF CONTENTS

ABBREVIATIONS

BL	British Library
CPR	*Calendar of Patent Rolls*
DNB	*Dictionary of National Biography*
Ec.HR	*Economic History Review*
OED	*Oxford English Dictionary*, unabridged
PRO	Public Record Office
REED	*Records of Early English Drama*
STC	*Short Title Catalogue*
TRHS	*Transactions of the Royal Historical Society*
VCH	*Victoria County History*

PART I
Introduction

I

English Towns in the Age of the Reformation

An effort to explore the relationship between the English Reformation and the provincial towns, especially from an urban perspective, seems long overdue. It has been, after all, more than two decades since the modern resurgence of interest in Pre-Modern towns began. Foundations laid by the formative work of, for example, Peter Clark and Paul Slack and their associates,[1] and of the Open University course (A. 322) on the same subject, have supported substantial further investigation in the form of graduate theses, monographs, and journal essays. Town 'biographies'[2] have begun to give way to more topical studies of the provincial urban experience, some founded on the study of particular towns, and some more widely inclusive.[3] Issues such as the nature of the urban economy and of particular social groups, the relation of town and nation, and the nature of urban popular and political cultures have become prominent concerns of current research, and have pushed our understanding of urban society in the Early Modern period a long way forward.

And yet we still have an imprecise sense of sequence about the

[1] e.g. esp. the essays in Peter Clark and Paul Slack (eds.), *Crisis and Order in English Towns, 1500–1700* (1972); and Clark and Slack's own *English Towns in Transition, 1500–1700* (1976).

[2] Some of the best of these include Wallace T. MacCaffrey's pioneering 1958 study of Exeter which, once scholarship caught up with it, was reprinted in 1975 by the Open University as *Exeter, 1540–1640*, and the following sampling: Alan Dyer, *The City of Worcester in the Sixteenth Century* (Leicester, 1973); John T. Evans, *Seventeenth Century Norwich* (Oxford, 1979); and D. M. Palliser, *Tudor York* (Oxford, 1979).

[3] Prominent examples include Charles Phythian-Adams's imaginative and precocious *Desolation of a City: Coventry and the Urban Crisis of the Late Middle Ages* (Cambridge, 1979); and the following works of the late 1980s and early 1990s: Peter Borsay, *The English Urban Renaissance: Culture and Society in the Provincial Town, 1660–1770* (Oxford, 1989); David Harris Sacks, *The Widening Gate: Bristol and the Atlantic Economy, 1450–1700* (Berkeley and Los Angeles, 1991); Robert Tittler, *Architecture and Power: The Town Hall and the English Urban Community, 1500–1640* (Oxford, 1991); and David Underdown, *Fire from Heaven: Life in an English Town in the Seventeenth Century* (London and New Haven, 1992).

subject: an absence of commonly accepted chronological boundaries, and an unrealized notion of what the salient features of
particular periods in 'Pre-Modern' urban history might be. While
one would not want to evoke either an overly Whiggish sense of
teleological development or an unduly rigid chronological scheme,
the business of periodization, the division of the past according to
the salient characteristics of chronological periods, does still form an
important way to define the nature and boundaries of past times.
Period labels continue to provide a useful shorthand for successive
eras. While these labels should never be applied too strictly, the task
of assigning them does compel us carefully to examine what seems
essential about a particular time.

The traditional periodization for English History as a whole, which
may be seen in the generic titles of our textbooks, derives from the
classic political, national, and narrative approach to history. Here
such phenomena as dynastic successions, major wars, and so forth
take centre stage. Yet labels designed for traditional chronologies
may not be very helpful when applied to new subjects. This has been
most pointedly observed in recent years by the late Joan Kelly-Gadol
who asked, reasonably enough, whether 'The Renaissance' should
be taken as a useful label for those exploring the field of Women's
History.[4] In her view—a view which many found overwhelmingly
persuasive—the answer was 'no'. Indeed, practitioners of many
newer approaches to the past have been moved to seek definitional
boundaries of their own, although some, pursuing a Braudelian preference for seeing things over the *longue durée*, seem more interested
in rejecting chronological boundaries than fixing them.

Like Women's History, Urban History is also a newish and non-
traditional sub-field. And like Kelly-Gadol, those who seek to
explore and chart the extent of English Urban History may not find
very useful the conventional period labels or the events on which
they have been predicated. In the Braudelian tradition, some have
preferred to emphasize the essentially unchanging nature of urban

---

[4] Joan Kelly-Gadol, 'Did Women have a Renaissance?', reprinted in R. Bridenthal, C. Koontz, and S. Stuard (eds.), *Becoming Visible: Women in European History*,
2nd edn. (Boston, 1987), 175–202. To pursue the analogy between urban and other
fields in this regard, it may be instructive to note that Kelly-Gadol's work and that of
a few others has generated debates about periodization and continuity in both
Women's History and Medieval History. A useful summary and contribution to
these continuing quandaries may be found in Judith M. Bennett, 'Medieval Women,
Modern Women: Across the Great Divide', in David Aers (ed.), *Culture and History,
1350–1600: Essays on English Communities, Identities and Writing* (London, 1992),
147–75.

society for the whole span between the end of the Middle Ages and the advent of Industrialization.[5] Yet this has been less apparent in the writing of English social and urban history than of Continental. Most who write in or about England have looked more closely for signs of change than of continuity. They tend to act like what J. H. Hexter once defined as 'splitters' rather than 'lumpers'.[6] Since the resurgence of interest in English Urban History in the 1970s, these splitters have employed a variety of period labels to demarcate one era from another while producing only partial consensus or precision regarding their use. Pioneers such as Clark and Slack have implicitly recognized a distinctive discontinuity with medieval patterns, but have remained tentative about defining boundaries. Tellingly, the titles of most of their works fell back upon the convenient but still arbitrary divisions provided by the centuries: 1500–1700,[7] 1600–1800,[8] 1700–1800,[9] and so forth. Although works such as Peter Borsay's *The English Urban Renaissance: Culture and Society in the Provincial Town, 1660–1770* have posited an appropriate periodization for a somewhat later chapter in this story, most who work on towns of an earlier time still fall back on such designations as, for example, 'Towns from 1500 to 1700', or 'Tudor Towns', or 'Tudor and Stuart Towns', as if 'Tudor' and/or 'Stuart' had particular meaning for what we do.

It must be admitted that in this fuzziness may rest great wisdom: perhaps more than one realized in setting out to assail it. But it does beg a number of questions, and one of them is the question of what the term 'Reformation' itself might usefully be taken to mean to the urban historian. This is less of a problem for those who write about doctrine. They now take 'Reformation' chiefly to mean the destruction of traditional Roman Catholic worship as the legal and normative faith, and the substitution of a form of Protestantism as the

---

[5] e.g. Jan DeVries, 'Patterns of Urbanization in Preindustrial Europe, 1500–1800', in H. Schmal (ed.), *Patterns of European Urbanization since 1500* (1981), 77–109; P. M. Hohenberg and L. H. Lees, *The Making of Urban Europe, 1000–1950* (Cambridge, Mass., 1985); and C. R. Friedrichs, *The Early Modern City, 1450–1750* (1995).

[6] Hexter, 'The Burden of Proof', *TLS*, 24 Oct. 1975, 1250–2. Hexter considered 'splitters' to be those who concentrated on the differences between two forms, and 'lumpers' those who emphasized the similarities instead.

[7] e.g. Clark and Slack (eds.), *Crisis and Order in English Towns*; Clark and Slack, *English Towns in Transition*; John Patten, *English Towns, 1500–1700* (1978); A. L. Beier and Roger Finlay (eds.), *The Making of the Metropolis: London, 1500–1700* (1986).

[8] e.g. Peter Clark (ed.), *The Transformation of English Provincial Towns, 1600–1800* (1984).

[9] Penelope J. Corfield, *The Impact of English Towns, 1700–1800* (Oxford, 1982).

normative persuasion of most English men and women, a watershed which consensus has recently located in the 1570s and 1580s rather than in the 1540s.[10] But to the urban historian it may bear additional or alternative connotations. In this the dissolutions of the 1530s and 1540s, central to what remains of the term 'Henrician Reformation', must be a prominent feature.

The object of this study is to see if the period at hand could be appropriately labelled for students not of national but of urban history, and—the metropolis of London being unique—of provincial urban history at that. Thanks especially to those pioneering works of the 1970s, we certainly do not lack salient characteristics for such a construct. The economic state of towns, the shifts in urban occupations and in the economic structure of the urban network, the consolidation of oligarchy in town governance, and the increasing political importance of towns in the affairs of the nation, have all commanded our attention in recent years. What has been lacking is a chronological framework upon which to hang such issues, and of course a more comprehensive conceptualization of the ideas and events which would support such a framework.

The potential for such a construct seems to have emerged from another direction entirely: not from urban historians working outwards from a prime interest in towns as such, but especially from one particular historian working from the standpoint of another subdiscipline and towards urban history. In delivering the Third Anstey Memorial Lectures in the University of Kent at Canterbury in May 1986, Professor Patrick Collinson deplored the peripheral position accorded by urban historians to the Reformation, and asked 'What did the Reformation do to or for the English towns?'[11] He appears to have directed his challenge to Clark, Slack, and their compatriots. Collinson noted, rightly enough, that, though the Reformation received 'due mention' in their work, it had also remained 'peripheral' to their main concerns. Those concerns were principally economic and social so that, to quote Collinson, 'the dominant theme in the literature is urban decay'.[12]

---

[10] Perhaps the most laconic statement of this view is Professor Collinson's own: 'I would even be prepared to state, crudely and flatly, that the Reformation was something which happened in the reigns of Elizabeth and James I', though many others now share that view (Patrick Collinson, *The Birthpangs of Protestant England* (London and Basingstoke, 1988), p. ix).

[11] Published as *The Birthpangs of Protestant England: Religious and Cultural Change in the Sixteenth and Seventeenth Centuries* (London and Basingstoke, 1988), 49.

[12] Ibid. 35.

In response to this thrust, Collinson sought to fill in the blank spaces on the other side of the equation, and thus to place religion closer to the heart of the story of sixteenth-century towns. 'It will somewhat redress the historiographical balance', he continued, 'if we insist that the Reformation was much more than a side-show'.[13] The remainder of his discussion emphasized several points which must be considered. First, Collinson took the Reformation principally to mean doctrinal change. Consequently, he considered it not to have come to fruition before the 1570s, when (as it now appears) that doctrinal change seems first to have prevailed as the majority view in at least most parts of the realm.[14] And finally, he posited an answer to his leading question. Although it by no means does justice to the complexity or eloquence of his argument so to describe it, the gist of this is that the Reformation provided the impetus for urban leaders to envision the ideal urban community as the 'city on the hill'. By the 1570s Protestantism had begun to provide an ideology for urban rule which was disciplined, moralistic, deferential, and doctrinally grounded. (It may of course be argued that sundry aspects of traditional Catholic ideology did no less in their time, but Catholicism obviously ceased being able to perform those functions by the Elizabethan era.)

It is very difficult to quibble with Collinson's argument so far as it goes, just as it is difficult to make more than relatively minor adjustments to the position of the urbanists on most of the issues which they have taken up.[15] But it seems obvious that the two approaches were not geared towards precisely the same ends, and thus are not, strictly speaking, entirely comparable. They differ in their fundamental perspective on the past, one being principally doctrinal and ideological, the other economic and social. They differ, too, in what they take the term 'Reformation' to mean (though, as Collinson says, his target group does not make much use of the term at all), and thus what precise time frame this term might embrace. To Collinson, emphasizing both doctrinal definition and the ascendancy of

---

[13] Ibid. 36.

[14] The passage must be cited in full: 'It is only in the 1570s that the historically minded insomniac goes to sleep counting Catholics rather than Protestants, since only then did they begin to find themselves in a minority situation. I would even be prepared to assert, crudely and flatly, that the Reformation was something which happened in the reigns of Elizabeth and James I' (Collinson, *Birthpangs*, p. ix).

[15] A conference held at the Institute of Historical Research to mark the twentieth anniversary of the publication of *Crisis and Order*, for example, expressed general admiration for how remarkably well the essential themes had stood the test of time.

Protestantism as the view of the majority, this begins somewhere around the 1570s. Clark, Slack, et al. are even less precise: they employ the labels 'Pre-Modern', 'Tudor and/or Tudor and Stuart', and so forth, and most of their titles add on the arbitrary dates '1500–1700'. Yet the two approaches do have a lot in common. They share an abiding interest in urban society, they take up a number of the same issues, and their efforts embrace both Collinson's entire time frame and more. If Professor Collinson has succeeded in righting the balance by putting the Reformation more centrally in the view of urban historians, he has not quite left us with a new synthesis with which to describe the state of English towns themselves—as opposed to the state of religion or popular belief in those towns—at the time.

It appears that more might be said to bring the two approaches closer together towards this goal. In the context at hand, religious doctrine ought not to be entirely divorced from economic, social, or political reality. The distinctive shapes of English Protestantism apparent by *c.*1600 may to some extent have come about by the pushing and pulling of forces in its immediate environment, certainly including the outlook of contemporary urban elites. In addition, by any definition and in any number of ways, the Reformation does seem a central and formative experience in almost every individual town.

In seeking to work through the dilemma proposed by the two approaches to Collinson's question, one might well propose a third position. This posits the identification of an 'era' in English *Urban* History and recognizes what appears to be a series of unifying characteristics in that time (the Reformation surely amongst them), but it does not pretend to offer a comprehensive study of all aspects of urban life. Though incorporating the concerns of both schools of thought, the suggested approach emphasizes characteristics of urban political culture and developments principally of a political, social, and economic nature. To the urban historian following this approach, the answer to Professor Collinson's question might well begin with the Henrician Reformation of the 1530s and 1540s, and with the great upheavals, not merely in doctrine, but in land ownership and jurisdiction in English towns set in motion by the ecclesiastical Dissolutions of that time. This adds a chronological boundary to the social and economic approach by recognizing the Dissolutions as the most seismic event for most towns in a very great while. It also suggests a context for Professor Collinson's concerns by marking a

point of acceleration in those events—the tightening of oligarchic rule and its extension to a greater number of towns—which made Protestant doctrine so welcome to the 'middling' and 'better sort' of townsmen a generation or two further on.

What has been proposed here might well be called 'The Age of the Reformation in English Urban History', beginning around the year 1540, and especially embracing two salient themes played out against a particular background. The first theme involves a sequence of events and responses set into motion by the sudden availability of a great amount of urban property, by way of the Henrician and Edwardian Dissolutions, throughout the realm. This was often followed by the pressing desire of those who governed in provincial towns to obtain such resources and to possess them for their communities (putting aside for the present desires for personal gain as well) in a secure manner. In turn, such acquisitive aspirations often required a greater formalization of local governing authority. It prompted a concerted quest for the requisite authority through a variety of legal and constitutional devices. Finally, local authorities utilized such a quest for authority not only in order to possess and manage new resources in the community, but also to fortify and extend their own positions of authority over their fellows. This theme, then, embodies questions of material resources, legal authority, and political power.

The second and closely related broad theme embraces elements of a social, ideological, and cultural nature. Prior to the 1530s medieval Catholic belief and practice had come to form an essential underpinning, not only for a religious culture and an attendant ideal of social harmony, but for the goals of hierarchy, order, and discipline, which were essential to a well-ordered society at every level. In all sorts of ways the abrupt statutory destruction of this distinctive political culture proved deeply crippling to traditional urban political life. It left governing authorities without their accustomed means of engendering loyalty, deference, and obedience. It left townsmen and women without their traditional recourse for social mediation. It created a gaping void where a viable political (as well as religious) culture had long served. These deprivations provided a characteristic and very grave challenge for the civil order of English towns, and for the civic authorities entrusted to maintain that order.

In effect, the consequent search for a new civic political culture, and especially for new discursive strategies to uphold the civic order, became a central preoccupation of town and central government

alike. It is to this search that Professor Collinson's observations about the civic ideology of Protestantism become particularly germane, though, as we will see, the consequent ideology of 'godly rule' was by no means alone in filling the void at hand.

Both of these themes, that of property, jurisdiction, and empowerment on the one hand and that of religious and then political culture on the other, emerged more or less directly out of the legislation of the Henrician and Edwardian Reformation, and especially from those statutes which dissolved various religious institutions and undermined many aspects of traditional faith and practice. Whether we take that legislative campaign as the beginning of the Protestant ascendancy or not, we cannot ignore its dramatic and destructive impact on the traditional culture and institutions of English local society. It allows us to take the Reformation events of the 1530s and 1540s as the titular and most compelling element in our thematic approach, and to treat these few years as a turning point in urban history.

In describing the contextual background against which these central themes must be understood, the dramatically accelerated pace of economic and social change apparent by the 1530s and 1540s, bringing to an end an era of relative stagnation extending well back into the previous century, seems especially striking. It, too, must be considered, and the fact that these developments followed a similar chronology strengthens the significance of the period from *c*. 1540 as a turning point. On the heels of those developments, led especially by a substantial and rapid rise in population, came the pervasive reality of epidemic disease, inflation, crime, rootlessness, and unrest (not to mention acute contemporary awareness of these phenomena) as prominent features both of contemporary life and political discourse. And though these factors pertained to all parts of the realm, they were most acutely experienced in the urban rather than the rural milieu.

An equally consequential factor lies in the centralization and expansion of the Tudor state in these years. We see this in many forms, but few are as dramatic as the staggering outpouring of regulatory proclamations and statutes emanating from Crown and Parliament from about this time forward. These had the collective effect of vesting an unprecedented range of new powers and responsibilities in the officials of the corporate towns and boroughs, and of transforming the traditional parish from an exclusively religious to a partially civic body of local administration. Such demands on local

officials arose especially as the relative social and economic stagnation of the fifteenth century gave way, by the 1530s and 1540s, to the much more dynamic changes of the sixteenth. In the case both of boroughs and parishes, these changes marked a sharp break with tradition.

And a third contextual factor, much less commonly remarked upon, lies in the relative weakness in England of traditions of urbanism of the sort which had emerged over the course of centuries in Continental cultures such as those of Northern Italy or the Low Countries. As Lawrence Manley has recently noted, 'Early Modern England was an *urbanizing* society lacking indigenous traditions of *urbanism*.'[16] Save for London, whose population rose from about 50,000 at the turn of the sixteenth century to between 300,000 and 350,000 by the outbreak of the Civil War 140 years later, England boasted virtually no urban areas in the population range of *c.*25,000 to 100,000 to take their place with perhaps a hundred of that size on the Continent. The predominant culture of the nation no less than its governing structure remained essentially feudal in nature and still agrarian and even chivalric in its values and assumptions. Its artistic and literary models continued to be dominated by neo-feudal and even chivalric themes well into the latter half of the sixteenth century. While some sixteenth-century writers absorbed a more positive appreciation of the urban milieu from their reception of Renaissance culture from abroad, most continued on into the last decades of the century with the idea that the city served both as a place to make one's fortune and then to be left behind for the more genteel and socially respectable milieu of the countryside.[17] If even the best of our studies on London have had little to say of the urban consciousness of its residents,[18] how strongly could it have been felt in the provincial towns of the realm? This shallowness of urban consciousness in a cultural milieu which was still essentially agrarian and aristocratic undoubtedly seriously impinged on the urban identity. It could only have hindered civic efforts to assimilate the large

---

[16] Lawrence Manley, *Literature and Culture in Early Modern London* (Cambridge, 1995), 15. Manley's use of the term refers to urban character or identity. It should not be confused with the French *urbanisme*, which connotes a concern for urban planning.

[17] These themes are developed in detail by Manley, *Literature and Culture*, *passim*.

[18] e.g. Steve Rappaport, *Worlds Within Worlds: Structures of Life in Sixteenth Century London* (Cambridge, 1989); and Ian W. Archer, *The Pursuit of Stability: Social Relations in Elizabethan London* (Cambridge, 1991).

number of migrants flocking in during this era, or to come to grips with myriad social and economic changes which were especially pronounced at the time.

Taken together, these sundry factors created a difficult situation for those who governed the six hundred and fifty or so English towns of the day, and for a ruling dynasty virtually obsessed with the problem of maintaining order. Sharp economic and social changes threatened instability just as Crown and Parliament uprooted the traditional and doctrinally based civic culture upon which urban governance had long relied. Both themes proceeded in the face of shallow traditions of urban identity and values to begin with.

Lest this seem too simplistic a model, and lest we forget W. G. Hoskins's wise caveat that only a fool would seek to generalize about the history of English towns, let us make at least a few qualifications before proceeding. First, we should recognize that the incidence of the social, economic, and political changes listed above was not by any means evenly distributed amongst towns of all types and sizes at the same time. In some (especially those oldest and most politically autonomous) towns, they took place well before the period at hand. The emergence of a more rigidly hierarchical political format, for example, especially in the guise of oligarchic rule, already had a long history by the sixteenth century.[19] In other towns, by contrast, it came later or not at all. For many of the very smallest of towns, particularly those like Cerne Abbas, Godmanchester, or Battle, whose very *raison d'être* was bound up with the operation of an ecclesiastical foundation, the Reformation virtually meant the end of urban status altogether. In addition, there were a goodly number of smallish seigneurial boroughs to whose lay control the Reformation made virtually no difference even up to and beyond the Municipal Corporations Act of 1835, and some others in which the transition from ecclesiastical to lay lordship allowed for similarly little autonomous development. As the argument unfolds below, further typological distinctions will become evident. In the meantime, in positing the salient characteristics of urban politics and

---

[19] Amongst scholars of medieval towns, it was noted in detail a full century ago by 'Mrs. J. R.' [Alice Stopford] Green, in *Town Life in the Fifteenth Century* (2 vols.; 1894), vol. ii, chap. 10, with reference to Lincoln, Lynn, Norwich, and Oxford, and by such more modern scholars as e.g. Francis Hill, *Medieval Lincoln* (Cambridge, 1965); Colin Platt, *Medieval Southampton* (1973); Robert S. Gottfried, *Bury St Edmunds and the Urban Crisis: 1270–1539* (Princeton, 1982); R. H. Britnell, *Growth and Decline in Colchester, 1300–1525* (Cambridge, 1986); and David Gary Shaw, *The Creation of a Community: The City of Wells in the Middle Ages* (Oxford, 1993).

political culture in this particular period, which is the chief point of the exercise, this study somewhat arbitrarily selects the most prominent tendencies of the conspicuously large number of towns under the lens. It is probably the best one may say of most time periods which may be labelled distinctive eras.

Having laid out the context and aims of the study at hand, we can move on to propose that the chosen themes seem to produce an overall shift in the political ethos or political culture of a good many English urban communities. Prior to that shift we find a strong sense of fellowship and civic identity amongst the freemanry, a generally malleable, fluid, and even egalitarian tone to political relations, and a doctrinally informed culture which more or less successfully harmonized inequalities amongst most residents. Following that shift we find that hierarchy, structural rigidity, and political as well as economic and social polarization became more prevalent, and that the harmonizing effect of traditional cultural forms had often been destroyed. Treading ever so carefully, so as not to invoke an antiquated picture of happy townsmen cavorting around the maypole in some mythical past, we might still characterize the former as reflecting something close to an ethos of 'community'; the latter as reflecting something closer to conventional notions of 'oligarchy'. This should be taken here to mean not only the literal 'rule by a few', but a number of related concepts as well: a political system which is strongly hierarchical, relatively static, and elitist; one in which the lines of authority flow vertically rather than horizontally; and one in which the general run, not only of residents but even of freemen, have relatively little influence over the course of government and administration.

The word 'community', as we know it, or *communitas* as it might have been rendered at the time, has been notoriously difficult to pin down with precision. One modern effort to do so came up with no fewer than ninety-four definitions, but found little consensus amongst them save for a common concern for people in a group, which does not get us very far.[20] The use of the term in the following pages will become clearer as the discussion unfolds, but a few points may well be made here at the outset.

Typical of the criticisms which have been made of the term's use is the recent sharp attack from a number of Medievalists and Early

---

[20] C. Bell and H. Newby (eds.), *Community Studies* (1984), 27, as cited in Alan Macfarlane with Sarah Harrison and Charles Jardine (eds.), *Reconstructing Historical Communities* (Cambridge, 1977), 2.

Modernists.[21] Yet that attack seems focused most sharply on the use
of 'community' in reference to the county—as in, for example,
Professor Everitt's notion of the 'county community'.[22] It has
additionally been questioned by those who read more into its use
than has often been intended, and by those who insist on definitions
which may be expressed in crisp, precise, and even statistical terms.[23]
One hopes its use in this study is sufficiently well defined to convey
useful meaning, but also sufficiently imprecise not to be subject to
this sort of postmodernist, particularist, and not in the end entirely
productive onslaught.

Be that as it may, those who still accept a valid use of the term
share some consensus on its meaning.[24] They emphasize especially
the ideas of mutual identity and obligation within a defined social
group. They emphasize, too, that 'community' by no means pre-
cludes either hierarchy or conflict,[25] or a degree of inequality in

[21] Especially and typically, Richard Smith, ' "Modernization" and the Corporate
Medieval Village Community in England: Some Sceptical Reflections', in A. R. H.
Baker and D. Gregory (eds.), *Explorations in Historical Geography* (Cambridge,
1984), 140–79; Miri Rubin, 'Small Groups: Identity and Solidarity in the Late Middle
Ages', in Jennifer Kermode (ed.), *Enterprise and Individuals in Fifteenth Century
England* (Stroud, Glos. and Wolfeboro Falls, NH, 1991), 132–50; and Christine Car-
penter, 'Gentry and Community in Medieval England', *Journal of British Studies*,
33/4 (Oct. 1994), 340–80.

[22] See e.g. Ann Hughes, 'Warwickshire on the Eve of the Civil War: A County
Community?', *Midland History*, 7 (1982), 42–72, and *Politics, Society and Civil War in
Warwickshire, 1620–1660* (Cambridge, 1987); A. J. Pollard, *Northeast England
During the Wars of the Roses* (Oxford, 1990), *passim*; Carpenter, 'Gentry and
Community'.

[23] Some of these demands on the use of the term appear in Rubin, 'Small Groups:
Identity and Solidarity in the Late Middle Ages', and Carpenter, 'Gentry and
Community'.

[24] Those who accept the term in one sense or another in reference to the period at
hand here are perhaps too numerous to catalogue exhaustively. However, amongst
the most accessible defences of the term as it may be applied to late medieval urban
life the following stand out: Susan Reynolds, *Kingdoms and Communities in Western
Europe 900–1300* (Oxford, 1984); Gervase Rosser, esp. in *Medieval Westminster
1200–1540* (Oxford, 1989) and 'Going to the Fraternity Feast: Commensality and
Social Relations in Late Medieval England', *Journal of British Studies*, 33/4 (Oct.
1994), 430–46; Christopher Dyer, 'The English Medieval Community and its
Decline', ibid. 407–29; Ben McRee, 'Charity and Gild Solidarity in Late Medieval
England', *Journal of British Studies*, 32/3 (July 1993), 195–225; and Shaw, *Creation of
a Community*.

[25] See e.g. G. Rosser, 'Communities of Parish and Guild in the Late Middle Ages',
in S. J. Wright (ed.), *Parish, Church and People: Local Studies in Lay Religion,
1350–1750* (1988), 29–55, and esp. 29–30; and Ben R. McRee, 'Unity or Division? The
Social Meaning of Guild Ceremony in Urban Communities', in Barbara A. Hanawalt
and Kathryn L. Reyerson (eds.), *City and Spectacle in Medieval Europe* (Minneapolis
and London, 1995), 189–207.

gender or in more general social and economic relations. Indeed, a goodly portion of the recent research on the late medieval town has emphasized characteristic elements of conflict and disharmony.[26]

Still, recent scholarship has also established that even when riven by strife, the local citizenry usually retained certain institutions, devices, and strategies designed to mediate social tensions, and that these mediatory instruments emanated from within rather than from outside the town.[27] Guilds and fraternities, for example, took care to resolve disputes amongst members, to mediate between members and the freemanry as a whole, and even to provide a common ground for townsmen and powerful residents of the hinterland. Their charitable activities defused potential discord stemming from economic deprivation; their codes of conduct helped establish and enforce an essential standard of civility.[28] Ceremonies and rituals, most of them linked to late medieval popular religion, provided similar strategies for mediation amongst townsmen, and between them and others, and even between the living and the deceased members of the same community.[29] A common sense of heritage, including the

[26] See e.g. A. F. Butcher, 'English Urban Society and the Urban Revolt of 1381', and B. Dobson, 'The Risings in York, Beverley and Scarborough, 1380–81', both in R. H. Hilton and T. S. Ashton (eds.), *The English Rising of 1381* (Cambridge, 1984), 84–111 and 112–42; Stephen Rigby, 'Urban "Oligarchy" in Late Medieval England', in J. A. F. Thompson (ed.), *Towns and Townspeople in the Fifteenth Century* (1988), 62–86; Gottfried, *Bury St Edmunds and the Urban Crisis*, chap. 6.

[27] This is emphasized in general in Ben McRee, 'Religious Gilds and Civic Order: The Case of Norwich in the Late Middle Ages', *Speculum*, 67 (1992), 69–97; 'Religious Gilds and the Regulation of Behavior in Late Medieval Towns', in J. Rosenthal and C. Richmond (eds.), *People, Politics and Community in the Late Middle Ages* (Gloucester, 1987), 108–22; and, most recently, 'Peacemaking and its Limits in Late Medieval Norwich', *English Historical Review*, 109 (1994), 831–66, the last-named work drawing in part on e.g. Phythian-Adams, *Desolation of a City*, pt. III; Rosser, *Medieval Westminster*, esp. chap. 9; Edward Powell, esp. in *Kinship, Law and Society: Criminal Justice in the Reign of Henry V* (Oxford, 1989); and Lorraine Attreed, 'Arbitration and the Growth of Urban Liberties in Late Medieval England', *Journal of British Studies*, 31/3 (July 1992), 205–35.

[28] This is emphasized, for example, in McRee, 'Religious Gilds and Civic Order'; 'Religious Gilds and the Regulation of Behavior', in Rosenthal and Richmond (eds.), *People, Politics and Community*; Barbara Hanawalt and Ben R. McRee, 'The Guilds of *Homo Prudens* in Late Medieval England', *Continuity and Change*, 7/2 (1992), 163–79; and Susan Brigden, 'Religion and Social Obligation in Early Sixteenth Century London', *Past and Present*, 103 (May 1984), 67–112.

[29] Important contributions include Susan Brigden, *London and the Reformation* (Oxford, 1989), chaps. 1 and 4; Brigden, 'Religion and Social Obligation'; Charles Phythian-Adams, 'Ceremony and the Citizen: The Communal Year at Coventry, 1450–1550', in Clark and Slack (eds.), *Crisis and Order in English Towns*, 57–85; Mervyn James, 'Ritual, Drama and Social Body in the Late Medieval English Town', *Past and Present*, 98 (Feb. 1983), 3–29.

operation of a collective memory and also often linked to religious practice, engendered a respect for common traditions and values.[30]

Of all the efforts to define the term 'community' in its historical dimension the working notion developed by Susan Reynolds in her study of medieval communities in Western Europe could be considered as a useful point of departure. Reynolds considered a community to comprise

people engaged in collective activities . . . which are characteristically determined and controlled less by formal regulations than by shared values and norms . . . relationships between members of the community are characteristically reciprocal, many-sided, and direct rather than being mediated through officials or rulers.[31]

Reynolds clearly did not mean to preclude the operation of formal bodies altogether, for she applied her definition to parishes, guilds, fraternities, villages, and towns. Both in the much earlier period which she studied and in subsequent centuries those institutions remained essential to the fabric of the medieval town. Yet she emphasized in particular the overwhelming importance of shared values and goals within those bodies, and amongst their members. She emphasized as well the essentially informal and horizontal ties amongst members of such groups. Nor does her definition insist on equality amongst members of such groups, merely a sharing of values. These seem to have included common notions of rights and responsibilities, of economic and social interest, of fairness and, by implication, of due process. Finally, she provides us with a model of social and political structure which, if not necessarily democratic or harmonious or entirely inclusive by any means, was also not in its essence hierarchical, autocratic, inflexible, exploitative, or (in the narrow and literal sense) oligarchic. Perhaps it need not be emphasized that all sorts of groups might fit these definitions. We should not assume that communities could not be multiple and overlapping. A master butcher in a pre-Reformation provincial town might thus be part of the community of freemen in his town, of the Butchers'

[30] Eamon Duffy, *The Stripping of the Altars: Traditional Religion in England, c.1400–1580* (New Haven and London, 1992), 327–37; Phythian-Adams, *Desolation of a City,* 170–9. For a classic exposition of this link in a Continental urban experience, see Edward Muir, *Civic Ritual in Renaissance Venice* (Princeton, 1981), and esp. chaps. 1–2.

[31] Reynolds, *Kingdoms and Communities in Western Europe,* 2. The following discussion of Reynolds's ideas derives from the introduction and esp. the first two chapters of this book.

Guild, of his parish, of his religious fraternity, of the Christian fellowship, and so forth.

These latter identities suggest another dimension of community: a thing of the mind, especially embracing cultural and religious values. Certainly, as we will see below, they comprised a large share of what English townsmen and women held in common on the eve of Reformation and, in some cases, long afterwards. And, although these values usually came to be expressed in formal laws and to be conveyed by specific institutions, Reynolds saw them as initially informal, unwritten, and deeply rooted in custom.

Though not meaning to ignore any of these possible dimensions of communal identification, this study deals especially with the community of local residents—the freemanry and its members' dependants—whom contemporaries themselves would identify as the townsmen and women of a particular place. It is this understanding which was expressed, for example, when in the year 1284 the townsmen of Lichfield sent a letter to King Edward I in which they referred to themselves as 'the Community of the City of Lichfield'. Characteristically, the grants they received from Edward I in 1285 and 1290, and from Edward III in 1345, were to 'the burgesses and goodmen of Lichfield': which employs the same usage. Even by that last date the townsmen seem not to have formed any guilds or similar governing—as opposed to purely devotional—bodies which would have indicated the beginnings of autonomous institutions.[32]

The changes at issue in this study do not of course begin from a standing start: the effort to identify an 'era' in English urban history should not obscure the fact that what we have here is merely a stage, however distinct, in a long continuum. Reynolds's observation of communities extended back to the tenth century, in which time she saw them as normal and common constructs for local social and political activities throughout most of Western Europe. Yet even as early as the twelfth century she detected a tendency towards a greater formalization in these activities, customs, and values. Acting principally according to the dictates of circumstance and the requirements of petitioning townsmen, the emerging authority of kings and magistrates, seigneurs and lawyers, began to encourage precise formulations for what had been customarily understood. In the course of these events local societies embarked upon that long, bumpy, and still somewhat uncharted passage away from the

[32] *VCH, Staffordshire*, 14 (1990), 75.

informality, mutuality, and reciprocity which had once and long prevailed.

Needless to say, that passage bore many twists and turns between the terminal point of Reynolds's study, at about the year 1300, and the point where our study begins. Yet thanks at least in part to the demographic contractions of the fourteenth century and the relative stagnation of centralized political authority in much of the fifteenth, the tendencies towards greater formalization in the conduct of local affairs had not proceeded as rapidly as they might well have done.

There were, to be sure, some especially older and larger towns, including Exeter, Norwich, York, Gloucester, and Bristol, which had enjoyed very considerable political autonomy from an early point, whose social and economic structures had become much more complex, and whose governments had come under the aegis of a narrow, elitist, and even self-selecting segment of the community. Here formalization had proceeded with the greatest expedition. Even though such towns may not have had the sort of charters of incorporation which would come to be standardized, formalized, and very common in the sixteenth century (a characteristic shared, for example, by London itself, not incorporated till the seventeenth century) they certainly attained at a relatively early time the sort of polarized, hierarchical, and oligarchic characteristics which would come to prevail amongst a great many more towns — albeit mostly of the middling and larger types — in the sixteenth century and after.

Elsewhere in these two centuries the effort to gain greater local control over community resources had continually and collectively engaged townsmen in competition with seigneurial authorities.[33] And yet, the effect of these efforts on the sense and strength of community, as Gervase Rosser has noted, was far from incompatible with social change, as 'the potential for collective action in a perceived common cause may best be realized not . . . in places and periods of unbroken calm, but precisely in the response to social transformations'.[34] The stakes of victory in such contests for local privileges or autonomy, often secured by and measured in terms of charters or other formal enabling devices, further enhanced the authority of the better sort of citizens as well as of their communities.

---

[33] Well-documented examples include Bury St Edmunds, in Gottfried, *Bury St Edmunds*, chap. 6; Wells, in Shaw, *Creation of a Community*, chap. 4; and Bishop's [later King's] Lynn, in Susan Battley, 'Elite and Community: The Mayors of Sixteenth Century King's Lynn', Ph.D. thesis (SUNY, Stony Brook, 1981), 35–7.

[34] Rosser, 'Communities of Parish and Guild', 30.

Viewed from the threshold of the Henrician Reformation, this movement had been slow and uneven in the majority of towns. Most of those towns were still substantially under the direct governing authority of an external and superior authority: lay lords, ecclesiastical lords, or the Crown itself. At the same time townsmen in many places enjoyed well-established parallel or alternative institutions which afforded some degree of local autonomy under that broader aegis. These included parishes, guilds and fraternities, aldermanic councils, and even mayoral courts, all of which generally functioned well as the most common and effective institutional expressions of a good many local interests.

In most instances officials who achieved positions of some authority, including aldermen and mayors, were still not decisively differentiated from the general run of the freemanry by dint of social standing, occupation, wealth, legal status, or similar criteria. The ties amongst members—the sense of loyalty, the common heritage and mutual responsibility, as well as bonds of kinship, patronage, and other associations—still frequently bore many of the hallmarks of interaction which Reynolds described as 'reciprocal, many-sided and direct'. In addition, the cultural underpinnings of English townsmen and women, including their religious outlook and their sense of the past, were still held predominantly in common and continued to be expressed by collective as well as individual activities.

But the years following that threshold, dominated by the Reformation itself and spurred on by many aspects of that event (as well, of course, as by the rapid economic and social changes of the same era), yielded a sharply accelerated transformation of urban government, society, and culture along lines already laid down. A great many more towns, especially those which were larger and more complex, now moved more decisively away from the sense and form of the communal ideal and towards a more formalized, hierarchical, rigid, and decidedly oligarchic pattern. A considerable political, not to say social and economic, distance ensued between the governors and the governed. Individuals came more often to interact more formally and through the mediatory role of superiors. Political activity came to be characterized by more formally defined labels, structures, and constraints than by informally shared identities. Vertical lines of social and political interaction, while never absent, proved more emphatic and forceful than the more pronounced horizontal lines of an earlier age. Though townsmen and women might still feel and might often express something of the old sense of common

values, these came to be superseded as underpinnings of the emerging political culture. By the early seventeenth century, as we will see, an appeal to traditional values as often as not emanated from polemical needs of those in power, and masked the reality of their demise. The old ethos had changed: the spirit and values which had prevailed in most towns at an earlier time tended to give way to the spirit and values of a new and more polarized system.

This broad shift invites our attention for several reasons. It reminds us that bodies such as guilds, fraternities, parishes, and especially towns themselves once carried out on the basis of custom and tradition many of the responsibilities which, for those such bodies which survived at all, came later to require more formal authority. These included such activities as the holding and letting of land, the collection of tolls, the adjudication of local disputes, the passage of by-laws, the regulation of behaviour, the formation of deliberative assemblies, and the delegation of specific functions by those assemblies to particular individuals or bodies. More formal authority followed as well from the shifting role of corporate towns and boroughs in the emergent Tudor state, a state which relied more heavily than ever on small groups of reliable men at the grass-roots level to carry out its expanding role of governance.

In this sort of transition, even allowing for differences of time and circumstance, towns were not alone. These tendencies are not unlike what Mervyn James has described as the transition from lineage-based to civil-based society and what Christopher Hill has seen as the transition from a traditional and personally directed sense of loyalty to the monarch to an impersonal loyalty to the modern state.[35] This transition meant nothing less than a redefinition of the political role of towns in that more modern type of state.

And, ironically, at the same time that the move towards greater local autonomy diminished the extent of traditional seigneurial authority in borough affairs, groups which were not as traditionally a part of the urban milieu, including regional gentry, professionals, and court officials, made more frequent inroads into the ranks of those ruling elites. They did so in ways which, while not seigneurial in nature, remained nevertheless highly political, and often detrimental to long-standing custom.

---

[35] Mervyn James, 'The Concept of Order and the Northern Rising of 1569', *Past and Present*, 60 (Aug. 1973), 49–83; Christopher Hill, 'The Protestant Nation', in *Collected Essays II: Religion and Politics in Seventeenth Century England* (Brighton, 1986), 28–9, as cited in Collinson, *Birthpangs*, 2.

A final concern in this broad picture concerns the nature of the civic identity, and the political culture which conveyed such an identity. Although the claims for a sharp discontinuity in the political culture of England's provincial towns, also occasioned by the Reformation of the 1530s and 1540s, have lain on the table for the past two decades or so,[36] both the nature of urban political culture itself and the question of its continuity or discontinuity have still to be resolved.

It will be argued here that the pace of these changes in at least middling and more substantial urban communities accelerated dramatically both from the time of the Henrician Reformation and to a considerable extent because of it. The impact of the Reformation on the towns, on their political operation and culture as well as on their more familiar social and religious dimensions, seems sufficiently distinct and decisive as to help mark the era beginning around 1540 as a watershed in the history of English urban society.

Although it seems less germane to the dilemma at hand to posit a precise terminal point for the era under consideration, it would appear that in several respects the 1640s serves very nicely, and not only because of its obvious significance in the nation's political history. By at least that time, if not before, refashioned forms of civic consciousness, including both secular and Protestant religious elements, had come to provide an appropriate and legitimizing political culture in the provincial towns of the realm. By that time, the exercise of local political autonomy which had come to prevail in the intervening decades began to be overwhelmed by the intrusion of external authorities, Crown, gentry, and even larger towns.[37] By that time, too, the legislative effort to invest the officials of corporate

---

[36] Placed there esp. by Charles Phythian-Adams's path-breaking essay 'Ceremony and the Citizen' and, more generally, in the sharp picture of discontinuity drawn in the same author's *Desolation of a City*.

[37] The substantial and successful intrusion of, for example, the Crown, regional landowners, and even the non-native-born who come to ruling positions in urban government, has been noted in several studies of individual towns which, in this sense, seem reasonably typical of a great many more. They include John T. Evans, 'The Decline of Oligarchy in Seventeenth-Century Norwich', *Journal of British Studies*, 14/1 (Nov. 1974), 46–76; Peter Clark in ' "The Ramoth Gilead of the Good": Urban Change and Political Radicalism in Gloucester, 1540–1640', in Peter Clark, A. G. R. Smith, and N. Tyacke (eds.), *The English Commonwealth, 1547–1640* (Leicester, 1979), 174, 180–1; Underdown, *Fire from Heaven*; Sacks, *The Widening Gate*. Although the affairs of towns and townsmen were never carried on in isolation from the surrounding world, the tendency in earlier decades was for townsmen rather than outsiders to serve in local office (save for recorders), and for many independent towns to escape undue entanglement in shire or even national affairs.

towns and boroughs with royal authority had produced a substantial change in the standing of those officials in their communities, and thus in the nature of urban politics. And by that time, as will be argued throughout the following pages, the transition towards a more oligarchic form of governance had largely been completed in almost all but the small seigneurial towns of the realm.

In the remaining two chapters of this introductory section, the discussion turns first to a more extended description of the medieval urban community in both its institutional and cultural dimension. This seems an essential benchmark from which to measure and assess developments to follow. Once that has been established, the final introductory chapter considers the profound disruption of this traditional system, and also the vacuum in both political form and political culture left in the wake of that disruption.

2

The Ethos of Community on the Eve of Reformation

i

Both the cultural context and institutional expression of the urban community on the eve of the Henrician reforms, those factors which principally comprise the communal ethos of the age, have been rendered increasingly clear by the research of the past decade or so. Thanks especially to the anthropologically informed historical investigations pioneered in the late 1970s and early 1980s by such scholars as Mervyn James and Charles Phythian-Adams,[1] and the work on religion and urban society carried out in the 1980s and early 1990s by a host of other scholars, we are better able to understand the prevailing culture and institutional framework of the late medieval urban community than ever before. If we are fully to comprehend the way urban communities changed in the Reformation era, we must first remind ourselves of the way they had been beforehand.

To this sense of the late medieval town as a community there are many dimensions. Culturally speaking, they include both an ideological framework, which supplied a common purpose and ethical perspective, and a ritualistic and ceremonial dimension which reinforced and justified its shared beliefs. Politically, they included that matrix of institutions which served, expressed, and, in entirely pragmatic ways, helped community members to achieve their common goals. The aim of this chapter is to identify these factors, and to describe more fully their contribution to the civic culture of provincial towns on the eve of the Henrician and Edwardian reforms.

ii

More than by any other agency, men and women of pre-Reformation times, whether urban dwellers or not, remained bound by a shared

[1] Esp. Mervyn James, 'Ritual, Drama and Social Body in the Late Medieval

fellowship in Christ and the medieval Christian tradition. As Susan Brigden has put it with reference even to such a large and complex city as London, 'Communal religious observance marked the autonomy of the city, and faith might bind the citizenry as nothing else could.'[2] To discuss the ideological underpinnings of late medieval towns, thereby the better to comprehend the urban implications of the Reformation, we must begin with the nature and practice of late medieval Catholicism in the urban context. By the fourteenth and fifteenth centuries throughout most of Europe, with some difference in emphasis from place to place, a common and characteristic ideology had emerged out of the diverse possibilities of both traditional Christian theology and popular belief and practice. Tested by time and both resilient and flexible in the face of circumstance, this defining ideology fulfilled several crucial preconditions for social harmony and stability in local societies. It offered mediatory outlets for inherent social tensions; it encouraged works of charity and good fellowship; it facilitated the social interaction of individuals in all walks of life; and it provided ceremonial acknowledgement and reinforcement of prevailing values. In most of these functions late medieval religion and religious culture transcended the sometimes tenuous boundaries between rural and urban society. Indeed all but a very small proportion of the contemporary population, whether rural or urban dwellers, would have subscribed to them without hesitation. Yet, the cloister aside, the concentration of population and resources in the urban scene permitted in that particular milieu, rather than in the countryside, its greatest institutional flowering.[3]

Central to this shared system of belief lay such concepts as the doctrine of Purgatory, including what one might call 'the purgatorial imperative'. By this is meant the obligation to pray for the souls of the departed and thus to ease their passage from Purgatory to perpetual salvation. Other central concepts included the notion of the shared fellowship in Christ, as symbolized, for example, in the sacra-

---

English Town', *Past and Present*, 98 (Feb. 1983), 3–29; and Phythian-Adams, 'Ceremony and the Citizen', in Clark and Slack (eds.), *Crisis and Order in English Towns*, 57–85; and *Desolation of a City*.

[2] Brigden, 'Religion and Social Obligation', 71.

[3] For a stimulating but slightly different perspective on this issue, which appears to exaggerate the putative distinctions which have been made between urban and rural religious culture in the medieval era, see Miri Rubin, 'Religious Culture in Town and Country: Reflections on a Great Divide', in D. Abulafia, Michael Franklin, and M. Rubin (eds.), *Church and City, 1000–1500: Essays in Honour of Christopher Brooke* (Cambridge, 1992), 3–22.

ment of communion, and the goal of remaining in a state of spiritual harmony, sometimes referred to as a state of charity, with others of that fellowship. It is in relation to ideological foundations such as these that the culture and ethos of the community must be understood. Let us consider them in turn.

Like many other tenets of late medieval Catholicism, the notion of Purgatory had come a long way by the opening years of the sixteenth century. Men and women of that time took it to denote a condition or place where the soul resided after death until, by the suffrages and good works of the faithful (and especially by the sacrifice of the altar), it might be absolved of its sins and thus achieve eternal salvation. Most writers on the subject have emphasized the terrors of the purgatorial state—the blood-chilling description in Thomas More's *Supplication of the Souls* often being offered in support[4]—and the consequent fear which the very thought of it struck in the hearts of the faithful. Some, on the other hand, have emphasized a more positive approach. They have noted that the doctrine had evolved to provide a welcome alternative to the stark poles of heaven and hell, and that it provided a positive motivation for pious activity of a voluntary sort.[5] Especially from the former perspective, but also from the latter, this core belief, and the intensity with which it was taken to heart, gave rise to an almost obsessive concern for the eternal fate of the soul.

One of the chief effects of the doctrine of Purgatory was the encouragement of a wide range of penitential practices (including prayer, numerous forms of charity, the sacraments in general and the mass in particular) and institutions (including, especially, the chantry, guild, and fraternity). By facilitating in one way or another the performance of good works, such penitential devices allowed individuals to build up a store of merit and thus to reduce the punishment which awaited their souls. The gains derived from such good works could be extended to the souls of the departed as well, further broadening their appeal.[6]

---

[4] e.g. A. G. Dickens, *The English Reformation*, rev. edn. (1987), 19; and C. S. L. Davies, *Peace, Print and Protestantism, 1450–1558* (1976), 146, as cited in Clive Burgess, ' "A Fond Thing Vainly Invented": An Essay on Purgatory and Pious Motive in Late Medieval England', in S. J. Wright (ed.), *Parish, Church and People: Local Studies in Lay Religion, 1350–1750* (1988), 58 and n. 8.

[5] Chiefly Burgess, ibid., *passim*.

[6] Miri Rubin, *Charity and Community in Medieval Cambridge* (Cambridge, 1987), 64–5; Burgess, 'A Fond Thing Vainly Invented', in Wright (ed.), *Parish, Church and People*, 66.

The extensive framework of penitential practices and institutions encouraged by this belief became integral to medieval society in general and—because of its greater concentration of wealth and population—to medieval urban society in particular. It gave rise to still a third perspective on Purgatory, and of the necessity for penitential works, which of course bears profound secular and social implications as well. Not only did penitential activities determine the fate of the soul, but they also had their social and secular uses. They allowed men and women to alleviate the suffering of their neighbours and contemporaries through charitable acts, and they permitted individuals to promote their own reputations in their immediate, worldly surroundings. It goes without saying that pious bequests made up much of the contemporary capacity to cope with poverty and similar distress. At the same time, such display rarely if ever came forth anonymously. To many a donor, it served as much to enhance personal reputation on earth as to alleviate the suffering of souls after death.[7]

Despite this emphasis on the actions of the individual, both the purgatorial belief and the penitential recourse to it necessitated responses which were more likely to be collective and cooperative than individualistic and merely personal. The mass itself, symbolizing in the elevation of the Host the redemption and renewal of the world and of the immediate community, must be considered a communal as well as a personal act.[8] And, if most medieval parishioners took communion themselves but once a year or so, often at Easter, many attended the daily mass offered at their parish church. It had commonly become part of their daily routine.[9] The very cost of charitable works invited sharing, and they were also considered essential expressions of God's love for one's friends and neighbours as well as one's self. In addition, acts of charity required recipients just as much as they required donors. Even the very wealthy, though they might employ their own priests, maintain their own household chapels, and endow their own charities, required the regular cooperation of others to fulfil this purgatorial imperative of charitable giving.

For those who were not sufficiently well off to endow their own benefactions, which is to say for the vast majority, the same belief

---

[7] P. W. Fleming, 'Charity, Faith and the Gentry of Kent, 1422–1529', in T. Pollard (ed.), *Property and Politics: Essays in Late Medieval English History* (Gloucester, 1984), 52–3.
[8] Duffy, *Stripping of the Altars*, 91–3.   [9] Ibid. 99–100.

necessitated even more of a collaborative response: to support priests, masses, buildings, and institutions for the appropriate performance of redemptive works; to form a fellowship to which they could contribute and on which they could rely for support; to collaborate in providing the appropriate opportunities and circumstances. And, though the wealthy might well contribute more than the poor, and though the poorest of all might be net recipients rather than contributors, all shared (and with considerable equality) in that community identified as the fellowship of Christ.[10]

Thus the doctrine of Purgatory elicited a response which was highly social, binding together the members of the living community. The same response may also be seen as historical, binding the present members of the community with their forebears. The fellowship of Christ took in the deceased as well as the living. It followed that purgatorial acts to save the souls of the departed were public acts, and that the particular identity of the departed whose souls remained at issue was not only known, but constantly remembered in a public manner. Indeed, one of the great fears was that the departed, and his or her soul, would soon be forgotten. This concern gave rise to both a language and a ceremony of memory.[11] Even the act of dying was often quasi-public in itself. Members of family and community strove to be present in order both to witness the event and to give strength and courage to the dying.[12] Many of the common rituals following the event worked to perpetuate the memory of the departed, not only so that his or her earthly fame might linger, but also so that prayers for the soul would not be neglected. These included the tolling of bells to announce the departure, and the funeral cortège itself which bore the corpse from the home to the church.[13]

This concern took many forms. Some were material in nature: brasses, inscriptions, candles or torches, plate, and vestments. Some were commemorative events: lights, anniversaries, and obits. A particularly important form of remembrance lay in the common adoption of the bede-roll: a written list of the departed members of

---

[10] See a particularly full and helpful discussion of this in Duffy, *Stripping of the Altars*, chap. 4.

[11] Ibid. 327–37.

[12] Ibid. 322–3; Richard Wunderli and Gerald Broce, 'The Final Moment before Death in Early Modern England', *Sixteenth Century Journal*, 20/2 (1989), 268.

[13] See the convenient summary in Robert Dinn, 'Death and Rebirth in Late Medieval Bury St Edmunds', in Steven Bassett (ed.), *Death in Towns: Urban Responses to the Dying and the Dead, 100–1600* (Leicester, 1992), 154–8.

the community for whose souls parishioners were enjoined regularly to pray. This record appears to have been read out publicly before the congregation, name by name, for that purpose, sometimes taking many successive Sunday services before the reading of the whole roll could be completed, whereupon the cycle began again. In providing a continuity with past generations the bede-roll preserved for the parish and community a vivid and usefully legitimizing collective memory, one wholly 'integral to the parish's sense of identity'.[14]

Connected to its purgatorial concerns, this shared faith also provided imperatives for the assertion of personal identity and the regulation of social interaction amongst living members of the community. Particularly striking here, and closely tied to the concern for the eternal fate of the soul, lies the crucial imperative to be in the state of charity: the loving affinity between the individual and God, the soul and the body, and—especially germane to our concerns—between the individual and his or her fellows.[15] The constant reminders of the imminence of death, provided in sermons, paintings, carvings, sculptures, and oral tradition as well as the frequent prayers in all their forms, reaffirmed the importance of remaining in charity in ways which were both constant and vivid. To die out of charity was to incur the substantial risk of eternal damnation or at least a prolonged lingering in Purgatory.[16]

By their diligent and frequent acts of confession and penitence those 'in charity' worked towards their own reward, building up a store of good works which could be drawn on to ensure eternal salvation. But what might in the end be seen as an essentially self-serving goal worked in practice towards a highly positive form of social interaction. Once again, harmonious relations within the community, devoted to the ideals of concord, peace, 'good neighbourhood', and the like, weighed heavily in one's favour, and were earnestly pursued.[17] Contemporary religious practice supported this goal amongst its most sacred responsibilities. The sacraments, and especially the mass, symbolizing the individual's fellowship in Christ

---

[14] Duffy, *Stripping of the Altars*, 334–6.

[15] Brigden, 'Religion and Social Obligation', 69–111; John Bossy, 'The Mass as a Social Institution, 1200–1700', *Past and Present*, 100 (Aug. 1983), 29–61, *passim*. For an excellent and fuller discussion of the material in the next several paragraphs, see Brigden, *London and the Reformation*, chap. 1.

[16] Burgess, 'A Fond Thing Vainly Invented', in Wright (ed.), *Parish, Church and People, passim*; and Duffy, *Stripping of the Altars*, 355–7.

[17] Brigden, 'Religion and Social Obligation', 67 and *passim*; Bossy, 'The Mass as a Social Institution', *passim*.

and communion with his or her fellows, helped to attain this charitable state. Religious services and a variety of less formal observances reinforced the sundry relationships which defined and characterized social interaction amongst neighbours and townsmen. Some such activities seem obvious and are well known. The imperative to perform charitable acts towards the less fortunate, along with the efforts of family and kinship networks, lay at the heart of whatever care of the poor, sick, and otherwise dependent that the times could provide.[18]

One less obvious way in which people affirmed and avowed their state of charity with their fellows was through the practice of oath-taking. In traditional English society the oath affirmed the loyalty and responsibility of the individual as he or she passed from one stage of life to the next: to marriage, parenthood, employment or apprenticeship, and to office both ecclesiastical and civic. Well precedented not only at earlier times in Western society but in other societies and at all times, the oath constituted a solemn promise which was both morally and legally binding. It constituted a ritualized affirmation of responsibility and loyalty towards the welcoming group or person: the master's household for the apprentice, the guild for the journeyman or master, the freemanry for the town official, and so forth. In this manner the oath perpetuated the communal ideal. It reinforced the idea of the wholeness of the community. It affirmed recognition of boundaries and constraints which were spiritual and moral every bit as much as they were geographic or political. No less than the charitable donation or the intercessionary prayer for the departed, the oath affirmed one's state of charity with the community.[19]

To these devices for affirming the Christian fellowship we must also consider the metaphoric and ritualistic aspects of the age. To anthropologically informed students of the subject like Mervyn James, for example, the metaphor of 'body' has seemed very central in this consideration. The civic body of the medieval community

---

[18] See e.g. Marjorie K. McIntosh, 'Local Responses to the Poor in Late Medieval and Tudor England', *Continuity and Change*, 3/2 (1988), 228–30; Burgess, 'A Fond Thing Vainly Invented', in Wright (ed.), *Parish, Church and People, passim*; and McRee, 'Charity and Guild Solidarity'.

[19] See esp. Brigden, 'Religion and Social Obligation', 86–9. Oaths were amongst the most important documents to be recorded in the records of the medieval town, where they were usually bound up with excerpts from the Gospels upon which they were administered; G. H. Martin, editorial introduction to Andrew Brent, *The Doncaster Borough Courtier*, i (Doncaster, 1994), p. ii.

found its spiritual expression in the body of Christ.[20] We see this in several ritual forms, but in none so clearly as in the celebrations of Corpus Christi, literally, of course, 'the body of Christ'.[21] A ritual observed so widely in England (and, indeed, Europe) obviously had many variations, but by the fifteenth century a common pattern had emerged. This saw the day begin indoors with a mass and end with a commensal feast, both of which involved the participation of all 'full' members of the community—that is to say the adult freemen—as equals in their Christian fellowship. In the former event each partook equally in the blood and body of Christ; in the latter, each joined to break bread with his fellows.

In between those bookends of the occasion came the procession of the Host, in which the symbolic display of spiritual and moral equality gave way to the more prosaic side of social relations within the community. The procession recognized the social, economic, and political inequalities which inevitably pertained amongst its members. In this sense, the procession has been seen (especially by Phythian-Adams and James) as a metaphoric display of the whole social body in its complete and precise order, a mirror of the community and a walking blueprint of its structure, carried out before those from outside (country dwellers of all social groups and even townsmen from elsewhere, but also wives and children of the freemen themselves) who lined the route to watch.[22]

By its very order of march, the procession was designed to display the precise social distinctions amongst members and groups of the community. Each person thus walked in a place determined by his own status and identity, and by the status and identity of those bodies to which he belonged, with the most honoured place being nearest the Host. Members of the same guild walked together, identified by the characteristic theme of their pageant display. Appropriate

---

[20] James, 'Ritual, Drama and Social Body'. See also Duffy, *Stripping of Altars*, 91–2.

[21] In addition to James's work, this discussion draws upon V. A. Kolve, *The Play Called Corpus Christi* (Stanford, Calif., 1966); Alan H. Nelson, *The Medieval English Stage: Corpus Christi Pageants and Plays* (Chicago, 1974); Phythian-Adams, 'Ceremony and the Citizen', in Clark and Slack (eds.), *Crisis and Order in English Towns*, 74–85; Alexandra F. Johnston, 'The Guild of Corpus Christi and the Procession of Corpus Christi in York', *Mediaeval Studies*, 38 (1976), 372–84; and Miri Rubin, *Corpus Christi: The Eucharist in Late Medieval Culture* (Cambridge, 1991), esp. chap. 4.

[22] M. James, 'Ritual, Drama and Social Body'; Phythian-Adams, 'Ceremony and the Citizen', in Clark and Slack (eds.), *Crisis and Order in English Towns*; and, for a close Continental parallel, Muir, *Civic Ritual in Renaissance Venice*, esp. 190–201. See also Rubin, *Corpus Christi*.

divisions of status within the guild were further denoted by the exact position of each member of the group. Town officials also marched together as a body, again in strict sequence of responsibility, authority, and honour. The most honoured place of all, save for the clergy, went to the mayor, nearest the priest bearing the Host just behind him.

Far from denying the divisions and tensions of the urban community or encouraging anachronistic images of egalitarian relations, these processions, like other rituals, provided ceremonial and symbolic strategies for mediation. They at least tried to create the boundaries within which such distinctions could be permitted to exist. In the case of the Corpus Christi processions, recognition came with the literal display of social hierarchy within the procession itself. Mediation ensued well before the event in the effort to work out the precise order of march by dint of status. This required an annual and formal consideration (ultimately by the town council) of the waxing and waning of particular guilds, and of the occupations which they represented. This, too, fulfilled an integral function of the governing ideology. It acknowledged that, though the ideal of the commonalty might be the harmony, cooperation, and unity of the whole, reality necessitated divisions and inequalities as well. Though it cannot be said always to have succeeded in these mediatory aims,[23] ceremony of this sort seems at least partly designed as a strategy for managing that reality.

Throughout all of this the metaphor of the body remained crucial. It likened the urban community to the Church Universal. It emphasized the more literal metaphor of the human body, the *corpus humanum*, subject to its sundry vulnerabilities and depending for its welfare on the effective interaction of its parts. In this thoroughly familiar medieval organic analogy each part had to work with the others regardless of its relative standing or function. The whole had to be governed by the head so that the organism might survive and flourish.

Though we also find examples and versions of these organizing

---

[23] Rubin esp. emphasizes the frequent failure of such a mechanism and, by dwelling on the exclusivity of the occasion, disputes Phythian-Adams, James, and others in seeing Corpus Christi processions as mirrors of the community (Rubin, *Corpus Christi*, 263–6). One wonders if her sense of community leaves too little room for the hierarchy and inequality, tension and conflict, which were, at least to a degree, also part of the mix. For another perspective on the mixed success met by these processions, see also McRee, 'Unity or Division?', in Hanawalt and Reyerson (eds.), *City and Spectacle*, 190–207.

mythologies in rural communities, they appeared more readily in
the urban context, and they did so for reasons which were more than
merely pragmatic. Late medieval townspeople probably found in
these strategies something of a substitute for the lineage, lordship,
and fealty, or (more commonly) for the tenurial standing, which
more clearly defined the identity and status of their country cousins.
The placement of an individual in the urban procession served the
same function as the periodic identification of his community status
in the annual view of frankpledge in agrarian society. Lacking both
the traditional attributes of seigneurial authority on the one hand and
the personal benefits conveyed by such factors as lineage, title, and
landholding on the other, those townsmen selected to govern their
fellows found in this religiously borne mythology a critical support
for their authority. Both societies of course depended heavily on
some sort of device which legitimized precedence and authority.
The leaders of the urban community, in whatever institutional guise
might apply at particular times and places, had to be able to govern
the *corpus civile* as Christ ruled the Church and as the head ruled the
corpus humanum. The greater material resources at their disposal
allowed them to mount ritual occasions of this sort which the rural
parish would be hard-pressed to emulate, and for which religious
houses in the countryside would be hard-pressed to find sufficient
lay participants.

Thanks to the bevy of scholars who have worked them through,
the Corpus Christi processions, particularly in York and Coventry,
have become the most familiar and most dramatically compelling of
all the ritualistic and ceremonial observances of this guiding mythology. Yet they are not the only such observances, or the most common or widespread.

In some precocious and evidently isolated cases, we can already
see a movement of civic ceremonial away from its liturgical foundations and towards the more laconically civic and secular. An interesting and perhaps precocious example of this has been described
for Bristol, very much at the top of the urban league save for London
itself, by Professor Sacks.[24] Here even by the opening of the fifteenth
century we find the ritual approximation of Corpus Christi in the
election and swearing of the new mayor, a ceremony in which the
metaphor of the body of Christ played but a minor role. The swear-

[24] David Harris Sacks, 'Celebrating Authority in Bristol, 1475–1640', in Susan
Zimmerman and Ronald F. E. Weissman (eds.), *Urban Life in the Renaissance*
(Dover, Del., 1989), 187–223.

ing came more directly to emphasize the relations between government and the governed, with more concern to emphasize the nature and force of authority than to smooth over inequalities of status. Symbolically, though the idiom of that celebration remains at least partially religious, it is the idea of hegemony itself which was celebrated more centrally. The sense of civic wholeness which in most towns still depended on the Church had in Bristol already begun to depend upon the civic magistracy.[25]

It should be said that in its ability to present a common urban pattern, the case of Bristol may be more striking than helpful. Its large size, wealth, political maturity, influence beyond its borders, and more direct links to a national commercial network place it amongst the most politically advanced of English urban centres in moving somewhat away from the medieval view of *communitas*. To the common run of fifteenth-century towns, Bristol represented the wave of the future.

Though the model of Coventry's Corpus Christi in particular provides colourful and well-documented ritual, the underlying ideology which it conveys could be found much more pervasively and constantly elsewhere. In a much broader sense, the governing social ethic of late medieval Catholicism, including such imperatives as the need to remain 'in charity' with one's fellows and to observe the requisites of 'good neighbourhood',[26] operated much more widely, and was much more internalized into individual behaviour, than any ceremony, however regularly performed, could be. Taken together, these practices justified a wholeness to the community and a fellowship amongst its members which, at least in theory, both countered and transcended other, more fractious, elements of urban society.

iii

In addition to these beliefs and practices and to the various occasions upon which they were expressed, we must consider the institutional forms by which they were conveyed. In addition to enhancing the spiritual welfare of contemporary parishioners, these institutions were also essential to the social relations, economic activities,

---

[25] On this theme, see e.g. Phythian-Adams, 'Ceremony and the Citizen', in Clark and Slack (eds.), *Crisis and Order in English Towns*, 79–80; and M. James, 'Ritual, Drama and Social Body', 24–6.

[26] As e.g. in the Liverpool town by-law of 1541 whereby 'all and every person shall make and doe neyburhode', as cited in J. A. Twemlow (ed.), *Liverpool Town Books . . . 1550–1802* (2 vols.; Liverpool, 1918 and 1935), i. 11 n. 35.

and political behaviour of English men and women before the Reformation.

The most obvious of these is of course the parish, that time-honoured unit of ecclesiastical administration whose religious, social, and even political functions contributed so much to local identity.[27] In smaller towns, the parish and town were often coterminous; in larger towns there might be as many as a dozen or more, which allowed them to form the cultural nucleus of the neighbourhood as well as the town. In addition to a multiplicity of other religious functions, and in comparison with all other institutions, the parish conventionally provided the most regular and accessible recourse to penitential and charitable activities. It provided both the space and the occasion whereby good works—prayer, anniversaries, obits, charitable relief, and the observance of the sacraments—could most regularly and reliably be rendered. It frequently bore the name of a patron saint who had particular significance for the local community.[28] It housed in its church virtually all the material objects required by Christian worship, and it provided the institutional 'framework in which believers executed their religious obligations'.[29] The very church building which lay at its centre and the boundaries which defined its spatial limits, provided essential loci of identity, while its church and churchyard, its bede-roll, statuary, bells, memorials, and plate served as 'sites of memory',[30] linking the present with the past.

Parishioners had much to gain by supporting the local priest and contributing to the upkeep and management of the church, and they obviously understood this very well. Whether measured by bequests to support the upkeep of parish churches, or by the rate of repair or rebuilding, or by the popularity of burial under its aisles, lay support for parish churches obviously remained very strong in the early

---

[27] The current proliferation of interest in the subject of parishes by a host of younger scholars seems poised to propel our understanding of it by geometric leaps in the near future. It is regretted that the following two works have appeared too late to be considered fully here: Beat A. Kumin, *The Shaping of a Community: The Rise and Reformation of the English Parish* (Aldershot, 1996); and K. L. French, G. G. Gibbs, and B. A. Kumin (eds.), *The Parish in English Life, 1400–1600* (Manchester, 1997).

[28] For a good example of a community's identification with its patron saints, see Shaw, *Creation of a Community*, 179–80.

[29] Rubin, *Charity and Community*, 237–8.

[30] Pierre Nora, *Les Lieux de mémoire* (7 vols.; Paris, 1984–96). For a short summary of Nora's use of the term, see his essay 'Between Memory and History: Les Lieux de mémoire', *Representations*, 26 (Spring 1989), 7–25.

decades of the sixteenth century.[31] Service to the parish engendered cooperation amongst neighbours and a community of purpose which transcended status or wealth. The church warden, that lay factotum of the parish, effectively became an official of the community as well as of the parish. Eventually, of course, his civic responsibilities took on statutory authority as the Tudor state co-opted parochial organization, and the community identity which it fostered, bringing it into the formal governing process of each community.[32] The common man and occasionally woman who served that office came thereby to exercise authority which was both extensive and considerable.

Often, especially in the middling and larger towns, the parish served to inform the local identity not only in and of its own resources, but by offering both facilities and space to other, more specialized institutions working towards some of the same ends: guilds, fraternities, and chantries. All emerging to some extent to facilitate the purgatorial imperatives of the age, these institutions also performed crucial roles in tending to the practical requirements of charity and fellowship. As building blocks for the larger social constructs of their communities, we may count such bodies, along with, for example, the family, household, and parish, as integral to the rich social fabric of the late medieval town, and as essential components of its political and social structure.[33] Once again, of course, institutions of this sort were also to be found widely in rural society in the same period, but the greater concentration of wealth and population, and the more complex demands of urban administrative requirements, made them especially common in and essential to the urban scene.

In these institutions even more than in the parish itself, the doctrine of Purgatory in general and the intercessionary potential of the mass in particular remained the central concerns. Both functions contributed greatly to the local sense of fellowship, to the

---

[31] See e.g. Rosser, 'Communities of Parish and Guild', in Wright (ed.), *Parish, Church and People*, 29–55; Duffy, *Stripping of the Altars*, 131–54; Robert Whiting, *The Blind Devotion of the People: Popular Religion and the English Reformation* (Cambridge, 1989), 83–105; Katherine French, 'Local Identity and the Late Medieval Parish: The Communities of Bath and Wells', Ph.D. thesis (University of Minnesota, 1993), *passim*. I am grateful to Dr French for permission to cite her thesis and for shedding light on this issue in conversation.

[32] See esp. Kumin, *Shaping of a Community*, chaps. 2, 5–6.

[33] This is nowhere better described than in Phythian-Adams, *Desolation of a City*, part III, 'Anatomy of a City'.

connection of both the living with the dead and of the more and less affluent. The single most essential function of the chantry was the performance of masses for the souls of the deceased, and equally integral functions of guilds and fraternities had to do with keeping anniversaries, lights, obits, and similar forms of remembrance. The anniversary, for example, consisted of a mass celebrated by pre-arrangement, usually in the parish church of the deceased, on two consecutive and specific days of the year. Its terms were usually spelled out by the will of the deceased. Payment for the service usually derived from rents on land left to the parish[34] or to feoffees or sometimes to the officers of the corporate town, for the purpose.[35] Often the bequest sufficed to support additional observances for the soul of the deceased, including the ringing of bells, the burning of candles, and the provision of alms for the poor who would, in turn, offer their prayers for the benefactor. In practical terms, these intercessionary bequests became a means of transferring lands for purposes which were in part charitable. In some cases anniversary bequests even allowed for surplus rents on such lands to be left for the use of local government, and thus became a source—sometimes a very considerable source—of civic income.[36]

The most functionally specific of these institutions remained the chantry.[37] Designed principally to facilitate the regular singing of masses for the souls of the departed, chantries responded directly to the purgatorial imperative. They may even be seen as a historical and functional outgrowth of the anniversary. In its most essential form, the chantry consisted of an endowed ecclesiastical benefice left for a priest to perform the desired mass for the soul of the

[34] Clive Burgess, 'A Service for the Dead: The Form and Function of the Anniversary in Late Medieval Bristol', *Transactions of the Bristol and Gloucestershire Archeological Society*, 105 (1987), 183–5 and 189–90.

[35] Ibid. 200–1.

[36] Burgess, 'A Fond Thing Vainly Invented', in Wright (ed.), *Parish, Church and People*, 75–9; Barbara Harvey, *Westminster Abbey and its Estates in the Late Middle Ages* (Oxford, 1977), 29–30; S. R. R. Jones, 'Property, Tenure and Rents: Some Aspects of the Topography and Economy of Medieval York', Ph.D. thesis (York University, 1987), 186–9.

[37] In general, see A. Hamilton Thompson, *The English Clergy and their Organization in the Later Middle Ages* (Oxford, 1947); K. L. Wood-Legh, *Perpetual Chantries in Britain* (Cambridge, 1965); Alan Kreider, *English Chantries: The Road to Dissolution* (Cambridge, Mass., 1979); C. R. Burgess, ' "For the Increase of Divine Service": Chantries in the Parish in Late Medieval Bristol', *Journal of Ecclesiastical History*, 36 (1985), 46–65; R. B. Dobson, 'Citizens and Chantries in Late Medieval York', in D. Abulafia, M. Franklin, and M. Rubin (eds.), *Church and City, 1000–1500* (Cambridge, 1992), 311–32.

departed benefactor. Legal developments of the fourteenth century permitted chantry administrators to hold such endowments, usually in the form of lands or rents, with licence to acquire in mortmain, and thus to act in an enhanced legal capacity in administering that endowment.[38] If a benefactor wished to endow a stipend without the legal complications of a formally endowed benefice, as was often the case, he could leave his bequest instead to one or more feoffees: the dean or chapter of a cathedral, the members of a religious fraternity or guild, or the mayor and officers of a town often served in this capacity.[39]

Of course this arrangement often extended to much more than the service of prayers for the deceased. Chantries of any size almost always necessitated the construction or demarcation of a physical space, in a cathedral, monastery, abbey, chapel-at-ease, hospital, or parish church, where the endowed observances could be held. Prominent amongst such physical institutions, for example, especially in the later Middle Ages, was the chantry college. Though far smaller and less splendid than such traditional colleges as the collegiate minsters of Beverley or Ripon, these nevertheless accommodated and supported several chantry priests in residence.[40]

In addition to the establishment of the chantry as a physical space, the considerable sums which went into these endowments—Wood-Legh notes that £200 was quite common even as early as the fourteenth century[41]—frequently permitted a surplus large enough to be expended on other, more strictly secular, functions. Many a town enjoyed sufficient surpluses even after the fulfilment of testamentary obligations to bring a tidy sum to the general coffers. In Bristol, for example, Geoffrey Thompson's chantry endowment of £200 plus a messuage in 1521 entailed an annual outlay of but £15. 13s. 4d. for a chaplain, leaving most of the balance for the City Corporation to manage as it wished.[42] In York such endowments enabled the City government to invest heavily in rental properties throughout the late fourteenth and fifteenth centuries.[43] Not all chantries by any

[38] Wood-Legh, *Perpetual Chantries*, 1–15. It may indeed be, as Susan Reynolds has recently suggested, that the need to hold such funds with the security of mortmain proved one of the driving forces behind the development of the legal notion of incorporation, probably as late as the 15th cent. I am grateful to Miss Reynolds for sharing her insights into this subject with me.

[39] Wood-Legh, *Perpetual Chantries*, 16–20.

[40] Kreider, *English Chantries*, 6–7.

[41] Wood-Legh, *Perpetual Chantries*, 46.   [42] Ibid. 178.

[43] Dobson, 'Citizens and Chantries', in Abulafia, Franklin, and Rubin (eds.), *Church and City*, 325–6; and S. R. R. Jones, 'Property, Tenure and Rents', 190–6.

means were intended to be perpetual. Many even of those which were so intended languished or even disappeared through inept management or adverse economic conditions. Nevertheless, it now seems not to have been unusual for such funds to survive for a century and more.[44]

Finally, not all chantry endowments came in the form of cash. Perhaps even the lion's share came in the form of income-bearing properties of one sort or another, with the recipient of the endowment receiving both the proceeds and seisin of the property itself. Such endowments commonly included town properties like burgage tenements, and other residential properties, shops, shambles, and market stalls. In Taunton, Somerset, it has been calculated that of the £90 brought in annually by the town's ten chantries at Dissolution, roughly 57 per cent derived from residential holdings, 30 per cent from lands in general, and 13 per cent from business premises.[45] Endowments of agrarian property might include such elements as orchards and gardens as well as residential and other agriculturally productive lands.

It goes without saying that chantries existed in rural as well as urban areas, but again the defining characteristics of urban society concentrated them most thickly in the town. Few towns could have been without at least one active chantry at the Reformation, most towns of any consequence could be expected to have a number, and the largest provincial centres could count their chantries by the score. Professor Dobson has identified at least 140 in York, possibly more than in any other provincial centre, of which nearly four dozen were administered by the City government.[46] Furthermore, because of the gravity with which contemporaries regarded the intercessionary imperative, the great majority seem to have been conscientiously administered. In sum, perpetual chantries, many of fairly recent foundation, not only served as spiritual institutions, but they brought in addition both income and extensive powers of patronage to their administrators. As was the case in Coventry and York, those administrators often included the governing bodies of particular towns.

Guilds and fraternities present some problems of definition. Not

[44] Wood-Legh, *Perpetual Chantries*, 128–9.

[45] G. H. Woodward, 'The Dissolution of the Chantries in the County of Somerset', M.Litt. thesis (Bristol, 1980), 30.

[46] Dobson, 'Citizens and Chantries', in Abulafia, Franklin, and Rubin (eds.), *Church and City*, 314 and 316.

only were and are still the two terms often used interchangeably, but both (and especially the first) might connote organizations which were essentially occupational or economic rather than religious. Like chantries, both organizations were specific to their host communities, though membership frequently extended to the immediate hinterland and occasionally, in the case of some of the larger guilds, virtually to the whole realm. In that handful of the very largest religious guilds, such as Norwich's Guild of St George, Ludlow's Palmers' Guild, Lichfield's Guild of St Mary and St John, or Coventry's Trinity Guild, this might be a substantial contingent indeed.[47] And, at least in theory, the ability of the religious guilds and fraternities in particular to include members from the immediate hinterland proved an important integrating device between town and countryside.[48]

Insofar as they emphasized spiritual over secular goals, guilds and fraternities were especially concerned to provide for the souls of the departed, and they provided anniversary masses, lights, and prayers for that purpose. In addition, members of these organizations attended the funerals of their brethren, supported families of the deceased, engaged in ceremonial feasting and similar rites of mutual bonding, and in general worked to achieve the spiritual well-being of the membership. Thus they contributed to the sense of the identity of their communities, including a keen sense of their history, acknowledging the spiritual worth and material contributions of members both living and deceased.

In a similar vein we now know them to have been important instruments in the regulation of behaviour. This, too, contributed mightily to the local sense of well-being and harmony. It goes without saying that guild by-laws routinely enjoined members not to transgress against the interests and honour of either the guild or the community which embraced it. But in addition, they held their members to strict standards of personal conduct, discouraging such activities as

---

[47] Mary Grace (ed.), *Records of the Gild of St George in Norwich, 1389–1547*, Norfolk Record Society, 9 (1937); Michael Faraday, *Ludlow, 1085–1660: A Social, Economic and Political History* (Chichester, 1991), 80–93; A. G. [Gervase] Rosser, 'The Town and Guild of Lichfield in the Late Middle Ages', *Transactions of the South Staffordshire Archaeological and Historical Society*, 27 (1987 for 1985–6), 39–47; Mary Dormer Harris (ed.), *The Register of the Guild of the Holy Trinity . . . Coventry*, Dugdale Society, 13 (1935); and Geoffrey Templeman (ed.), *The Records of the Guild of the Holy Trinity . . . Coventry*, Dugdale Society, 19 (Oxford, 1944).

[48] R. H. Hilton, 'The Small Town as Part of Peasant Society', in id., *The English Peasantry in the Later Middle Ages* (Oxford, 1975), 76–94; Phythian-Adams, *Desolation of a City*, 139–40.

gambling, drunkenness, disrespect towards authority, or consorting with strangers of the opposite sex. Guild brothers and sisters were to be treated with respect; aggressive, lewd, or intemperate language was to be avoided; fractious behaviour had no place. These were no mere pious wishes. While felonious behaviour could of course be met with formal legal action from the appropriate court, most guilds of any size undertook to mediate disputes amongst members and to punish transgressions before they got out of hand. Failing successful intervention by senior guildsmen, quarrelsome or provocative behaviour could provoke expulsion from the guild. Considering the extent of guild authority within a particular community, and the frequently close ties between guilds and town or manorial government, this posed a substantial sanction. These efforts seem clearly intended to preserve the good public image of the guild itself, and thus of the community.[49] As these activities were also much more common in urban than in rural guilds,[50] we must now consider the guilds as a substantial force for the maintenance of harmony, order, and stability even at times of considerable social and economic stress in the pre-Reformation town.[51] At a time when many towns still lacked much in the way of their own administrative or judicial authority, as opposed to the manorial, they may often have played the largest part of all in maintaining the local peace and tranquillity.

And, though not as prominently as in most of the Latin countries of Europe, English guilds and fraternities often came about in part through the celebration of the life of a particular saint. Such figures might have seemed inspiring to local benefactors who would have learned of them abroad, or might, as with the adoption in the port of Great Yarmouth of St Nicholas—patron saint of fishermen—hold associations for local occupations, and some had other local associations. The prominence with which figures of such saints were depicted and displayed in the parish church or guild chapel firmly imprinted their association with the town in the popular mind. They served as icons of local pride and identity; their deeds often became integral to the collective memory of particular communities.[52]

---

[49] Sylvia Thrupp, 'Social Control in the Medieval Town', *Journal of Medieval History*, 1 *Supplement* (1941), 40–2; Brigden, 'Religion and Social Obligation', 96–8; McRee, 'Religious Gilds and the Regulation of Behaviour', in Rosenthal and Richmond (eds.), *People, Politics and Community*, 108–22.

[50] McRee finds that 'Rules governing the behaviour of members were an almost exclusively urban feature' (ibid. 116).

[51] See esp. Hanawalt and McRee, 'Guilds of *Homo Prudens*', 163–79.

[52] Duffy, *Stripping of the Altars*, 155–63.

The secular functions of the guild ran but a short stride behind the religious and behavioural in their importance to the medieval community. As was the case with endowed chantries, guilds, too, came to hold extensive property in many a town, as we will see, in the form both of rental properties and their own guildhalls. And of course in some communities guilds formed the organizational structure which had come through the years to assume many of the functions of secular self-government. As we will note at greater length below, many a borough government of the later sixteenth century could trace its roots to the structure and responsibilities of its leading guild or fraternity of days gone by. This, too, formed part of the communal ethos which typified many pre-Reformation towns.

Amongst major guilds in the more substantial communities, Coventry's Trinity Guild (officially the 'Guild of the Holy Trinity, St Mary, St John the Baptist and St Katherine') illustrates this as well as any. The amalgamation of the four founding guilds, some of them primarily religious guilds and at least one, the Trinity Guild itself, primarily a guild merchant, took place in the 1360s. From an early point the members of the Court Leet which represented the interests of the townspeople, and which had been recognized in the early incorporation of 1345, were closely associated with the leadership of the Guild. And from an early point, too, the Master of the Trinity Guild came always to be a former Mayor of the borough. The Trinity Guild paid the stipend of the Recorder and the annual farm to the Prior for his half of the City, taking its payment in part from bequests and partly from the rent roll which accrued to its possession during these decades.[53] Right up to the eve of Dissolution, the Master of Trinity Guild sat on public occasions only below the Mayor; even the Recorder held less prestige. The Master was always a JP, always sat on the Leet Court jury, and was often designated as one of the keepers of the common chest.[54] In other words, the operation of the Trinity Guild was very closely intertwined with the self-governing institutions of the City itself. Similar instances of the political role of guilds may be found in Lichfield,[55] Boston,[56] Stratford-upon-Avon,[57]

[53] Harris (ed.), *Register of the Guild of Holy Trinity*, pp. xiii–xix.

[54] Templeman (ed.), *Records of the Guild of the Holy Trinity*, pp. xvii–xix, 23–5.

[55] Rosser, 'Town and Guild of Lichfield', 39–47.

[56] Claire Cross, 'Communal Piety in Sixteenth Century Boston', *Lincolnshire History and Archaeology*, 25 (1990), 33–8.

[57] Levi Fox, *The Borough Town of Stratford-upon-Avon* (Stratford-upon-Avon, 1953), chap. 11.

Norwich,[58] Ludlow,[59] and other towns.[60] In all of these some elements of oligarchic rule may already be detected. Yet in almost all cases the *cursus honorum* prevailed as the road to civic office, and one still had to gain prominence in the guild before gaining authority in the town.

In sum, then, the religious guild or fraternity served the late medieval urban community in ways which were religious, social, economic, and political. One might see the guild as a collectivity of freemen, and often the wealthier and better-established freemen at that. Yet we ought not to jump to conclude that it was overly exclusive in form. Many guilds remained accessible to non-freemen as well as freemen. Some took in women as well as men.[61] Even when guilds restricted entry to freemen, it should be understood that each freeman in the guild served also as a head of a family and household, thus bringing women, children, apprentices, journeymen, and others at least indirectly into its orbit and under its aegis.[62]

With the discussion of the role of guilds we round out the description of two conspicuous elements, one cultural and one institutional, which shaped the medieval urban community. Institutions such as the parish, guild, fraternity, chantry, and, indeed, the household and family, comprised the very fabric of urban society. Doctrines such as the belief in Purgatory and the necessity of performing the sacraments and doing good works contributed an essential part of the urban character. Elements of both institutions and practice contributed to civic harmony and, more prosaically, to the civic treasury as well. We may now appreciate more fully what was at stake, not only for ecclesiastical and quasi-ecclesiastical institutions themselves, but also for the towns of the realm with which they were so closely tied, when Henry VIII embarked on his campaigns of destruction in the 1530s and 1540s.

[58] Grace (ed.), *Records of the Gild of St George*. One awaits the forthcoming study of this guild by Ben McRee.

[59] Faraday, *Ludlow*, 80–93.

[60] See Ben McRee, 'Religious Gilds and Civic Order', 72–3.

[61] This is summarized esp. well in Hanawalt and McRee, 'Guilds of *Homo Prudens*', 166–9.

[62] See e.g. how this worked in Coventry in Phythian-Adams, *Desolation of a City*, part III, esp. chaps. 6–8 and 13.

3

Traditional Perspectives and New Approaches

i

For historians of the national scene, it is no longer appropriate to think of the English Reformation as having taken place in the reigns of Henry VIII or Edward VI. Few now locate in that era the establishment of Protestantism as the predominant perspective of English men and women.[1] Yet for the urban historian, for whom the Reformation means much more than a revolution in doctrine, the picture remains somewhat different. The legislative onslaught especially of those years brought most of the finely balanced religious foundations of late medieval urban society tumbling to the ground. In the early 1530s all was more or less as it had been. Two decades later a very great deal had changed in the institutional, social, political, and cultural dimensions of urban life. Four decades further on, urban communities were continuing to evolve in ways heavily influenced by the Reformation, and even the doctrinal changes had only just become firmly established. If traditional religious belief itself seems often to have remained more resilient than one used until very recently to think, the circumstances in which such beliefs had evolved and been sustained for a very long time had changed for ever. The nature and sequences of those changes seem familiar enough in their broad outline, but it will not hurt to recall them concisely so that we may better consider events in their wake.

That complex series of events usually referred to by the shorthand term 'The Dissolution of the Monasteries', or simply 'The Dissolutions', seems the place to begin. Some precedents may be offered for

---

[1] See e.g. Patrick Collinson, *The Religion of Protestants* (Oxford, 1982); J. J. Scarisbrick, *The Reformation and the English People* (1984); Christopher Haigh (ed.), *The English Reformation Revised* (1987); Collinson, *Birthpangs*; Duffy, *Stripping of the Altars*; and Christopher Haigh, *The English Reformations: Religion, Politics and Society under the Tudors* (Oxford, 1993).

dissolution of the occasional monastery in earlier times. A systematic campaign against the religious houses had been urged by John Wycliffe in the fourteenth century, and the notion surfaced again in both the fifteenth and early sixteenth centuries. Yet the wholesale dissolution of ecclesiastical and lay religious institutions themselves began in 1536. By the statute 27 Henry VIII, c. 28, the government closed down and appropriated the smaller religious houses: all those with yearly revenues of less than £200. In 1539, by 31 Henry VIII, c. 13, the larger houses ('Monasteries, Abbathies, Priories, Nonries, Colleges, Hospitalls, Houses of Friers and other religious and ecclesiastical Houses and Places') followed. With these houses came their diverse properties, both agrarian and urban, as well as other possessions: 'Manors, Londes, Tenements, Rentes, Revercions, Tythes, Pencions, Porcions, Churches, Chappels, Advowsons, Patronages, Rights, Entrees, Condicions & all other Interestes and Hereditamentes'.

The second wave of confiscations consisted of the dissolution, again by Crown initiative, of both the remaining intercessionary and much of the charitable apparatus of the medieval Church, by statutes of 1545 ('An Acte for dissolucion of Colledges', 37 Henry VIII, c. 4) and 1547 ('An Acte wherby certaine Chauntries Colleges Free Chapelles and the Possessions of the same be given to the Kinges Majestie', 1 Edward VI, c. 14). These Acts terminated the activities and provided for the Crown's confiscation of both those institutions now rendered increasingly vestigial by doctrinal change, and others which depended upon the first sort. These institutions included religious (though not economic) guilds and fraternities, colleges, chantries, schools, hospitals, almshouses, free chapels, and the like, and the funds for lights, obits, and anniversaries. The Crown now also took in all the residential properties, funds, and appurtenances with which these establishments had been endowed. Most of those institutions, especially many schools and hospitals, which had operated under the aegis of these bodies went as well. Even the parish did not escape these years unscathed: not only did a vast and valuable array of material artefacts disappear, but an Act of 1545 allowed for the consolidation of two or more neighbouring parishes into one.[2] Though this was not to be done for urban parishes without the written consent of the borough corporations, such consolidations did nevertheless take place. They effectively disrupted the continuity of parish life and the sense of community thereby engendered through the years.

---

[2] 37 Henry VIII, c. 21 (1545), 'An Act for the Union of Churches'.

Changes wrought in official doctrine, if not in widespread popular belief, were entirely more complicated. By 1553, the end of the reign of Edward VI, the traditional Catholic doctrine of Purgatory and all implied therein, the essential doctrine of salvation by the performance of good works, and a great deal besides, had been legislated away.[3] The majority of people may have managed to retain their beliefs for some time thereafter, but it was much more difficult to maintain the visible, institutional, and material aspects of those traditions in the wake of legislation rendering them illegal or obsolete, or calling for their physical destruction. All those institutions, material objects, and indeed people which or who had been employed in sustaining that bedrock of the medieval faith had been either swept away as well or had their roles and functions substantially redefined. Gone was the traditional interpretation of the mass, which had sustained a sense of fellowship amongst all believers in Christ. Gone was the sanctioned belief in intercessionary powers which had supported the Purgatorial imperative. Gone at least in theory were the various ceremonies and processions which had as their side-effect achieved a degree of social harmony amongst neighbours. Gone at least from permissible use (and thus largely either hidden or destroyed) were the great variety of material objects which made up the paraphernalia of traditional worship, both from the church itself and even from individual homes. And gone were the institutions — including chantries, religious guilds, and fraternities (at least in their traditional forms) — which had served the whole.

In the wake of these losses lay an enormous void, the filling of which in one way or another, as it concerned the state of English provincial towns, forms a central concern of this book. In particular, these changes fall into two broad themes which are most germane to this study. The first of these is the confiscation of vast amounts of urban property by the Crown, and the instigation of a process of sale and resale which would drive the English land market with unparalleled force in the century to come. The property in question of course extended beyond the very lucrative revenue-bearing residential, agrarian, commercial, or 'industrial' properties which changed hands in most of the towns of the realm to one extent or another. It took in as well schools, hospitals, and almshouses, which were more likely at least in the short run to face dissolution than resale in their

---

[3] Excellent recent summaries of this complex story include: Dickens, *English Reformation*, chaps. 7–11; Duffy, *Stripping of the Altars*, chaps. 11–13; and Haigh, *English Reformations*, chaps. 7–10.

accustomed form. And along with this vast transfer of property went legal jurisdiction, especially the lordships of a good many towns or parts of towns.

The second theme is the abolition of much of the medieval form of Christian belief, and with it the institutions both lay and clerical which had evolved to serve that belief. Whether people continued for some time in their loyalty to the old faith, as it now appears, or not (and save for the Indian summer of official Catholicism in the reign of Mary), the practical opportunity to continue active public worship in the accustomed manner all but disappeared in most parts of the realm. Most of the material paraphernalia of traditional Christian worship, remarkable in its extent and complexity, was either confiscated if it held material value, destroyed if it did not, or hidden from those who might carry out either action. Of those institutions through which that faith had been expressed and served, and which had provided for the community the ritualized and ceremonial provision of social mediation, charity, and fellowship, most disappeared. Only those few chantries, guilds, and fraternities which townsmen managed to redefine and thus save as secular institutions, or managed to define as exceptions, survived to serve again, if not precisely in the same form or fashion as before.

This much is too well known to be belaboured here. What is more controversial and uncertain are the consequences of both these themes. Scholars have expended no little effort in explaining the significance of the Dissolutions for both central themes at issue here: the disposition of property on the one hand and the spiritual and political culture of English townspeople on the other. Yet standing explanations, sometimes founded on strong polemical biases, remain distinctly open to question or at least to investigation. Let us consider those explanations, and thus the state of current thinking, on each of these two issues in turn.

ii

Certainly the question of the impact of the Dissolutions on the disposition of property and jurisdiction has received about as much attention as any economic or political phenomenon of the sixteenth century. Yet save for the quasi-antiquarian studies devoted to particular towns, little of this attention has targeted the urban milieu itself. It has come instead from the agendas of several different debates. These have not been well integrated with each other, nor

have they dealt with urban issues in anything more than an incidental manner. They include studies written from the Roman Catholic
perspective as well as from other, more neutral approaches, and
most of them see the Dissolutions as pretty much of a disaster for
urban as well as for rural society.[4]

The emphasis here has certainly remained on elements of disruption and discontinuity, though there has been a reluctance to look
beyond the reign of Henry VIII or, at best, Edward. This view
emphasizes the point that, save for a few achievements in Edward's
reign, the promise to convert church property to useful, secular purposes went largely unfulfilled. Also unfulfilled was the refoundation
of most social institutions which had previously operated under one
or another form of ecclesiastical control. In addition, towns were
also seen to be impoverished by the loss of economic activity generated by monastic establishments, shrines, chantries, fraternities, and
the rest, some fatally so. Even Peter Clark and Paul Slack, for example, whom it would be difficult to accuse of strong ideological bias in
this regard, are amongst those who have emphasized the loss of pil-
grim trade to the economy of former ecclesiastical towns.[5]

This rather negative (though by no means entirely inaccurate)
approach to the impact of the Reformation on the towns continues
with the theme that the acquisition of dissolved properties, chiefly
by the gentry and aristocracy, often meant a simple licence to pillage
standing structures as a source of building materials for country
houses. It also entailed the large-scale investment in urban rental
property which allowed such agrarian interests to exert more control
over, if not responsibility for, urban communities than ever before.

A second historiographic perspective has derived from those pre-
Revisionist historians interested in tracing the causes of the Civil
War. This interest led to the study of land-owning, social change,
doctrinal allegiance, and political factionalism in particular counties.
Coloured as well by the debates of the 1950s through the 1970s about
the 'Rise of the Gentry/Crisis of the Aristocracy', such studies paid

---

[4] Dom David Knowles, *The Religious Orders in England* (3 vols.; Cambridge,
1950–9), esp. vol. iii; G. Constant, *The Reformation in England* (New York, 1940);
Fr. Philip Hughes, *The Reformation in England*, i (1950); M. Aston, 'English Ruins
and English History: The Dissolution and the Sense of the Past', *Journal of the Warburg and Courtauld Institutes*, 36 (1973), 231–55. Though writing from an essentially
Roman Catholic perspective, Scarisbrick pursues a more balanced view in *The Reformation and the English People*. See also Duffy, *Stripping of Altars*; and J. H. Bettey,
The Suppression of the Monasteries in the West Country (Gloucester, 1989).

[5] Clark and Slack (eds.), *Crisis and Order in English Towns*, 12.

particular attention to the acquisition of lands by the gentry and
aristocracy, but some of them at least took note of urban properties
as well.[6] Other studies have treated the disposition of lands of particular ecclesiastical foundations, some in urban settings,[7] while a
very few studies placed the distribution of urban property at the
centre of their focus.[8]

Amongst the conclusions of this research has been the view that
urban properties made up a very small part of the dissolved lands to
begin with, and that an even smaller proportion of those who came
to possess such lands after sale by the Crown could be counted as
urban interests, whether individual residents or governing bodies.

---

[6] Pioneering studies include S. B. Liljegren, *The Fall of the Monasteries and the
Social Changes in England Leading up to the Great Revolution* (Lunds Universitets
Årsskrift, N.F., Avd i, Bd. 19/10, 1924); R. H. Tawney, 'The Rise of the Gentry,
1558–1640', *Ec.HR* 11 (1941), 1–38; and H. J. Habakkuk, 'The Market for Monastic
Property, 1539–1603', *Ec.HR*, 2nd ser., 10 (1958), 362–80. More modern works
include the following sampling, though there are few counties to which studies of
some value have not been devoted in the last three decades: C. J. Kitching, 'Studies in
the Redistribution of Collegiate and Chantry Property in the Diocese and County of
York at the Dissolution', Ph.D. thesis (Durham University, 1970); and Kitching, 'The
Disposal of Monastic and Chantry Lands', in F. Heal and R. O'Day (eds.), *Church
and Society in England: Henry VIII to James I* (1977), 119–36; Katherine Wyndham,
'The Redistribution of Crown Land in Somerset . . . 1536–1572', Ph.D. thesis
(London, 1976); and Wyndham, 'The Royal Estate in Mid-Sixteenth Century Somer-
set', *Bulletin of the Institute of Historical Research*, 52/126 (1979), 129–37; Michael
Zell, 'The Mid-Tudor Market in Crown Lands in Kent', *Archaeologia Cantiana*, 97
(1982 for 1981), 53–70; G. H. Woodward, 'Dissolution of the Chantries'; G. H. Wood-
ward, 'The Disposal of Chantry Lands in Somerset, 1548–1603', *Southern History*, 5
(1983), 95–114; G. W. O. Woodward, 'A Speculation in Monastic Lands', *English
Historical Review*, 79 (1964), 778–83; David Thomas, 'The Administration of the
Crown Lands in Lincolnshire under Elizabeth I', Ph.D. thesis (London, 1979);
G. A. J. Hodgett, 'The Dissolution of the Religious Houses in Lincolnshire', *Lincolnshire Architectural and Archaeological Society Transactions*, 4 (1951), 83–99; Joyce
Youings, 'The City of Exeter and the Property of the Dissolved Monasteries', *Trans-
actions of the Devonshire Association*, 84 (1952), 122–41; Youings, 'The Terms of the
Disposal of Devon Monastic Lands, 1536–1558', *English Historical Review*, 69 (Jan.
1954), 18–38; R. B. Outhwaite, 'Who Bought Crown Lands? The Pattern of Purchases, 1589–1603', *Bulletin of the Institute of Historical Research*, 44 (1971), 18–33;
P. A. Cunich, 'The Administration and Alienation of Ex-Monastic Lands by the
Crown, 1536–1547', Ph.D. thesis (Cambridge, 1990); Richard Hoyle (ed.), *The Estates
of the English Crown 1558–1640* (Cambridge, 1992).

[7] For those in urban settings, see esp. L. F. R. Williams, *The History of St Albans
Abbey* (1917); R. V. H. Burne, *The Monks of Chester* (1962).

[8] Exceptions include Janis C. Housez, 'The Property Market in Bury St Edmunds,
1540–1600', MA Original Essay (Concordia, 1988), and brief discussions in scholarly
histories of particular towns in the 16th cent., such as e.g. Palliser, *Tudor York, passim*;
Wallace T. MacCaffrey, *Exeter, 1540–1640*, 2nd edn. (1975), chap. 8; Adrienne
Rosen, 'Economic and Social Aspects of the History of Winchester, 1520–1670',
D.Phil. thesis (Oxford, 1975), *passim*; and Youings, 'Exeter and the Property of the
Dissolved Monasteries'.

Like the proponents of the Catholic approach, this perspective neither took in the urban scene in and of itself, nor produced a picture
which would encourage others to do so.

Several reasons may be offered for this unfortunate neglect, and
most of them seem more appropriate to pursue in subsequent parts
of the discussion. But it is worth noting here that most studies of dissolved lands failed to pursue the changes in landholding beyond the
first generation of sales, and the lion's share of them dwelt exclusively on the sales of monastic lands rather than those very diverse,
and arguably much more urban, properties dissolved in the wave of
the 1540s.[9] These approaches have produced short-range and, in the
end, not entirely accurate conclusions. Perhaps this scholarly hiatus
may also be explained in part by the fact that most of the studies
cited above came before the expansion of interest, since the mid-
1970s, in pre-industrial urban society as a subject of its own. A few
studies have looked more closely at the impact of the Dissolutions
on urban society, but none yet could be said to have followed up systematically on Colin Platt's suggestion of two decades ago that post-
Dissolution redistribution of resources may well have amounted to
a virtual 'tenurial revolution' in urban communities.[10] Clearly, the
invitation to look further remains open.

The following discussion will offer some new perspectives on
these issues. For one, it will examine the urban scene directly, and
not as ancillary or incidental to other concerns. It goes without saying that urban communities made up only a small fraction of the total
area in the realm to begin with, and also that, save for London—
which has been excluded from this study in part for this very reason—English towns were very small by Continental standards. But
if it is those communities rather than the whole realm which we seek
to investigate, then the dissolved properties within their bounds
become a great deal more important.

A second important point is that, despite the occasional tendency
to speak of towns in the abstract, not all towns by any means
responded to the Dissolutions in the same way. For those numerous
small towns whose *raison d'être* had been bound up closely with
the very ecclesiastical establishments gobbled up in the 1530s, for

---

[9] A point made by Kitching, 'Disposal of Monastic and Chantry Lands', in Heal
and O'Day (eds.), *Church and Society in England,* 128–33. As indicated in the title of
the work cited in the previous note, even Youings, for example, relegated her study of
dissolved lands in Exeter to monastic lands: Youings, 'The City of Exeter and the
Property of the Dissolved Monasteries'.

[10] Colin Platt, *The English Medieval Town* (1976), 181.

example, dissolution brought few benefits. For them the Reformation often meant sudden and often prolonged crisis. The fate of these towns, the Ramsays and Cerne Abbases of the realm, has long dominated our common impressions of the social and economic impact of the Reformation on the towns. Having economies which remained one-dimensional and political structures largely dominated by the monastery or abbey, they too often had nothing upon which to fall back when dissolution struck. Those towns which depended for their livelihood on provisioning its brethren, administering its assets, or serving those who came on pilgrimage, were suddenly bereft. The more fortunate exchanged an ecclesiastical lord for a lay seigneur upon whom their economy, perhaps differently defined, and governance continued to depend. Many fared much worse, some effectively losing their urban character altogether. They more than any other type have provided the (perhaps over-emphasized) picture of rack and ruin.

For other, more substantial towns, however, the Dissolutions proved a watershed in ways which were much more complex and, in the long run, even beneficial. These were typically of middling or larger size and importance. Their economies were sufficiently diversified so as to rebound from the loss of their ecclesiastical business, and they had more often than not already established substantial indigenous governing institutions, albeit often still under the technical aegis of a landlord. Their size, diversity, and complexity allowed them more often than not to make a silk purse out of the sow's ear of dissolution. Though towns of this type must surely add up to at least a substantial minority of all, and comprised a strong majority of the more substantial towns of the day, their story nevertheless remain less familiar to us. They include the sorts of communities with which this study will be most concerned.

Some additional communities, of course, were little affected in any direct sense by the Dissolutions. Most of these were smaller and less complex towns under the firm hand of a lay landlord. Though they may have experienced loss of chantries and some few social and educational institutions, neither their economies nor their governance changed much in the event. Our concern rests to some extent with these towns, too, at least insofar as they partook, as many of them did, in the political and social changes described below.

A third perspective has to do with the factor of timing: the chronology with which urban rather than rural interests acquired dissolved properties in their own communities. In general neither

individual townsmen nor borough corporations appear prominently as original purchasers of dissolved properties. In the City of York, for example, only one or two of the original thirty or so purchasers of property formerly belonging to the City's religious houses were York citizens, the great majority being country gentry. But within a single generation the majority of those same lands had come into the hands of local men and, in some cases, the City itself.[11] This pattern of purchases by non-resident individuals is especially vivid if we focus on the first wave of Dissolutions, those of the religious houses, which took place in the 1530s: the monasteries, abbeys, nunneries, priories, and the like.[12] Indeed, the 'Particulars for Grants' by which towns were expected to petition for the purchase of such lands may be found for but seven towns in Henry's reign and fifteen in Edward's.[13]

Yet the further in time we follow the disposition of dissolved properties, and especially the properties devolving from the second wave of Dissolutions of the latter 1540s (the chantries, guilds, fraternities, and even such more obscure but numerous funds as obits, lights, and anniversaries), and the more we look at private as well as Crown sales, the more we may be able to see them coming into the hands of either individual townsmen or urban governing bodies.[14] In reality, it now seems more appropriate to suggest that these urban interests were much more likely to be secondary, tertiary, or even subsequent purchasers. Their acquisitions would thus be more likely to come in the mid-century and beyond, and from private parties rather than from the Crown. As the extended discussion of this issue

[11] *VCH, City of York* (1982), 117–18 and 357–65.

[12] The observation made by W. G. Hoskins nearly four decades ago, that in the early 16th cent. it would be difficult 'to detect any sustained interest in urban property as an investment', but that greater interest became forthcoming towards mid-century, seems still essentially correct (Hoskins, 'English Provincial Towns in the Early Sixteenth Century', *TRHS*, 5th ser., 6 (1956) 10–11). The point has been echoed in Palliser, *Tudor York*, 265; and Platt, *The English Medieval Town*, 182–3.

[13] In Henry's reign we have Bristol, Canterbury, Coventry, Faversham, Gloucester, Lincoln, and Warwick, and in Edward's, Chichester, Colchester, Coventry again, Crediton, Derby, Dorchester, Exeter, Ludlow, Newcastle-upon-Tyne, Norwich, Shrewsbury, Stamford, Winchester, Wisbech, and York. All are listed in the Exchequer records in the Public Record Office in manuscript class E. 318.

[14] To be fair, this is not always easy to do. As Michael Zell has noted in studying the redistribution of lands in Kent, when lands were sold from primary to secondary and subsequent purchasers, they were often alienated in socage, which did not require a licence of alienation. As such licences are a major means of tracing such alienations, these subsequent purchases are much harder to detect. He concludes that 'the numbers would be appreciably higher if resales could be followed into the 1560s and '70s' (Zell, 'Mid-Tudor Market in Crown Lands in Kent', 66).

presented in the next chapter will show, there are several explanations for this timing.

In sum, a serious effort to examine the local impact of the dissolution and redistribution of urban properties must adopt several particular perspectives if it is to break new ground. It should look at least to the end of the century. It should recognize distinctions between one type of town and another. It should treat the activities of towns in and of themselves rather than as part of some wider focus. Finally, it should remain unencumbered by the sorts of ideological predispositions which have all too often beclouded consideration of doctrinal change or the provenance and meaning of the Civil War and/or Revolution to come. The discussion to follow in Part II will proceed from these perspectives.

iii

The second important theme to be considered is the destruction of the cultural or mental world of late medieval urban society, and of that Christian fellowship and of those institutions which had evolved to serve that outlook. Here it seems appropriate to begin with the work of those, especially Charles Phythian-Adams and Mervyn James,[15] who have done the most to demonstrate the contributions of traditional Christian worship and doctrine to the social harmony of the late medieval town. Both see in the destruction of the traditional system a formula for dramatic social change and, especially in Phythian-Adams's case, for a virtual catastrophe in the political culture of English towns. In his view the destruction of the organic whole which formed the culture of medieval Coventry could lead only to interpersonal conflict: 'By the seventeenth century the claims of community . . . were yielding first place to class loyalties.'[16]

James's picture draws less on the exhaustive study of a particular town and remains entirely more theoretical. As noted in the previous chapter, one of his signal contributions has been to elucidate the ways in which the metaphor of body—so integral, for example, to

---

[15] Phythian-Adams, 'Ceremony and the Citizen', in Clark and Slack (eds.), *Crisis and Order in English Towns*, 57–85; and *Desolation of a City*; James, 'Ritual, Drama and Social Body in the Late Medieval English Town', *Past and Present*, 98 (Feb. 1983), 3–29. Others writing in the same vein have dwelt especially on London. They include Michael Berlin, 'Civic Ceremony in Early Modern London', *Urban History Yearbook* (1986), 17–25; and Brigden, *London and the Reformation*, esp. chaps. 1 and 4.

[16] Phythian-Adams, 'Ceremony and the Citizen', in Clark and Slack (eds.), *Crisis and Order in English Towns*, 80.

the mass and to the role of the Host in the Corpus Christi processions and elsewhere—served to integrate and harmonize the disparate parts of the urban community. In his view, Reformation iconoclasm not only obliterated the heavily iconocentric nature of late medieval worship and belief, but it threw out at the same time the opportunity to identify the wholeness of the civic community with God, the Church, and the Fellowship of Christ.

In place of those traditional and essential underpinnings to the civic identity, as James saw it, there emerged the pragmatic and secular realities of law and magistracy, in which 'the Corpus Christi becomes the Body of the Realm; and urban rituals, like religious rituals, tend to become progressively secularized, privatized and monopolized by the magistracy'.[17] James rounded out his thesis with the suggestion that the elite ruling groups which came to the fore after the Reformation were not merely hostile to the ritualistic and essentially non-literate culture of the late medieval Church. In addition, they seemed anxious to replace it with a political culture which they could more easily control and in which participation would be more restricted. This meant an emphasis on the civic over the religious heritage, on literate as well as non-literate forms of communication, and perhaps eventually on a new and much more highly disciplined religious ethic as well: the familiar 'godly rule'.[18]

To be sure, the approaches of Phythian-Adams and James, emphasizing as they do the essentially harmonious nature of the pre-Reformation urban community, have had their critics, especially amongst some medievalists. In the effort to challenge the assumption of civic harmony, several scholars have now described the emergence of oligarchic tendencies in London and amongst a number of provincial towns in the decades prior to the Reformation, pointing to developments in both government itself and even the same sort of civic ceremonies which Phythian-Adams and James themselves had discussed.[19] These findings would de-emphasize the impact of

[17] James, 'Ritual, Drama and the Social Body', 23.   [18] Ibid. 23–9.

[19] Such works include, but are not limited to, Maryanne Kowaleski, 'The Commercial Dominance of a Medieval Provincial Oligarchy: Exeter in the Late Fourteenth Century', *Medieval Studies*, 46 (1984), 355–84; Rigby, 'Urban "Oligarchy" in Late Medieval England', in Thompson (ed.), *Towns and Townspeople*, 62–86, and *English Society in the Later Middle Ages: Class, Status and Gender* (1995), 174–6; Jennifer Kermode, 'Obvious Observations about the Formation of Oligarchies in Late Medieval English Towns', in Thompson (ed.), *Towns and Townspeople*, 87–106; Sheila Lindenbaum, 'Ceremony and Oligarchy: The London Midsummer Watch', in B. A. Hanawalt and K. L. Reyerson (eds.), *City and Spectacle in Medieval Europe* (Minneapolis, 1994), 171–88.

the Reformation, and lead us to wonder if there is a longer and more continuous unfolding of urban oligarchy than one had suspected. We must then examine this movement at the various stages along that road which stretched in time and place from Professor Phythian-Adams's Coventry processions, through Professor Sacks's precocious ceremony for swearing in the mayor in pre-Reformation Bristol,[20] to the full-blown sway of godly rule in Professor Underdown's Dorchester a century and a half later.[21]

These alternative approaches having been set forth so clearly by students of late medieval society and culture, our task must be to consider the implications of their views for the development of urban communities in subsequent decades. Do the descriptions of late medieval urban oligarchy obviate the notion of the Reformation as a watershed in the history of urban politics and political culture? Contrarily, does the Reformation make a sufficiently sharp difference as to render common what was once but an exceptional condition in a handful of England's largest and most precocious towns? Does it enhance the possibilities which have been observed in pre-Reformation oligarchies so as to place the whole notion on a different and more comprehensive plane? And did the destruction of traditional religion, so essential to the very essence of late medieval towns, prove as consequential and deleterious as Phythian-Adams has suggested, or were many towns able to develop new discursive strategies for mediating social conflict and preserving harmony and order? Finally, if the latter alternative proves more accurate, what forms did such strategies take, and how did they come about?

iv

Though it may have been useful to treat these two themes—one concerning material resources and the other concerning political culture—at least from an introductory and historiographical perspective in this single chapter, it will avoid untold confusion if we deal with one at a time hereafter. The first issue in this scheme proves to be much the largest and most complex. It entails not only the question of acquiring resources itself, but also the very central consideration of the political implications of those acquisitions. Part II of this study has therefore been devoted to the issue of material

---

[20] See above, pp. 32–3; and Sacks, 'Celebrating Authority in Bristol', in Zimmerman and Weissman (eds.), *Urban Life in the Renaissance*, 187–223.

[21] Underdown, *Fire from Heaven*.

resources: their acquisition (Chapter 4), the problem of enabling authority encountered in the course of that acquisition (Chapter 5), and the state of local resources thereafter (Chapter 6). Part III will take up the connected question of the implications of these acquisitions. It will seek to connect the acquisition of additional resources with the enhancement of local political autonomy (Chapter 8). It will seek to connect both of those factors with the strengthening of earlier tendencies towards oligarchic rule, thus to understand such rule as the prevalent format for borough government by the opening of the seventeenth century (Chapters 9 and 10). Once we have understood this broad transition in the patterns of urban politics, we will then be best able to return in Part IV to consider the second principal theme at hand, the mental world and thus the political culture of the post-Reformation town. That final section will take up in turn the role of the built environment (Chapter 12), the re-creation of a legitimizing collective memory (Chapter 13), and the triumph of a culture of order and deference (Chapter 14).

PART II
Material Implications of the Reformation

4

Dissolution and the Strategies of Acquisition

On the face of it, the interest taken by town officials in acquiring dissolved properties seems logical enough. Yet the nature and circumstances of that interest, the barriers to its fulfilment, and the strategies employed in its pursuit prove more complex than they might seem. Crucial to these complexities is the distinction which must be kept in mind between the significance of the first and second waves of dissolutions—that of the religious houses in the late 1530s, and that of the chantries, guilds, fraternities, and associated institutions in the late 1540s—and the contrasting attitudes which many townsmen took towards each.

Those institutions and their properties which were dissolved in the first wave had not been as closely integrated with the community as those dissolved later on. While they may often have lain physically within particular towns, have stimulated local economies, and greatly have been valued by townsmen and women, they had often been held and run by authorities who dwelt elsewhere. Their support derived from bequests and other sources which had often been made so long in the past as to have lost their identity with the resources of the community itself (and in that sense the Dissolutions may be seen as acts of resumption for some communities[1]). They could rarely be drawn upon at will either by members of the community or the governing bodies which acted on the behalf of such members.

This may well account for the very mixed reception with which these dissolutions were greeted. On the one hand, for example, many people feared and some resisted the event. These institutions had sustained many towns economically, providing employment for generations of local laity, prompting the traffic of pilgrims and others, and consuming goods and services from their immediate surroundings. They operated many of the schools, hospitals,

---

[1] Joyce Youings, *The Dissolution of the Monasteries* (1971), 13.

almshouses, and other institutions. They held many of the lands (including rental properties) and other physical resources. Finally, of course, they offered, to a greater or lesser extent and along with other local institutions, some institutional focus for local religious life. Stories of local acts of loyalty to such institutions under threat of imminent dissolution, of hiding and burying valued relics and the like, of dissembling before the King's commissioners who came to survey resources, and of physical resistance on a scale ending with the Pilgrimage of Grace, cannot be dismissed.[2]

On the other hand, we also know that the queue of potential purchasers of dissolved ecclesiastical lands had begun to form even at the whiff of rumour before the event. We know, too, that many who thus licked their lips did so quite apart from theological loyalties. And, although most research on the subject has focused on the acquisitions of the landed classes, it strains credibility to imagine that urban interests, both individual townspeople and towns as civic bodies, were any less keen.

The town leaders in Winchester, for example, had long been, and long continued to be, religiously conservative and supportive of traditional doctrine. Yet they willingly cooperated in the surveys of the royal commissioners prior to the dissolution of religious houses in their city. Though they protested the loss of the Hospital of St John, they worked ardently and, in the end, successfully to regain its material resources and wealth for the community.[3] In Coventry, where the religious houses held a very considerable amount of property, there seem to have been as many instances of cooperation with the dissolutions of the 1530s as opposition to them, though the City government itself united vigorously against the dissolution of the chantry lands in the following decade.[4]

No doubt some of the interest taken by urban governing bodies in ecclesiastical possessions reflected motives of a political nature. After all, if monastic establishments had often been economically beneficial and socially beneficent to their surrounding communities, there had also been a history of frequent conflict and competition between them and the governing bodies of those communities. Many abbots, priors, and bishops had been lords either of whole

---

[2] See e.g. Duffy, *Stripping of the Altars*, 482, 490–2; Haigh, *English Reformations*, 143–4.

[3] Rosen, 'Economic and Social Aspects of Winchester', 64–5.

[4] Mark Knight, 'Religious Life in Coventry, 1485–1558', Ph.D. thesis (Warwick, 1986), 254–9.

towns or of parts and precincts thereof. They had controlled markets and fairs, the courts of law, housing, and rental income. In many cases local governing institutions emerged only at their leave, often by hard-fought victories in conflict with them. In some places no such emergence had been permitted.[5] In many places jurisdictional squabbles had long endured. They frequently showed little sign of abating in the opening decades of the sixteenth century.[6] If only by providing a force for townsmen to rally against, many of these squabbles contributed mightily to the sense of community which townsmen shared prior to the Reformation.[7] We will take up these issues of political jurisdiction in Chapter 8 below.

More to the immediate point, and in addition to their sundry char-itable institutions, many religious houses held substantial rentals and other properties which would no doubt have been coveted by the indigenous governing bodies of such communities. In Bath, for example, the Priory had held over 150 houses, making it easily the largest single landlord in the town.[8] In Coventry, the Priory had held lands worth nearly £350 a year, making it the wealthiest property owner, though two other religious houses in the city plus five others located outside also held lands within its bounds. The Corporation of Coventry itself, by contrast, held lands worth only £76 per annum.[9] In Bury St Edmunds, it has been estimated that the Abbey held £251 worth of rents in and around Bury in the fifteenth century and that some 70 per cent of townsmen had lived in properties held of the Abbey at Dissolution in 1539,[10] though Bury's failure to gain incorporation in the sixteenth century and the financial strength of

[5] Examples of such institutional retardation include Lincoln, St Albans, Read-ing, Bodmin, Shaftesbury, Cirencester, Romsey, Leominster, Peterborough, and Banbury.

[6] See e.g. the important essay of Harold Garrett-Goodyear, which shows that the early Tudor revival of *quo warranto* may be explained in considerable measure by the desire of towns and ecclesiastical authorities to challenge the jurisdictional claims made by the other party, using this legal device as a means towards that end. The Crown, of course, remained anxious to proceed with such clarification, and thus hap-pily availed this means to contentious parties (Harold Garrett-Goodyear, 'The Tudor Revival of *Quo Warranto* and Local Contributions to State Building', in M. S. Arnold, T. A. Green, S. A. Scully, and S. D. White (eds.), *On the Laws and Customs of Eng-land: Essays in Honor of Samuel E. Thorne* (Chapel Hill, NC, 1981), 231–95).

[7] Amongst other sources, the point is well made in Rosser, 'Communities of Parish and Guild', in Wright (ed.), *Parish, Church and People*, 30.

[8] A. J. King and B. H. Watts (eds.), *The Municipal Records of Bath, 1189–1604* (n.d.), 59. The Priory had held a number of important non-rental properties as well, including a grammar school.

[9] M. Knight, 'Religious Life in Coventry', 5–6.

[10] Housez, 'The Property Market in Bury St Edmunds', 50–1 and *passim*.

the regional gentry made it difficult for the town to acquire much of this from the Crown. And in York the three largest landholders were the Dean and Chapter of the Minster itself, St Mary's Abbey, and St Leonard's Hospital, with the last of these alone controlling as much as 20 per cent of the City's rents in 1542. In all, the monastic estates of York held on the eve of dissolution well over 400 individual properties worth nearly £250.[11]

The second wave of Dissolutions, those of the 1540s taking in the guilds, fraternities, and chantries, presents a somewhat different situation. Such institutions and their resources were more often of as well as in the community. Their properties, funds, and possessions were often more directly the result of lay bequests, often made in the relatively recent past and by local men and women, many of them still remembered at least by reputation. They were often dedicated to patron saints who also bore local significance, and who could be thought of as 'kynd neyghbour[s] and of our knowynge'.[12] Added to the frequent custom of accompanying intercessionary bequests with the obligation to enter the name of the deceased beneficiary on the bede-roll, where it would be read out to parishioners on a regular basis, it is easy to see how these bequests came to form part of the collective memory, and hence the very particular identity, of specific communities.[13]

Contemporaries often seemed to feel that only the laity could be trusted to see that such charitable and intercessionary bequests would be carried out by the clergy. In consequence, laymen often placed their bequests for chantries, obits, and anniversaries in the care of autonomous bodies of laymen rather than church officials or ecclesiastical institutions.[14] Then, too, some lay benefactors thought twice about leaving their bequests to a hierarchy whose upper echelons might be geographically distant and whose most visible officers were often but paid bailiffs. Many such bequests were thus held and administered through the parish and other, lay-governed, institutions: religious fraternities and guilds, chantries (many of which were run by guilds and fraternities), trusts of lay feoffees, and in many cases the mayor and aldermen of specific communities.[15]

[11] S. R. R. Jones, 'Property, Tenure and Rents', 142, 152, and table 4.1, pp. 179–80.
[12] Edmund College and James Walsh (eds.), *A Book of Showings to the Anchoress Julian of Norwich* (1978), ii. 447, as cited in Duffy, *Stripping of the Altars*, 164.
[13] See e.g. Duffy, *Stripping of the Altars*, chaps. 4, 5, and 9.
[14] Dobson, 'Citizens and Chantries', in Abulafia, Franklin, and Rubin (eds.), *Church and City*, 316–18.
[15] See e.g. C. Burgess and B. Kumin, 'Penitential Bequests and Parish Regimes in Late Medieval England', *Journal of Ecclesiastical History*, 44 (1993), 610–30;

Holdings of this sort could also be very extensive. Professor Dobson has noted the numerous chantry bequests of wealthy York merchants from the late fourteenth to the early sixteenth centuries, some for as much as 500 marks, which were to be administered by the officers of the City Corporation. Largely invested in rental properties, these seem not only to have produced income sufficient for the intended charitable purposes, but also a substantial surplus for the City's coffers.[16] Professor Palliser has estimated some five hundred houses in York had been held by the chantries prior to Dissolution.[17] Though it is doubtful that chantry bequests made directly to civic authorities anywhere else in the country could match these accumulated in York, the practice of entrusting the administration of chantry or similar intercessionary funds to lay officials seems more widespread than has been recognized.[18]

These properties too were, and were probably considered to be, much more in the nature of community resources already in hand than most of the holdings of the religious houses themselves. The threat of their dissolution, with the subsequent likelihood of their sale by the Crown to extra-mural purchasers, was thus much more likely to be feared, resisted, and even circumvented before the event. This was perhaps even more emphatically the case because, by the time these dissolutions took place in the mid- and latter 1540s, the press of population growth and poverty in many communities had begun to create shortages in local housing and raise rental values. After all, the Henrician Poor Law of 1536[19] and five of the seven rebuilding statutes of the same reign[20] were passed through Parliament in reaction to these intensified pressures just in the short span between the inception of the dissolution process in 1535 and the first of the so-called Chantry Acts in 1545. These were tumultuous times indeed! Both because the resources implicated in the second wave of Dissolutions were often seen as more integrally a part of the local community to begin with, and because the need to control and augment local housing had become more acute even in the intervening

---

Dobson, 'Citizens and Chantries', in Abulafia, Franklin, and Rubin (eds.), *Church and City*, 311–32.

[16] Ibid. 322–8.   [17] Palliser, *Tudor York*, 239.

[18] See e.g. the practice in the much more modest and in many ways more typical town of Faversham as related in Fleming, 'Charity, Faith and the Gentry of Kent', in Pollard (ed.), *Property and Politics*, 39.

[19] 27 Henry VIII, c. 25.

[20] 27 Henry VIII, c. 1; 32 Henry VIII, c. 18; 32 Henry VIII, c. 19; 33 Henry VIII, c. 36; 35 Henry VIII, c. 4.

few years, it seemed more important to control such resources after the second wave of Dissolutions than the first.

And yet, town governments were often not in a position to compete effectively in the race to purchase properties which, once confiscated, were usually thrown onto the open market. Often they could not do so until much later in the century. For this there could be many reasons, and they bear examination so that we may better understand the alternative strategies which such towns often adopted. Some of these explanations had to do with traditional attitudes on the part of urban officials; some with the strategy of the Crown in selling lands; and some with a simple lack of resources available at the right time.

Given the common and long-standing history of friction over local resources between townsmen and (especially ecclesiastical) landlords, is perhaps a little surprising to note that investment in large blocs of rental property had not often been a favoured strategy of townsmen acting either individually or collectively. Especially in middling-sized towns, the strategy of investment had not fared well through what were often many decades of stagnating rents and widespread physical dereliction. Jurisdictional squabbles between townsmen and landlords often concerned such issues as powers of self-government, control of schools, gaols or prisons, hospitals, and similar institutions. Much less often do they seem to include contention over income-bearing properties.[21] In consequence, while it seems logical for townsmen suddenly to have lusted after valuable rental properties which came onto the market in these years, and while there is a good deal of evidence that the leaders of at least some towns acted in just this way, in other cases it took some time before the barrier of old attitudes, much less a number of more practical encumbrances, could be overcome.

Crown policy in selling lands often proved one of those encumbrances, for the Crown's agenda in carrying out those sales allowed scant consideration of the state of England's towns or of their need to make particular acquisitions. The early preference, for example, was to sell confiscated properties with the obligation of knights' service, which was of course unattractive to most

---

[21] Thus e.g. it is again useful to remember the difficulty which W. G. Hoskins had in detecting amongst townsmen 'any sustained interest in urban property' before the mid-16th cent. (Hoskins, 'Provincial Towns', 10–11). See also Platt, *The English Medieval Town*, 181–3; Palliser, *Tudor York*, 265; and Housez, 'The Property Market in Bury St Edmunds', 2–3.

towns.[22] Another factor was the increasing preference on the Crown's part that corporate purchasers acquire lands in mortmain, which the majority of towns had not obtained licence to do. This intricate legal requirement will be discussed in greater detail below. Many towns simply lacked the financial wherewithal. The fiscal resources of almost all urban communities of this age were meagre, fragile, and relatively inelastic. They served to produce balanced budgets only some of the time, and income and expenditures were never very far apart in annual reckonings. Most towns were incapable either of raising large sums without extraordinary and imaginative strategies, or of doing it quickly under almost any circumstances. In consequence, such potential civic purchasers often had to wait until lands came onto the market a second or even a third time before they could step forth with cash in hand.[23] This is well illustrated, for example, by the experience of the City of York, which still suffered from economic decay when local lands first came onto the market. The City confiscated what lands it could prior to dissolution, but had to wait until its finances rebounded towards the end of the century before it could make larger purchases.[24] This experience seems to have been shared by many other towns as well.

By contrast, many private individuals, especially members of the landed classes and court circle who made most of the early purchases or even individual townsmen acting on their own behalf, often enjoyed far greater resources, and far greater flexibility and fluidity in their use. Fortunately for corporate urban interests, many of those private purchasers who made the running in the early days of the land rush seem to have had to sell off many of their purchases later on. This prompted a trickle-down effect which endured over the course of the century and more. It perpetuated an active market for dissolved lands well beyond the point of first sale. Thus it increased the chances that particular properties would eventually come into urban hands when local resources and attitudes became more favourable.[25]

And, fiscal considerations being what they were, the decision to invest precious resources made mayors and aldermen look very

---

[22] Youings, *Dissolution of the Monasteries*, 120; M. Knight, 'Religious Life in Coventry', 294; Cunich, 'Administration and Alienation of Ex-Monastic Lands', 149.

[23] Emphasized esp. in Zell, 'Mid-Tudor Market in Crown Lands in Kent', 67.

[24] D. M. Palliser, *The Reformation in York, 1534–1553*, Borthwick Papers, 40 (1971), 17–25.

[25] See e.g. Zell, 'Mid-Tudor Market in Crown Lands in Kent', 64.

carefully at the quality of the properties on offer at a given time. Particularly in the early years after dissolution, when the laws of supply and demand had not yet worked to upgrade and expand the housing stock to meet the frequent demand of rising population, much of the urban property on the market proved derelict and marginal. There are some suggestions that lands which had been held by ecclesiastical landlords, often lying in small parcels which were not geographically contiguous with each other or with larger blocs of land under the same authority, had been especially poorly maintained and administered.[26] Arranged in years of stagnant population and low rental values and with an eye to protecting the landlord against further losses, leases tended to be long-term. At the same time, the depressed population in many towns up to the early decades of the sixteenth century had depressed rental values, doing little to make urban property an attractive investment.[27] Town officials no doubt walked past such properties many times in the course of a working week: past crumbling mortar, sagging joists, cracked tiles, and leaking roofs. They must have known when renovation and upkeep would require more outlay than local coffers could support. Absentee purchasers from amongst the landed aristocracy or court officials who made most of the earlier purchases were less likely to be so knowledgeable. While striving for legislation which would compel renovation of such properties by their private owners on the one hand, urban corporations often waited until fiscal conditions improved and housing shortages emerged before they strove to purchase.[28]

From the time of the Dissolutions forward, of course, the situation evolved with considerable rapidity. The growth of immigration and net population in many towns soon accentuated the need for housing and other services. At the same time, traditional sources of civic revenue proved unequal to many of the tasks of local governance. Under these circumstances the importance of purchasing and renovating urban properties inevitably came into ever sharper relief.

[26] e.g. R. B. Dobson, 'Cathedral Chapters and Cathedral Cities: York, Durham and Carlisle in the Fifteenth Century', *Northern History*, 19 (1983), 35–6.

[27] Platt, *The English Medieval Town*, 182; Stanford Lehmberg, *The Reformation of the Cathedrals: Cathedrals in English Society, 1485–1603* (Princeton, 1988), 172–6; Joseph Kennedy, 'The Dissolution of the Monasteries in Hampshire and the Isle of Wight', MA thesis (London, 1953), 171; Dobson, 'Cathedral Chapters and Cathedral Cities', 35–6; G. H. Woodward, 'Dissolution of the Chantries', 168 and 177.

[28] Robert Tittler, ' "For the Re-edification of Townes": The Rebuilding Statutes of Henry VIII', *Albion*, 22/4 (Winter 1990), 591–605.

Acquisitions would not only contribute to the proportion of the housing stock under local control, but could also provide a much needed fillip to corporate finances in the latter decades of the century. Not for nothing did some of the Tudor Poor Laws encourage local authorities to purchase revenue-bearing properties, especially former chantry lands, so as to support the relief of poverty.[29]

For any and all of these reasons, many towns thus began later in the century and built their rental holdings slowly and steadily, in some instances working for many years to acquire a particular piece of property. Similar considerations applied to civic buildings and the institutions which they housed: schools, hospitals, almshouses, guildhalls, and even the structures of former ecclesiastical or fraternal buildings which could be recycled to other uses.

In sum, some delays in the acquisition of dissolved properties came by deliberate choice, but many more appear to have come out of necessity. This impression emerges even more clearly when we examine the imaginative strategies which some towns employed to acquire lands right at the beginning, often before the actual dissolution could proceed. For many, as local officials well knew, it would be the last chance for a long time if not for ever. In these circumstances it was not uncommon for some towns to pre-empt vulnerable properties or endowments before they could be confiscated, or to conceal knowledge of such properties from the agents of the Crown. Let us turn to the dubious but widespread businesses of pre-emption and concealment.

Though pre-emptive sales of lands to be dissolved were specifically declared illegal by statute (27 Henry VIII, c. 28, clause iv) there are some indications that officials even of religious houses themselves took such actions in the efforts to thwart dissolution of their establishments. This assumes, as one may do, that there was a widespread suspicion on the eve of the event that dissolutions were to take place. It is the same sort of suspicion which led the townsmen of Louth to attack the royal commissioners who came to assess the wealth of the local church, provoking the Lincolnshire Rising of 1536. Thus, for example, there are indications that the Prior of Spalding Monastery, Richard Palmer, sold off as many leases of priory lands as he could and for whatever he could get before the

---

[29] Ibid., with reference to the Henrician Rebuilding statutes, *passim*; Valerie Pearl, 'Social Policy in Early Modern London', in H. Lloyd-Jones, V. Pearl, and B. Worden (eds.), *History and Imagination: Essays in Honour of H. R. Trevor-Roper* (1981), 122.

royal commissioners beat him to it, for, as a contemporary observed, 'all the time he was prior the suppression was dailie loked for, ffor preachers did openly preach that the little houses were gon & the greate would followe'.[30]

But the examples of actions which were (consciously or unconsciously) pre-emptive seem more frequent and more vivid when they pertained to chantries, guilds, and the like in the 1540s, or even the plate and other material resources of such foundations, than when they pertained to the religious houses per se of the earlier wave. Most often prompted by rumour and fear for the loss of local resources, the lion's share of these pre-emptions came between the first and second waves of dissolution. In Hull and Southampton townsmen confiscated and sold church ornaments and plate before they could be confiscated by the Crown, using the proceeds for street pavement and other public works.[31] The unincorporated town of Richmond seized in 1544 six chantries, two chapels, and ten obits.[32]

Carmarthen financed its successful quest for a charter of incorporation in 1546 by a similar seizure.[33] The Town Guild of Lichfield transferred numerous lands to trustees for the unincorporated town in 1545 before they could be confiscated, securing them more permanently by the subsequent incorporation of 1548.[34] In the southwest, both Plymouth and Dartmouth seized plate to finance the purchase of required military ordnance during the French War of the early 1540s[35] and Looe confiscated lands set aside for obits to finance repair of its bridge in 1544.[36] Virtually a third of the more than two hundred churchwardens' accounts examined by Ronald Hutton, in rural and urban parishes alike, record the sale of ornaments and vestments before they could be taken.[37] Even before 1540 the precociously Protestant leadership of Canterbury replenished civic coffers with proceeds from the sale of goods and property from

[30] Testimony of Miles Raby, former Clerk of the Priory, in a concealment case of 1572–3; PRO, E. 134/14 & 15 Elizabeth, Mic. 15. The Warden of the Franciscan Friary in Chester seems to have done the same thing with leases to Friary lands; *VCH, Chester*, 3 (1980), 173.

[31] Platt, *The English Medieval Town*, 180–1.

[32] L. P. Wenham, 'The Chantries, Guilds, Obits and Lights of Richmond, Yorkshire', *Yorkshire Archeological Society Journal*, 38 (1955), pt. 2, p. 210.

[33] PRO, C. 1/1222/34, *Goodale* v. *Mayor of Carmarthen*.

[34] Rosser, 'Town and Guild of Lichfield', 45; PRO, C. 66/811/m.29.

[35] Whiting, *Blind Devotion*, 67 and 180. Whiting also notes the continued confiscation of church property after the Dissolutions, as in e.g. Exeter in both 1552 and 1559; ibid. 216.

[36] Ibid. 31.

[37] Ronald Hutton, *The Rise and Fall of Merry England* (Oxford, 1994), 92.

chantry, fraternity, and chapel. In addition, it invited a textile manu-
facturer to set up shop in the Blackfriars, and it used rents from
former monastic properties to help the poor.[38] The declining
Lincolnshire port of Boston pulled off one of the most substantial
pre-dissolution acquisitions of all. After securing a charter of
incorporation in 1545 expressly for that purpose, the borough purchased for £1,646, to be paid out over twelve years, extensive guild
and other resources worth £525 a year: a relative bargain at the
time.[39]

A familiar and important example of this sort derives from the
City of York. As was widely the case elsewhere, very few of the
initial purchasers of dissolved ecclesiastical property in that City
were townsmen, much less the government of the City itself.[40] We
must infer from this not so much that the City officials were unwilling
to make such purchases but that they were unable to do so in the
event. Undoubtedly recognizing ahead of time the difficulties they
would face in purchasing after surrender, officials successfully carried out in 1536 a municipal dissolution of some local chantries and
obits so that they could be absorbed into the City's holdings. When
the income of those endowments declined, the City simply turned to
Parliament for a statute which would allow it to divest itself of the
burdens of maintenance while keeping the endowments. Coming
well before the chantry dissolutions of the next decade, this was a
perfectly legal, and by no means unique, strategy.[41] Whether this was
done in the fear—one could hardly say foreknowledge—that
chantries would go the way of the smaller monasteries or not is difficult to tell. Yet it does surely illustrate the perceived desirability of
bringing such properties under local control, and of deriving from

[38] Peter Clark, 'Reformation and Radicalism in Kentish Towns', in W. J. Momm-
sen, P. Alter, and R. Scribner (eds.), *Urban Classes, the Nobility and the Reformation*,
Publications of the German Historical Institute, 5 (1979), 119, and *English Provincial
Society from the Reformation to the Revolution: Religion, Politics and Society in Kent,
1500–1640* (Hassocks, Sussex, 1977), 44. Chantry property was also confiscated in
Sandwich (Clark, 'Reformation and Radicalism', 124).

[39] This is despite the fact that the town's petition for grants in the Augmentations
indicates lands worth but £65; PRO, E. 318/5/143. But see details of further acquisitions in *Letters and Papers of Henry VIII* (1545), grants nos. 648 and 51, and
C. 66/771/m. 32, Patent Roll entry of Boston's charter indicating these properties.
A discussion of the purchase, which was contested by some local interests, may be
found in PRO, STAC 3/Bundle 5/11, petition of John Browne of Boston.

[40] Above, p. 51; *VCH, City of York* (Oxford, 1961), 117–18.

[41] A. G. Dickens, 'A Municipal Dissolution of Chantries at York, 1536', *Yorkshire
Archaeological Society Journal*, 36 (1944–7), 164–73. See also Palliser, *Reformation in
York*, 4–6.

them what the town's officials would have seen as the maximum benefit for the community.

Another means of preserving these resources for local control lay in concealment. During and after the Dissolutions, many local authorities intentionally concealed from the Crown's commissioners knowledge of various sorts of vulnerable properties and institutions. Typically, they simply kept quiet or had lapses of memory before commissioners whose tight schedules in surveying a large region made thorough investigation impossible. Then they quietly appropriated those resources for local use. This widespread practice proved more effective with smaller properties than larger, though such highly visible targets as the lands and buildings of guilds and fraternities were concealed as well as those of, for example, chantries, obits, and anniversaries. Sometimes even lands listed in the *Valor* were in effect concealed when the Crown simply forgot about them, allowing them to be retained in local hands by default. Such was the efficiency of Crown land administration in the mid-century![42]

Concealment often allowed town governments to come out ahead in two ways. It not only permitted the retention of property or associated endowments, but sometimes it allowed towns easily to divest themselves of the financial obligation to employ the traditional chantry priests and other clerics, whose activities had of course been curtailed. In Hull, for example, the Corporation had been taking an annual loss because the obligatory costs of supporting chantries, anniversaries, and obits had come to exceed the value of the rental income attached for that purpose. At dissolution, the town managed to conceal the bulk of chantry endowments from the King's commissioners, thus keeping those revenues without enduring the expenses for which they had been intended.[43]

In a similar fashion the Mayor and Aldermen of Walsall were accused in 1560 of having concealed not only the chantry lands of the former Guild of St John, worth over a hundred pounds per annum, but the Guildhall itself.[44] The government of Bury St Edmunds

[42] David Thomas, 'The Elizabethan Crown Lands: Their Purposes and Problems', in Richard Hoyle (ed.), *The Estates of the English Crown, 1558–1640* (Cambridge, 1992), 69. For concealment of parish properties, which often wound up under borough control, see Beat Kumin, *The Shaping of a Community: The Rise and Reformation of the English Parish, c.1400–1560* (Aldershot, 1996), 210–12.

[43] Rosemary Horrox (ed.), *Selected Rentals and Accounts of Medieval Hull, 1293–1528*, Yorkshire Archeological Society Record Series, 141 (1983 for 1981), 17.

[44] PRO, E. 133/1/61 (*c.*1565).

(though not empowered by incorporation until 1606) evidently did the same thing, appropriating the Guildhall for town use.[45] Even the smallest towns engaged in concealment. The officials of God-manchester burned the property deeds of both religious guilds to prevent them being traced after the town seized the lands, while nearby St Neots concealed the lands of the Jesus Fraternity as well.[46] And concealments were so common in the lands controlled by the Duchy of Lancaster that Duchy officials launched no fewer than seventeen separate investigations of them—applying to agrarian as well as urban jurisdictions—before the century's end.[47]

Though the more visible institutions dissolved in the 1530s— monasteries, priories, abbeys, and the schools, hospitals, and similar institutions attached to them—were more difficult to conceal, many of them were successfully retained as well. The Borough of Andover, for example, concealed and appropriated the lands and rents of the Hospital of St John the Baptist, which had been financed partly by the Guild Merchant of the town. This ruse lasted until 1574, when the Earl of Leicester claimed title, compelling them to com-pound for their acquisitions.[48] Bedford concealed St Leonard's Hospital, whose lands brought in £20 a year.[49] The officers of Win-chester managed to appropriate the fifty or so properties of the Hos-pital of St John, along with the Hospital itself and some additional resources, prior to their dissolution.[50] The townsmen of Beverley concealed properties whose value had reached £195 by the time they were discovered late in the century.[51]

Intercessionary institutions technically subject to dissolution were by no means always listed in the *Valor Ecclesiasticus*. After all, this catalogue had been primarily designed to list the holdings of the religious houses, while perhaps the majority of intercessionary

---

[45] Margaret Statham, *Jankyn Smith and the Guildhall Feoffees* (Bury St Edmunds, 1981), 7.

[46] Haigh, *English Reformations*, 172.   [47] Ibid. 171.

[48] *VCH, Hampshire*, 4 (1911), 356.

[49] *VCH, Bedfordshire*, 3 (1912), 24. In view of the very modest corporate incomes of the day, this was a considerable sum, probably amounting to one-half or one-third of the annual average revenue of the Borough corporation at the time of conceal-ment.

[50] The lands were confirmed in the Borough's possession by the town incorpora-tion of 1588; Rosen, 'Economic and Social Aspects of Winchester', 66, 79–80. See also *CPR, Eliz.*, ii. 155.

[51] *VCH, Yorkshire, East Riding*, 6 (1989), 69. As was often the case when such lands were discovered, the Crown compounded with the Borough, allowing it to retain the properties for a fair consideration.

bequests had been entrusted to other sorts of institutions, including the chantry, parish, guild, fraternity, and the town itself. Given the laxity with which the Crown managed its landed estates, even some which may be found in the *Valor* remained unconfiscated and, in effect, concealed.[52] Yet in those instances when it is possible to compare municipal records after the Dissolutions with the official record of pre-dissolution ecclesiastical holdings as compiled in the *Valor*, we find numerous properties noted in the former but missing from the latter.[53] A great many of these represent concealments.

Especially in the Elizabethan years the Crown did try with some vigour to discover concealments. Many were discovered, though of course we have no reliable means of assessing what proportion of all concealments these represent.[54] In most Exchequer cases, the local, concealing interests were more likely to be allowed to compound for them, as was the case with Andover, than to have them repossessed by the Crown. Beverley presents another example. When its concealed lands, formerly belonging to several local chantries, were discovered around 1585, the Crown allowed the Borough to compound for them, thus recognizing its possession of them.[55]

Though the actual fact of dissolution itself was obviously and widely feared, especially when it threatened resources which had become such an important part of the community, only two towns, King's Lynn and Coventry, succeeded in gaining exemptions from such acts. In exchange for their agreement to drop opposition in Parliament to the dissolution bill of 1547, both were exempted from the ultimate statute with the promise that their lands would be granted back after the fact. In addition, we must assume, to having had unusually astute spokesmen in Parliament and perhaps at court, both towns had been able to demonstrate how vital the incomes from those properties had become to essential functions: repair of piers and sea walls in Lynn and upkeep of two parish churches in Coventry.[56] (In the event, however, though Lynn received

---

[52] D. Thomas, 'Elizabethan Crown Lands', 69.

[53] John Caley and Joseph Hunter (eds.), *Valor Ecclesiasticus* (6 vols.; 1810–34).

[54] e.g. cases regarding alleged concealment in Beverley, Yorkshire, PRO, E. 178/2816; Dunstable, Bedfordshire, E. 178/367; Liskeard, Cornwall, E. 134/9 Eliz., Hil. 4; Windsor, Berkshire, E. 134/31 Eliz., Hil. 12. Further details are often to be found in PRO, E. 302, 'Particulars for Concealments'. See also C. J. Kitching, 'The Search for Concealed Lands in the Reign of Elizabeth I', *TRHS*, 5th ser., 24 (1974) 63–78.

[55] 27 Eliz. I, PRO, C. 66/1254.

[56] *Acts of the Privy Council*, NS, vol. ii, entry of 6 May 1548. Coventry had failed in its earlier attempt to prevent the surrender of the Priory or Cathedral, which had been

its due according to the agreement,[57] Coventry did not. Instead of receiving them as a gift as agreed, it had in the end to purchase the desired lands, worth £100 per annum, at the substantial price of £1,300. 15s. 20d.!)[58]

An examination of the strategies and circumstances surrounding the acquisition of urban properties thus reveals some subtleties which have not commonly been appreciated. We can see that somewhat different conditions governed local intentions towards the two waves of dissolution. In the case of the later dissolutions, properties pried loose from traditional authorities, or dissolved altogether, seemed much more central to the resources of the community. Local governing authorities seemed both more anxious and more able to prevent their alienation from the community to begin with or, failing that, more determined to acquire or restore them under local control in subsequent years.

Failing either pre-emptive acquisition before the Dissolutions or concealment during and afterwards, town governments had at least in theory the more visible and at least putatively straightforward possibility of simple purchase. To this prospect, as we have already begun to recognize, there were a number of impediments of a legal and attitudinal as well as a fiscal nature. It is to the first and last of these factors which we must now turn.

the largest property owner in the City and was worth £350 a year in rents and other income. The surrender took place on 15 January 1538/9 (M. Knight, 'Religious Life in Coventry', 239–40, 248).

[57] *CPR, Edward VI*, ii (1924), 21 May 1548, 11–13.

[58] M. Knight, 'Religious Life in Coventry', 312–15; PRO, E. 318/27/1548 and see also an additional and very substantial purchase described in PRO, E. 318/8/321.

5

The Problem of Enabling
Authority

The effort to consolidate and control the varied resources of individual communities could prove a substantial challenge for almost any provincial town of the age. To do so with legal security, and to be empowered to manage such resources effectively—e.g. to renovate, lease, or even sell properties—posed even more complex challenges. These efforts obviously required substantial capital outlays. They also required a legal status or authority which could withstand litigious challenges to the title, management, or disposition of the resources in question.

Prospective purchasers of dissolved lands and other resources also often required certain clarifications of title of the properties or rights to particular jurisdictions.[1] Though this may seem odd to us today, the situation seemed real enough in the many towns which had suffered severe economic stagnation or decay, or even mere administrative laxity, in the decades leading up to the Reformation era. There are more signs of urban prosperity in the pre-Reformation decades than one used to think,[2] but the ranks of decayed and

[1] A. R. Bridbury, 'English Provincial Towns in the Later Middle Ages', *Ec.HR*, 2nd ser., 34/1 (Feb. 1981), 24.

[2] The debate on urban prosperity, or the absence of it, in the late Middle Ages includes the following contributions: M. M. Postan, *The Medieval Economy and Society* (1972); A. R. Bridbury, *Economic Growth: England in the Later Middle Ages* (1962); D. M. Palliser, 'A Crisis in English Towns? The Case of York, 1460–1640', *Northern History*, 14 (1978), 108–25; Phythian-Adams, *Desolation of a City*; and 'Urban Decay in Late Medieval England', in P. Abrams and E. A. Wrigley (eds.), *Towns in Societies: Essays in Economic History and Historical Sociology* (Cambridge, 1978); R. B. Dobson, 'Urban Decline in Late Medieval England', *TRHS*, 5th ser., 27 (1977), 1–22; S. H. Rigby, 'Urban Decline in the Later Middle Ages?', *Urban History Yearbook* (1979), 46–59; Bridbury, 'English Provincial Towns', 1–21; R. Tittler, 'Late Medieval Urban Prosperity', *Ec.HR*, 2nd ser., 37/4 (Nov. 1984), 551–4, and A. R. Bridbury, 'Late Medieval Urban Prosperity, a Rejoinder', ibid. 555–6; D. M. Palliser, 'Urban Decay Revisited', in J. A. F. Thompson (ed.), *Towns and Townspeople in the Fifteenth Century* (1988), 1–21; M. Bailey, 'A Tale of Two

impoverished towns still seem well subscribed. It was not uncommon in the less favoured provincial towns of the day for at least some rental properties (as well as e.g. markets, fairs, courts, etc.) to have yielded so little revenue that their holders, especially when they were absentees, had simply neglected to go to the trouble of collecting negligible rents.[3] Some were simply inattentive administrators of the lands and entitlements which were legitimately theirs, eventually losing track of their possessions and entitlements. Often such inattention eventually became customary, bringing into question landlords' entitlement to do what they had not done on a regular basis and over a long period. In that void of administrative control, officials of the town itself, intimately familiar with local conditions, often stepped in and assumed jurisdiction. Though they may have gotten away with this possession by default at the time, it did little to clarify their legal entitlement to such authority.

When the economies of many of those towns revived in the sixteenth century and when rising populations began to drive up rents once more, those revenues once again began to be worth the trouble of collection. Legitimate landlords of long standing began to reassert their claims. At the same time, a great many new landlords, those who had purchased dissolved lands from the Crown, were much more aggressive in demanding the revenues, powers, and perquisites to which, in their view, their purchases entitled them. In these circumstances, conflicts over control of local institutions and resources became quite common, with such issues as title to properties and the right to collect rents, hold court, and enjoy the revenues of the market at stake. Such conflicts often entailed the collision of local custom with legal entitlement, as documented by deed or other writ.

For these and similar reasons, a great many post-Reformation towns not only found themselves wanting to challenge the putative holdings of superior authorities, but they themselves faced constant challenges to their own jurisdiction. Such challenges ensued regardless of whether that jurisdiction had accrued through practice or had been conveyed more formally. Even when such towns had not effectively encroached in this manner, the circumstances of the era brought

Towns: Buntingford and Standon in the Later Middle Ages', *Journal of Medieval History*, 19 (1993), 351–71. The recent summary by Alan Dyer clarifies some issues, but cautions against definitive statements (*Decline and Growth in English Towns, 1400–1640* (Cambridge, 1995)).

[3] This and the following two paragraphs are based on Alan Everitt, 'The Marketing of Agricultural Produce', in J. Thirsk (ed.), *The Agrarian History of England and Wales,* iv. *1500–1640* (Cambridge, 1967), 502–6.

their claims to authority under greater scrutiny than ever before. This followed because of the increasing value of urban properties and economic activities in this era. It followed, too, because a new generation of landlords, brought in through the Crown's sale of dissolved properties, aggressively pursued what they saw as their entitlement. Though Professor Everitt has identified the period from about the 1570s as particularly characterized by litigation of this sort, scrutiny of different classes of court cases from those upon which he relied has allowed us to push back the dates of this litigious period several decades.[4] A few examples will suggest the nature of these battles.

In the absence of strong manorial control by the Abbot of Bury St Edmunds, the inhabitants of the small Suffolk town of Beccles had for a least a generation or two come to utilize and to control the fenland surrounding their community. When William Rede purchased Beccles Fen following the dissolution of the Abbey, the actual grant merely called for the terms of his jurisdiction to be worked out over a five-year period. Yet having spent a great deal for the property, Rede assumed a close and complete jurisdiction from the very beginning of his tenure. He appointed his own reeves, had them collect various fines and profits from people using the fen, and let out part of the lands—which the townsmen had long utilized as common land—at lucrative rents. The townsmen had traditionally used the fen for pasture, firewood, building materials, and other things. They naturally resented what they viewed as Rede's encroachment. Litigation rapidly ensued, but was by no means rapidly resolved. Marked by actions in both Chancery and Exchequer and the acquisition of not one but two charters of incorporation for the townsmen, the case carried on into the third generation of the Rede lordship before some resolution could be found.[5]

A similar story emerges from the purchase by Sir Thomas Pakington of the lordship of the town of Aylesbury. Having come into possession of his new domain, he was surprised and disappointed to find that the townsmen, his tenants, had come to exercise considerable powers of self-government. Pakington had worked hard to gain his

---

[4] Everitt, 'Marketing of Agricultural Produce'. See also Diarmaid MacCulloch, *Suffolk and the Tudors: Politics and Religion in an English County, 1500–1600* (Oxford, 1986), 322–6.

[5] *Letters and Papers of Henry VIII*, 15, p. 175; PRO, C. 3/29/109 (1564 ff.); C. 3/30/4; E. 133/4/658 (28 Elizabeth, East.); E. 134/28 Eliz., East 21 (1586); E. 123/14/23a; E. 123/14/120; E. 123/14/203–5; E. 123/13/46; E. 123/13/145; E. 123/13/235; E. 123/13/244; E. 123/13/247; E. 123/12/29; E. 123/12/43; E. 123/12/108–9; E. 123/12/123; E. 123/12/227; E. 123/12/297–8; E. 123/11/154.

purchase against the efforts of rival claimants to begin with,[6] and he naturally wished to receive the maximum benefits to which he felt entitled. He thus brought suit against the townsmen for what he alleged was their use of a forged custumal: the document which recorded local understanding of custom, and thus came to serve as an instrument of local government.[7] The burgesses found themselves in a difficult position. They had long exercised the rights in question, and yet they had scant legal grounds beyond claims of precedent, recorded in their custumal, upon which to rest their case.[8]

Still a third case in the same vein derives from the Devon borough of Barnstaple, one of the chief ports of the Bristol Channel. Following his purchase of Magdalen Priory which lay within the borough, Lord William Howard was distressed to learn that the burgesses had operated their own court of record, regulated weights and measures, punished vagrants, and collected both fines against offenders and rents on some local properties. These were all powers which Howard understood to have devolved from the Prior's jurisdiction to his own by dint of his purchase. He thus urged his bailiff and tenants to harass the town's officials in the performance of their duties until they should give them over. Faced with this aggressive stance, the burgesses pushed back. After a few violent scuffles, they sued to retain their accustomed powers.[9]

In a number of cases of this type the plaintiff was the Crown itself, especially when concealed lands were at issue. In view of the Crown's poor record in managing its own urban properties there is more than a little irony in this.[10] Nevertheless, cases of this sort are quite common throughout the period at hand in the Court of Exchequer, which held jurisdiction over Crown lands. Many of them result from the work of local informants who hoped to purchase the lands

[6] *Letters and Papers of Henry VIII*, 20/2, p. 6.2 99; *Cary, Lord Hunsdon* v. *Pakington*, PRO, C. 3/47/52.

[7] *Pakington* v. *Walwyn* (1553), PRO, C. 1/1373/11. The custumal survives in the Birmingham Reference Library, Hampton Collection MS no. 505423 ('Customary of the Manor of Aylesbury'). I am grateful to Mr Hugh Hanley of the Buckingham County Record Office for bringing this to my attention.

[8] In the end, they got around Pakington's suit by successfully petitioning for a charter of incorporation (R. Gibbs, *A History of Aylesbury . . .* (Aylesbury, 1885), 116–22; and *VCH Buckinghamshire*, 3 (1925) 6–9).

[9] *Drewe, Mayor of Barnstable et al.* v. *Golde, Hayne and Savell* (34 Henry VIII), PRO, STAC 2/13/88–91; *Mayor of Barnstable* v. *Savell, Golde and Oliver* (temp. Edward VI), STAC 3/3/9. For a general introduction to Tudor Barnstaple, see Joyce Youings, 'Tudor Barnstable: A New Life for an Ancient Borough', *Report and Transactions of the Devon Association*, 121 (1989), 1–14.

[10] Hoyle (ed.), *Estates of the English Crown*, 39–40.

in question if the town's rights could successfully be challenged.[11] In this manner, for example, the Crown challenged the possession by the City of Gloucester of the former Fraternity of Our Lady of Chipping Sodbury, claiming it to be concealed.[12] It challenged the Cornish borough of Liskeard with concealment of various chantry lands,[13] and also the mayor and burgesses of Walsall for concealing lands worth over a hundred pounds as well as the guildhall.[14] A host of similar examples may be found in the records of the Exchequer.

One coveted asset in these hard-fought contests was the right, established by licence, to obtain and hold land in some form of tenure which was at least relatively unencumbered. The right to acquire and hold in mortmain had loomed as especially important since the 1391 Statute of Mortmain had prescribed this form of tenure for towns, guilds, fraternities, and similar bodies as well as for religious and spiritual persons.[15] It not only meant holding property without such feudal obligations as knights' service, but also the freedom to alienate at will and without further permission. Indeed, it could be difficult for towns and similar corporate groups to acquire and manage rental property and some other holdings without a licence to hold in mortmain, making that licence itself a highly coveted prize. Thus, for example, when the wealthy Hereford resident (tailor, draper, and six times mayor) Richard Phelips wished to give to that City a considerable amount of his property in 1535, he granted it for only a limited period until the Mayor and Aldermen could secure a licence to hold it in mortmain. As an experienced official and successful man of business, Phelips well knew that his bequest would be open to question without that safeguard.[16] Once the licence had been obtained, in July 1536, he re-bestowed his gift, this time in perpetuity.[17]

Many towns already possessed the right to acquire lands in mortmain by the opening of our period. Yet though Hereford, still an unincorporated borough, was able to secure such a licence as late as

---

[11] Esp. in the documentary categories E. 134, Depositions taken by Commission, and E. 178, Special Commissions of Enquiry. See also D. Thomas, 'Elizabethan Crown Lands', in Hoyle (ed.), *Estates of the English Crown*, 69.

[12] PRO, E. 134/15 Eliz./Trin. 3 (1573).   [13] PRO, E. 134/9 Eliz./Hil. 4.

[14] PRO, E. 133/1/61 (c.1565).   [15] 15 Richard II, c. 5.

[16] F. R. James, 'Copy of a Deed by Richard Phelips, Dated 1535', *Transactions of the Woolhope Field Naturalists' Club* (1934), 100–4.

[17] Historical Manuscripts Commission, *Thirteenth Report, Appendix*, 4 (1892), 'Report on the Manuscripts of the Corporation of Hereford', 287; F. R. James, 'Copy of a Deed by Richard Phelips', 100–4.

1535 to meet the conditions of Phelips's bequest, the Crown's policy towards such licences seems to have changed very shortly thereafter. In most instances after about 1540 the Crown seems to have preferred that towns in a similar situation acquire a full charter of incorporation, of which the right to obtain lands in mortmain had by then become a common feature, rather than a mere licence by itself. Not only could the Crown charge more for a charter of incorporation than for a licence to acquire in mortmain, but incorporation allowed the Crown to invest local officials with much fuller authority, and thus to help ensure order and tranquillity in the community to a much fuller extent, than by a mere licence to hold in mortmain.

Only a decade after Hereford acquired its licence in 1535 the Borough of Warwick petitioned the Court of Augmentations for the right to purchase certain dissolved lands. The Chancellor of the Augmentations, Sir Edward North, insisted on the need 'to make a corporation for the said towns to receyve the Landes and possessions aforesaid', which, in the event, included the right to possess lands in mortmain.[18] The City of Exeter, for all its claims of ancient status and despite its preliminary incorporation in 1537, met a similar response in petitioning for the purchase of certain lands in 1550. The Augmentations considered it necessary 'for doubts that may arise [re:] their corporatyion that they nowe have to make a good and sufficient graunt [of] corporacion'. A second, fuller, incorporation ensued in that year, granting the right to acquire lands in mortmain to the sum of £100, along with the specific lands in question.[19]

By the time of the Dissolutions the right to acquire lands in mortmain or in other secure forms, a right which had long been well employed by religious corporations, was also well established in at least some boroughs. The same could be said for incorporation itself. Yet this was still not true in most boroughs. Even some of the most important provincial centres enjoyed no such rights. They were perhaps especially unlikely to have been held by those towns which had laboured under the governance of an ecclesiastical landlord, a condition which often seriously impeded the acquisition of local governing authority. In view of this and other legal shortcomings, to acquire and hold property securely, and notwithstanding the efforts of many towns to practise simple concealment in the hope of getting

---

[18] PRO, E. 318/22/1187; and also *VCH, Warwickshire*, 8 (1969), 490, where, however, the manuscript reference is given incorrectly. The grant of incorporation, dated 10 May, 37 Henry VIII, is in *Letters and Papers, 37 Henry VIII*, 20, item 846, no. 41.

[19] PRO, E. 318/28/1602; *CPR, Edward VI*, iii. 205–6.

away with it, the governing bodies of a great many towns, like Warwick and Exeter, thus found pressing motivation to fortify their legal
positions. The same may certainly be said as well for groups of leading townsmen in towns which had no real governing bodies as such,
or in which indigenous government remained weak.

Even if we include such institutions as schools and almshouses
along with rent-bearing properties, it would be misleading to discuss
this desire for legal formalization as deriving only from the need for
additional property. Towns held political, social, and other motives
as well, and these will be discussed in their turn. Yet from the perspective of town governing bodies faced with increasing civic costs,
the sudden opportunity to bid for local properties and other
resources, now available in such unprecedented numbers, sharply
focused local strategies of enablement. These circumstances vastly
enhanced the attractions of greater local autonomy. In many towns
they created a virtual crisis of authority.

For the most part townsmen employed three strategies to meet
this need: litigation, enfeoffment to uses, and incorporation by
charter.[20] As we will see, the significance of such steps would come to
apply to much more than new properties alone. Yet towns undertook them at this particular time first and foremost either to acquire
such resources or to defend resources, old as well as new, already in
hand. Each of these three courses of action bears closer scrutiny.

We have already observed the marked increase in litigation which
seems evident after *c.*1540 between landlords (including the Crown)
who had acquired ecclesiastical properties and perquisites on the
one hand and groups of townsmen, acting on their own or on behalf
of their communities, on the other.[21] While most such cases tended
to be brought against towns rather than by them, there are certainly
some towns which undertook litigation in order to gain rental properties and other resources.

In the Suffolk market town of Sudbury in the mid-1540s, for

---

[20] Incorporation could also be acquired by statute, but the difficulties of so doing
made this a very rare occurrence. For the obstacles involved in towns getting any
legislation through, see R. Tittler, 'Elizabethan Towns and the "Points of Contact":
Parliament', *Parliamentary History*, 8/2 (1989), 275–88.

[21] See Everitt, 'Marketing of Agricultural Produce', in Thirsk (ed.), *Agrarian
History*, iv. 502–6, who places this increase in litigation in the last three decades of
the century, and my own work, which places it several decades earlier by looking
at different classes of court documents: Tittler, 'The Incorporation of Boroughs,
1540–1558', *History*, 62/204 (Feb. 1977), 24–42; and Tittler, 'The End of the Middle
Ages in the English Country Town', *Sixteenth Century Journal*, 18/4 (Winter 1987),
480–2.

example, the Mayor, William Smyth, brought suit in the Court of Chancery against William Ayloffe, whose father had willed extensive properties, apparently of former charitable endowments, to the town for the relief of the local poor. The Mayor and burgesses who had received the lands in question had indeed used them for relief of the poor and other charitable purposes. They claimed that after a few years Ayloffe the younger had subsequently entered the lands, expelled the borough's tenants, and taken both possession and profits for himself. The townsmen now wanted the lands back, according to the terms of the initial bequest. While the younger Ayloffe did not deny the allegations against him, he claimed that the town's officers had forfeited their rights by not fulfilling all the conditions of the bequest. No decree survives to tell us the outcome of this case, but it is worth noting that the townsmen sought an incorporation a few years later which strengthened their title to lands in their possession.[22] Though no connection between the litigation and the incorporation can be proven, it must at least be suspected.

In the complex litigation over the control of the Beccles Fen, noted above, the townsmen were plaintiffs[23] as well as defendants,[24] as each side sued the other for acknowledgement of perceived rights. Newcastle-upon-Tyne, where the mayor and burgesses carried on protracted litigation against the Bishop of Durham over rights to certain properties, amongst other things,[25] and Chester, where the townsmen challenged to gain the tithes of a collegiate church,[26] illustrate the same tendency.

In sum, this was indeed an especially litigious time for the governing officials of English towns and for those, individual landowners and the Crown itself, who challenged the holdings and jurisdiction of those towns. Most boroughs, corporate or not, had constantly to be ready to defend their lands and jurisdiction against legal assault. No doubt this litigiousness was encouraged by the lawyers and government officials of the day, and obviously the process could be dauntingly expensive for most communities. Yet litigation of this sort had become more of a reality of urban government than

---

[22] *William Smyth, Mayor* v. *William Ayloffe, gent.*, *c.*1544–7, PRO, C. 1/file 1160/61–2. Sudbury was incorporated in May 1554, *CPR, I Mary*, 141–3.

[23] PRO, C. 3/29/109, *Beccles* v. *Gresham* (1564), and C. 3/30/4, *Beccles* v. *Rede* (1564).

[24] *Rede* v. *Baase*, E. 133/4/658 (1586).

[25] PRO, E. 134/23 & 24 Eliz./Mich. 17; and 8 James I, East 41. (These are two separate cases revolving around the same dispute.)

[26] E. 134/38–9 Eliz./Mich. 30.

ever before, and the total number of such cases seems rapidly to have increased from the fourth or fifth decades of the sixteenth century. As we will see further on, it encouraged towns to engage experienced lawyers as Recorders and to attract powerful patrons as High Stewards. It also provided a continual motivation to seek more permanent protection by legal means.

A second strategy whereby towns tried to secure and defend the possession of property and other resources in this era was enfeoffment to uses. This meant the creation of a trust: a self-perpetuating body of individuals or feoffees—in this case almost always townsmen—legally entrusted with control of particular resources by the authority of a deed of enfeoffment. Trusts certainly existed prior to the Reformation, when both individual families and also such institutions as the inns of court and university colleges did a great deal to expand their use. In its effort to prevent evasion of common-law practice which favoured the interests of the Crown, Parliament passed the Statute of Uses in 1535.[27] Yet in practice, the common lawyers chose to interpret this statute narrowly, applying it less to secular bodies than to private individuals.

After the Dissolutions, the greater burdens which befell urban communities, coupled with the sudden availability of local rental properties on the market and the importance of refounding charitable institutions, made trusts particularly useful devices for townsmen as well. They allowed groups of townsmen to hold land legally and with at least some of the entitlements of a corporation, yet without the greater difficulty and expense of incorporation itself.[28] We thus find townsmen forming trusts to gain and administer particular lands or institutions acquired or regained after the Dissolutions.

The formation of most of these trusts followed a common pattern. First, a group of townsmen secured sufficient funds to purchase from the Crown the desired properties. The Crown then granted the land to two or three of the townsmen who had been delegated by their fellows to receive it. These receivers then conveyed the same lands by formal deed to a larger group of named townsmen, usually a dozen or more, who then became the trustees or feoffees of that property. The deed in question conveyed to the feoffees not only the lands themselves, but also the powers of governance over them and con-

[27]   27 Henry VIII, c. 10.

[28]   This and the preceding paragraph are based on F. W. Maitland, 'Trust and Corporation', in H. A. L. Fisher (ed.), *The Collected Papers of F. W. Maitland* (3 vols.; Cambridge, 1911), 321–404.

trol of rental income from them. In addition, such deeds also provided for the perpetuation of the feoffees, usually by co-option of replacements in their own numbers. In effect, deeds of trust granted both lands and governance and often served as de facto governing instruments for the whole community. In some cases these endured, without incorporation or further enhancement, right up to the modern era.[29] Ironically enough, the very fact that towns which were governed chiefly by their trusts, rather than by corporations, made them ineligible for the application of the Municipal Corporations Act of 1835, allowed many to survive well beyond that time.

Effective trusts came to operate at this time in, for example, Bicester, Bury St Edmunds, Coggeshall, Fowey, Great Torrington, Hungerford, Lostwithiel, Melton Mowbray, Peterborough, Rotherham, Sheffield, Tewkesbury, and many other middling-sized and smaller towns.[30] Some of them were created for the purpose of holding rental properties, some to found and operate schools and similar institutions, some even to serve as effective governing instruments for the whole community. Within these general patterns there were of course numerous variations: in the scope of authority, the powers of governance, the relations with other governing institutions, and other such matters. A few examples should suggest the broad possibilities opened up by this device.

[29] Tittler, 'End of the Middle Ages', 484–5; Maitland, 'Trust and Corporation', in Fisher (ed.), *Collected Papers*, 321–404; Dorothy Pockley, 'The Origins and Early History of the Melton Mowbray Town Estate', Ph.D. thesis (Leicester, 1964) (hereafter 'Melton Mowbray [thesis]'); Kevin Grady, 'The Records of the Charity Commissioners: A Source for Urban History', *Urban History Yearbook* (1982), 31–3; Statham, *Jankyn Smith and the Guildhall Feoffees*, 3–10.

[30] For Bicester, *VCH, Oxfordshire*, 6 (1959), 37; Bridlington, J. S. Purvis (ed.), *Bridlington Charters, Court Rolls and Papers* (no place of publication, 1926), 29–35; Bury St Edmunds see Statham, *Jankyn Smith and the Guildhall Feoffees, passim*; Coggeshall, *Returns Comprising Reports of the Charity Commissioners* [hereafter *Reports of the Charity Commissioners*], *Thirty-Second Report* (1837), 630; Fowey, *Report of the Charity Commissioners, Thirty-Second Report* (1837), 450; Great Torrington, PRO, C1/File 1418, pp. 14–18; Melton Mowbray, Dorothy Pockley, 'The Origins and Early Records of the Melton Mowbray Town Estate', *Transactions of the Leicestershire Archaeological Society*, 45 (1969–70), *passim*; Rotherham, M. H. MacKenzie, 'Records of the Feoffees of the Common Lands of Rotherham', unpublished typescript (Rotherham Public Library, 1960), copy in National Register of Archives, citing enfeoffment of 1584; Tewkesbury, Tewkesbury Borough Archives, MS A. 1, 'Minute and Order Book no. 1, 1575–1624', *passim*; Lostwithiel, *Report of the Charity Commissioners, Thirty-Second Report* (1837), 466; Sheffield, J. S. Leader, *Records of the Burgery of Sheffield, Commonly Called the Town Estate* (1897), *passim*; Peterborough, W. T. Mellows (ed.), *Peterborough Local Administration, Parochial Government from the Reformation to the Revolution, 1541–1689*, Northamptonshire Record Society, 9 and 10 (1937–9), *passim*.

In the Yorkshire town of Bridlington, the formation of a trust came about as a means of gaining some measure of local control over what had become a royal manor after the fall of the local Priory. In this case the town remained extremely poor and decayed for much of the period at hand. When the Crown tried to manage it through its own steward in the 1540s, many rents went uncollected through default. The Crown then passed on the problems of collecting revenues by leasing the whole manor to the townsmen in 1566. By the lease of 8 July in that year the townsmen were to pay a yearly rent of £153. 17s. 5½d., plus another £40 for the parsonage, and to post a recognizance against default of £2,000. In return for this sum they were empowered to maintain the harbour and pier (and allowed to levy a tax for this purpose), and to hold and let both the tenements belonging to the manor and profits of the fair. In the end, continuing poverty compelled the townsmen to forfeit the lease.[31]

A generation later, another group of townsmen gathered together to take a second lease on the manor in 1595, and in 1630 the Crown formally sold the manor to their successors. After holding it on their own for six years, this group finally drew up a deed of conveyance and enfeoffment, officially creating the governing trust. The deed named thirteen inhabitants as feoffees, who were empowered to administer the manor and town on behalf of their fellows, with powers akin to those of a manorial lord.[32]

For Bridlington the device of enfeoffment to uses solved problems of governance for both townsmen and the Crown. The townsmen, who were never well off as a group, gained substantial powers of self-government, including landholding, when a charter of incorporation was either not on offer or not within financial reach. For the Crown (which, perhaps because of Bridlington's strategic value as a north-east coast port, chose to retain title of the manor and thus lordship of the town after dissolution), lease and then enfeoffment solved the problem of providing a governing body where revenues had been difficult to collect.

In towns like Bridlington, Hungerford, and (at least between dissolution of the Abbey and acquisition of the 1606 charter) Bury St Edmunds, the powers conveyed to the feoffees were more extensive than the mere holding and administration of resources. Hunger-

---

[31] Purvis (ed.), *Bridlington Charters*, 29–35; *VCH, Yorkshire, East Riding*, 2 (1974), 32.

[32] Purvis (ed.), *Bridlington Charters*, 37–52; *VCH, Yorkshire, East Riding*, 2 (1974), 68–9.

ford's Trust, which evolved from the mid-1570s and reached its mature form in 1613, had authority to elect both a jury as a ruling body and an official called a 'constable' whose powers were much greater than most of that designation. The Constable of Hungerford was empowered to serve as coroner, feodary, escheator, and clerk of the market on behalf of the Crown, and eventually (i.e. after the enfeoffment of 1613) he enjoyed authority tantamount to the office of the mayor.[33]

In a common variant on the purchase of lands from the Crown, numerous towns which were governed by manorial jurisdiction first leased and then purchased the manor from the lord, forming a trust to enable them to hold it with legal impunity. The small Leicestershire town of Hinckley, and the middling-sized Tetbury in Gloucestershire, exemplify this pattern.[34] In other cases trusts existed within communities which already had a chartered governing authority, or which continued to operate as integral and perpetual bodies even after previously unincorporated towns gained incorporation. In these cases the trust became a semi-autonomous but limited element of existing local government. This is exemplified in Bury St Edmunds, where the Feoffees of the Guildhall, founded in the fifteenth century as the result of the bequest of a leading townsman, continued to exist and function not only after the borough's eventual incorporation in 1606, but right into the twentieth century![35]

Unlike the case of Bridlington, Bury's Trust was not the only effective instrument with governing powers over the town and townsmen. Manorial jurisdiction still played a part, as did, of course, the jurisdiction of the Liberty of Bury, the County of Suffolk, and other authorities. Yet it still managed to exercise a broader range of powers than some trusts, where competing jurisdictions were so thick on the ground as to leave but a very narrow area of jurisdiction.

In Peterborough, for example, there were three local governing authorities already in place, and in competition, when the Trust became established in 1572. One of them was the Dean and Chapter of the Cathedral, which survived the Reformation without dissolution and retained an active and strong presence in the town. Here the Feoffees of 1572 were little more than a governing body in the

---

[33] *VCH, Berkshire*, 4 (1924), 185–6.
[34] Pockley, 'Melton Mowbray [thesis]', 20–6.
[35] Statham, *Jankyn Smith and the Guildhall Feoffees*, 11–14.

parish, which was coterminous with the manor. They held lands, but for the most part the scope of their actions in administering the revenues from those lands remained effectively restricted to charitable works on behalf of the parish church and their fellow parishioners.[36] In other cases, however, such parochial trusts, in which the parish vestry and the trust tended to be coterminous, came to exercise virtually autonomous authority over the community.[37]

In Sheffield there were also competing authorities and, as in Bury, the town trust, called the Burgery, pre-dated the Reformation: it has even been traced in one form or another to before the Conquest. But here even by mid-century the townsmen succeeded in converting the trust into something more powerful. In 1554 Mary Tudor granted a charter which incorporated the traditional Burgery into a much tighter oligarchy — election giving way to co-option as the means of selecting the ruling twelve — and which granted the fuller powers one normally associates with corporate status.[38]

In many cases, townsmen succeeded in forming a trust primarily for the purpose of administering lands or such institutions as schools and almshouses which they managed to hang onto after the Dissolutions, or to regain shortly thereafter. In Devizes a trust permitted townsmen to retain or re-acquire former chantry lands, and to administer them on behalf of the townsmen until incorporation could be secured and even, under the watchful eye of the corporation, for a time thereafter.[39] Both Melton Mowbray's Town Trust and Rotherham's Feoffees of the Common Lands provide further examples of a trust's prime function in the holding and administration of town lands without incorporation.[40]

Trusts like Bury's Feoffees of the Guildhall long pre-existed the Reformation, but took on new powers and properties after the Dissolutions. Bury's Feoffees came to hold considerable lands, employ and reward town officials, answer writs to the Crown, provide poor relief (as much as £100 in 1594), and keep up rents and buildings which it held as part of the terms of its creation. As in Bridlington, its

[36] Mellows (ed.), *Peterborough Local Administration*, 9 (1939), pp. xlvii–lv. Mary Bateson's 1906 statement that the Peterborough Trust came essentially to govern the town seems an exaggeration in the light of Mellows's work. Bateson, in *VCH, Northamptonshire*, 2 (1906), 428.

[37] Pockley, 'Melton Mowbray [thesis]', 19. For a more general picture of parish enfeoffment, see Kumin, *Shaping of the Community*, 206–9.

[38] Leader, *Records of the Burgery of Sheffield*, pp. xxix–xxxii.

[39] *VCH, Wiltshire*, 10 (1975), 270–1, 307.

[40] Pockley, 'Melton Mowbray [thesis]'; Mackenzie, *Records of the Feoffees of the Common Lands of Rotherham*.

authority served in place of a charter when repeated efforts to secure such a boon failed throughout the Elizabethan period.[41]

In sum, trusts lacked the jurisdictional breadth and legal standing of full incorporations. They did not serve to the same extent as authorized agents of local government in all its parts and responsibilities. As the Feoffees of the Melton Mowbray Town Estate found on several occasions, town trusts could sometimes face legal challenges to their rights to possess lands.[42] Yet deeds of trust were more easily and inexpensively obtained, and—as they were not necessarily enrolled in the patent rolls—possibly less easy to trace, and thus to challenge, than full charters of incorporation. And, despite what must have been a period of concern after the passage of the Statute of Uses, contemporary legal interpretation, guided by the imperative of sheer necessity, continued to recognize the legality of towns or delegated groups of townsmen as trustees for lands or charitable institutions.[43]

However useful it may have been to win or defend title to coveted lands by litigation or to secure their possession by enfeoffment to uses, there can be little doubt that the most secure form of authority lay in a charter of incorporation. 'Prescription and pretended Immemorial Custom or Visages avail not', in the words of the Tory historian Robert Brady (d. 1700), 'when there are charters . . . which show . . . they are mere conjectures, words of course, and the popular affections of . . . men'.[44]

Like enfeoffment to uses, incorporation was by no means a new device by the sixteenth century.[45] The standard modern account dates the first boroughs to be incorporated to the middle of the fourteenth century, with Coventry and Hedon being the pioneers.[46] Yet it must be admitted that these early charters were sketchy

---

[41] 'The Feoffees Minute Book', West Suffolk Record Office, MS H2/6.2, vol. i; Statham, *Jankyn Smith and the Guildhall Feoffees, passim.*

[42] Pockley, 'Melton Mowbray [thesis]', 37–8 and 42–50.

[43] Maitland, 'Trust and Corporation', in Fisher (ed.), *Collected Papers*, iii. 397, citing Porter's Case from 1, Coke's *Reports*, 60.

[44] Robert Brady, *An Historical Treatise of Cities and Burghs or Boroughs*, 2nd edn. (1704), p. ii. Brady was writing from a Tory perspective, attempting to fortify the view that all powers of boroughs rested ultimately in the Crown. Yet the general acceptance of his view seems verified by the seriousness with which boroughs took incorporation in his time and before.

[45] Though we have agreed to differ on a number of points, and though she should by no means be held accountable for what follows, my understanding of incorporation has been greatly enhanced by communication with Susan Reynolds.

[46] According to the definition of incorporation employed by Martin Weinbaum in *The Incorporation of Boroughs* (Manchester, 1936), 46.

documents at best, and that it took a long time for the concept of incorporation to catch on and evolve. Indeed, its development over the course of time seems to have been guided less by legal theory than by the demands of political or economic necessity of the sort experienced by many towns in the era at hand. Even then the practice became formalized only by fits and starts. Under the Tudors, only thirteen boroughs gained what were called incorporations for the first fifty-five years of the dynasty (1485–1540). (See Table I.) Though the pace quickened dramatically in the years thereafter, with 149 borough incorporations and 72 re-incorporations in the century between 1540 and 1640, there remained throughout the sixteenth century a disconcerting imprecision to the concept. The identification of the 'five points' which have been taken to distinguish charters of incorporation from other charters seems firmer in the minds of legal theorists like Blackstone in the eighteenth century and historians like Martin Weinbaum in the twentieth than in the minds of lawyers and government officials in Tudor times. It remains true that some sixteenth-century charters were considered and labelled 'incorporative' while lacking one or more of the five putatively distinguishing points, and true as well that even in the sixteenth century all five may be found from time to time, though rarely all together, in charters which are not labelled charters of incorporation. These anomalies increase in frequency the further back before that time one chooses to go.

Yet we should by no means dismiss incorporation as a mere empty label in this era. Even with this imprecision, the term seems well enough understood at least in a broad sense in the language of both the charters themselves and the locally derived petitions which instigated their acquisition from the Crown. The language of contemporary statute and proclamation repeatedly recognizes a distinction between corporate and other towns or boroughs. Not only were 'towns corporate' listed separately from mere 'towns' in the conventional wording of statutes from the 1540s and after, but in numerous statutes of the mid and latter decades of the century 'towns corporate' received powers and privileges which were denied to other towns: another obvious reason for seeking formal incorporation.[47] Elsewhere, at least two petitions for licences to acquire lands in mortmain were denied in favour of a Crown demand for incorpora-

---

[47] I am indebted to Professor Norman Jones for his view on this issue, and for pointing to the following early Elizabethan statutes to illustrate the point: 1 Eliz., c. 21 (esp. secs. 8 and 19); 5 Eliz., c. 4 (sec. 36); 5 Eliz., c. 5 (sec. 20); 5 Eliz., c. 8 (sec. 34).

tion, which was fast becoming the only acceptable means of securing such licences.[48] And the dramatic post-1540 explosion in the quest specifically for charters 'of incorporation', often in the face of considerable expense and powerful opposition, leaves little doubt as to the importance which that status held for contemporaries.

These points both of doubt and reassurance suggest that in the very lengthy history of the concept of incorporation from the medieval to the modern period, the years after 1540 marked a stage of accelerated formalization and standardization, albeit one which still fell short of invariable precision or absolute uniformity. Even by 1640 the definition of incorporation was by no means as precise as it would become. Yet its meaning—to which the 'five points' became steadily more central—nevertheless became much more standardized, its usage more precisely understood, and its acquisition much more highly valued, than ever before.

As applied to the incorporation of towns, a close examination of those charters issued even in so short a time as between 1540 and the accession of Elizabeth eighteen years later bears out the rapidity of these developments. Almost all of Henry VIII's last 'incorporations' convey only partial powers; nearly all of Mary's convey all five points and lots besides (a pattern continued under Elizabeth and thereafter), with the pattern of Edward's charters falling about half-way between.[49] Very likely the driving force in this movement lay with the lawyers of the day, ever anxious to secure new business and often successful in convincing local authorities of the greater necessity of this device in an undeniably very litigious age. To consider charters of incorporation in the period at hand is thus to see a legal concept at a particular stage in its lengthy development.

It is also worth considering that, like many other charters, those conferring corporate status were often at least as much descriptive as they were prescriptive. They confirmed and sanctioned existing practices as much as they created new ones from scratch. They were thus commonly able to provide greater authority for a host of practices, jurisdictions, possessions, and the like which had been claimed and exercised, but which remained open to challenge. In practice this could mean that if townsmen had effectively exercised certain rights and privileges for a long enough time, they stood at least some

---

[48] These are Exeter and Warwick; see above, pp. 79–80.

[49] Though I would not now defend as readily some of the arguments contained therein, these charters are examined in Tittler, 'Incorporation of Boroughs', 24–42, and are listed in Appendix A, 41–2.

chance of getting a charter which would recognize them, whether or not those rights and privileges had formerly pertained to the manorial lord. By the same token, a ruling elite within a town could use a charter to sanction the assertion of governing powers over fellow townsmen even if such powers had not otherwise formally been conveyed.

The initiative in obtaining a charter and in defining its terms lay almost always with the townsmen themselves, whence it came in the form of a petition, rather than with the Crown. For that reason, charters spoke very specifically to the needs of the individual community, and especially (for communities were never monolithic) to the needs of the particular group within that community who launched the effort to incorporate. As it took a lot of funding to acquire a charter, the sponsoring townsmen were almost always amongst the wealthy elite of the community: a very important point when we consider the terms of specific grants. (For one, most charters named the 'charter officers' of the corporation, whose names almost always coincide with those on petitions for incorporation. This point will be pursued below in considering the use of incorporation in the advancement of oligarchy.)

One of the several factors which account for this striking advance of incorporation in the mid-sixteenth century, where 45 boroughs received incorporation between 1540 and 1558 alone (see Table I), is the suddenly pressing contemporary need to acquire real property or charitable institutions with a secure and appropriate form of tenure, which is to say, in mortmain.[50] Charters had long been linked with the legal burdens of landholding, and there can be no doubt that incorporation afforded this advantage. The right to acquire and hold in mortmain, which provided such security and flexibility of use, and the right to sue as a corporate body in defence of such possessions, are prominent features of these charters. For a variety of reasons, therefore, it is not surprising that we find a more intense interest in incorporation after *c*.1540. These included the sudden and very extensive expansion in the land market after Dissolution, the Crown's growing unwillingness to grant mortmain licences apart from broader governing responsibility, the insecurity to landholding authorities wrought by the recent Statute of Uses, and, finally, the snowballing economic and social pressures of the era.

---

[50] This and the remainder of the discussion is based on Tittler, 'Incorporation of Boroughs', unless otherwise noted.

Of course even within the century under consideration here incorporation pertained to a wide variety of local requirements. We will come back to consider some of them below. But those towns seeking incorporation in the approximate period c.1540–1560, for example, did so especially in the context both of the effort to regain and control local resources, and also the effort to gain greater political autonomy with which to hold and utilize those resources. While these factors remained important, additional motives began to compete for primacy of place in ensuing decades. Let us look at the first of these factors for the moment and return to the second in Chapter 8 below.

In the mid-sixteenth century, where the issue has been examined most closely, more than half of the towns seeking charters of incorporation seem to have been under some form or other of social or economic duress. We can only assume that they saw the chance to augment and manage local resources with the powers of incorporation as a means to economic recovery. Often the precise nature of the economic distress, and the precise resources in question, are noted in the charter itself.

These distressed communities, comprising at least twenty-four of the forty-four boroughs incorporated between 1540 and 1560 alone, ranged in size from such modest communities as Seaford and Colnbrook, on the one hand, to such substantial provincial centres as Boston, Reading, and Worcester, on the other. The nature of the difficulties themselves ranged almost as widely. Colnbrook, Abingdon, Maldon, Sheffield, Boston, Beaumaris, and Barnstaple had become unable to maintain essential public works. Louth, Saffron Walden, Thaxted, and Sheffield again could not provide alms for growing numbers of local indigents. Abingdon, Brecon, Higham Ferrars, St Albans, Stafford, Saffron Walden, Louth, Seaford, and Wisbech had experienced difficulties in paying their fee farms or other fiscal obligations to the Crown. St Albans, Stafford, Saffron Walden, Wisbech, and Louth wished to refound their grammar schools and required help in order to do so.

With the growing integration of regional economic activities within England, and even of England's economy within Western Europe, some of these towns found themselves being dominated by regional rivals in the competition for commercial activity. Barnstaple and Torrington vied for the trade of North Devon and the West Country. Leominster found its regional marketing activity squeezed out by the merchants of Hereford and Worcester. Boston

and Aldeburgh were threatened commercially by King's Lynn, and many towns aspiring to incorporation were threatened industrially by the growth of manufacturing in the countryside.[51]

These difficulties were extremely diverse in nature. In some cases they extended back many years. Some were and some were not created or exacerbated by the Dissolutions. Incorporation promised a variety of remedies, some of them especially facilitated by the greater availability of lands following the dissolutions. Aside from sanctioning local control of the market place, a complex and lucrative asset, and granting trading rights to freemen of corporate communities, many charters confirmed the grant of specific properties. Others provided a vehicle for the refoundation of schools, almshouses, and the like, or for the repair of such structures as sea walls and bridges. Almost all granted the right to acquire lands, usually in mortmain.

The coveted licence to acquire land in this form facilitated the acquisition, possession, and management of local rental properties which either had already come, or could be expected soon to come, into the hands of the corporation. Nearly all of the forty-four boroughs incorporated in this twenty-year period thereby gained licences for the acquisition of lands. In addition, some specified a grant of particular lands; others specified a ceiling on the amount which could be obtained under this aegis. (See Table II.)

In other instances, the acquisition either of lands themselves or the right to acquire them followed not immediately but still close enough in time to suggest that the incorporation had served as a conscious means to it. The Borough of Leominster worked for several years to purchase the lands of three chantries whose estimated value came to £53. 11s. a year, which would probably have more than doubled the income of the town. The eventual grant, in the reign of Mary, came at roughly the same time as the incorporation of 1554.[52]

We must assume that many or even most towns on this list lost little time at least in trying to acquire lands to which their new charters entitled them. Perhaps the most spectacular case is that of Boston, incorporated in May 1545, and purchasing extensive local guild lands almost immediately thereafter. Control of these intrinsically valuable lands was an obvious reason in itself for the town to seek incorporation, and the opportunity to undertake both initiatives had presented itself after the town's long-dominant landlord, the Priory

---

[51] Tittler, 'Incorporation of Boroughs', 35–6.
[52] Hereford Record Office, MS B 56/12, fo. 47ʳ; *CPR, Mary I*, 395–8.

of St John of Jerusalem, had been removed a few years earlier. It may be, too, that the timing followed from either the fear or fore-knowledge that these guilds would be dissolved, and thus lost to the community. A fear of confiscation was certainly possible, and such a motive would be alleged two years later when a local plaintiff, John Browne, brought suit against the Mayor and aldermen concerning the control of the lands in question.[53] Certainly the petitioning offi-cials spoke of no such concern, nor would they have done. As they explained in defending themselves against Browne's suit in Star Chamber, and as is reflected in the wording of the charter itself, they hoped that the acquisition of guild lands within the town would help them pay for repairs to sea dykes and houses which had been destroyed in recent flooding, and for which no help had been forth-coming from Westminster. They offered the notion that the Duke of Suffolk, a long-time friend to the town, had urged them to take such a step, and noted his help in securing the charter.[54] In their view the annexation of the guild lands was thus a perfectly legal act, war-ranted by their new charter. As events transpired, the charter had been sealed (14 May 1545)[55] well before the Parliament which ulti-mately passed the statute dissolving guilds (37 Henry VIII, c. 4) had even been convened.

In the end, though the court's decree has not survived, the Bor-ough's grip on these lands seems to have been affirmed, and we next find the mayor and aldermen taking their revenge on Browne by suing him in turn for illicitly pulling down buildings without licence.[56] If this is indeed the case, as seems likely, Boston was not doing much more than the City of York had done a few years ear-lier,[57] though unlike York, which was already so empowered, Boston required a charter before its officers could act.

One of the very first acts of the new Corporation was to undertake a survey of the existing town lands with a view towards their en-closure, 'to the common use and profit of the town', a step which it was for the first time in a strong legal position to take.[58] Shortly

[53] Petition of John Browne in Star Chamber, 1547, PRO, STAC 3/5/11.

[54] Answer of Roberts and Wendon, defendants, PRO, STAC 3/8/18.

[55] *Letters and Papers of Henry VIII*, 20/1, p. 418 (14 May 1545).

[56] Discussed in a letter from the Mayor and Burgesses to the young William Cecil, around the time of his first appointment to the Privy Council but already a 'friend at court' with close ties to the community, *c*.1551; PRO, SP 10/15/109.

[57] Dickens, 'Municipal Dissolution of Chantries at York', 164–73. See also above, p. 69.

[58] Though Boston's charter is dated 14 May 1545, there seems to have been some delay in setting up its government as provided therein: an indication of how little

thereafter the Borough purchased lands of five local guilds, plus the Manor of the Town of Boston, St Botolph's Church along with its vicarage and rectory, together worth £526 a year. Though the cost of incorporation could not have been slight, and the lands themselves cost £1,646. 15s. 4d. payable over twelve years, this nevertheless (assuming some stability in rental values) assured the Borough of over £300 in annual income both during the repayment period and ever after: enough to ensure fiscal stability even in a borough whose glory days as a trading centre were well behind it.[59] And as icing on the cake, the Borough petitioned at the same time for an additional purchase of lands formerly held in the town by Rivaulx, Fountains, and Durham Abbeys, and both the Augustinians and the White Friars of Boston itself, valued by the Crown at over £160 p.a.[60]

Other charters in this period during and immediately after the Dissolutions referred specifically to the refoundation, new establishment, and/or support of schools, hospitals, and other institutions of the sort often disrupted in the 1530s and 1540s. Thus, for example, surveying the twelve incorporations from Edward's reign alone, we find that Louth, Saffron Walden, St Albans, Stafford, Stratford-upon-Avon, and Wisbech received rents or were legally empowered to support grammar schools,[61] while Stratford-upon-Avon was also authorized to support an almshouse.[62] We will return to this theme in the next chapter.

Finally, the evidence for the importance of incorporation both at this time and for these reasons stands out with particular clarity when one considers the difficulty and expense of the process. Incorporation usually took a goodly time to obtain, with some towns working towards a charter for several years. Furthermore, both in absolute and — given the decayed state of many towns who sought it — relative terms, they were costly. In the words of one scholarly study,

notwithstanding the comparatively modest nature of . . . individual fees, the total expenditure in payments and gratuities for the entire process not infrequently placed a severe strain upon a borough's financial resources. . . .

self-government had been permitted under the rule of the former Prior. The act of the Borough Assembly to carry out the survey is found on the third page of the Assembly Minute Book, dated 25 March 1545 (i.e. 1546, new-style dating). John F. Bailey (ed.), *Transcription of the Minutes of the Corporation of Boston* (3 vols.; Boston, 1980–3), i. 3.

[59] PRO, STAC 3/5/11 and STAC 3/8/18 (1547); Hodgett, 'Dissolution of the Religious Houses', 83–99.

[60] PRO, E. 318/5/143.

[61] *CPR, Edward VI*, iv. 119–20; ii. 211–12; v. 33–4; iv. 21–2; v. 279–81; iii. 339–40.

[62] *CPR, Edward VI*, v. 279–81.

The renewal of a charter or the obtaining of a new grant was with few exceptions the largest financial liability a borough was ever likely to incur.[63]

Most of the evidence which has come to light regarding the cost of incorporation has appeared for the early seventeenth century, where sums reached as high as £522 for the Shrewsbury charter of 1638.[64] Yet we also know, for example, that the Borough of Beverley expended about £360 over an eleven-year period, 1562–1573, towards acquisition of its charter in the final year. This sum included about £135 for the long period of negotiating for the document over that span, much riding back and forth to Westminster, employment of lawyers and provision of gifts for those involved at the process at court, and £233. 1s. 10d. for the procurement of the document itself in the final year of this marathon effort.[65]

We should consider, too, that the impressively high number of incorporations which were granted in the period immediately following the dissolutions would be higher still if all boroughs which applied for a charter had received one. Most of the few such instances of failure which have come to light, resulting from the opposition of a local landowner or a dissident faction of townsmen, derive from the early seventeenth century: we will consider them below in the context of urban politics in that later period. Though we have no way of knowing how many failed in the sixteenth century, the experience of Bury St Edmunds, which failed several times despite the intervention of Sir Nicholas Bacon, Elizabeth's Lord Keeper,[66] and Thetford, which received it on the sixth try in 1574,[67] cannot have been unique.

---

[63] Shelagh Bond and Norman Evans, 'The Process of Granting Charters to English Boroughs, 1547–1649', *English Historical Review*, 91 (1976), 120.

[64] *Historical Manuscripts Commission, Fifteenth Report*, Appendix, 10/38 (Norwich, 1899). Kidwelly, in Carmarthenshire, spent the even higher sum of about £600 in the 1610s but, as the lawsuit which records this cost tells us, this seems to have been inflated considerably by the corruption of local officials; PRO, DL 44/1032.

[65] Humberside Record Office MS BC/II/7/3, fo. 58ᵛ and BC/II/6/30; D. J. Lamburn, 'Politics and Religion in Sixteenth Century Beverley', Ph.D. thesis (York, 1991), 184 and 183.

[66] R. Tittler, *Nicholas Bacon: The Making of a Tudor Statesman* (1976), 150; and letter from Bacon to Clement Higham et al., 29 Nov. 1562, West Suffolk Record Office, Bury St Edmunds Branch, MS C4/1. Bacon presented the feeling at court that there were already too many incorporations, but in view of the many which were granted thereafter, this seems more of a contrived excuse to Higham and others on the local scene than an accurate assessment. The Wells case is noted by Shaw, *Creation of a Community*, 109 n. 18.

[67] J. S. Craig, 'The "Godly" and the "Froward": Protestant Polemics in the Town of Thetford, 1560–1590', *Norfolk Archeology*, 41 (1992), 281.

What may we conclude from all this? Needless to say, many towns acquired bequests or former ecclesiastical properties without seeking incorporation, forming a trust or successfully defending in the courts tenuous claims to lands whose control had informally been assumed. Either by concealing title or active pre-emption, some managed to maintain schools and other such institutions. Though they did not necessarily gain the most desirable forms of possession in so doing, they nevertheless managed to avoid what could be very considerable costs entailed in such processes. Many either had the right to acquire lands in mortmain already, acquired or held them in other forms of tenure, or purchased a simple licence to hold as the need arose and took their chances on the security of their tenure. These will be considered below.

Yet the fact remains that many towns pursued these three strategies of enhancing legal enablement, litigation, enfeoffment to uses, and incorporation, with particular vigour in the period at hand. It appears, too, that the attainment of these goals considerably enhanced the legal ability of a great many towns to gain, regain, and manage particular lands and other resources within their boundaries.

Just as urban governing elites were anxious to acquire local resources in a secure form of tenure in this period, so did they also require the authority to manage such resources effectively: to renovate and restore dilapidated buildings and thus enhance the housing supply, whether such buildings lay within civic or private control. Such powers were also sought and obtained in these very years, in the form of what have come to be known as the rebuilding statutes of the reign of Henry VIII. They enabled local officials of over a hundred specifically named towns to enforce the upkeep and repair of urban properties which lay in private hands, and even to confiscate them if their landlords could not be identified or failed to comply. Parenthetically, they also demonstrate another means whereby the Crown and Parliament came, from about this time, to show their concern for the state of the urban communities of the realm.[68]

It is clear as we have seen above that the physical state of many towns, including housing and other rental property, had become very poor indeed by the time under consideration. This may have been especially true of the older centres of industry which were

---

[68] This theme is explored in R. Tittler, 'The Emergence of Urban Policy, 1536–1558', in J. Loach and R. Tittler (eds.), *The Mid-Tudor Polity, c. 1540–1560* (1980), 74–93.

facing economic competition from the countryside, provincial ports
either silting up or losing out to London, and towns generally in the
south and east which received the heaviest flow of subsistence
migration. Of this common condition there could be no better witness than the antiquary and traveller John Leland, whose journeys
throughout the realm, carried out in precisely these years, frequently describe such conditions of decay and dilapidation.[69]

In general it is likely that properties owned by ecclesiastical landlords or even guilds, fraternities, and parishes might have suffered
even worse neglect than those held in lay hands. Platt, for example,
points out that 'The clergy . . . were notoriously soft landlords', often
holding lands for so long that the level of rents came to be set by custom and precedent rather than true economic worth.[70] This is not to
suggest that they were negligent in the modern sense, but often that
their interests in holding urban properties—especially those deriving from charitable bequests, as a great many holdings did—were
primarily charitable and intercessionary rather than financial. That
approach reflected the charitable derivation of many such lands in
ecclesiastical or fraternal hands to begin with. It encouraged a management strategy geared to the saving of souls rather than maximiz-
ing profits.[71]

Letting at very long-term leases, sometimes for three or four lifetimes, and passing on obligations to repair in return for such long-
term leases, had become common amongst ecclesiastical authorities
especially (and sometimes amongst civic authorities as well) right
through the late fifteenth and early sixteenth centuries. When rising
population pushed up rental values thereafter, they often left long-
term leases at far below their true market worth.[72] Certainly the
many small, individual urban properties which accrued to ecclesiastical control over the years made for difficult administration and
high costs of management and repair.[73] Reduced income from such

[69] The standard modern edition is Lucy Toulmin Smith (ed.), *The Itinerary of John
Leland in or about the Years 1535–1543* (5 vols.; 1906–8).

[70] Platt, *The English Medieval Town*, 182. See also Dobson, 'Cathedral Chapters
and Cathedral Cities', 35–6.

[71] This was very much the pattern in York, for example, where a very substantial
proportion of the City's housing stock was held by ecclesiastical authorities. S. R. R.
Jones, 'Property, Tenure and Rents', 232–3.

[72] Lehmberg, *Reformation of Cathedrals*, 172–6; S. R. R. Jones, 'Property, Tenure
and Rents', chaps. 5 and 6.

[73] Margaret Bonney, *Lordship and the Urban Community: Durham and its Overlords, 1250–1540* (Cambridge, 1990), chap. 4, *passim*; Dobson, 'Cathedral Chapters
and Cathedral Cities', 15–44.

lands also reduced the capital available for repairs and renovations and the incentive to carry out such work. In sum, it appears that a substantial proportion of urban properties which had been left for charitable and intercessionary purposes were considerably decayed at the point of dissolution.[74]

These conditions might well have endured for many decades further without causing particular distress in urban communities, but the era of the Dissolutions placed the issue in a very different light. The general revival of population which seems to have accrued at roughly the same time as the Dissolutions and to have accelerated thereafter, the subsequent press on the housing supply, especially in England's urban communities, and the sudden availability of urban properties on the market, all now made these conditions of physical decay intolerable. Town officials required the power to command renovation and even confiscation just as urgently as they required the power to obtain and securely to hold property itself. This would allow them to improve the local housing stock and also to bring problem properties under civic control.

Traditionally town officials had two sorts of remedies to fall back on against such conditions. Neither proved sufficient. One lay in the customary usage whereby some medieval boroughs had come to exact fines on those who left property in a decayed state, failed to build on a lot which had become similarly derelict, or failed even to pave in front of their tenements.[75] A few towns even secured acts of Parliament enabling them to utilize such powers, though each act pertained only to the petitioning community.[76] As far back as the fourteenth century it had come to be recognized that either the Crown or the borough government could actually distrain lands and rents left void and unrepaired. This, too, came to be enshrined in statute for a handful of individual towns which petitioned (individually) for parliamentary sanction.[77] By the early sixteenth century

---

[74] G. H. Woodward, 'Dissolution of the Chantries', 168, 177, 188. Woodward notes that in Somerset, chantry lands worth £46 had to be written off by the Crown because of the high costs of repairs and extreme state of decay, most of these lands being in Taunton; ibid. 188.

[75] Mary Bateson (ed.), *Borough Customs* (2 vols.; Selden Society, 1904 and 1906), i. 278.

[76] A. P. Wright, 'The Relations between the King's Government and the English Cities and Boroughs in the Fifteenth Century', D.Phil. thesis (Oxford, 1965), 206, citing Northampton, Southampton, Winchester, and Bristol, all in the 15th cent.

[77] Bateson (ed.), *Borough Customs*, i. 279; Wright, 'Relations between the King's Government and the English Cities', 208, citing acts for Northampton in 1431, and Southampton, Winchester, and Bristol later in the century.

the experience of towns such as Dartford, Guildford, York, and Southampton attests to the wide understanding that good repair lay as a condition of tenure. This was considered part of the imperative of 'good neighbourhood'. It often shifted the burden of repair from local authority to the tenant himself.[78]

A second source of remedial action lay with the statutory initiatives which had been taken from the latter years of the fifteenth century in regard to the 'pulling down of towns'. Despite their headings, which employ the term 'town' in the contemporary rather than the much narrower modern sense, these several statutes referred primarily to the perils of enclosure in the countryside. They decried the decline of tillage and the accompanying practice of engrossment, in which the houses of husbandmen, smallholders, and labourers had come to be pulled down.[79] The last two of these Acts, passed respectively in 1515 and 1516, introduced mention as well of 'Cytees & Market Townes brought to grete ruyn & decaye', and included boroughs along with 'towns', villages, and hamlets.

Yet even these Acts seemed insufficient by the decade of the 1530s, when population growth in many communities became much more emphatic and troubling, and when large numbers of urban properties, many of them decayed, began to appear on the market. Clearly urban governing authorities throughout the realm now came to require enabling legislation to permit them to deal with such problems more effectively. Hence we have the Henrician rebuilding statutes.

The first of these came just on the eve of the first dissolutions, secured on its own behalf by the City of Norwich. Though motivated by the need, after nearly three decades of presumably slow population growth, to rebuild grounds and housing which had been destroyed by the great Norwich fire of 1507, the Norwich bill included almost all the elements which would be sought by other towns in the years ahead. Amongst those was the requirement that owners of void grounds or dwellings rebuild within two years or forfeit possession to the City Corporation.[80] This was no empty

---

[78] e.g. Devon Record Office, North Devon Branch, MSS 61296, 61303, 61306; E. M. Dance (ed.), *Guildford Borough Records* (1958), 42; S. R. R. Jones, 'Property, Tenure and Rents', 232; A. L. Merson (ed.), *The Third Book of Remembrance of Southampton, 1514–1602*, i (1952), 28–9, item 106; ii (1955), items 160, 170, etc.

[79] Tittler, 'For the Re-edification of Townes', 593–5. The statutes in question are 4 Henry VII, c. 19, 6 Henry VIII, c. 5, and 7 Henry VIII, c. 1.

[80] 26 Henry VIII, c. 8 (1535).

threat: it was frequently enforced. Local historians consider it to have marked the beginning of substantial improvement in the quality of the City's housing stock.[81]

The second of the rebuilding statutes also dealt with but a single town, in this case King's Lynn.[82] Its preamble explained that the 'ravages of the sea' had destroyed many houses along the waterline, and that landlords refused to repair them lest they be damaged again in the same manner. In the event, the town had long held a substantial number of decayed properties which lay abandoned and, if habitable at all, were at least severely damaged.

The subsequent statutes, coming on the heels of acute distress over housing in towns such as York, Shrewsbury, and Great Yarmouth,[83] were directed more widely. The first of these, 27 Henry VIII, c. 1, named seven towns, widely scattered geographically. It was followed by 32 Henry VIII, c. 18, listing 36 towns and, in the same session, 32 Henry VIII, c. 19, listing 21 more, mostly in the south-west. 33 Henry VIII, c. 36, listed 9 towns plus the 7 Cinq Ports and the 'members' thereof, and finally, 35 Henry VIII, c. 4, listed 24 more, mostly in Wales and Lancashire. In all, 106 towns plus the member ports of the Cinque Ports came specifically under these statutes. All of them were at least said to have been impoverished with, *inter alia*, decayed housing and void grounds.

What is most likely to have happened in these parliamentary deliberations is that the representatives of specific towns simply rose at the appropriate time to have their own constituencies listed on bills which thus became almost general.[84] Someone must also have spoken for towns which lay unrepresented by their own MPs, for many of these are also listed. It remains possible that not all those towns which were listed suffered at the time of passage such acute decay of housing as described. For some at least these Acts must have been seen as enabling statutes in the case of future need. But for many and perhaps most of the listed towns, conditions must already have seemed sufficiently dire at the time.

Because the statutes make no reference to reporting of enforcement in any of the central courts, it is virtually impossible to arrive at

[81] William Hudson and J. C. Tingey (eds.), *Records of the City of Norwich* (2 vols.; Norwich, 1906 and 1910), vol. i, pp. lxx–lxxii.

[82] 26 Henry VIII, c. 9.

[83] Tittler, 'For the Re-edification of Townes', 598–9.

[84] G. R. Elton, *Reform and Renewal: Thomas Cromwell and the Common Weal* (Cambridge, 1973), 108.

any systematic idea of their enforcement. Our only source is the records of the listed boroughs themselves, where such records exist: obviously a spotty source permitting only an impressionistic idea of enforcement patterns. Nevertheless such records yield sufficient mention at least to permit the suggestion that most enforcement seems to have come, not at once, but a few decades further on in the century: roughly at the time, as we have seen, when towns themselves were more likely to take their most active interest in urban rental property. There are in these years several examples in which towns confiscated derelict properties according to the statutes. We may assume that these examples are typical of wider enforcement of that type.[85] Finally, there can be little doubt that, like the legal devices employed in the quest for forms of secure title—the litigations, enfeoffment to uses, and incorporations—the powers conferred on local governing bodies by the rebuilding statutes cannot but have aided in the extension of governing powers in those communities.

This discussion of legal devices enabling borough governments more effectively to acquire and manage local resources also contributes to the notion of this era as something of a watershed. Though precedents may be offered for much of what we have described here and the period offers little which was new in kind, these years after about 1540 exhibit a sharp revival of concern for the issues at hand. We also find here responses which were pragmatic, decisive, and prompt. More than that, they came about through an informal but effective partnership of interests between the towns of the realm and the central government. Anchored by charter and statute, this common purpose reflected the changing nature of authority at both ends of the equation. It stood in contrast to the frequently conflictive nature of town/Crown relations which pertained through most of the fifteenth century.[86] Local, ad hoc, and tentative remedies now became widely adopted, enshrined in both the policy and law of the Tudor state. From the Crown's perspective, much progress had been made in identifying and empowering local bodies with enforceable authority to carry out proclamation and statutory law. And from the other end of the telescope, they allowed an ever increasing number of

[85] Summarized in Tittler, 'For the Re-edification of Townes', 601–3.
[86] Portrayed with particular clarity, for example, by Wright in 'Relations between the King's Government and the English Cities and Boroughs'.

communities to acquire and manage substantial resources for their own needs, and to exercise fully sanctioned governing powers in their own milieux. They could now do so without the encumbrances of intercessionary bequests or the policies of intermediate authorities, and in a manner which was at least in theory economically viable and self-sustaining.

6

Totting Up: Local Resources after the Dissolutions

It cannot be denied that the combined effect of the Dissolutions remained enormously destructive of former ecclesiastical property which lay in towns as well as elsewhere, and enormously disruptive at least in the short run to a host of charitable, educational, and similar social institutions. Nor can it be claimed that either towns or townsmen came to possess the majority of those urban properties confiscated and then resold by the Crown. But in considering these implications for community resources, several related points nevertheless remain more open to debate. To what extent did towns eventually come to possess at least some of these local properties and resources? Did such acquisitions allow a considerable number of towns, especially of the upper or middling ranks, thus to control more of their own resources than before? Was the experience of acquisition and control significant enough to mark a turning point in the self-direction of many English towns in this era? Some aspects of these issues, especially regarding poverty, charity, and education, have been explored fairly extensively. Others, especially concerning the disposition of properties and wealth in general, have not. The task at hand, therefore, is to shed as much further light as possible on the latter, while assessing and summarizing the more complete picture of the former.

In taking up first the question of property and other assets, we must remain sensitive to the patchiness of the sources. They make it impossible to be as certain and precise as one would like. Nevertheless, a wealth of evidence from a variety of town types, both for the acquisition of resources and for their application to provincial town government and political culture, produces rather a different picture than has conventionally been drawn of this problem.[1]

---

[1] See above, pp. 46–52.

i

Though we may readily enough reconstruct the acquisition of new jurisdiction and authority in the hands of urban officials, it proves more of a challenge to investigate the acquisition of economic and financial resources. It requires a frame of reference for understanding the acquisition of those resources by towns as corporate bodies, and that framework differs from what we might apply to acquisitions by private individuals. After all, we can hardly pretend that the acquisitions which seemed so important to many towns following the Dissolutions often reached the magnitude of purchases by members of the aristocracy, the gentry, members of the court circle, or even the wealthier ranks of individual townsmen themselves. With the literature on the 'getting and spending' of the landed classes of this era so abundant and familiar, we easily forget just how meagre and fragile were the financial resources of England's towns and boroughs. And with the considerable sums which were required to purchase most desirable properties from the Crown, it helps to have some understanding of financial resources and strategies.

We may place the scale of these resources in perspective by considering a 'composite' example of finances in those smaller and middling communities which made up the vast majority of English towns at that time. Most of these would be technically seigneurial in governance but would nevertheless have enjoyed some elements of self-rule. Their populations probably fell into the range of 1,200–2,400, and they would typically have been amongst the four or five most important towns — but not the most important town — in each shire. A composite of this type has been drawn from a close examination of financial records in seven towns roughly conforming to that description — Kingston-upon-Thames, Poole, Lyme Regis, Bridport, Blandford Forum, Marlborough, and St Albans.[2] In the decade prior

---

[2] Sources are as follows. Kingston: Kingston-upon-Thames Chamberlains' Accounts, 1567–1637, Surrey Record Office MS KD5/1/1; and Peter Clark and Jean Hosking, *Population Estimates of English Small Towns, 1550–1851*, rev. edn. (Leicester, 1993), 145. Poole: Poole Borough Archives, Civic Centre, Poole, MS 23(1) ('Old Record Book' no. 1, 1490–1553) and 26(4) ('The Great Boke', 1568–76) plus various individual yearly accounts and for population, Poole Borough Archives MS 92(48) giving 1,354 people in 1574 and PRO, SP 12/38/9:1, fo. 438, giving *c*.1,222 in 1565. Lyme Regis Mayor's Accounts, Dorset County Record Office, MS B7/G2/3a Bridport: Bridport Borough Archives, Dorset Record Office MS B3/H1. Blandford Forum: Blandford Forum, uncatalogued Chamberlains' Accounts, Dorset Record Office, *passim*. Marlborough: Marlborough Borough Records, Wiltshire County Record Office MS G22/1/205/2. For St Albans: the 'Mayor's Court Book, 1589–1633',

to the first Dissolutions, the 1520s, gross annual income and expenditures in this sampling ran in a normal range of only about £20 to £40 per annum. A half a century later, in about the 1570s (and when surviving records allow us to add Stratford-upon-Avon[3] and even the somewhat larger Chester[4] to the list), this would have more than doubled, presenting a still very modest normal range of £50 to £90.

A similarly constructed composite may be made for larger towns: typically those county towns and most provincial centres with populations in the mid-century of roughly 2,500 to 5,000 and with a substantial degree of self-governing authority. These would include, for example, Oxford, Leicester, and, from the 1560s, Bath,[5] but it would stop short of the handful of largest towns (always save for London) like Bristol, Norwich, York, Exeter, Newcastle, and perhaps Salisbury. This grouping would show ranges of income and expenditure at something on the order of twice these figures: £40 to £80 in the 1520s and £80 to £160 in the 1570s.

Not until the last decade or two of Elizabeth's reign and on into the early seventeenth century did several factors combine to move this range upwards at an almost geometric rate, so that even some towns below the biggest five or six could reach annual totals of expenditures and income in the several hundreds of pounds.[6] Factors prompting this often dramatic upswing of course included inflation, but also the somewhat artificial bulge given to both income and expenditures in particular years by the special causes which became

acquisition no. 312 in charter case, St Albans Old Public Library Local History Room. Even Leicester, which almost certainly had more than 2,000 inhabitants at this time and which was also the county town, had receipts and expenditures which fell well within this range: its total receipts did not exceed £40 until 1547–8; Mary Bateson (ed.), *Records of the Borough of Leicester*, iii (Leicester, 1905), 4, 20, 25–6, 27–8, and 56.

[3] Richard Savage (ed.), *Minutes and Accounts of the Corporation of Stratford-upon-Avon, 1553–1620*, Dugdale Society, Oxford, 3 (1924), 43–9, 56–60, 66–9, 73–8, 95–9, 103–7, 113; and 4 (1926), 11–17 and 40–9; Clarke and Hosking, *Population Estimates of Small Towns*, 157 (where Stratford's population is given as 1,680 in 1563).

[4] Chester City Record Office, MS TAC/1/14–16.

[5] H. E. Salter (ed.), *Oxford Council Acts, 1583–1626*, Oxford Historical Society, 87 (1928); Bateson (ed.), *Records of the Borough of Leicester*, iii; F. D. Wardle (ed.), *The Accounts of the Chamberlains of the City of Bath, 1568–1602*, Somerset Record Society, 38 (1923).

[6] In Leicester, for example, income in the 1570s averaged £120 a year, with a high of £230 and a low of £89; expenditures during the same decade averaged £102, with a high of £186 and a low of £63. But four decades on, we have income averaging £652 for the three years in which figures are readily available, and expenditures averaging £544 (Bateson, *Records of the Borough of Leicester*, iii. 131–80, *passim*; and H. Stocks and W. H. Stevenson (eds.), *Records of the Borough of Leicester* (Cambridge, 1923), 156–7, 182–3, and 194–5).

so frequent at that time: for military assessments, multiple parliamentary subsidies, tenths and fifteenths, and, in the case of income, a sharp increase in the level of entry fines for new leases and an often augmented rent roll resulting from acquisitions of additional lands.

In the fiscal reckonings of virtually all towns, deficits were common.[7] For towns in both sample groups, surpluses and deficits were usually within 10 or 12 per cent of breaking even, though most towns experienced some years where extraordinary circumstances provoked extreme deviations from that norm. And, though some forms of income and expenditure were relatively fixed—e.g. rents on the income side and fee farm on the expenditure side—other categories could show very considerable differences from year to year. The common system of accounting in these towns certainly permitted surpluses and deficits to be carried over from one year to the next, yet few towns had much of an opportunity to set money aside for a rainy day. Years of very great surpluses seemed not to provide any safe hedge against a reversal of fortunes in a very few years down the road. Some of these swings could be quite sharp. In Bath, for example, a modest deficit of £14. 5s. in 1573, about 10 per cent of total income for that year, became a surplus of £88 in the next year, followed in turn by a slight deficit in 1575.[8]

Some further idea of what this all meant may be gleaned by surveying briefly the chief items of income and expenditure. Rental property of course provided an important component of income: the single largest category in many towns. Most towns of any substance had at least some property at their disposal. Especially in towns whose landlord still received most emoluments, it could by default easily form the largest proportion of income.[9] Some of this derived, as we have seen, from intercessionary bequests in which the obligatory expenditures had previously left the town little if any remainder. As for example with Hull,[10] such a circumstance could even mean an annual loss. But not all pre-Reformation bequests were intercessionary and some came free of any obligations.[11] Interces-

---

[7] In Bath, for example, there were an even number of surplus years and deficit years between 1569 and 1597, and only a run of five straight years of surpluses allowed the City to end the century on a positive fiscal note (Wardle, *Accounts of Bath, passim*).

[8] Wardle, *Accounts of Bath*, 23–9.

[9] This is well illustrated, for example, by the revenues of Stratford-upon-Avon, where a rent roll made up between 96% and 45% of the total revenues in the Elizabethan years (Savage, *Minutes and Accounts*, 3 and 4, *passim*).

[10] Horrox (ed.), *Selected Rentals and Accounts of Hull*, 17.

[11] This was quite common, for example in Wells, where wealthy townsmen bequeathed property to the Borough Community without religious intent, partly as a

sionary bequests themselves of course faded out following the 'abolition of Purgatory'. In addition to domestic rentals, such property might include mills, shops, storehouses, bakehouses, agricultural lands, and other income-bearing resources. And the value of rental properties as such extended to more than mere rents themselves. As the century progressed, for example, entry fines played an increasing part in property-derived receipts. Town governments commonly raised entry fines from one tenant to the next while leaving annual rental levels themselves relatively constant. The receipt of an entry fine on the incoming side of the ledger and the high proportion of defaults in years of deprivation on the other side, account for much of the volatility in income from this source.

The revenues of the market place were also vital, though they, too, were vulnerable to short-term economic fluctuations. These included fees for picage, stallage, lastage, and murage from traders, local customs on certain trade goods, rental of shops, stalls, shambles, pentices and other commercial premises, and fines and fees from courts of market and fair. In most cases there seems to have been a steady increase in such emoluments as population grew, a factor which pushed up both food prices and the volume of market activity, from mid-century on. Less directly the fiscal benefits from commercial activity included licences from certain kinds of businesses and fines from the town courts. Fees for such activities as entry into the freemanry or evading office provided an additional, if modest, source.

The balance between these sundry sources depended a lot on the political and constitutional status of each town. In those seigneurial towns which had few constitutional powers and therefore few emoluments which they were entitled to collect, rental income could constitute almost the entire annual revenue. Until its re-incorporation in 1589, the Somerset borough of Wells provides a good example of this pattern.[12] The overall impact of the Reformation era on the

means of recognizing the authority of the collectivity against the formal authority of the bishop as lord of the City (Shaw, *Creation of a Community*, 125–7).

[12] Shaw shows that as much as 96% of Wells's borough income derived from rents throughout much of the 15th, and presumably early 16th, cent. (ibid. 128–9). Bath, incorporated in 1590, shows a similar if less emphatic pattern for some years prior to its incorporation: in 1575 and 1576, respectively, for example, its regular annual income from rents of £101. 7s. 11d. comprised a similarly large proportion of total income which reached only to £105. 15s. 8d. and £105. 17s. 3d., respectively, in the same two years. From then on, however, while the rental income remained virtually fixed, other sources came on stream to raise the total. Rents thus became a smaller (if still dominant) proportion (Wardle, *Accounts of Bath*, 23–33). This is confirmed in

self-direction of these towns, especially if it led to incorporation and an expansion of constitutional powers, usually brought new revenue sources under local control and thus reduced the proportion of income derived from rents. In towns with older traditions of self-government, by contrast, the town coffers already received numerous kinds of income depending from their political jurisdiction. These towns had much more to gain proportionately from additional accretions of property, rendering the increase of rental income of relatively greater importance. In both sorts of towns, of course, several factors commonly worked to increase income in an absolute sense as the century progressed: rising values in an era of population growth, increases in the absolute amount of rent-bearing property under local control, and a general increase in entry fines.

Expenditure, too, helps us appreciate the fiscal position of Reformation-era towns. Ordinary expenses were dominated in most communities by the payment of the fee farm to the Crown and/or annual rentals to the manorial lord. Though it could often be deferred until circumstances became favourable, the maintenance of public works often came a close second. This included not only the reparations on town rentals and other property, but also the maintenance of the roads and bridges, streets and marketsteads, conduits, quays, and warehouses upon which the commercial life of the towns depended. Maintenance needed to be carried out, too, on guildhalls and market halls, schools, and other meeting places under local control. Stipends to the mayor, town clerk, and recorder, to the schoolmaster and eventually the preacher, as well as to less prominent officials, employees, and casual workers, could also be substantial. Ceremonial events, certainly including the mayor's annual dinner (only some of which obligations he defrayed himself), gifts to local patrons—for which wine, sugar loaves, capons, a sturgeon, or a deer served as common coin—and the cost of legal fees, loomed large. The burdens of poor relief and such social expenditures as education became more prominent throughout the period, the former especially tending to become oppressive by the later decades of the sixteenth century. And for boroughs enjoying the parliamentary franchise the costs of sending MPs to Westminster could also prove substantial, though it became increasingly common to find MPs

A. J. Scarse, *Wells: The Anatomy of a Medieval and Early Modern Property Market*, Faculty of the Built Environment, University of the West of England, Working Paper no. 30 (1993), *passim*.

willing to pay their own way for the privilege.[13] In almost all of these cases, and even without factoring in the element of inflation, obligations rose steadily.

Inevitably every town also faced extraordinary expenses which accrued from time to time. They included the unplanned and very considerable as well as those to which deliberate forethought had been given (though these could also be very considerable). The need for major repairs, relief in times of fire, pestilence, or acute poverty—especially during the decades of the 1550s, 1590s, and 1620s—and of course such ad hoc demands as ship money which might be imposed by the Crown and Parliament, could place severe strains on local resources in even the best-prepared of towns. Even such pre-determined projects as major litigation, the quest for legislation in Parliament[14] or a charter from the Crown,[15] the building of a town hall[16] or school, and certainly the purchase of substantial properties proved major challenges.

Extraordinary costs of this order became both more common and more substantial towards the end of our period. The vast expansion in the costs of national government, in which war and inflation played prominent parts, inevitably passed from the Crown to local authorities. Requests for multiple parliamentary subsidies, tenths and fifteenths, became commonplace in these years, along with sundry special assessments for purposes which were national as well as local. Factors of this sort made it much more difficult for contemporaries to tabulate annual income and expenditure. Because

[13] J. E. Neale, *The Elizabethan House of Commons* (1949), chap. 11.

[14] Tittler, 'Elizabethan Towns and the "Points of Contact" ', 277.

[15] Some sample costs of incorporation, which rose steadily through the period 1500–1640, are as follows: Beverley: renewal of standing charter, 1559, £48. 15s. 10d.; acquisition of new charter, 1573, £360 (Humberside Co. Record Office, MSS BC II/7/2, fos. 20ʳ and 22ᵛ and II/7/3, fo. 58ᵛ; Lamburn, 'Politics and Religion in Beverley', 184 and 189); Carlisle: acquisition of a new charter, 1635, £273. 8s. 2d. (Carlisle Chamberlains' Audit Book, Cumbria Record Office (Carlisle Branch), MS Ca/4/1, fo. 87ʳ); Exeter: confirmation, 1625, £160; new charter, 1627, £201 (MacCaffrey, *Exeter*, 28 and n. 3); Guildford: confirmation of 1519, £17. 8s. 0d. (E. M. Dance (ed.), *Guildford Borough Records, 1514–1546*, Surrey Record Soc. 24, (1952)); Kidwelly: raised towards cost of new charter, £133. 4s. (R. S. Ferguson (ed.), *A Boke off Recorde . . . of Kirkbie Kendall*, 7 (1892), pp. viii and 1–17); Oxford: acquiring new charter, 1605, £150; new charter, 1621, £101.16s. 6d. (Salter, *Oxford Council Acts* (1928), pp. xlvii–xlviii, 388–9; Hobson and Salter, *Oxford Council Acts* (1933), 419); Stafford: acquiring a new charter, 1614, c.£320. (Staffs. Record Office, MS D(W) 1721/1/4, fos. 87–8); Shrewsbury: acquiring new charter, 1638, £521. 19s. 2d. (Historical Manuscripts Commission, *Fifteenth Report*, Appendix, 10/38).

[16] For sample costs of building town halls and a wider discussion of town finances in that regard, see Tittler, *Architecture and Power*, chap. 3 and esp. table 3, p. 52.

extraordinary expenses were often recorded separately from the ordinary, the task becomes more difficult still for us. The numbers on either side of the ledger become larger, but they also tend to camouflage the regular and ordinary features of local funding which were most often but a small part of yearly totals.

Regular sources of income could rarely stand up to fiscal demands of this sort, placing great strains on local ingenuity. In meeting this challenge, however, the resourcefulness of particular communities seems bound only by the limits of magisterial imagination, political expediency, and, at least most of the time, legal propriety. In a pinch, towns might always hope for testamentary bequests or voluntary contributions by members of the freemanry, but these occurred unpredictably and irregularly. More regular devices included the sale of property (including an enormous amount of church plate[17] and even buildings), increased entry fines on corporate rentals, fund-raising entertainments such as ales, and of course formal loans from wealthy individuals both within and outside the community. All of these no doubt played their part in facilitating the purchase of additional lands and resources, in much the same manner as they supported the costs of other extraordinary expenses,[18] during these decades. At the same time, large debts run up in the same process appear to have seemed neither disastrous nor, in many cases, long-standing. Still, as with central government, rising demands for revenue placed great strains on traditional mechanisms for raising funds in a great many towns at this time. Town accounts constantly convey the impression that every shilling counted. In sum, at a time when few towns operated with an annual income equivalent to that of the average country gentleman, purchases which would seem very modest to the individual man of means could easily increase the annual income of a recipient town by a substantial percentage.

ii

With this perspective in mind, we may now turn to the main business: the acquisition of additional resources, especially income-producing resources, by individual urban communities in the decades following both the first and second waves of dissolution. Though the evidence for such activity remains extensive, it is also

---

[17] See esp. Kumin, *Shaping of a Community*, 211–12.
[18] See e.g. on the finance of major building projects, Tittler, *Architecture and Power*, chap. 3.

widely scattered, making it impossible to offer even rough estimates for nationwide figures. The best approach may be to consider, one by one, the several means by which such acquisitions came about, and to sample as far as the evidence will allow what each category may have yielded up. Arbitrary as these categories might seem, this process offers a number of insights into the extent of the acquisitions in question, and their significance. That significance, it must be remembered, must not be measured against the sum of all property transfers or against those acquisitions made by other groups and parties at the time, but in relation to the circumstances of the urban communities themselves.

The most readily accessible listing of lands which were at least bid for by towns may be found in the 'Particulars for Grants' as filed in the Court of Exchequer, catalogued in the Public Record Office as class E. 318. The towns in Table III initiated this procedure when their governing authorities formally asked to purchase specific properties from the Crown through the Court of Augmentations. Faced with this request to purchase, Augmentations officials surveyed the lands in question, estimated their annual value, and arrived at a sale price. These surveys and evaluations were called 'the particulars'. They formalized the offer of sale and sometimes imposed conditions on such offers as well.[19] In at least two such cases (Exeter and Warwick), as we have seen,[20] Augmentations officials required towns to obtain corporate charters prior to purchase. Considerable dickering could also ensue regarding the actual value of the properties in question, the term of payment, or even the very nature and description of the lands at issue. Both parties seem to have had room to manoeuvre. Deals could be struck. When the Crown calculated the purchase price of coveted lands in Canterbury at £424. 8s. 4d., the Archbishop of Canterbury intervened on the City's behalf and gained a reduction of 50 per cent, bringing the price down to £212.[21] Yet in the end most such negotiations seem to have been completed within a few months, sometimes (e.g. Norwich in 1547[22]) within weeks, with the town proceeding to purchase.

---

[19] The authoritative account is Walter C. Richardson, *History of the Court of Augmentations* (Baton Rouge, La., 1961), esp. 233–5.

[20] See above, pp. 79–80, 89.

[21] PRO, E. 318/7/236; *Letters and Papers of Henry VIII*, vol. 17, item 881:23, p. 489; see also Zell, 'Mid-Tudor Market in Crown Lands in Kent', 62.

[22] The list of particulars is dated 16 Apr., 1 Edward VI, the subsequent grant followed on 7 May of the same year. But here the terms seem not to have changed

Because this process became less common after the Court of Exchequer absorbed the Augmentations in 1554, and because there were other ways of going about the task of acquisition, the number of towns suing for Particulars remained modest. And right from the start some purchases were distinctly minor. Two cases, Newcastle and Faversham, seem puzzling at first because the annual rental accruing to the Crown equals the annual return on the lands in question, thus obviating any profit. Here the purchasing towns sought jurisdiction rather than income: different towns undertook to acquire dissolved lands for different reasons, and there will be more to say about this below. But the fact that the size of the purchase would have seemed small potatoes to any gentleman or aristocrat worth his salt, while true enough, remains beside the point. Contemporary town officials had to consider the annual income value of many such acquisitions to be substantial in relation to the sum of other fiscal resources available to them, and so they very frequently were. Despite purchase prices which the Crown routinely set at many times the annual assessed value (normally at twenty times in Edward's reign, twenty-five in Mary's, and thirty in Elizabeth's),[23] this very likely proved the case with towns such as, for example, Bristol, Canterbury, Coventry, Crediton, Derby, Lincoln, Ludlow, Norwich, Warwick, and Wisbech.

We should bear in mind that however alluringly accessible this listing may be, it also remains severely limited in its use and extent. It records but a small minority of towns seeking to purchase lands from the Crown. It covers but those few years (1536–54) in which the Court of Augmentations existed apart from the Exchequer. If we looked no further, we might well conclude that only that small list of towns which bid in this way for purchases received dissolved lands at all. Nothing could be further from the case.

Towns which gained resources through the filing of Particulars usually received their eventual acquisitions by letters patent. Yet the vast majority of towns receiving by letters patent, and even some which did not, are not to be found listed in the Particulars. This latter group forms a second category of acquisition: lands received from the Crown by other means than the filing of Particulars for Grants. Nearly all these transactions may be traced in the Patent Rolls, at least until the modern published calendars of those rolls run

from the beginning to the end of the process, making this a straightforward case in every respect (PRO, E. 318/5/143; and *CPR, Edward VI*, i. 13–17).

[23] Richardson, *Augmentations*, 234 n. 51.

out in the middle of Elizabeth's reign. They include resources granted as part of charters of incorporation, also conveyed by letters patent.

Though some of these grants included funding for such institutions as schools and hospitals, which we will consider below, perhaps the bulk of them merely referred principally to the general needs and condition of the town, and especially to its sources of rental income. Winchester's experience proves typical in this regard. Its cathedral was not dissolved during these years, but a great number of rental and other properties within the City had been held by institutions which were dissolved. The impending dissolution of St John's Hospital looked to be a great loss in both symbolic and financial terms: it held over fifty properties worth some £30 a year. However, though the formal grant cannot be found, the City clearly regained the Hospital and its properties in short order, a reality confirmed in the City's incorporation of 1588.[24] In addition, the townsmen petitioned Edward for all ecclesiastical lands which remained unsold in 1552, and the grant was eventually made in the first year of Mary's reign.[25] By the end of Mary's reign the town received rents from some ninety individual properties, bringing in close to £20 rent a year: a substantial sum for a still unincorporated seigneurial town.[26]

In Colchester, where the Guild of St George had been an important institution and a substantial landholder from the middle of the fifteenth century, Dissolution no doubt provoked great consternation. Yet when in 1549 the Crown allowed the 'Mayor and Citizens' (for so they were styled) to buy back their lands, the town not only regained an important, if not enormous, source of income, but also the control of that substantial quasi-religious body whose possessions had largely been earmarked for intercessionary purposes.[27] Experiences of this sort were shared by such other 'middling' towns as, for example, Bath,[28] Chichester,[29] Maidstone,[30] and Saffron Walden.[31]

[24] Rosen, 'Economic and Social Aspects of Winchester', 65–6.
[25] *CPR, Mary I*, i. 186–7.
[26] Rosen, 'Economic and Social Aspects of Winchester', 74.
[27] *CPR, Edward VI*, iii. 420. The town made further acquisitions of dissolved property in 1552, formerly owned by the Archbishop of Canterbury in one case and the Knights of Jerusalem in the other (*CPR, Edward VI*), iv. 288.
[28] *CPR, Elizabeth*, vi. 89.
[29] *VCH, Sussex*, 3 (1935), 92–3.
[30] *CPR, Edward VI*, ii. 174–6.
[31] Ibid., ii. 211–12.

As with those grants made via the Particulars for Grants, these awards by letters patent are not difficult to uncover: they all come in one way or another from the Crown as initial purchases of dissolved properties. But a third general category of acquisitions, much more extensive, amorphous, and eclectic in nature, includes all those not made directly of the Crown. In these cases towns served as the secondary, tertiary, or even subsequent purchasers of lands which, as was the case with most dissolved lands, had first been acquired by private individuals. When those earlier purchasers—typically members of the landed classes, professionals, or courtiers—or their descendants could no longer keep up their holdings, they sold at least some of them off. This created a sequence of land transfers from one purchaser to another which went on throughout the century under study here, but which is perhaps most intense in the first or second generation of those families which made such purchases initially. It is thus not only the initial and virtually unprecedented splash in the land market which gave towns a chance at acquisition, but the subsequent ripples which followed—albeit in diminishing magnitude—for decades thereafter.

In contrast to the first two of our categories, acquisitions of this sort prove extremely difficult to examine and virtually impossible to do so comprehensively. First, cities, boroughs, and towns corporate were exempt from the legislation requiring licences for 'bargains and contracts of lands and tenements', and thus such purchases were not necessarily enrolled so that the modern researcher might systematically retrieve them.[32] In other words, it is hard to track down this sort of transaction without going to local record repositories, in which the rate of survival has been far lower, and the access more difficult, than for the central archives.

Secondly, it is often impossible to be certain whether an intermediate purchaser of such lands acted on his own or on behalf of the town. In numerous instances what appears to be a purchase by a private party is in fact a purchase from the Crown by an agent of the town government, with the purchase and subsequent resale to the town recorded in the name of the agent. In the vast majority of these cases there are only hints that the town itself is the true purchaser: a short interval between the purchase from the Crown and the resale to the town, or a purchase by a townsman known to be active in town government at the time, are likely indicators (though, conversely,

---

[32] 27 Henry VIII, c. 16 (1535–6).

any townsman active in local government at the time could also probably afford to purchase on his own). References in local records of payment to the buyer is of course proof positive, but these turn up more by chance than by any more obvious or systematic means. Yet despite these problems of evidence, we may be certain that such purchases were common amongst at least the middling and larger towns of the realm, and that they continued right through our period. Enough examples have come to light in the records of specific towns to show how they could have been made, and how they contributed both to the control of local resources and to the support of the local economy in years to come.

When the Borough of King's Lynn paid £30 to Thomas Waters (1495–1563/4)—one of its leading citizens, three-time mayor and eight-time MP[33]—for the houses and estates of the friaries in the town, we may be pretty sure that he acted as an agent in making the purchase in his own name from the Crown just a short while before. In this particular case, as we learn from the Borough Minute Book, the plot was even somewhat more complicated than that: it reminds us how complex such arrangements could be. Evidently having on hand only £30 when the desired lands came up for sale, the Mayor and Aldermen also arranged with Waters that he would purchase additional friary lands for £133 more. They would pay him back the principal when they could, and he would retain the lands of the Blackfriars for his trouble.[34] King's Lynn employed several other townsmen in a similar manner, essentially deriving the required capital from some of its wealthier citizens to purchase a considerable part of the dissolved property in its midst early on in the resale derby.[35]

On the whole, in fact, intermediate holders in the early years after Dissolution, like Waters, are probably more likely to have been acting as agents than for themselves. Some people purchased directly for a quick resale on a rising market. But the course of events

---

[33] Profiles may be found in S. T. Bindoff (ed.), *The House of Commons, 1509–1558* (3 vols.; 1982), iii. 555–6; and P. W. Hasler (ed.), *The House of Commons, 1558–1603* (3 vols.; 1981), iii. 588.

[34] King's Lynn Borough Archives, MS KL/C7/5, fo. 11ᵛ, 35 Henry VIII. This may seem very generous of the town, but Waters had served it long, well, and with equal generosity. In the 1520s, battling in the courts for greater independence from episcopal control, the Borough borrowed heavily from several of its leading citizens, including Waters. It ended up owing him £54: a very substantial sum at the time. He remitted £34 of this sum when the town's debts proved burdensome (King's Lynn Archives, MS KL/C7/5, fos. 274ᵛ and 275).

[35] King's Lynn Borough Archives, MS KL/C7/5, fos. 55ᵛ and 106ᵛ.

whereby a primary purchaser from the Crown had to sell off because of his own declining position, or where his survivors sold off either because of debts or lack of an heir, almost always took time to come about. Purchases from third parties in the Elizabethan years and after are thus much more likely to result from a sequence of this sort. They may be very difficult to discover, but they almost certainly accounted for a large share of corporate purchases in the latter decades of the century.

Such purchases from third parties could be very substantial, both in size and in importance. Exeter, for example, fared poorly in the early running of the post-Dissolution land market and then used purchases from a third party to catch up later on. On the eve of the first wave of Dissolutions, income from property brought in about one-third of the City's annual average revenue of about £250 and local officials clearly hoped to gain a good share of confiscated lands to add to this resource.[36] In the event, town officials were only able to purchase St Nicholas's Fee, worth but £12 a year, while private parties snapped up the remainder. In 1545 two townsmen, John Haydon and Thomas Gibbs, paid very close to £900 for all the remaining monastic lands in the City. They, in turn, transferred their purchases to two central government officials, Sir John Williams and Henry Norryce. City officials, who watched this all very closely, seemed to like their chances with Williams, and they made him an offer to purchase the lot. In 1549, for £1,460. 2s. 3d., he and Norryce sold to five feoffees designated by the Mayor and aldermen lands worth between £90 and £95 per annum, nearly 40 per cent of current revenues. As part of the arrangement, the City Chamber and thirty-two wealthy citizens undertook to come up with the funds to reimburse the feoffees. The modern historian of Tudor Exeter suggests that they acted to acquire these lands not only to gain revenue, but also to prevent any single person from purchasing the lot and thus exerting undue influence on the affairs of the City.[37]

In acting to prevent domination by an outsider, Exeter successfully avoided the situation in which Coventry found itself for several decades after the dissolution of its rich ecclesiastical and chantry lands. Yet even in Coventry the townsmen eventually overcame a series of setbacks in their long efforts to control property in their midst, and arguably ended up in a stronger fiscal position than

---

[36] MacCaffrey, *Exeter*, 59.   [37] Ibid. 184–5.

before the Dissolutions.[38] The tale of these events exemplifies how long and complex the effort to acquire local resources in a single town could be. They also point up the wide variations in financial strategies employed by provincial towns, and the consequent difficulty offering blanket explanations for such events.

Coventry had been especially well served by ecclesiastical institutions prior to the Reformation. These included a priory which in turn held several churches, two friaries, and a considerable amount of rental property held by these bodies. In addition, and as was true in many of the more substantial towns and especially cathedral cities, ecclesiastical institutions which were not themselves located in Coventry held additional rentals in the City. The Priory in particular commanded very extensive local holdings. It was, in fact, the largest single property owner in the City, with annual rental income of nearly £350 on the eve of dissolution. At the same time the City Corporation itself, by contrast, earned an annual rental income of only £76. And in addition to these properties of the regular clerical bodies, dissolved in the first wave of dissolutions, the City's guilds, especially Holy Trinity and Corpus Christi, were also especially well endowed.[39]

As was also the case elsewhere, when the first wave of dissolutions hit Coventry a number of the leading citizens helped the King's Commissioners take stock, and then expeditiously joined the queue for purchases. The City itself was able to acquire some of the Priory lands in 1542, thereby virtually doubling its income from rental properties,[40] and it gained some additional bits and pieces over the next few years.[41] But the largest share of all ecclesiastical properties went to the court official and scholar John Hales, then at the start of what looked to be a promising political career.[42] Hales bought up most of the Whitefriars holdings, including both lucrative properties and also leet jurisdiction over about one-third of the City. He also acquired the sites and buildings of St John's Hospital, worth £195 a year, and some additional properties as well.[43]

---

[38] The following is based on *Letters and Papers*, 37 Henry VIII, vol. 20/1, 666; *CPR, Edward VI*, ii. 81 and iv. 337–8; M. Knight, 'Religious Life in Coventry', 307–9, 312.

[39] Ibid. 4–6, 17–18.

[40] The City paid £1,466. 3s. 8d. for lands worth £77. 12s. 4d. (ibid. 275–6).

[41] Ibid. 276–8.

[42] Hasler, *House of Commons, 1558–1603*, ii. 238–9; *DNB, vide* Hales, John (d. 1572).

[43] M. Knight, 'Religious Life in Coventry', 278–94.

This turn of events confirmed the City's worst fears. An outsider from Hertfordshire, with strong connections at court but no previous ties to Coventry, Hales suddenly became the largest individual landholder in the City. Now holding both the property itself and the legal jurisdiction which came with it, he had come from nowhere to become a dominant force in local affairs. And, though he tried to assuage the sensitivities of his new neighbours by offering to refound the dissolved grammar school, he never followed through on his promise.

When the chantries came up for dissolution in the following decade, Coventry departed sharply from its earlier support and met the prospect with concerted opposition. These holdings were not only substantial in a monetary sense, but townsmen considered the chantry possessions to be much more integral to the identity of the community.[44] In addition, they cannot but have feared that Hales or someone like him would dip into them too, further strengthening the influence of wealthy outsiders. Coventry's role in the opposition to the Crown's chantry bill in the Parliament of 1547 proved so forceful that, in return for its acquiescence, the Crown agreed to re-grant chantry lands to only two boroughs: King's Lynn and Coventry.[45] In the event, as we have seen in Chapter 4, the Crown kept its promise to Lynn, granting it in 1548 the extensive properties once belonging to the two dominant guilds of the town, Holy Trinity and St George's, and thus assuring the town's future fiscal security.[46] But it failed to keep its word to Coventry. The City had to buy those lands as they became available under Edward.

In its long effort to regain and augment local resources, Coventry's fiscal fortunes—if not its economy as a whole—improved in the 1550s. They did so not because more land could be bought from the Crown, but because Hales's own volatile career placed his personal financial position in some jeopardy. During the Marian years the Protestant Hales went into exile. Shortly after his return at Mary's death he fell afoul of Elizabeth, living out most of his remaining years either in prison or under house arrest. These tribulations ate up his resources at a great rate, forcing him to sell off his holdings, bit by bit, for ready cash, until his death in 1572. In the end the City was able to regain a large share of those lands he had held. By 1572 the

---

[44] 'Religious Life in Coventry', 254–61.

[45] The story is recounted in *Acts of the Privy Council*, NS, II, 6 May 1548; and Dickens, *English Reformation*, 289.

[46] *CPR, Edward VI*, ii. 11–13.

City Corporation came in this way to gain leet jurisdiction over about three-quarters of its area—something which it had never possessed before Dissolution—which included extensive parts of the dissolved lands.

It cannot be said that its former prosperity ever entirely returned to Coventry during the course of the sixteenth century, as its traditional manufacturing base had substantially been undermined.[47] But these acquisitions placed the City finances on a much firmer footing by about the mid-1570s than it had enjoyed for many years, and gave its officers greater judicial control than ever before. Finally, the spectre of political and fiscal domination by an outsider of Hales's ilk came to an end. Like many others who made large initial purchases, he could not sustain his investments over the long run, and the Mayor and Burgesses were able in the end to pick up many of the pieces of his former 'empire'.

Like Coventry, the Borough of Leicester came late to obtaining former ecclesiastical lands in its midst, and like Coventry, it was under some economic duress when it did so. Leicester lingered under the authority of the Duchy of Lancaster in several respects, and it was the Duchy, rather than the Crown, which held the rents of most of its former colleges and chantries. By the 1580s, and possibly before, Leicester found itself in decline, with particularly severe decay of its building stock. Landlords obviously had insufficient funds or motivation to keep up their buildings. Not only did this lead to the deterioration of some 235 houses, in the estimate of a Duchy Commission established to study the problem in 1587,[48] but it had begun to make it difficult for the City Chamberlains to collect rents on City property.[49]

Recognizing the gravity of their plight, the town's governing officials drew up a series of petitions to the Queen asking for a grant of additional lands in and around the town, most of which had been held by colleges, hospitals, and chantries.[50] In February 1589, the Queen acceded to their requests and granted Leicester its first

---

[47] Phythian-Adams, *Desolation of a City*, part I; and Ronald M. Berger, *The Most Necessary Luxuries: The Mercer's Company of Coventry, 1550–1680* (University Park, Penn., 1993), chap. 2.

[48] Bateson, *Records of the Borough of Leicester*, iii. 239.

[49] The problem became no easier even after the Borough gained its grant of additional lands in 1589 (ibid. 300–1).

[50] Sundry drafts of this petition, dated by the editor to c.1587, are printed ibid. 233–9.

incorporation.[51] The grant included virtually all the lands, rents, authority, and jurisdiction the townsmen had requested. Added to dissolved lands formerly purchased of Francis Hastings,[52] this gave the new corporation a considerable stock of property. A rental of 1594 indicated theoretical rental income of £166. 16s. 8d.,[53] nearly three times higher than the Borough's total revenues (£58. 7s. 11d.) in 1587–8, the year it petitioned for incorporation.[54] And, though many of the new holdings were in poor condition, the new charter conveyed the authority to renovate them and thereby increase their rental value.

The survival of the Borough Chamberlains' Accounts allows us some insight into the financial impact of the new acquisitions. They show that after a healthy start in Elizabeth's reign, Leicester ended with a deficit in each of the six consecutive years before the grant, from the fiscal year 1584–5 to 1589–90. Although expenditures still exceeded revenues for three of the four years immediately following the grant these may be attributed to the Borough's struggle to pay the Crown £137. 13s. 7¾d. for the charter as well as to defray the expenses incurred in the long process of obtaining it. Regular budgetary surpluses returned by 1594–5.[55]

Nor did Leicester's government sit back after obtaining this grant of 1589. Ten years later it successfully petitioned for a second incorporation, in which an additional remnant of the dissolved institutions—if not rental property as such—came into its control and jurisdiction. This was the liberty of 'The Newarke', a former hospital and college with its own privileges of self-government within the boundaries of the Borough.[56] A further and very substantial purchase in James's reign gave Leicester the fee farm of The Newarke Grange Estate, adding yet again to its resources.[57]

In the end it cannot be said that this late Elizabethan turnabout in civic finances rescued the Borough's economy as a whole. Like Coventry again, Leicester seems to have remained depressed for some time. But systematic renovation of the many decayed properties thus brought under its control promised something of a nest-egg for the future, as the Borough Chamberlains proved much more diligent managers of local property than the officials of the Duchy had ever been.

[51] Printed in Bateson, *Records of the Borough of Leicester*, iii. 247–52.
[52] *VCH, Leicestershire*, 4 (1958), 63–4.
[53] Bateson, *Records of the Borough of Leicester*, iii. 304–15.
[54] Ibid. 245–6.   [55] Ibid. 273–5, 287–8, 292–3, and 303–4.
[56] *VCH, Leicestershire*, 4 (1958), 347.   [57] Ibid. 64.

Another place which did poorly in acquiring dissolved lands in the immediate aftermath of Dissolution only to make substantial gains in the longer run is Oxford. Most of the numerous properties of dissolved religious houses in and around Oxford went initially to the colleges or to individual speculators from outside the community, with townsmen getting a few chunks and the City almost nothing at all. But in the longer term the process of percolation of ownership followed in Oxford as it had in Coventry and Leicester, with both the City and individual townsmen acquiring more and more as time went on. For the sum of £610 in 1587 the City was able to acquire from William Frere the lucrative holdings of the Austin Friars.[58] These were not easy years for those faced with the task of balancing the City budget. Trade dwindled to the point where receipts from the annual fair fell from around £10 in the 1580s to a mere few shillings by 1603, and other revenue-producing assets produced unsteadily. Yet normal expenses remained relatively constant. It appears that the City Chamberlains finished with a surplus in only about two years out of three in the period *c*.1584–1617,[59] making frequent borrowing a necessity.[60]

In this financial context the revenues from the Friary lands, purchased in part with borrowed money but let on very lucrative terms, kept Oxford from an even more serious situation. Though they obviously failed to rescue the City from its constant fiscal balancing act, the new revenues seem to have been the major factor in keeping it solvent. They allowed Oxford to sustain a series of extraordinary expenses in subsequent years. These included the substantial purchase of armour and armaments on the eve of the Spanish Armada, a visit by the Queen in 1592 which cost at least £155, and the purchase of a new charter for £150 (excluding expenses) in 1605.[61] The newly acquired lands were carefully managed, being let quickly and lucratively. It is very difficult to imagine how Oxford would have fared without them. When in 1610 the City faced an opportunity to purchase valuable lands in nearby Eynsham, it sold these same Friary properties as a means of raising capital for that purchase.[62]

In some cases there could be a good many links on the chain which

---

[58] Salter (ed.), *Oxford Council Acts*, p. xli; *VCH, Oxfordshire*, 4 (1979), 311.
[59] Calculated on the basis of totals given in Salter (ed.), *Oxford Council Acts*, *passim*.
[60] Ibid. 382, 388–9.   [61] Ibid. 388–9.
[62] The City sold it to Dorothy Wadham, who used it in the original endowment of Wadham College; *VCH, Oxfordshire*, 4 (1979), 112–13, 142, 311, 368; Salter (ed.), *Oxford Council Acts*, pp. xli and 402.

led from the primary purchase from the Crown to the eventual acquisition by the town. This also makes it difficult to trace such activities. Frere was the fifth person to hold Oxford's Austin Friars after Dissolution: it had been leased by the Crown to Thomas Cardon, then granted to Henry Brandon, Duke of Suffolk and his partner. They sold it in 1552 to Henry Bailey, and he in turn just months later sold it to Frere's father Edward, who of course left it to Frere himself.[63]

The lands and buildings of the Abbey of Abingdon also went through several landlords during the years immediately following its dissolution, almost all of them court figures, before coming to the town itself. In November 1560, William Blacknall (who had bought them from Sir Thomas Wrothe, and he from Sir John Mason, and so forth) sold the property to the Corporation for £10. Six months later he leased to the Corporation the Chapel House of St John's Hospital for 1,200 years at a peppercorn rent: a different process altogether and one to which we will return below. Blackwell, a Berkshire gentleman with a seat at Swallowhold, near Reading, had numerous local interests in Abingdon. He himself held these properties in fee simple, and alienated them in that form. In any event, the Corporation made good use of these properties, and applied for a royal pardon in 1585 to cover any ambiguities which might arise concerning the security of their tenure.[64]

A similarly long chain of landholding applied in Bedford, whose trustees designated for the purpose finally bought the lands of Caldwell Priory in 1620. These had been held by William Gostwick and his wife, Anne, from 1538 and then by Thomas Leigh and his son John from 1563. Worth £11. 15s. 6d. at Dissolution, they had greatly increased in value by 1620.[65] They must have been very welcome additions to one of the smallest and least prosperous county towns in the realm.

The City of Bath supplies a final example of this sort of process of acquisition.[66] Here the resources at stake were not only the lands and site of the dissolved Priory, but also the school, numerous rental

[63] *VCH, Oxfordshire*, 4 (1979), 368.
[64] Berkshire Record Office, Preston MSS, D/EP 7/36, 2, 6–7; and D/EP 7/36 no. 82, 2–3.
[65] *VCH, Bedfordshire*, 3 (1912), 21.
[66] James Stokes and Robert Alexander (eds.), *REED: Somerset and Bath* (2 vols.; Toronto, 1996), ii. 458–61. I am indebted to both editors and to Dr Sally-Beth MacLean of REED for allowing me to examine the manuscript of this work prior to publication.

properties, and even the rights to the baths themselves. All of this came up for grabs at the Dissolutions, and almost all of it lay at that time outside the City's financial grasp. It remained for the City to undertake a long, slow process of acquisition which ensued for many years. Bath gained directly from the Crown the properties to support a refounded grammar school in 1552, the rights to the lucrative baths came in litigation in the following year (costing the City £90 in settlement), and additional former properties of the Priory accrued in 1572, 1573, and 1583.

These seven examples demonstrate the ways in which the middling and upper ranks of provincial towns slowly but steadily gained control of local resources over the course of several decades. A fourth and final general category of acquisitions, also very difficult to trace systematically, consists of acquisitions made through bequests of one sort or another from those favourably inclined towards a particular town. Although the intercessionary motives of former times no longer applied, many such benefactors, like William Blacknall—who, as has been noted above, 'leased' an important holding to the Borough of Abingdon for twelve hundred years at a peppercorn rent—were local landholders who wished to do something for their communities before their death, or who wanted something in return during their lifetimes. Some were landed gentry or aristocracy seeking to extend their influence into town affairs. Others were native sons who had either prospered in the community or left it to establish themselves at court or in the London business world.

A good example of this sort of acquisition comes from the Devon Borough of Totnes, where the all-important Priory and its lands had been sold at Dissolution to the Champernon family. The Champernons sold the Priory in 1542 to the wealthy townsman Walter Smith, who eventually conveyed it back to the Crown so that it could be granted to the Borough.[67] Another comes from Bristol, where George Owen purchased the site and extensive holdings of the Hospital of St John and then conveyed them, with royal licence, to the Borough in 1548.[68]

A much fuller example may be found in the bequests made by Richard Pates (1516–88) to several towns of his native Gloucestershire.[69] Pates (or 'Pate', as he is sometimes known) exemplifies as

[67] *CPR, Edward VI*, v. 227–8; Bindoff (ed.), *House of Commons, 1509–1558*, i. 75.
[68] *CPR, Edward VI*, i. 375–6.
[69] A. L. Browne, 'Richard Pates, MP for Gloucester', *Transactions of the Bristol and Gloucestershire Archeological Society*, 56 (1935 for 1934), 201–25; Arthur Bell,

well the 'new men' of the Tudor Age who turned a good education and some useful connections into a successful government career. Pates was a Cheltenham man who never lost touch with his home turf. After a year or two at Corpus Christi, Oxford, at which he took no degree, he proceeded in 1541 to Lincoln's Inn. Distracted by getting on with other activities, he then took a long time rising through the *cursus honorum* before receiving his call to the bar in 1558. But in the intervening years he forged close links with both royal and local administration in Gloucestershire, serving as under-steward of the manorial courts of Cirencester Abbey (1544), and of the Manor and Borough of Tewkesbury (1546). This put him in line for an appointment as a chantry commissioner for Gloucestershire, also in 1546. His own acquisitions of chantry properties, made jointly with his fellow official Sir Thomas Chamberlain, began in 1549 with purchases amounting to £1,134.[70]

Unlike some of the many court officials who got in on the ground floor of purchases from the Crown, including men like John Hales, Pates strengthened rather than weakened his ties to local affairs. He married the daughter of the Gloucester Sheriff and Mayor John Rastell, and became Recorder of that City by 1554.[71] He kept a residence there, served as its MP in several Parliaments, and when he died he was buried in Gloucester Cathedral. He also retained close ties to Cheltenham, where he established the School and Hospital which still bears his name,[72] and to Chipping Sodbury, where he bought at second hand the property and possessions of the Guild of the Blessed Virgin Mary—possibly as a mere agent—and resold them to the Borough for the same amount he had paid.[73]

Some of the lands which these three towns gained from Pates were acquired by sale. Others may be counted bequests. Pates's Foundation in Cheltenham, which includes the School and Hospital, is the most obvious, surviving in a slightly altered form into the present century. He was generous as well to the City of Gloucester, conveying to it most of his acquisitions from amongst the chantry lands of

---

Tudor Foundations: A Sketch of Richard Pate's Foundation in Cheltenham (Chalfont St Giles, Bucks., 1974); Hasler (ed.), *House of Commons, 1558–1603*, iii. 185–6; Gloucester Borough Records, MS GBR G 12/1.

[70] *CPR, Edward VI*, iii. 260–7.

[71] Browne claims this came about in 1556, but City records show him as Recorder by 1554; MS GBR F 4/3, fo. 62ʳ.

[72] *CPR, Eliz.*, vi. 297–8.

[73] F. F. Fox, 'On the Gilds of Sodbury and Dyrham', *Transactions of the Bristol and Gloucestershire Archeological Society*, 13 (1888–9), 9.

that City, amounting to slightly more than £100 in annual rental income,[74] and leaving in his will funds to support the City's poor, repair certain buildings, maintain prisoners, and build at least part of a new prison.[75]

Many similar examples may be culled from the histories of individual towns. The activities of men like Smith, Owen, and Pates not only demonstrate the role of local benefactors in buying up dissolved properties and then conveying them, in one form or another, to their own communities. They allow us insight into yet another way in which an individual town might gain or regain local properties and other resources in the several decades following the Dissolutions.

Even aside from being on the receiving end of Pates's generosity, the City of Gloucester exemplifies the admirable persistence of many towns in acquiring lands, not merely in the immediate aftermath of the Dissolutions, when a single purchase in 1542 for nearly £500 brought in a number of former ecclesiastical properties,[76] but for decades thereafter. Its surviving deeds and financial records do not allow us to reconstruct in complete detail its acquisitions of dissolved properties or to assess their value, but they do provide some substantial information. Even when we may not be certain precisely how and when they were obtained, we know, for one, that the City managed to acquire specific properties from chantries and other dissolved institutions over the course of several decades. Table IV shows both those, especially chantry properties, whose annual rental value after acquisition has not been found, and those often more substantial acquisitions where that value may be reconstructed on the basis of existing rentals or other financial records.

If the record of St Bartholomew's is any guide to the rest, those whose values we can reconstruct proved sound investments, becoming steadily more valuable through the century. They greatly enhanced the City's total revenue from the collection of rents, which had been reckoned in 1494 as only £29. 19s. 1½d. and in 1544 at £97. 3s. 9¾d. This last figure already includes St Margaret's Hospital, acquired well before Dissolution, plus the acquisitions of 1542 for which the City paid £493.[77] In the end, these possessions allowed Gloucester more than to double its income from rents and

---

[74] W. H. Stevenson (ed.), *Calendar of the Records of the Corporation of Gloucester* (Gloucester, 1893), 208.

[75] A copy may be found in the City archives, MS GBR G 12/1, fo. 269ʳ.

[76] *Letters and Papers, Henry VIII*, 17, item 881:20, p. 488.

[77] *VCH, Gloucestershire*, 4 (1988), 56.

associated sources, and to keep its own finances afloat at a time of considerable economic uncertainty.[78]

The third largest city in the realm throughout most of this period was Bristol, one of those five or six communities at the very top of the provincial town population table. Not only was Bristol larger in population than any other provincial community but Norwich, but its finances exemplify as well as any other the impact of acquiring dissolved lands in the decades following their surrender.[79] Yet even a town of Bristol's size and wealth could not purchase the larger share of dissolved lands when they came on the market. Local chantry properties alone yielded to the Crown the staggering sum (staggering at least for an urban community) of £4,258. 17s. 6d.: well beyond the means of even such a large centre as Bristol. But by judicious planning and persistent attention to possibilities for other purchases, it had substantial success in both acquiring other properties and in managing them effectively thereafter.

The first of these purchases came as early as 1541, when the City acquired the Carmelite and Franciscan friaries and Gaunt's Hospital, including the manor of Hamp and other country estates. These the Crown allowed the City for a price of £1,000 and the charge of a single £20 knight's fee.[80] Four years later Bristol purchased the former property of the Hospitallers of St John known as Temple Fee, plus some lands which had been held by the late Lord Lisle. These went to the City for £789. 17s. 10d. and were valued in sum at £71. 16s.[81] And in 1548 the Corporation bought the Chapel on the Bridge for an additional £40, along with the quit rents with which the Chapel had been endowed.[82] The total purchases came to £1,829. 17s. 10d. Aided by sale of church plate which the City somehow managed to preserve from confiscation, and by substantial loans from the extremely wealthy members of its own merchant elite, Bristol's

[78] Though not as economically distressed as many communities at this time, mid-16th-cent. Gloucester experienced the decline of its traditional textile industry and related industries and worked to encourage in its place the emergence of marketing and service-related activities. It faced a mild economic crisis in the 1590s and a very severe one in the 1620s (Clark, 'The Ramoth Gilead of the Good', in Clark, Smith, and Tyacke (eds.), *English Commonwealth, 1547–1640*, 167–88).

[79] The following discussion derives from D. M. Livock (ed.), *City Chamberlains' Accounts in the Sixteenth and Seventeenth Centuries*, Bristol Record Society, 24 (1966), pp. xv–xix.

[80] *Letters and Papers, Henry VIII*, 16, item 878, no. 10; and Livock (ed.), *City Chamberlains' Accounts*, p. xvii.

[81] *Letters and Papers, Henry VIII*, 19, part I, item 1035, no. 79, and 18, part I, item 436.

[82] Livock, *City Chamberlains' Acounts*, p. xviii.

chamberlains were able to pay the Crown in full by the end of 1548. And although some further purchases were made over the remainder of the century, none seem to have been of formerly dissolved lands.

Though this seems a large investment at the time, the success with which Bristol's mayors and chamberlains managed their new assets in an inflationary era made it the basis both of substantial income and substantial property development in decades to come. The steep and steady increase of entry fines, for example, raised annual income from this source from a mere £8 in 1556–7 to £538 by 1627–8, so that it amounted to over one-third of total income by the latter date. Part of this increase may be attributed to the City's decree of 1575–6 that the maximum term for leases on City property should be twenty years, where anything up to ninety-nine years had previously been the norm. This meant at least four entry fines in a century instead of one, and it certainly had the desired effect. Though the rental income per se from Gaunt's Hospital and its associated estates rose only from £191. 3s. 1½d. in 1556–7 to £228. 4½d. in 1627–8—an increase which failed dismally even to cover the impact of inflation over those years—entry fines on those properties increased over the same span from a mere £1 to £463. 3s. 4d.[83]

iii

In view of this sort of evidence we must obviously reconsider the assumption that towns gained little from the Dissolutions because they made relatively few of the initial purchases from the Crown. Towns acquired dissolved lands over a long period of time and by several means; they were inspired to do so by a variety of motives. In acquisitions made directly from the Crown, through purchase and/or charter, such motives are often stated in the petition for the desired properties. The upkeep of roads and bridges, the re-founding and maintenance of schools (and, to a lesser extent, hospitals and almshouses), the employment of a chaplain or lecturer, and support of the indigent figure prominently in these cases. The ensuing grant conveyed either formally or informally the expectation that the resulting resources would be applied to the stated objective. As the Mayor and Aldermen of Colchester learned to their chagrin, the Crown seemed willing to investigate allegations to the contrary.[84]

[83] Ibid., pp. xvii–xviii.

[84] In 1584, for example, the Exchequer launched an investigation to ascertain whether lands granted to Colchester to found a school had actually been devoted to

But in many instances of course acquisitions did not come by purchase of the Crown, or grants and purchases were not earmarked for specific purposes. Here the variety of uses to which communities put new resources seems even more diverse. Bristol's Friary properties, for example, seem to have consisted in large measure of agricultural land, much of it on the outskirts of the City itself. As we have seen, these properties bore but modest rental income, but they proved very valuable nonetheless for the entry fines which tenants were willing to pay, and because they allowed the City to control future suburban development in important locations.[85] Along with their other priorities for new resources, Coventry and Exeter had motives which were partly political. They were anxious to prevent wealthy and powerful outsiders from purchasing and thus controlling the lands in question. In Coventry's case, as we have seen, this had already happened once.[86] Newcastle and Faversham seem to have been particularly interested in extending their legal jurisdiction over properties which had been 'in but not of' the town in times past.[87] And Oxford, Beverley, Worcester again, and Colchester exemplify those communities which chose — or were compelled — fairly soon to resell at least some of their acquisitions, thus liquefying their assets in difficult times.[88]

But paramount for many towns, including Leicester, Chipping Sodbury, Hull, Worcester, and Winchester,[89] remained the need to derive additional rental income, and we may expect towns like this

this purpose. Though neither the genesis of the investigation nor its conclusion are recorded, it cannot but have come from local initiatives (PRO, E. 178/829).

[85] R. C. Latham (ed.), *Bristol Charters, 1509–1899*, Bristol Record Society, 12 (1947), 22.

[86] For Coventry, see above, pp. 117–18; MacCaffrey, *Exeter* (1958, 1975), 184.

[87] This is the obvious conclusion to be drawn from the fact that the annual value of the lands for which they petitioned equalled the rent paid for them to the Crown (Newcastle, PRO, E. 318/32/1815; and *CPR, Edward VI*, v. 299; Faversham, PRO, E. 318/10/433; and *Letters and Papers*, 21, pp. 75–6). Newcastle also received lands on which they did make a profit (*CPR, Edward VI*, ii. 203).

[88] The City of Oxford sold off the properties of the former Augustinian Friary for £600 in 1609–10. The ruling elite of Beverley sold off some former church lands to local gentry, though they may have done this as much for political as for financial reasons. Worcester sold off the building materials from some of the friary buildings in its possession for a total of £350 while keeping the rental properties (Salter (ed.), *Oxford Council Acts*, 400–1; Lamburn, 'Politics and Religion in Sixteenth Century Beverley', 227; Dyer, *City of Worcester*, 218; Jennifer C. Ward, 'The Reformation in Colchester, 1528–1558', *Essex Archaeology and History*, 15 (1983), 88).

[89] *VCH, Leicestershire*, 4 (1958), esp. 63–4; F. F. Fox, 'On the Gilds of Sodbury and Dyrham', 9; *VCH, Yorkshire, East Riding*, 2 (1974), 127–8; Rosen, 'Economic and Social Aspects of Winchester', 97.

to have taken close care for the renovation of derelict properties and the active management of leases. If not carried out on the scale of Bristol's operations, some of these efforts nevertheless seem particularly successful. Following its acquisition of dissolved lands by the end of Mary's reign, rents and entry fines comprised the largest single source of Winchester's income for the rest of the century.[90] And in Worcester, the City leaders managed to purchase dissolved religious properties, despite declining profit margins due to fixed, long-term rents, which still brought in roughly two-thirds of the City's income by the end of the sixteenth century.[91]

iv

Though the necessarily circumstantial nature of the evidence makes it impossible to measure it in anything approaching precise terms, the combined material resources rescued from the dissolution process through concealment and pre-emptive acquisition on the one hand, and the acquisition by grant, purchase, or bequest on the other, seem clearly to have brought a substantial shift of income-bearing resources to the control of urban governing bodies. It cannot be claimed that this shift was anywhere near as great as that transfer of wealth to individual lay purchasers, but that may to a considerable degree be beside the point. From the perspective of towns and their governing authorities, many such material acquisitions proved important elements in the assertion of greater local control in ensuing decades. In this sense the gain in material resources went hand in hand with the attainment, through enfeoffment to uses, litigation, and incorporation, of greater legal jurisdiction and governing authority over the same period.

This broad transfer of resources had a number of implications. For one, civic control over income-bearing properties afforded a basis for civic finance which promised both security and growth. This would be extremely significant at any time. It was all the more so in the face of both rapid economic changes in general and marked increases in the costs of governing both town and nation. Save for the 1550s, these years also witnessed a steady growth in population, and thus a steady rise in property values (one feature of the economic restructuring) which generally occurred at an even greater rate in urban than in rural areas. Under these conditions land

[90] Rosen, 'Economic and Social Aspects of Winchester', 59–66, 97.
[91] Dyer, *City of Worcester*, 217–18.

became a very good investment, all the more so if let on shorter-term leases than in previous periods. Contemporary townspeople familiar with the local property market seem to have understood this very well. Just a few decades earlier property values had sunk so low, and the rate of default had become so high, as to render collection of rents more trouble than it was worth. Now rents and entry fines on rental property together seem to have become the single most important source of revenue for many or even most communities, often replacing traditional perquisites of market, freemanry, or court in pride of place.[92]

Possession of such properties themselves also allowed borough governments to exert greater control both over the condition of local housing, as was explicit in the rebuilding statutes of the 1530s and 1540s, and over the sorts of people contracted as tenants. Borough officials could now define the conditions for the award of leases or the sale of properties, and to choose the recipients. They now had much greater authority to demand appropriate upkeep on borough properties, and to enjoin tenants to refrain from housing strangers or vagrants. These themes become commonplace in contemporary town by-laws and to some extent in property leases as well. At a time when the maintenance of order, under the aegis of what Clark and Slack have called 'small knots of reliable men', loomed paramount in the eyes of government authorities from the Crown on down, this was no small advantage.

Aside from its potential for social control (and, indeed, as we will see in Chapter 9, also for corruption), the augmented power to grant leases or even sell off unprofitable lands also allowed borough authorities greater flexibility in managing local resources. In some cases it provided the sort of financial liquidity which, as we have seen, allowed Oxford's mayor and burgesses to sell off one property in order to purchase another. In other cases a free hand in the award of leases might allow a town's officials to cultivate the shire gentry, and thus to encourage greater gentry support for its interests. In Beverley, for example, several mayors of the 1580s took it upon

---

[92] e.g. Oxford: *VCH, Oxfordshire*, 4 (1979), 140–1; and Salter (ed.), *Oxford Council Acts, passim*; Beverley: *VCH, Yorkshire, East Riding*, 6 (1989), 69; Kingston-upon-Thames: Kingston Chamberlains' Accounts, Surrey Record Office, MS KD5/1/1, *passim*; Winchester: Rosen, 'Economic and Social Aspects of Winchester', 97; Gloucester (where the City's rental income increased from £89 to £204 in the quarter century between 1550–1 and 1575–6): Stewards' and Chamberlains' Accounts, Gloucestershire Record Office, MS GBR F4/3; Bury St Edmunds: Summary of Accounts, West Suffolk Record Office, MS H2/3/1.1.

themselves to sell off choice pieces of former ecclesiastical land to local magnates in the hope of cementing political and personal ties between the Borough and the county community, though this may have worked against the Borough's interests in the long term.[93] Nevertheless, such practices undoubtedly had continuing implications for such matters as parliamentary representation, patronage of diverse sorts, and the social and cultural influence of gentry in urban affairs.

V

Finally, we must try to draw some conclusions about the fate of educational, charitable, and similar social institutions. One must still bow to Professor Scarisbrick's conclusion that 'We will probably never have a complete picture of the effect of the Reformation [on English schools and hospitals] and never be able to draw up a definitive balance sheet of losses and gains.'[94] Yet there is a somewhat better-established record of scholarly investigation on these issues than on questions of property alone, and it is a record which further research seems more to support than to challenge.

The founding or re-founding of schools, for example, represented a major priority for a great many towns. Admittedly, a substantial debate still rages concerning the impact of the Reformation on education and schools.[95] Nevertheless it has become clear that, though the Crown did not follow through on its own promises in this

---

[93] Lamburn, 'Politics and Religion in Beverley', 221–30.

[94] Scarisbrick, *Reformation and the English People*, 112.

[95] Most of the debate revolves more around the question of the state of the schools and of education generally prior to the Dissolutions than around the question of re-foundations, though the latter, too, remains moot. Consideration of the former question begins with the work of A. F. Leach, esp. *English Schools at the Reformation* (1896); and Leach, *Schools of Medieval England* (1915); and of criticisms and/or at least partial defences of his work in the following: Joan Simon, *Education and Society in Tudor England* (Cambridge, 1967); Nicholas Orme, *English Schools in the Middle Ages* (1973); and Orme, *Education in the West of England, 1066–1548* (Exeter, 1976); A. R. Morris, 'The Effect upon Schooling in Sussex of the Legislation Dissolving the Religious Houses and Chantries', *Sussex Archeological Collections*, 119 (1981), 149–56; Joann Hoeppner Moran, *Education and Learning in the Diocese of York, 1300–1500*, Borthwick Papers, 55 (York, 1979); and Moran, *The Growth of English Schooling, 1340–1548: Learning, Literacy and Laicization in Pre-Reformation York Diocese* (Princeton, 1985).

Claims for dramatic advances in the foundation or re-foundation of schools after the Dissolutions, and for advances in education thereafter which strike some as 'revolutionary' in extent, derive esp. from the work of Simon as cited above and from Lawrence Stone's provocative essay 'The Educational Revolution in England, 1560–1640', *Past and Present*, 28 (July 1964), 41–80.

regard, it did respond to local initiatives in several ways. In consequence, education seems much less disrupted than one used to think.
In a number of cases the Augmentations, exercising powers specifically vested in it by the Crown in 1548,[96] simply endowed with an
annual stipend schools which had either survived the Dissolutions in
one form or another or which required re-foundation. Most of these
endowments came as stipends to pay the schoolmaster.[97] In other
cases schools were either sustained or re-founded by charter, again
at local initiative. These might be given to the town as a whole, sometimes as part of an incorporation,[98] or to feoffees charged with the
responsibility for running a particular school. In other such cases we
find the organization of school trusts as bodies in and of themselves,
operating under the terms of a deed of enfeoffment rather than a
borough charter.[99] In numerous cases feoffees of one sort or another
were invested as well with the power to appoint the schoolmaster,
albeit sometimes in mandatory consultation with some formal, often
university or ecclesiastical, authority. Since the feoffees were often
appointed by, or were even the same people as, the mayor and aldermen, this had the effect of placing the control of such schools at least
indirectly in the hands of the local government.[100]

In addition to these direct cash endowments, the Crown often

---

[96] *CPR, Edward VI*, 3 (1925), 215. See also Richardson, *Augmentations*, 176–7 and
193.

[97] Returns have survived for but 23 counties plus North and South Wales in PRO,
E. 319/Files 1–26. Schools receiving fixed annual sums under this aegis rather than
income-producing lands, and which were in towns (as not all of them were), include
the following: Alnwick, Basingstoke, Bedale, Bodmin, Bradford (Wilts.), Brecknock,
Bromsgrove, Bromyard, Chipping Norton, Coventry, Crewkerne, Darlington,
Dylwin, Evesham, Higham (Kent), Houghton (Beds.), King's Norton, Ledbury,
Northallerton, Nottingham, Oundle, Pembridge, Penryn, Rothwell (Northants.),
Saltash, Shenston (Staffs.), Southwell (Notts.), Stamford, Stratford-upon-Avon,
Thorneton (Lincs.), Towcester, Trowbridge, Walsall, Wimborne, and Wisbech.
Some of these eventually proved insufficient.

[98] These included: St Albans, Stafford, Saffron Walden, Higham Ferrars, Wisbech, and Maidstone, as summarized in Tittler, 'Incorporation of Boroughs', 35–6.

[99] Examples include Blandford Forum, cited in PRO, C. 93/1/11 (42 Elizabeth);
Bury St Edmunds (in which the Town Trust paid the schoolmaster's wages), 'The
Minute Book of the Feoffees of the Guildhall', West Suffolk Record Office, MS
H2/6.2, vol. i, *passim*; Grantham, John Bernard Manterfield, 'The Topographical
Development of the Pre-Industrial Town of Grantham, Lincolnshire, 1535–1835',
Ph.D. thesis (Exeter, 1981), 7; and Melton Mowbray, Dorothy Pockley, 'Early
History of Melton Mowbray', 37–8, 50.

[100] The view that the Dissolutions precipitated a shift in the control of schools from
ecclesiastical to lay authority, arising impressionistically from a reading of the *Calendar of Patent Rolls*, is confirmed in current secondary scholarship, ably summarized in
Nicholas Orme, 'The "Laicization" of English School Education', *History of Education*, 16/2 (June 1987), 84.

permitted some host towns to hold lands generating the required revenues, at least up to a certain stipulated value. In other cases it granted specific lands directly, usually drawing them from the resources of dissolved chantries or guilds. The latter group has been identified in Table V. Tabulated only for as many years as the published *Calendar of Patent Rolls* will permit, even this extensive list must be considered illustrative rather than comprehensive. Though we cannot expect that schools continued to be re-founded at quite the same pace under Elizabeth, there were almost certainly a good many more foundations or re-foundations in that period, and in the latter years of her reign, for which Patent Rolls have yet to be calendared.

The general thrust of this evidence supports the emerging consensus that the Dissolutions provided at the worst but a brief interruption at the grammar school level, and that many or most schools were no worse off afterwards than before.[101] It supports as well the view that these years resulted in a substantial shift from ecclesiastical to lay control, and that such lay control often rested in the hands of mayors, aldermen, and their appointees, or of trusts in the same communities. This role extended beyond the re-foundation and funding of such schools. It applied as well to the appointment of schoolmasters, to setting the conditions of their employment, and, especially with the triumph of Protestantism in the mid-Elizabethan years, to determining of a good part of the curriculum as well.

Another form of education which became increasingly important as the century wore on took place not so much in the grammar school as in the parish church; it was directed not merely to schoolchildren but to entire communities. The concern exhibited by the leaders of many towns for moral reform, and thus for a preaching clergy which could enjoin the entire community to join in building the New Jerusalem, became more important than ever before in the years at hand. Although the efforts in scores of towns to appoint lecturers or control the appointment of parish clergy in the latter decades of the sixteenth century and opening decades of the next have long been

---

[101] Simon, *Education and Society*, esp. chap. 11; Morris, 'Effect upon Schooling in Sussex', 149–156; Rosen, 'Economic and Social Aspects of Winchester', 76; *VCH, Leicestershire*, 3 (1955), 243; Woodward, 'Dissolution of the Chantries', 227–30; Scarisbrick, *Reformation and the English People*, 111–17. A dissident note has been issued by J. P. Anglin in 'Frustrated Ideals: The Case of Elizabethan Grammar School Foundations', *History of Education*, 11/4 (1982), 267–79, but he deals mostly with schools after re-foundation and takes his examples from London rather than the provincial towns.

familiar,[102] it is worth noting that some towns saw this need almost immediately after the opening salvos of Reformation legislation: examples have been identified at Ipswich, Leicester, and Warwick.[103] Civic control of advowsons in urban parishes does not seem to have been especially common before the Reformation.[104] Yet a considerable number of towns had been able to acquire advowsons to local livings with their initial purchases of dissolved lands, with their post-dissolution incorporations, or with simple grants from the Crown.[105] These typically included both the right to appoint incumbents and to hold endowments for their support. Towards much the same ends of augmenting civic control over the local ministry and strengthening the role of that ministry, the statute of 1545, permitting the consolidation of parishes less than a mile apart, proved an additional boon.[106]

The story of the hospitals during the Reformation years also remains complex and marked by many local variations.[107] Hospitals as such were not especially targeted for dissolution until 1545,[108] though many of them were thrown out with the bathwater when institutions to which they had been attached were themselves dissolved in the 1530s. Yet throughout the sixteenth century sympathy remained strong at all levels of decision making for the hospitals as institutions and for the work which they carried out for the sick and disabled. Henry VII had been a noted supporter and patron of

---

[102] For civic patronage of ministers and preachers in general, see Christopher Hill, *The Economic Problems of the Church from Archbishop Whitgift to the Long Parliament* (1956), esp. 57; Patrick Collinson, *The Elizabethan Puritan Movement* (1967); id., *Birthpangs*, chap. 2; and id., *Religion of Protestants*, chap. 4; Claire Cross, *Urban Magistrates and Ministers*, Borthwick Papers, 67 (1985); MacCulloch, *Suffolk and the Tudors*; W. J. Sheils, 'Religion in Provincial Towns: Innovation and Tradition', in F. Heal and R. O'Day (eds.), *Church and Society in England: Henry VIII to James I* (1977), 156–76; Paul S. Seaver, *The Puritan Lectureships: The Politics of Religious Dissent, 1560–1662* (Stanford, Calif., 1970), esp. chap. 4 and appendix A. In this last appendix, counting only those boroughs with parliamentary franchises, Seaver lists seventy-five which founded lectureships in the years 1560–1640.

[103] Seaver, *Puritan Lectureships*, 80–1.

[104] The traditional view that such civic patronage may have been altogether unknown prior to the Reformation has but recently been corrected. Kumin, *Shaping of a Community*, 44–5.

[105] See e.g. Norwich and Crediton in 1547, Ludlow in 1552, Stratford-upon-Avon in 1553, Clitheroe in 1554, Higham Ferrars in 1556 (*CPR, Edward VI*, i. 13–17 and 43–5; iv. 346; v. 280; and *CPR, Mary*, ii. 192; *Philip and Mary*, iii. 200–3).

[106] 37 Henry VIII, c. 21; D. M. Palliser, 'The Union of Parishes at York, 1547–1586', *Yorkshire Archeological Journal*, 46 (1975), 87–102.

[107] The following derives largely from Nicholas Orme and Margaret Webster, *The English Hospital, 1070–1570* (London and New Haven, 1995), 155–66.

[108] 37 Henry VIII, c. 4.

hospitals. Henry VIII had not opposed them directly and his reign saw several fervent supporters express their views in writing. Edward and Mary's reigns saw serious and partly successful attempts to sustain those hospitals still left and, especially in Mary's reign, to re-found many which had ceased to function. These policies continued on into Elizabeth's reign.

'On the whole', as the most recent authorities on the subject have concluded, 'the impact of events on hospitals seems to have been similar to that on schools. Individual places sometimes suffered badly, but the whole interest was only partly affected and remained as before in many respects.'[109] It might be added that in local communities efforts to re-found such institutions continued for some time to come. And as with schools, the re-foundation or further support of hospitals often came via the charter of borough incorporation.

The picture regarding other aspects of poor relief must also be considered. The vast majority of those institutions which had provided poor relief in one form or another had disappeared in the 1530s and 1540s, precisely the time when accelerated economic changes brought the incidence of poverty itself to new heights. Here the disruption of traditional systems was more sweeping than with educational institutions, many of which had been in lay hands prior to the Reformation and were thus undisturbed by it. Yet the poverty problem became so much more pressing in these decades that even the preservation of the entire system as it had been could not have turned the tide by the latter half of the sixteenth century. The problem rapidly overwhelmed either the simple provision of relief on a small and local scale or the resources encouraged by traditional religious imperatives.[110] It would take remedies of an entirely more complex nature and on a national scale — in short, the culmination of legislative efforts as they evolved to the Elizabethan Poor Laws of 1597 and 1601 — to formulate a reasonable response. This same could be said as well for the provision of poor relief in states all over Europe, where even states that remained Catholic had to resort to some form of civic control of poor relief as a supplement to traditional charitable dispensations.[111]

---

[109] Orme and Webster, *The English Hospital*, 163. This conclusion echoes that made by Scarisbrick, *Reformation and the English People*, 115–16.

[110] See e.g. Paul Slack, *Poverty and Policy in Tudor and Stuart England* (1988), 40–55.

[111] See e.g. Nicholas Terpstra, 'Apprenticeship in Social Welfare: From Confraternal Charity to Municipal Poor Relief in Early Modern Italy', *Sixteenth Century*

Yet while Parliament experimented with national remedies in a sequence of statutes issuing forth between 1531 and 1601, both individual townspeople and local communities undertook initiatives as never before. The thrust of these initiatives, eventually supported by statute, was to found or re-found appropriate charitable institutions under civic aegis: to seek and to receive the authority both to run them and to raise compulsory alms for that purpose. Though the parish became the most common jurisdiction for exercising such powers (thus enhancing its role as a unit of civil administration), officials of the town also came in for a greater share of responsibility as well. Some local schemes for poor relief, including well-known examples in Norwich and Ipswich, blossomed under borough authority in these years, while in many other communities officials of the parish and the borough worked closely together towards the same end.[112]

In sum, we should not allow our prime focus on the implications of the Reformation to blind us to these other, equally profound and contemporary events. The rapid economic and social changes of this era brought to the governing authorities of English towns and boroughs much greater concern for problems like economic dislocation and poverty, crime, rootlessness, unrest, and the general apprehension which came with them. If the Reformation changed dramatically the ways in which these problems could be faced, it also (and indirectly) armed many local officials with new sources of revenue, especially in expanded rental income, and facilitated greater civic jurisdiction over social institutions. As the business of managing those resources effectively lies more in the realm of politics and government than in finance, we must now turn to those issues.

Journal, 25 (1994), 101–20; Kathryn Norberg, *Rich and Poor in Grenoble, 1600–1814* (Berkeley, 1985); Brian Pullan, *Rich and Poor in Renaissance Venice: The Social Institutions of a Catholic State to 1620* (1971); Maureen Flynn, *Sacred Charity, Confraternities and Social Welfare in Spain, 1400–1700* (1989), chaps. 2–3; C. F. Black, *Italian Confraternities in the Sixteenth Century* (1989), chaps. 7–10; Linda Martz, *Poverty and Welfare in Habsburg Spain: The Example of Toledo* (1983).

[112] In addition to Slack, *Poverty and Policy*, and a host of standard works on the subject, see Marjorie K. McIntosh, 'Local Responses to the Poor in Late Medieval and Tudor England', *Continuity and Change*, 3/2 (1988), 209–45; J. F. Pound (ed.), *The Norwich Census of the Poor, 1570*, Norfolk Record Society, 40 (1971); and John Webb (ed.), *Poor Relief in Elizabethan Suffolk*, Suffolk Record Society, 9 (1966); and Kumin, *Shaping of a Community*, chap. 6 and conclusion.

Part III
Politics and Authority

7

Introduction

It should by now be obvious that the events discussed in the first two parts of this study had profound implications for the political life of most of England's larger and middling-size towns. We turn in Part III to a consideration of some of those political ramifications.

Broadly speaking, the political development of a good many English towns from the Dissolutions to the early seventeenth century appears to proceed in sequential stages. Through the late medieval period and on to the middle decades of the sixteenth century, most towns experienced a strong presence and often a general domination of their government and resources by external, especially manorial, authorities. Shortly following the Henrician Reformation and contemporary social and economic developments, many towns resumed and redoubled earlier efforts to secure a greater degree not only of control over local resources, as we have seen in the preceding section, but also of political autonomy in a wider sense. By the middle of the Elizabethan era the results of these renewed efforts had begun to tell. In a good many towns we see a consolidation of newly won political and constitutional authority in the form of strengthened indigenous institutions. We see, too, a narrowing of the political process, and a move towards a more elitist approach to local affairs.

Once again, of course, these phenomena applied not so much to the bottom ranks of the urban table, but especially to towns of middling or greater size, substance, and complexity. These were the towns best able to take some positive initiatives when faced with the dissolution of local institutions. Most often these were also the towns whose citizens were sufficiently numerous and politically resourceful to capitalize on the opportunity thus provided. In some cases, especially in towns formerly run by ecclesiastical landlords, such efforts met success for the first time, making a particularly sharp institutional break with past practice. In perhaps the majority, they added substantially to earlier gains.

Along with most efforts to generalize about the political or social characteristics of pre-modern towns, however, this evolutionary paradigm should not be construed too rigidly. It does not mean, for example, that the tendency towards oligarchic rule could not be found in some towns before *c.*1540, or that it triumphed completely thereafter. There can be little doubt that oligarchic rule of a sort — especially in the narrow and literal sense of rule by the few — had already come to prevail in many towns by the end of the fifteenth century.[1] A number of towns had already come to be dominated by small groups of men, while the exclusion of many town-dwellers before the Reformation, and especially of non-freemen, women, and children, has also been widely observed. It has even been argued that the sort of 'communal' ceremonies which, for example, Charles Phythian-Adams and Mervyn James have seen as promoting social cohesion may either not have accomplished their objective or may even have done just the opposite.[2]

Yet in large measure it still seems fair to say both that contemporaries did not so much mind being ruled by a small number of people (a situation rendered 'natural' because of the wealth required for the assumption of governing responsibility) so long as elements of participation, consent, and delegation remained implicit in the mix.[3] In this context oligarchy in the sense of a corruption of appropriate authority (i.e. oligarchy in the Aristotelian sense) appears to have remained relatively uncommon and highly objectionable prior to the Reformation. A number of examples may be offered of pre-Reformation townsmen resisting the sundry forms of this corruption, and for the most part the impression arises that they did so with considerable success.[4]

---

[1] Representative works include: Platt, *The English Medieval Town*, 120–4; Gottfried, *Bury St Edmunds and the Urban Crisis*, chap. 4; Rigby, 'Urban "Oligarchy" in Late Medieval England', in Thompson (ed.), *Towns and Townspeople*, 62–86. Important qualifications to the nature and meaning of oligarchy in the same period come from Susan Reynolds, as cited in n. 3 below, and from David R. Carr, 'The Problem of Urban Patriciates: Office Holders in Fifteenth Century Salisbury', *Wiltshire Archeological and Natural History Magazine*, 83 (1990), 118–35.

[2] For London, for example, see Lindenbaum, 'Ceremony and Oligarchy', in Hanawalt and Reyerson (eds.), *City and Spectacle*, 171–87.

[3] This line of argument is usefully explored by Susan Reynolds in *An Introduction to the History of English Medieval Towns* (Oxford, 1977), 135–7; and in Reynolds, 'Medieval Urban History and the History of Political Thought', *Urban History Yearbook* (1982), 14–23. See also Rigby, *English Society*, 170–1; and Shaw, *Creation of a Community*, chaps. 5–6.

[4] The thrust of these points, and of the numerous studies from which they derive, is conveniently summarized in Rigby, *English Society*, 170–6.

The more common experience of English towns on the eve of Reformation still recognized a local communal identity, heavily informed by traditional religious elements. Where a degree of self-government under seigneurial aegis permitted, an informal consensual support of local government by at least the freemanry, if not necessarily all residents, still remained the wide and general expectation. We find this expectation embodied in the term 'commonalty', often employed both in the language of litigation and testimony and in such documents as charters of incorporation on into the mid-sixteenth century.[5] It is difficult to know how much significance we should attach to this usage. Yet we may presume that, as charters derived from the petitions of the townsmen themselves, this reflected the language of local description for the community in its political and legal form. Furthermore, as many towns employing that term in the charters of the mid-sixteenth century were still modest in size and apparently not very polarized politically, the implication of a sense of community in the word 'commonalty' is likely to have been more consciously descriptive than coincidental.

That is to say that, in most middling and larger towns around the turn of the sixteenth century, the freemanry as a whole still shared (and expected to share) widely in the powers of whatever government pertained. They expected mayors and aldermen to honour their oaths of office, rule in the common interest rather than in their own interest, observe the traditional *cursus honorum* to prominence, and respect a relatively inclusive and participatory process of selection. Even where considerable self-rule had been obtained, it was still expected that major decisions, concerning such issues as market regulations, local levies and tolls, and even the disposition of leases on community-owned property, would be taken through the deliberations of both the councils which conventionally comprised the structure of those boroughs. Despite obvious gradations of wealth, status, and achievement, which were by no means incongruous with this ethos of community, the freemanry shared broadly in the rights and opportunities at hand. They also shared a collective responsibility for the well-being of the whole.[6]

---

[5] In labelling the recipient towns, nine of the sixty-two charters of incorporation granted to urban communities in the period 1540–75 still employed the term 'commonalty': Saffron Walden (1549), Sheffield (1554), Launceston (1556), Thaxted (1556), Tamworth (1560), Henley-on-Thames (1568), Poole (1568), Hythe (1575), and Tewkesbury (1575). But such usage became less common thereafter.

[6] As Paul Slack has reminded us, this has been noted esp. with reference to the

It remained true that some freemen held civic office while others did not. Yet the former remained in close touch with the rest and were frequently reminded of their obligations to the whole. Oaths of office, for example, were not only taken as sacred obligations, but also as commitments to honour the rights and interests of the whole community, rich as well as poor, freeman as well as non-freeman, in an even-handed manner. Progress from office to office, usually along the paths of some commonly understood *cursus honorum*, depended as much on individual effort and achievement as on family connections, more on some sort of election than blatant co-option, more on seniority than queue-jumping, nepotism, or outright patronage.

The parish, too, had long exhibited these characteristics of community, perhaps even more so than the towns of which they were a part, thus reinforcing that common identity as it applied more generally. Parish government remained freer of external authority than most towns. Parish officials on the whole still came from a broader spectrum of the local population than did town officials as such, and the electoral principal often applied more comprehensively to parish councils than to borough councils. Parish offices provided an early foothold in the civic *cursus honorum* for those who would go further. For others they afforded at least a taste of civic participation and further encouraged the sense of belonging.[7] As Tudor legislation enhanced the civic functions of the parish, its relationship to the government of the town itself, and of its officials with the town's, grew steadily closer.

Fostered by these means, harmony amongst the parts in the pre-Reformation community may not invariably have been obtained, but it remained an attainable and practical ideal. The concept of 'being in charity' with one's neighbours may have emerged along with the notion of spiritual grace, but its practical expression as a secular and social ideal had also become an important animating force in the community.[8] Townsmen spoke commonly of 'neighbourhood' or 'doing neighbourhood',[9] and took exception to violations of that

economically disadvantaged members of the local community, right up to the middle of the 16th cent. (Slack, *Poverty and Policy*, chap. 2).

[7] Phythian-Adams, *Desolation of a City*, 167–9; Whiting, *Blind Devotion*, 83–92; Shaw, *Creation of a Community*, 109–10; Kumin, *Shaping of a Community*, chaps. 1–5.

[8] Brigden, 'Religion and Social Obligation', 67–112.

[9] i.e. of being good neighbours or sustaining good relations amongst neighbours (*Oxford English Dictionary*, *vide*, 'Neighbourhood', nos. 1–2). Thus, for example, a Liverpool by-law of 1541 reminds all residents of the traditional expectation 'that all

notion. In many boroughs political friction between townsmen and seigneurial or ecclesiastical authorities no doubt strengthened local loyalties. Religious guilds and fraternities did a great deal to encourage these values, serving as important elements in the perpetuation of civic harmony and urban identity.[10] And of course the prevailing view still has civic ceremony, often sponsored by those local guilds and fraternities, serving as an important device towards the maintenance of civic harmony.[11]

We see the notion of community at work in numerous settings and in numerous towns throughout the pre-Reformation era: as represented by the forms of the *liber burgi* and the *firma burgi* in the early stages and by the forms of town guilds or formal borough structures themselves in many communities later on. A few examples illustrate the point.

In Newcastle-under-Lyme, for example, authority within the community by the fourteenth century seems to have been exercised by a mayor, two bailiffs, and twenty-four burgesses who constituted a common council. Yet the name employed to describe the whole was 'The Mayor and Community of Newcastle-under-Lyme'. We might well wonder whether the name had already become a mere euphemism for what was in fact rule by an inner circle. But when major decisions had to be taken, the consent of the whole body of freemanry seems to have been considered necessary and—as with a decision to enclose the town's common lands in *c*.1379–80—it was duly solicited. Even by the late fifteenth century the newly emerged body of inner councillors known as 'The Twelve'—a common enough formulation for the time—represented in its voice 'the whole assent and consent of the cominalte' to acts taken by the mayor and what had become two councils. Only by the mid-Elizabethan period, when the Twelve inflated to twenty-four and pulled away from the freemanry at large, did the means of electing such a body seem to have become indirect.[12]

In Lichfield the formulation of a 'community' within the purview of the manorial structure headed by the Bishop may be traced to

and every person shall make and doe neyburhode' (Twemlow (ed.), *Liverpool Town Books*, i. 11 n. 1).

[10] See esp. McRee, 'Religious Gilds and the Regulation of Behavior', in Rosenthal and Richmond (eds.), *People, Politics and Community*, 108–22.

[11] The classic works remain Phythian-Adams, 'Ceremony and the Citizen', in Clark and Slack (eds.), *Crisis and Order in English Towns*, 57–85; and M. James, 'Ritual, Drama and Social Body', 3–29.

[12] *VCH, Staffordshire*, 8 (1963), 25–26.

c.1221. Though the details are few, it seems clear that throughout the twelfth and most of the thirteenth centuries the townsmen had a quasi-formal structure of their own while remaining in most respects under manorial jurisdiction. In letters to the kings of those times they expressed this identity as 'the Community of the City of Lichfield' or 'the burgesses and goodmen' of the same.[13] In a pattern repeated at Norwich,[14] Coventry, Ludlow,[15] and widely elsewhere, this community of townsmen came by the end of the fourteenth century to be embodied in a religious guild, in this case the Guild of St Mary and St John the Baptist, established *c*.1387. While the Bishop's jurisdiction continued to provide judicature and other essential aspects of governance, the townsmen, through their Guild, strove to provide both religious and social services. In these and other ways they shared a concern and a responsibility for the peace and harmony of the community. By 1448 the Guild Master and 'his brethren' formalized ordinances for the peace of the community, probably simply codifying in written form what had come to pass by the accretion of practice. These described the mediation of disputes amongst brethren ('brethren' in this case including women as well as men, as both were included as full members of the Guild) as well as numerous other services and activities devoted to the common good.[16]

In contrast to many such arrangements, there does not seem to have been much jurisdictional rivalry or other friction between the Bishop (who served as lord of the manor and, hence, of the City) and the Guild. Yet with the Reformation, even though Lichfield remained a diocese and the Bishop remained on his throne, things changed rapidly. The Guild itself was dissolved, and the townsmen gained incorporation as a borough in and of itself shortly thereafter.[17] The new corporation appropriated many of the functions of the former Guild, and certainly the individuals who had come to direct the Guild continued on as officers of the new corporation. Yet these years rapidly closed out the period in Lichfield which exemplified a community ethos. When we follow the Borough's progress in the ensuing decades below, it will be to illustrate a very different tendency.[18]

[13] *VCH, Staffordshire*, 14 (1990), 73–5.
[14] Grace (ed.), *Records of the Gild of St. George*, 8–20.
[15] Faraday, *Ludlow*, 79–81.   [16] *VCH, Staffordshire*, 14 (1990), 75.
[17] On 2 July 1548; PRO, C. 66/811/m. 29.
[18] *VCH, Staffordshire*, 14 (1990), 76–8. See also Rosser, 'Town and Guild of Lichfield', 39–47; *CPR, Edward VI*, i. 386–7.

Finally, in the episcopal Borough of Salisbury, where the townsmen managed to develop considerably mature governing institutions of their own despite continual friction with the Bishop from the very inception of the community in the twelfth century, only some glimpses of a more oligarchic mode seem visible in the fifteenth century. The mayoral office, dating from *c.*1306, and other institutions were well in place in at least early forms, but the sense of communal responsibility and ideals of harmony and accessibility still prevailed. Many senior officials were drawn from the wealthy, from mercantile occupations, and from the ranks of those who had come up through an informal sequence of lesser offices. Yet not all the senior officials displayed these characteristics, nor did the townsmen in general seem to think this unusual or oppressive. Those in office remained accountable to the freemanry at large, and the political frictions were very much still between townsmen and Bishop rather than amongst townsmen themselves.[19]

These examples stand in sharp contrast to the oligarchic sort of rule which lay at the other end of the political spectrum. Though it may have shared the attributes of 'rule by a few', it did so in an increasingly corrupt form which was by no means as acceptable to those outside that small number. The tendencies in urban government during the period from about 1540 work prominently in two directions. First, we find a narrowing of the elite in a great many more towns than before: a tendency which was not in itself especially objectionable to most contemporaries. But now we also find a narrowing of vision amongst the ruling elite, a hardening of lines and widening of distance between them and the rest, and numerous transgressions against local tradition in order to accomplish and sustain those developments. We find decisions coming forth from a very small number of the freemanry, almost always amongst the wealthiest and best connected, even when they affected the whole community.

Typically elections came in this era more commonly to become 'selections'. The few who ruled thereby perpetuated their positions by excluding the many, thus exercising what amounted to mere co-option and denying the traditional *cursus honorum*. This may be seen most frequently from about the 1580s or 1590s, when mayors once elected by the freemanry itself, or by some substantial part of that body, came now typically to be chosen by one or both of the two councils which dominated town government. There were many

---

[19] Carr, 'The Problem of Urban Patriciates', 118–35.

variations on the essential theme, but members of the upper council frequently came to select replacements to its number from the lower council, and members of the lower frequently selected theirs from favoured members of the freemanry.

Barred from their former avenues of civic expression and community service, frequently thwarted in their normal progress up the *cursus honorum*, townspeople risked losing their loyalty and the old spirit of collective responsibility. Those who ruled moved from the acknowledgement of collective responsibility to the spirit of patriarchy. While not necessarily by any means denying the interests of the whole, the governing vision often focused on goals more specific to the economic interests and/or moral and behavioural outlook of their own sort of people. Though there are numerous examples of these characteristics occurring at an earlier time, they seem not to have become prevalent until the middle of the sixteenth century or after. In addition, we now see much more evidence of ruthlessness in eliminating a wider participation in government, and in fending off challenges from those who were out of power.

Not only do we see these tendencies in the institutions of the borough government, conventionally structured into two councils, one smaller and more powerful than the other, plus a mayor. We see it too in the institution of the parish, which gained from the Crown in the post-Reformation years functions which were new to it, secular, and very vulnerable to oligarchic influences.[20] This placed the parish on an entirely new footing in the urban administrative structure, marking a sharp break with past practice. It ushered in an era lasting well beyond the Civil War in which the parish served particularly to focus the local forces of oligarchic rule.

In these and other ways, a great many town governments characteristically moved in this era from what we might think of as the Aristotelian concept of rule by aristocracy—rule by a few but with full regard to due process and the interests of the whole—to the Aristotelian concept of oligarchy, a corruption of the former. The fact that these tendencies came as often through legal and constitutional means as not makes them no less vivid or consequential for the direction of civic government. Many towns seem to have moved even further on the same spectrum: from a structure which was not even aristocratic, in the Aristotelian sense, to begin with, to one which was oligarchic by the seventeenth century.

[20] See esp. Kumin, *Shaping of a Community*, chap. 6.

To investigate the sense in which this era marked a watershed in governance for many towns, we must turn especially to the middle years of the period at hand, and thus again to the sorts of legal devices which were so commonly employed by towns at that time: litigation, enfeoffment to uses, and especially incorporation. While all three were common enough amongst towns throughout the century under consideration (1540–1640), it would appear that their primary political function tended to change after the first few decades of that span.

From *c*.1540 into the early Elizabethan years, as we have noted above, these devices seem chiefly to have been employed in order to gain (or regain) control of local resources and of political autonomy from such external forces as, for example, the Church, early individual purchasers of ecclesiastical lands, and manorial lords of both ancient and recent vintage. (Ironically, if only because it tended to eliminate intermediate authorities, such autonomy often made for firmer rather than weaker links between towns and the Crown.) But from about the mid-Elizabethan era the political aims of borough governing elites made them devote their energy more to consolidating their own authority than to any broader representation of the freemanry. This tended more often to take place at the expense of the freemanry in general, of groups within the social or political framework, and against the idea of community itself.

One apparent result of this broad transition was a corresponding move from the earlier, relatively participatory and egalitarian ethic, to one which was much more exclusive and oligarchic. In its most extreme forms this tendency towards a tighter oligarchy gained strength with the adoption of a Puritan ideology as its justifying force, resulting in the 'godly rule' which characterized many communities by the early seventeenth century. We have, then, even by the end of the sixteenth century some sharp contrasts of vision regarding local governance, visions which either did not appear at all prior to this period, or which were still largely rudimentary.

These themes suggest a natural order for the discussion of Part III. Chapter 8 will take up the drive for local autonomy which seems so characteristic of English towns from *c*.1540 to the early years of the Elizabethan era. It will take up several questions. Of what did such a drive consist? How and why did it come about? How and why does it help mark the era at hand as distinctive in the evolution of political forms and practice amongst English towns?

Chapter 9 will consider the oligarchic tendencies which came into

their own especially in the last third of the sixteenth century and first four decades of the seventeenth century. It will consider the shifting meaning of oligarchy in these decades, how it was achieved, whose interests it served, what climate of political opinion it engendered, and towards what sort of political culture it led. Chapter 10 will consider how the increased tendency towards oligarchic rule played itself out in the operation of local government. It will explore changes in the administration of local affairs in general, and in the developing roles of specific town offices.

8

The Drive for Local Autonomy,
c.1540s–1560s

i

We have already noted in passing the frequency with which local governing bodies came under sharp scrutiny in the years following the Dissolutions. This was emphatically the case with conflicts over local resources, social institutions, and legal jurisdiction. These conflicts often came about through imprecise definitions of authority, which were in turn encouraged by rival legal claims or a history of lax administrative practices. In many places the changing circumstances of the post-1540 era brought matters to a head. Rising population and its attendant social pressures, large-scale changeovers in the possession of lands and resources, the ever present concern for law and order, and the vast corpus of regulatory legislation directed by the Tudor Parliaments towards local officials all proved vexatious to the local governing officials of the day.

Under these circumstances local officials felt more than ever the need to assert their positions or to formalize customary assertions of jurisdiction. And again they often relied upon such legal recourses as litigation, enfeoffment to uses, and incorporation. Having observed how quickly these devices were revived, and how important they were in securing control of local resources, it is now time to turn to an even more fundamental use to which they were put in this era: the attainment of local autonomy. This is not to suggest absolute autonomy so much as legal hegemony in local affairs, under the Crown of course, but not chiefly, as had often been the case, under the lord of the manor or the officials of the shire. Of these three legal devices the importance of enfeoffment to uses and of litigation should already be clear from the previous discussion, but in the somewhat different context of this chapter more especially needs to be said about incorporation. The accelerated move towards local autonomy, facilitated and recognized particularly by

incorporation, presents one of the most salient themes in urban affairs following the initial stages of the Reformation. We see it most dramatically in the quarter century or so following about 1540 and prominently in the decades thereafter. (See Table I.) Again, of course, these tendencies turn up more readily in some sorts of towns than others, and we have to explore a typology of urban communities with this in mind. This chapter will begin by exploring such a typology and then move on to investigate the meaning of incorporation in those many towns where it applied.

ii

As has been noted in passing already, the six or seven hundred towns of sixteenth-century England were far from uniform in most respects, and this was certainly the case with regard to their political configurations. At either end of the political spectrum we would find those towns for which the events of the Reformation era had least political consequence, either (*a*) because their autonomy was already too far advanced for further gains to be forthcoming, or (*b*) because they were too much under the thumb of a lay landlord to be able to seize the moment and make any gains. In between we would find (*c*) those towns which tended to be governed very closely by ecclesiastical lordships of the 'regular' (as opposed to secular) clergy before the event and be given opportunity for the acquisition of self-governing institutions and authority thereafter, and (*d*) those towns with some degree of self-government which could make further advances in the four or five decades following the Dissolutions. Here we would find that earlier institutions of self-government, particularly including guilds and fraternities, were often able to be redefined and formalized as the central governing structures of corporate boroughs. We would also find that external authorities which had held considerable formal authority had now effectively to renegotiate their role.

In the first category (*a*) we would find most of the oldest and politically self-contained towns of all, those in which, parenthetically, the harbingers of oligarchy, as defined above, would first have been visible. In these instances the impact of the Reformation will have been felt in the opportunity to acquire more land and resources and in the demise of economically important ecclesiastical institutions. But even where incorporation may have ensued in this era, the direct implications for political change in these towns lay largely in formal-

izing, confirming, and/or relabelling of established structures and consolidating forms of government already long in being. We find here, too, a consolidation of resources, including those of fraternities, guilds, and chantries, under indigenous civic control and in a form unencumbered by former religious, fiscal, and political obligations.

Exeter, recorded even in Domesday as having held land as a recognized civic entity, provides a fine example of this first type. Exeter received its first royal charters under Henry II, and by the early thirteenth century it already had a mayor and four stewards. By the mid-fifteenth century Exeter had a strong and stable city council, and could without any risk be called a tightly run oligarchy by the turn of the sixteenth. As we have seen above (p. 116) it was able to capitalize on the availability of dissolved lands and considerably expand its holdings by the end of the sixteenth century.[1] York, Bristol, Gloucester, and Norwich provide equally useful illustrations of the same type.

The second category (*b*), in which the Reformation had but mild political impact but for quite different reasons, consists of those very different towns with a tradition of manorial rule so tight as to preclude the extensive development of self-governing institutions in earlier times, and without the resources or initiative which might have led to substantial gains thereafter. Here, typically, the lord or his bailiff, and not the mayor, would have presided over local courts. These would have been essentially manorial in form: especially the leet court and view of frankpledge. The same officials will usually have collected most perquisites of the market or fair as well as the courts. Outside of such bodies as parishes, guilds, and fraternities, townsmen would have had relatively little scope to determine and administer their own affairs. Even many of these towns experienced some changes around this time, but with such thin traditions of self-rule upon which to build, few of them made dramatic gains in the decades following the Reformation.

Here we would find tight control by landlords drawn from the laity, secular clergy, and regular clergy alike. Lay seigneurial towns like Petersfield in Hampshire, which was coterminous with the manor of Petersfield and Lymington in the same shire,[2] Brackley in

---

[1] Summarized in MacCaffrey, *Exeter*, 16–17.
[2] *VCH, Hampshire*, 3 (1908), 114–18.

Northamptonshire,[3] Orford in Suffolk,[4] Reigate in Surrey,[5] Arundel, Bramber, Horsham, New Shoreham, and perhaps Winchelsea in Sussex,[6] and Cricklade, Devizes, Westbury, Wilton, and Wootton Bassett in Wiltshire,[7] all fit this description. So do many towns with landlords who were 'secular' (as opposed to 'regular') clerics who would have maintained their authority unabated. These would include places like Penryn, held by the Bishop of Exeter;[8] Havant, Farnham, and Taunton, held by the Bishop of Winchester;[9] and Croydon, held by the Archbishop of Canterbury.[10] Towns held by officials of the regular clergy would have reverted to the Crown and been sold to a lay landlord thereafter, again without substantial political gains by the townsmen. In this manner the lordship of Newport (Cornwall) changed hands from the Prior's lordship, via the Crown, to the Duchy of Cornwall;[11] Dunstable's lordship went from the Prior to the Crown;[12] Tavistock's went from the Abbot via the Crown to the Russell family;[13] Shaftesbury's abbatial jurisdiction came to be distributed amongst several lay lords;[14] and Cirencester's went from the Abbott via the Crown to Sir Thomas Seymour.[15]

This is not to say that the political form of these towns remained entirely unchanged or that townsmen remained completely subservient to their lords. Some of them made modest gains or received a parliamentary franchise (though their representatives would frequently have been selected by the manorial lord) and a few, like Salisbury, came by the early seventeenth century (1612) to enhance their status by incorporation.[16] But in general towns of this sort failed to gain the more substantial elements of local autonomy in the decades immediately following Dissolution. Such advances as they did make, one supposes, might well have been accomplished sooner or later had the Dissolutions not taken place.

---

[3] Hasler (ed.), *House of Commons, 1558–1603*, i. 215–16.

[4] Bindoff (ed.), *House of Commons, 1509–1558*, i. 192.

[5] *VCH, Surrey*, 3 (1911), 231–7; Hasler (ed.), *House of Commons*, i. 254–5.

[6] Bindoff (ed.), *House of Commons*, i. 201–2 and 263; Hasler (ed.), *House of Commons*, i. 255–7, 259, 261.

[7] Bindoff (ed.), *House of Commons*, i. 220, 221, 231–3.   [8] Ibid. 57.

[9] *VCH, Hampshire*, 3 (1908), 123; Bindoff (ed.), *House of Commons*, i. 183; Hasler (ed.), *House of Commons*, i. 236–7.

[10] *VCH, Surrey*, 4 (1967), 217.

[11] Bindoff (ed.), *House of Commons*, i. 52; Hasler (ed.), *House of Commons*, i. 131–2.

[12] *VCH, Bedfordshire*, 1 (1904), 376.

[13] Bindoff (ed.), *House of Commons*, i. 74.   [14] Ibid. 84.

[15] Ibid. 95.   [16] Ibid. 230.

Closer to the centre of the spectrum of post-Dissolution political change lay a great many boroughs—types (c) and (d)—which, though to some extent still technically manorial in form, nevertheless made substantial strides. Often the driving force behind those gains remained the desire to gain lands or resources which would provide a sound base for civic finance, or a restoration of important educational or social institutions. In addition (and in distinction to the sort of ecclesiastical towns listed above) most of these were sufficiently large, complex, and populated by citizens of some wealth and substance, to seize the moment in a way that the Petersfields, Orfords, and Reigates could not. Though not all such gains by any means came through incorporation, the survival of charters for that process provides an especially convenient and revealing insight into the changes which were forthcoming in communities like these. Towns of this sort account for most of the conspicuous bulge in the number of charters and enfeoffments in the decades following Dissolution; they lend the greatest weight to the overall argument.

In point of size, complexity, and the wealth and initiative of their residents, these towns comprise at least a substantial minority of all urban communities and perhaps a majority of the more consequential. It is in their regard that the Reformation era marked an especially decisive period in the acquisition of self-governing powers. In one case after another we see towns with at least some institutional framework for self-governing authority already in place on the eve of Reformation, and a much stronger, autonomous, and complete governing structure emerging in the decades thereafter.

The most dramatic cases include those towns which had been governed by such restrictive ecclesiastical landlords that almost no effective institutions of self-government had been allowed to emerge. Here we may look at such places as Banbury, Beverley, Bodmin, Boston, Bury St Edmunds, Leominster, Reading, Romsey, and St Albans, where the impact of the Reformation era on local political powers was little short of revolutionary. Save for Bury St Edmunds (which was not incorporated until 1606 and whose town trust, the Feoffees of the Guildhall, shouldered the burdens of local government between the dissolution of the Abbey and that time), Beverley (1573), and Bodmin (1563), all were incorporated within a decade of dissolution, thus gaining comprehensive powers of self-government for the first time at the very outset of our era.

The Borough of Beverley furnishes an example which not only proves the point, but one whose exceptionally full documentation

makes it accessible and familiar to us.[17] On the eve of Reformation the townsmen lingered under the seigneurial jurisdictions of the Archbishop of York and, to some extent, the Provost of the College of St John's. The few self-governing privileges they possessed (which, sparse as they were, still exceeded those of some towns) came via several non-incorporative charters from the Archbishop or the Crown.

Yet if not expressed very well institutionally, the townsmen's common identity, interaction, and conscious self-interest had long been apparent. The sense of *communitas* had not only been well understood and applied in Beverley from an early time, but the term itself was employed in the ordinances of 1359. These by-laws were perpetuated in a second version in 1498. They spelled out structures of self-government including a small, inner council of twelve keepers or governors and a larger, common council of twenty-four. The members of the twelve were elected annually by that commonalty— all freemen—who could actually be fined if they failed to vote. Together the two councils were known as the 'thirty-six'. Amongst their limited powers were the right to receive rents and make assessments on local properties within their purview, and to make by-laws and punish those who transgressed against them, though these had to be carried out with the consent of the commonalty.

Even within this limited range of authority the system was not without its problems, and disputes over the definition of powers were not uncommon. Yet the rudimentary governing structure which it defined remained flexible, responsible and accountable to the inhabitants at large. Not only was there a broad franchise for electing members of the inner council, but those 'governors' were barred from succeeding themselves after their year in office. It has even been argued that this flexibility and adaptability derived to some extent from the absence of an incorporative charter.[18]

Parallel to and also entwined with these structures, as in many towns, lay the guilds. The guilds held regulatory powers over their own occupations and their own members, but as all freemen were

---

[17] The following account derives from Martin Weinbaum, *British Borough Charters, 1307–1660* (Cambridge, 1943), pp. xxx–xxxi; A. F. Leach, *Beverley Town Documents*, Selden Society, 14 (1900); G. Poulson, *Beverlac, or the Antiquities and History of the Town of Beverley* (1829); George Oliver, *History and Antiquities of the Town and Minster of Beverley* (1829); *VCH, Yorkshire, East Riding: The Borough and Liberties of Beverley*, 6 (1989); Lamburn, 'Politics and Religion in Beverley'.
[18] By Lamburn, 'Politics and Religion in Beverley', 37.

necessarily guildsmen as well, the guilds often expressed—and claimed to express—the voice of the commonalty in dialogues with the two councils. But the temptation to envision the structure of local government prior to the Reformation as a question of townsmen versus manorial authority does not get us very far. In fact, the townsmen themselves were not institutionally or, at least some of the time, politically united, while seigneurial rule itself remained divided between the two authorities, the Archbishop and the College. These characteristics were reasonably typical of pre-Reformation towns of this type.

Although we will not take up the latter stages of Beverley's pre-Modern political development until the discussion of oligarchy in a subsequent chapter, some events from later in the century will bear description here. Notwithstanding some fascinating political manoeuvres during the time of the Pilgrimage of Grace, the critical time for decisive change in Beverley's governance came in the 1540s. The Archbishop lost his lordship over the town in 1542 and dissolution befell the College in 1548. The Borough eventually came into the hands of the young Robert Dudley, later the Earl of Leicester. Yet Dudley was a busy man. He was never a resident landlord and had little first-hand experience with local affairs. In the inevitable void of active leadership left in his wake, additional powers of self-government emerged rapidly in the 1550s and 1560s. Governors and burgesses were allowed to elect a mayor. Governors came to serve for life and became elected by co-option rather than by a franchise of the whole freemanry. With the emergence of the mayoralty, a mayoral court of record came into being. The right to hold a prison and to have a recorder followed suit. By the mid-1560s the leading townsmen behind these changes began to work for the acquisition of an incorporative charter which would signify the Crown's formal recognition of recent gains and secure them in perpetuity. The resulting document of 1573, gained with the Earl's help (as a perfect example of mutually beneficial political patronage), allowed the emergent elite to build even further structures in the years ahead.

Though we are chiefly concerned with its political applications, it is worth noting that Beverley's charter had its economic and fiscal implications as well. These must have brooked large in the drive for incorporation. Left impoverished by the Dissolutions and bereft of several essential educational and social institutions, townsmen expended considerable energy between dissolution and incorporation in regaining what they could from the Crown. In 1552 the Crown

responded to local petitions and granted the profits of the Minster, which had been heavily endowed, plus two chantries, totalling some £54 a year: a considerable sum in the context of time and place. Probably at local urging, the Crown earmarked these funds to support the upkeep of the Minster itself as a parish church and grammar school. In addition, the Borough managed to acquire Holy Trinity Hospital by 1556 and St Mary's Poorhouse by 1557. Incorporation allowed it to hold these more securely than before, and also to acquire further resources in secure tenure: the Poorhouses of St John Baptist and St John Evangelist by 1585 and grants in 1579 and 1585 to further support the Minster and school as well as St Mary's Church.

In sum, the Reformation facilitated some dramatic changes in Beverley's governing structure. In twenty-five years it came from the status of a subservient community of long-standing but severely limited powers of self-government to an increasingly puissant and almost entirely self-governing borough. The economic implications were also striking for, although Beverley did not gain all the lands and resources which had been caught up in the Dissolutions, it did recover a goodly share of them within a few decades, and could now hold them more securely than ever before. (A third area of rapid change can also be seen here: not only in the move from commonalty to formal incorporation in a matter of about a quarter century, but from commonalty to oligarchy as well. This is a theme for the next chapter.)

Another dramatic example of the rapid accretion of governing powers derives again from the eastern parts of the realm: the Lincolnshire port of Boston. As with Beverley there is some irony in the fact that both towns had been extremely important as regional centres in the late Middle Ages. Beverley's Minster, of course, served as a powerful magnet for pilgrims and a major centre of devotional activity. Boston ranked as the fifth wealthiest town in the realm in the tax evaluation of 1334, as the most important port outside of London for the export of wool, and as hosting the only Hansa Steelyard outside London.[19] Yet, aside from the organization of its guilds, Boston had developed even fewer self-governing institutions than Beverley. It held very little in the way of local privileges or autonomy save for what had pertained to residents as manorial tenants. Governed by manorial institutions, the Fees of Tattershall, Croun,

---

[19] S. H. Rigby, 'Boston and Grimsby in the Middle Ages: An Administrative Contrast', *Journal of Medieval History*, 10 (1984), 51.

and especially the Honour of Richmond until the Reformation, Boston's incorporation of 1545 provided the first viable royal charter to the townsmen in their own right as distinct from their status as tenants of the Honour.[20] Whereas Beverley had at least sent members to Parliament in the fourteenth century, allowing the privilege to lapse thereafter, Boston had never done so until it received the franchise in 1547.[21]

Yet given the size and importance of the town in its heyday of the fourteenth and early fifteenth century and its still viable, if decayed, state in the early sixteenth, it is unlikely that Bostonians failed to develop a sense of community or to sustain it throughout this time. Indeed the lack of a well-developed institutional format for such an identity does not seem to have curtailed its emergence by less formal or alternative means,[22] and this no doubt helped considerably when the question of incorporation arose. If in the technical and legal sense Boston was only minimally a borough, it was certainly an urban place and a town of substantial, if reduced, importance.

In the context of the reign of Henry VIII, in which charters of incorporation were still often relatively sketchy and incomplete, Boston received by that document a relatively full complement of chartered rights and liberties. Its corporate structure was to consist of the conventional mayoral and bicameral form (in this case consisting of an inner, aldermanic council of twelve and an outer, common council of eighteen). Right from the outset it was to have a recorder and town clerk, as well as six constables, an escheator, a coroner, and a clerk of the market. The mayor served as escheator and coroner; he, the recorder, and aldermen served as JPs. In addition to the leet court, a holdover from manorial jurisdiction and now convened by the mayor, there was to be a court of record served by the JPs, and the borough was to have a gaol as a further aid to its powers of law enforcement. In fiscal terms, Boston's charter included a licence to acquire lands in mortmain up to the value of £100, with specific lands being conveyed in the reign of Philip and Mary to keep up some of the town's essential resources.[23] (Within a few years it regained virtually all the former monastic lands in its midst.) Here, then, the Dissolutions had a dramatic effect on

---

[20] Ibid. 58; Pishy Thompson, *The History and Antiquities of Boston* (Boston, 1856), *passim.*

[21] Bindoff (ed.), *House of Commons*, i. 133.

[22] Rigby, 'Boston and Grimsby', 60–2.

[23] *Letters and Papers, Henry VIII*, 20/1, p. 418.

governing structures. The initial bumbling over record-keeping, in which townsmen objected to the Mayor taking council minutes home to his house after each meeting, should not surprise us. It reflected a lack of experience in such matters, honestly come by.

If not quite as dramatically as Boston, a number of communities used the opportunity to extend what had been the governing authorities of local guilds and fraternities, effectively exercising substantial civic functions prior to the Reformation without legal sanction, into fully sanctioned civic institutions (often in the forms of corporations or governing trusts) thereafter. Examples of this are not as rare as one might think. As we learn more about the secular and civic role of late medieval religious guilds and fraternities, the point becomes ever clearer.

One such case, typical of that substantial number of towns which moved from guild to civic structures at the Reformation, is the Staffordshire borough of Lichfield.[24] Technically speaking, this small city, founded essentially to serve the cathedral in its midst, came under the seigneurial authority of the Bishop. That official held about one-third of the town's tenements and rental properties, the portmoot court (the sole governing institution recognized in law prior to Dissolution), the fee farm, and sundry other forms of influence and jurisdiction.

But as a political entity in and of itself, 'The Community of the City of Lichfield', as the inhabitants came to call themselves, may be traced to the early thirteenth century. Additional rights of self-determination accrued in royal grants of the later thirteenth and fourteenth centuries. In the year 1387, following the Peasants' Revolt, the Crown granted chartered status to Lichfield's amalgamated Guild of St Mary and St John the Baptist. Though allegedly a guild for spiritual and charitable purposes, this body became the effective instrument of local self-government in secular affairs as well. Its master usually served as one of the twelve jurors of the Bishop's Court, thus exercising some influence in the Bishop's jurisdiction, while at the same time the Guild's own governing structure took rapid shape. By the mid-fifteenth century this consisted of the master and a council of forty-eight, an arrangement confirmed in the

---

[24] The following is founded on Rosser, 'Town and Guild of Lichfield', 39–47; Ann J. Kettle, 'City and Close: Lichfield in the Century before the Reformation', in C. Harper-Bill and C. Barron (eds.), *The Church in Pre-Reformation Society: Essays in Honour of F. R. H. DuBoulay* (Woodbridge, Suffolk, 1985), 158–69; and *VCH Staffordshire*, 14 (1990), *vide* 'Lichfield'.

ordinances of 1486. Thus governed, the Guild's membership may at times have reached a thousand people (the City's population not having exceeded 2,500 at most) including many members of the regional gentry and aristocracy. It included women as well as men, non-residents as well as residents, and a correspondingly wide social spectrum.

Though not legally entitled to do so, the Guild effectively provided most of the secular governing functions for the community: the regulation of economic activity, public works, law and order, the punishment of moral offences, and the holding and management of considerable properties which had accrued to it through the years in the form of charitable bequests. Prior to Dissolution the Master and Council established a trust to hold some of these lands both in and outside of the city which were essential to its water supply. These authorities kept at least some records of their activities and they met regularly in the Guildhall to conduct their affairs.

This, then, was how Lichfield stood at the Reformation. The Guild was dissolved in 1547, though the Cathedral, being held by secular rather than regular clergy, escaped the same fate. In the hope of retaining and even augmenting their accustomed powers, the townsmen petitioned for incorporation, which the Crown granted in a charter of July 1548. Later in the same year the Crown persuaded the Bishop to grant the manor to the new corporation in exchange for an annual fee farm of £50. A second, more complete charter of incorporation came forth under Mary in 1553, and still a third in 1598. As with many similar incorporations, the 'charter officials' of Lichfield were largely the same men who had run the Guild to its last days, providing continuity of personnel as well as at least secular function. They continued to meet in the Guildhall, a building which seems to have been in use for over a century. The use of that term itself thus changed from its original and literal meaning, the hall of the Guild, to its newer and figurative meaning: the town hall.

In view of these elements of continuity, common to many other towns as well, one may be tempted to ask whether incorporation bore much significance at all, and to downplay the event as a milestone in name only. Though incorporation meant less of a drastic change for Lichfield than for towns like Boston or Beverley (and though, as has been noted in an earlier chapter, the concept itself was still distressingly imprecise at this time) we must avoid the temptation to pass it off as inconsequential. As applied to Lichfield, for example, the structure of government narrowed considerably so as

to make its work more manageable. The master and the cumbersome body of forty-eight gave way to two bailiffs and a council of twenty-four. Secondly, the legal authority of the whole took on greater definition, jurisdiction, and force. We see this in the establishment of a weekly court of record (the first court of any sort actually recognized by the Crown, and thus, in law); the right to hear pleas arising within the bounds of the Corporation, at least to a value of forty shillings; the right to fines and profits of those courts; and a prison. We see it, too, in myriad responsibilities conferred on towns corporate, but not necessarily on their still unincorporated neighbours, by the regulatory legislation of the Tudor Parliaments. Throughout the last two-thirds of the sixteenth century, statute after statute distinguished between towns with and without that status. And third, incorporation conferred on Lichfield for the first time the right to acquire lands to a yearly value of £20, thus lending considerable security to the possession of lands already in hand and opening up the potential for further acquisitions.[25]

Even more decisive were the additional powers conveyed five years later in the Marian incorporation, a charter granted in part, as its preamble tells us, because of the City's loyalty to Mary in the tense opening days of her reign and against the challenge of Jane Grey. This placed Lichfield amongst that select group of boroughs with the status of counties in and of themselves, with a sheriff as the chief judicial and administrative officer. Its court would now hold the status of a county court, with jurisdiction not limited to pleas to the value of forty shillings, but extending to the hearing and determining of all murders and felonies. In addition, it gained for the first time the right to have a recorder, a steward, JPs of its own, a clerk of the market, an escheator, and a commission for musters.[26]

Even with the long-term existence of effective local government as provided by the Town Guild of Lichfield, the Reformation proved a watershed in the town's constitutional and political development. Save for the acquisition of county status, similar observations could no doubt be made about most of those towns—including Ludlow, Reading, Wisbech, Chichester, Abingdon, King's Lynn, and others—which had enjoyed unsanctioned but extensive government by religious guilds prior to the Reformation, and which gained incorporation or similar legal recognition shortly thereafter.

[25] *CPR, 1 Edward VI* (2 July 1548), 386–7.
[26] *CPR, 1 Mary*, i. 50–2.

In sum, then, the changes in political status which unfolded in this era played themselves out in different ways for different town types. For those towns with a long history of local self-government, the attainment of legal autonomy often meant little more than a formal recognition of existing conditions. In some of these cases, as for example Exeter, self-government extended so far back in time as to pre-date the claims of seigneurial authority. In perhaps the majority of other towns, some degree of self-government had emerged over a long period of give and take between towns and their lords. Often such local control formed along the lines of guild authority in the late Middle Ages. Some other towns, like Beverley and Boston, formerly under ecclesiastical lordship, experienced a particularly sharp break with past practice, and welcomed the creation of institutions and jurisdiction for which there had been but modest precedent. And finally there were those numerous very small and sometimes marginally urban communities whose seigneurial status remained unchanged during this period. Once again these hold less interest for the present study.

The few decades from about 1540 to the early Elizabethan years were thus marked by gains in local political autonomy for a great many towns in a short space of time. In the decades thereafter, as we will see in the next chapter, such gains tended to be consolidated by the accretion of practice and experience, and also by the encroachment of oligarchy. Before we get to that contiguous development, we must also examine that mechanism which, more than any other, formalized the acquisition of governing authority for so many towns in the era at hand. Let us turn again to borough incorporation, attending this time to its implications for local political institutions, and also to its implications for autonomy from seigneurial authority both ancient and recent.

iii

As noted above in Chapter 4, there can be little doubt that borough incorporation revived dramatically in the years after 1540. (For details, see Table I.) After only thirteen borough incorporations in the first fifty-five years of Tudor rule, there were nine in the last seven years of Henry VIII, twelve (plus one re-incorporation) in the brief reign of Edward, and twice that number in the even shorter reign of Mary: a virtually geometric rate of increase. Though that pace slowed somewhat in the rest of the century, there were still

fifty-three incorporations (plus seventeen re-incorporations) under Elizabeth and fifty-one more (plus fifty-four re-incorporations) under the first two Stuarts up to 1640. In all, there were a hundred and forty-nine incorporations in the century prior to 1640. In addition, there were seventy-one re-incorporations, some of them having gained their initial incorporations prior to 1540. If we add in all those boroughs which gained mere confirmations of incorporations gained prior to 1540, the total would far exceed two hundred boroughs incorporated by 1640: almost all those urban communities enjoying notable political or economic significance.[27]

That aspect of incorporation most germane to the question of holding lands or similar resources, the right to acquire in mortmain, should by now be familiar. Yet it was but one of five fundamental elements which were rapidly coming to characterize formal incorporation and not, all things considered, necessarily the most important. Two of the others, the right of perpetual succession and the right to sue and be sued in courts of law as a body corporate, eliminated the legal risk and responsibility which might otherwise accrue to individual governing officials. They permitted the borough to have the status of an individual person before the law, and to enjoy that status perpetually. Save for a few cases in which local landlords successfully broached the validity of particular charters, incorporation provided the basis for local jurisdiction least vulnerable to challenge by rival claimants. As we will see, it often also facilitated a more oligarchic rule.

The last two 'points' of incorporation, the right to issue by-laws and the right to hold a common seal, were more likely to have been confirmations of existing practice. Incorporation by charter added that which, by the rapidly developing standards of the day, was the ultimate legal authorization short of statute itself. (Incorporation could technically be conveyed by statute, and this was at least alleged in an Elizabethan lawsuit to have been the case with Shrewsbury in Henry VI's reign,[28] but the success of incorporation by charter nipped this more expensive line of development in the bud.) The right to issue by-laws had long been exercised de facto by many town governments, but incorporation conveyed royal sanction on the

---

[27] Based on Weinbaum, *British Borough Charters*, pp. xxix–lv, as amended in individual cases on the basis of local records.

[28] PRO, STAC 7/Bundle 2/20, *temp.* Elizabeth; the statute in question must surely have been 1 Edward IV, c. 1, sec. 17, 'An Acte of Parliament for the Towne of Shrewsbury', which confirmed earlier privileges without stipulating them in detail.

practice. Though this may sound perfunctory, it became increasingly important that such powers came to be exercised de jure at this time. Incorporation helped sustain local authorities faced with the burden of enforcing an ever-expanding corpus of social and economic legislation pouring forth from Tudor Parliaments, and faced with increasing legal challenges from both within and without their boundaries.

A common seal permitted the borough government to certify the authenticity and force of such pronouncements, as well as such other devices as leases, return of writs, borough accounts, official correspondence, and so forth. Though in many cases a seal had long been employed on documents emanating from local officials, this opportunity for a royal affirmation of that right loomed important at the time. And, though this was not its avowed purpose, this formal sanction for such seals sometimes provided a chance to adopt a historical and pictorial image reflecting the community's heritage, as opposed to an image of a former civic authority, in the design of the seal itself.[29] In Norwich, for example, this era saw the replacement of the image of the Trinity on the town seal with that of the City's arms.[30] As we will see below in Part IV, this seems one of a piece with the contemporary innovations in civic portraiture, civic building, and civic furnishing. In all these media changes in form and style tended to emphasize the local heritage of the community, and the authority of its leadership, in ways which were often highly symbolic.

In addition to these five points, most charters of incorporation, emanating as they did from petitions of the townsmen themselves rather than some office of central government,[31] came to include specifically worded provisions for a full range of administrative jurisdictions and functions. These include the lands and other possessions which have been discussed above. In addition they addressed geographic boundaries of the town; the means for selecting officials; the courts and legal jurisdiction; fairs and markets; tolls, fees, and

[29] Though dealing with town seals of a different time and place, probably the best succinct treatment of this is nevertheless Brigitte Bedos-Rezak, 'Towns and Seals: Representation and Signification in Medieval France', *Bulletin of the John Rylands Library*, 72 (Autumn 1990), 35–48. I am grateful to Susan Reynolds for bringing this to my attention.

[30] Basil Cozens-Hardy and E. A. Kent (eds.), *The Mayors of Norwich, 1403–1835* (Norwich, 1938), 56.

[31] The process of acquiring a charter of incorporation in this era is best described in Bond and Evans, 'The Process of Granting Charters', 102–20, though some of their contentions are more valid for the later years of their study than for the earlier.

fines; rights relative to neighbouring authorities; and sometimes parliamentary enfranchisement.

The road towards a more oligarchic rule, in which incorporation became an important and almost invariable staging point, seems clear enough for many towns and over the course of the whole century at hand. Yet few had completed that journey in the first decades after the Dissolutions, and that destination does not always appear the prime motivating force for securing incorporation to begin with. Along with their concern for acquiring lands in mortmain, those townsmen who most often took the lead in seeking incorporations often did so for reasons which were more limited and precise. Equally important was the definition and confirmation of the essential governing authority, especially in the wake of post-dissolution transfer of lordship. In the end, oligarchy seems most often to have accrued in response to a variety of pressures, both internal and external, which threatened the integrity of local liberties and institutions. In that regard it seemed as much a response to the needs of the local community as a whole, as to the interests of 'the better sort' of townsmen. It became a more conscious aim of incorporation only in the last decades of the sixteenth century, especially when those townsmen saw a need to tighten up an existing charter by re-incorporation. Attending first to the earlier part of the whole period under consideration, roughly from *c.*1540 to the middle of Elizabeth's reign, and leaving aside concerns for economic and fiscal resources which have been treated above, let us look more systematically at some of these more fundamental motivations for incorporation.

Those towns seeking incorporation to remedy insufficiently defined or formalized governing structures were quite common in the decades after *c.*1540. Nearly half of the two dozen towns incorporated under Mary Tudor, for example, held no previous charters in their own right. True, some of them, such as e.g. Abingdon and Leominster, had effectively gained some privileges through charters granted to the heads of the religious houses which had ruled over them.[32] Yet most others had only the bulwark of custom, in the form of unsanctioned local institutions and claims to authority, to deflect

---

[32] Abingdon, Aylesbury, Banbury, Buckingham, Chippenham, Great Dunmow, Higham Ferrars, Ilchester, Leominster, Sudbury, Thaxted, and Torrington. Cf. Weinbaum, *British Borough Charters*, pp. xxx–lv; *Reports from the Commissioners Appointed to Enquire into the Municipal Corporations of England and Wales, Report I*, Appendix (1835), *passim*.

challenges to their liberties. Other towns incorporated in the mid-century era held non-incorporative charters, sometimes several of them, which they now found to be insufficient because of 'doubts' — the word is frequently employed in petitions for incorporation — which had arisen regarding their force. In Droitwich, which had eight such charters of one sort or another, such 'doubts' came through the intrusion into local affairs of investors who had gained control of much of the salt and cloth industries upon which the town largely depended for its livelihood.[33]

In the spirit of improvisation which had, for example, led many towns to conceal lands from the Crown's commissioners prior to dissolution, some towns at least tried to invent claims of authority. A few went so far as to claim charters which did not exist, or even to forge them. Medieval precedents for this have been found. Ms Reynolds has shown that Barnstaple, for example, forged no fewer than five charters by the fifteenth century.[34] It hardly challenges the imagination to suppose that numerous other towns might make unfounded or exaggerated claims regarding charters which they presumed or pretended to possess.

Yet whereas in earlier times it might well have been assumed that a forged or pretended charter could stand without further ado at its presumed face value, now it became increasingly vulnerable to the likelihood of legal challenge. In consequence, townsmen came to realize that the value of a forged or pretended claim would lie especially in its 'confirmation' at face value by a charter of incorporation. Thus even if the original, supposed charter were bogus, its confirmation in a new incorporation would recognize, and thus validate, its claims.

This seems clearly what the town fathers of Higham Ferrars intended in seeking incorporation to 'confirm' its 'undoubted' charter which they claimed to have been 'mislaid',[35] or what Sudbury's leaders had in mind in petitioning for a 'new' charter to replace one 'which had been embezzled'.[36] The chances that documents kept as

---

[33] Weinbaum, *British Borough Charters*, 123; T. R. Nash, *Collections for the History of Worcestershire* (2 vols.; 1781–2), i. 302–3; L. T. Smith (ed.), *Itinerary of John Leland*, ii. 92–3.

[34] Susan Reynolds, 'The Forged Charters of Barnstaple', *English Historical Review*, 84 (1969), 699–720.

[35] *CPR, Mary*, i. 141–3.

[36] Ethel Stokes and Lilian Redstone (eds.), 'Calendar of the Muniments of the Borough of Sudbury', *Proceedings of the Suffolk Institute of Archeology*, 13 (1909), 5–7.

securely as charters of incorporation could truly be embezzled or mislaid, documents upon which rested claims to virtually all rights and powers of local government, seem so remote as to be suspect. Even Barnstaple, pushed in these same years by challenges to its legal jurisdiction and by the need of a sounder control of its finances, at last sought formal incorporation in the reign of Mary.[37]

If anything, incorporation amongst many Welsh boroughs could mark even more dramatic changes. Since earlier legislation of Henry VIII's reign (27 Henry VIII, c. 26) had effectively destroyed the authority of the Welsh boroughs, they were especially bereft of sound local governing authorities. The incorporation of Carmarthen (1546), Monmouth (1549), Brecon (1556), Beaumaris (1562), and New Radnor (also 1562) may be attributed more or less directly to the effort to fill that void. In each instance incorporation re-established a viable governing structure.

iv

In addition to the desire to verify and augment governing authority as an end in itself, town leaders in this era often sought incorporation as a means of asserting their authority over that of external claimants. They meant not only to draw clear lines in the sand regarding jurisdiction, but effectively to redefine relationships between specific towns, on the one hand, and regional landowners, including landlords or the Crown itself, on the other.

Needless to say, at least some manorial lords and other powerful regional landholders posed prominent threats to borough liberties in this era. Anxious to secure the maximum value from their costly acquisitions, new landlords were not always willing to permit the perpetuation of de facto self-government which had often accrued through practice. New owners could be a good deal more earnest in their pursuit of their interests than their predecessors had been. After all, the population-driven increases in rental values, market activity, the perquisites of local courts, and similar sources of income raised the value of such acquisitions, while obligations to honour the intercessionary bequests once attached to particular grants had disappeared. In response, while some new lords proved well disposed to governing structures which they found in place, others did not. Especially if they were new to the region itself, as was often the case with purchasers of dissolved lands, they were often poorly informed

---

[37] *CPR, 3–4 Edward and Mary*, 391–2 (29 May 1557).

about local customs and unsympathetic to the complex give-and-take which had come to apply between townsmen, on the one hand, and previous landlords, on the other. Given the imprecision of title in many new purchases as well, it is not surprising that these conditions often led to jurisdictional conflict.

Of course there was little novelty in conflicts of this type. But the fact of dissolution itself, not to mention the ensuing political and constitutional activities which it opened up, probably made such battles much more frequent and, if anything, hard-fought.[38] Some of the ensuing conflicts, including those we have seen in such towns as Beccles, Aylesbury, and Barnstaple, revolved around the control of land and similar resources. Others concerned the even more fundamental question of who governed the community.

Some of these intransigent landlords and other landed magnates with traditional influence in particular towns worked to block incorporation before it could be won. We see this in Northamptonshire, where a group of five prominent shire gentry with interests in the Borough appealed to the Earl of Leicester to use his influence against the incorporation of Daventry in 1571.[39] We see it, too, in Ipswich and Sudbury in Suffolk,[40] and in the Dorset port of Poole. Though local traditions of self-government were by no means insubstantial beforehand, Poole's efforts to gain incorporation in the 1560s met bitter opposition from Lord Montjoy. Townsmen overcame this barrier only by prevailing upon another patron, the influential courtier Walter Haddon, to intercede with William Cecil at court and by sending a palliative 'gift' of £100 to soothe Montjoy's feelings in the event.[41]

In some cases seigneurial authorities fought incorporation more intensely after the event than before. The Aylesbury incorporation of 1554 did virtually nothing to improve relations between the townsmen and their lord, Sir Thomas Packington. Sir Thomas and his widow after him kept up a constant barrage of harassment and litigation against the full implementation of corporate authority. Though they themselves would not live to see it, their descendants of the

---

[38] This is noted specifically for Suffolk by Diarmaid MacCulloch, but is widely apparent elsewhere throughout the realm (MacCulloch, *Suffolk and the Tudors*, 323).

[39] Northamptonshire County Record Office, MS YZ 9118. The effort cannot have worked for long, as Daventry gained its incorporation five years later, in 1576.

[40] MacCulloch, *Suffolk and the Tudors*, 323–6.

[41] Poole Borough Archives, MS 25(3) fo. 10^r; British Library, Lansdowne MS 7, fo. 50^r, and Lansdowne MS 43, no. 19. I am grateful for the last two references to Professor David Palliser.

mid-seventeenth century turned the tide of battle at long last, managing to secure an annulment of the borough charter in 1664.[42] The Essex town of Thaxted had a similar experience. An incorporation of 1556, gained by the townsmen at a time of particular weakness in the seigneurial family, was bitterly and in the end successfully fought by that same family when it regained strong leadership later on.[43] The fourth Earl of Huntingdon, offended at what he saw as an erosion of his privileges, fought bitterly against an expanded corporate charter in the already corporate Borough of Leicester.[44] We see this, too, in those episcopal-run boroughs, like Salisbury and Durham,[45] where bishops continued to defend against clamorous townsmen.

Yet these examples should not by any means be taken as the whole story or even the general rule. For one, the act of incorporation itself did not necessarily bring about complete autonomy from seigneurial intervention. Even when it did, the pattern of seigneurial opposition seems more often to have been the path not followed. In perhaps the majority of cases incorporation 'took' in the sense both that the townsmen were strong enough to make a go of greater autonomy and in that landlords and regional gentry accepted the fact and adjusted their own political aspirations and behaviour accordingly. This seems especially true in the smaller and middling-size market towns which were particularly numerous amongst mid-century incorporations.

In the end it would be more accurate to say that incorporation often redefined the relationship between corporate towns and both their traditional lords and other regional powers. In the event, these men often found themselves as content to interact cooperatively with corporate boroughs, which they came to view as political jurisdictions of different composition but equal weight, as they were to press claims of their authority over 'subservient' towns.[46] They saw

---

[42] *VCH, Buckinghamshire*, 3 (1925), 9–10; L. J. Ashford, *History of the Borough of High Wycombe* (1960), 96.

[43] R. Tittler, 'Incorporation and Politics in Sixteenth Century Thaxted', *Essex Archeology and History*, 8 (1976), 224–32.

[44] Catherine F. Patterson, 'Leicester and Lord Huntingdon: Urban Patronage in Early Modern England', *Midland History*, 16 (1991), 51–2.

[45] Catherine Patterson, 'Urban Patronage in Early Modern England: Corporate Boroughs, the Landed Elite and the Crown, 1580–1640', Ph.D. thesis (Chicago, 1994), 191, 198–9.

[46] The point has been made before, esp. with reference to parliamentary enfranchisement of seigneurial or formerly seigneurial boroughs, in Mark Kishlansky, *Parliamentary Selection: Social and Political Choice in Early Modern England* (Cambridge, 1986), chaps. 1 and 2 for the 17th cent.; and in Tittler, 'Incorporation of

such arrangements as mutually beneficial for themselves and for communities in which they often had long-standing interests. (Indeed, it would not be entirely inappropriate to liken the range of landowners' attitudes under these circumstances to that of the great colonial powers faced with independence movements in the twentieth century: some eventually acquiesced with grace while others fought to the end.) In this manner both neighbouring gentry and actual landlords might enjoy continued influence of a less formal but equally extensive nature as before, not as overlord but as patron.

The consequent redefinition of relations between borough and landlord, or borough and regional gentry in general, proves interesting in a number of respects. In some cases, incorporation effectively terminated the exclusive grip of a single family on a town's affairs, ending an essentially feudal and, politically speaking, subservient relationship and opening up the borough to the influence of perhaps several regional landowners instead of one alone. In other instances ties to several such figures had already been well established. In either event, the legal reality whereby a town took on through incorporation the status of an individual person before the law thus had its political concomitant. Many boroughs now became linked in a newly defined political relationship with one or a number of important figures in shire or regional affairs. The parties to these relationships, either corporate or individual and gentle, now functioned essentially as political equals. The ties between them came to depend more on factors of economic and political interdependence than on political domination and subordination.

In many cases the political courtship which ensued in the wake of incorporation or similar empowerment amounted to an ardent wooing of a community's leadership, in which the sundry boons of 'good lordship'—boons which proved so beneficial to many a community—formed the proffered bouquet. In return, the townsmen, and especially those of its leaders empowered to extend such patronage, could hold open to the magnate in question such plums as patronage in the selection of MPs, recorders, town clerks, schoolmasters, preachers, and similar posts; loyalty in the arena of shire politics; and the sundry sturgeons, fat bucks, and sugar loaves which were the common coin of such relationships. In this manner the

Boroughs', 29–31; and id., 'Elizabethan Towns and the "Points of Contact" ', 283–4, for the Elizabethan era. Its fullest exposition is now in Patterson, 'Urban Patronage in Early Modern England'. I am grateful to Dr Patterson for permission to consult her thesis.

spate of incorporations and greater empowerment of so many boroughs did much to shape the patronal and political relations between many corporate towns and the important landed families of their region, whether such families had held the lordship of the borough or not. In some cases these relationships brought with them close connections to the shire leadership and even to the court circle itself. They permitted boroughs to enter more fully into the political activity of their shires and regions, and even of the realm as a whole, than might formerly have been the case, and to undertake such roles as important players.[47]

Even the smallest and least consequential towns receiving incorporation in this era might well be drawn into such patterns. The inhabitants of Beccles in Suffolk, a town which surely lingered closer to the bottom than to the top of the urban league tables, had carried on peacefully enough as unchartered tenants of the Abbot of Bury St Edmunds prior to incorporation and their battles with the Rede family. Yet within a few years, incorporation and its fallout drew that quiet backwater into the battles between contending puritan and reactionary factions of shire gentry, disrupting local traditional tranquillity for some time to come.[48]

In some cases powerful and politically aspiring magnates in the countryside might even help a borough gain incorporation as a means of offsetting the seigneurial influence or control of a rival, thus opening up the town in question for this sort of political courtship. This may well have been Walter Haddon's aim in helping Poole against the opposition of Montjoy (though Haddon himself may simply have been operating as an agent of the Earl of Bedford, who also enjoyed a fruitful relationship with Poole).[49] It seems almost certainly, for example, to have motivated the Stanleys to help the burgesses of Liverpool gain confirmation of earlier charters, in 1603, and then incorporation in 1626, against the interests of the

---

[47] Kishlansky, *Parliamentary Selection*, esp. chaps. 1 and 2; and Patterson, 'Urban Patronage', *passim*. See also C. G. Parsloe, 'The Growth of a Borough Constitution, Newark-upon-Trent, 1549–1688', *TRHS*, 4th ser., 22 (1940), 171–98; *VCH, Buckinghamshire*, 3 (1925), 476–8.

[48] The testimony of several deponents in the protracted case of *Rede* v. *Baase* makes it clear that Rede's efforts to control the Fen were widely supported by Sir Thomas Gawdy and other prominent East Anglian Catholic recusants. The townsmen, for their part, seem heavily to have leaned towards Puritanism. The townsmen's steward, William Downing, seems to have led this faction, and to have been supported by the local puritan minister Mr Fleming (PRO, E. 133/4/658). See the summary in MacCulloch, *Suffolk and the Tudors*, 326–7.

[49] Hasler (ed.), *House of Commons*, i. 153.

Molyneux family.[50] It clearly applies to the Earl of Pembroke, who helped the Wiltshire borough of Chippenham gain its charter of 1554 so as to shake it loose from its ties to his rival, Sir Henry Shering-ton, former lord of the borough. The burgesses responded by allow-ing Pembroke the choice of one of its two MPs thereafter as a token of gratitude.[51]

The tendency for incorporation to open up new relations between particular boroughs, on the one hand, and the shire and regional gentry, even the court, on the other, should not obscure for us earlier precedents and analogues. Some, especially wealthier, boroughs in the pre-Reformation era had enjoyed close ties to shire and regional gentry for a long time past. In addition, such ties often extended through at least one medium, religious fraternities and guilds, which had been wiped out in the Reformation. Though these might nom-inally be town-centred bodies, they often included members who came from the surrounding areas. The larger and more successful guilds, not only in the great towns of the realm like London, Norwich, and York but also in towns like Ludlow, with its Palmer's Guild and Lichfield with its the Guild of St Mary and St John the Baptist, attracted large numbers of men, and often women, from the surrounding countryside, other towns, and even in some cases from the court at Westminster.[52] Even the smallest towns had guilds or fraternities which drew some of their members from outside, though not, of course, from such a wide area.[53]

To some extent, therefore, the relations with outsiders cemented by the governing authorities of corporate towns in the subsequent era may thus be seen as something of a continuity in relations with particular magnates, or as a refashioning of traditional guild-centred ties which were cut with dissolution. There were, however, crucial differences to such ties after the Dissolutions.

---

[50] Barry Coward, *The Stanleys, Lords Stanley and Earls of Derby, 1385–1672*, Chetham Society, 3rd ser., 30 (Manchester, 1983), 133–4.

[51] *CPR, Mary*, i. 103–5; M. Rathbone (ed.), *List of Wiltshire Borough Records . . .* (Trowbridge, 1951), 4–9; Neale, *Elizabethan House of Commons*, 141; Joel Hurst-field, 'County Government, 1530–1688', in *VCH, Wiltshire*, 5 (1957), 80–1; S. T. Bind-off, 'Parliamentary History, 1529–1688', ibid. 116.

[52] Faraday, *Ludlow*, 78–91; Rosser, 'Town and Gild of Lichfield', 39–47. Rosser estimates that in its heyday of the late 15th and early 16th cent., the guild may have numbered as many as a thousand members, with a heavy representation amongst the gentry of Staffordshire and throughout the Midlands (ibid. 41–2).

[53] Hilton, 'Small Town as Part of Peasant Society', in *English Peasantry, passim*; Rosser, 'Communities of the Parish and Guild', in Wright (ed.), *Parish, Church and People*, 33–4.

In the case of individual patrons, links became much more important than ever before in the face of the greater integration of the more
substantial towns with both the central government, on the one
hand, and the emerging urban network of the realm, on the other.
Whereas the influence of borough patrons might once have been but
casually useful in regional affairs, now they became virtually essential, and in national as well as regional circles. And while local guilds
had forged links both within and without their towns amongst people of widely differing social status, the new associations extended
primarily between those of the ruling elite within and their counterparts without. This early form of networking effectively eased the
entry of the 'better sort' of townsmen into rural society just as it
eased the entry of countrymen into urban politics and society.

In addition, it appears that the ability of most towns to undertake
such mutually beneficial interaction greatly improved in the decades
following the Reformation. They were then more often legally as
well as politically autonomous. Myriad regulatory statutes of the
Tudor and early Stuart Parliaments made corporate towns much
more powerful and authoritative. They thus enjoyed in those years
more boons—as measured in offices, decision making, statutory
authority, and the like—to offer a patron in return for the benefits of
'good lordship'. On the other side of the equation their own interests
now much more commonly opened out to the region, town, and
nation—occasionally even to overseas—augmenting as they did so
their need for friends in the right places.[54]

Although such patronal interaction took place at many levels and
in regard to many borough activities, the most familiar area for such
activity concerns parliamentary selection and representation.
Though the point has not always been understood even in the most
recent scholarship,[55] incorporation did not necessarily entail the
award of a parliamentary franchise, nor did the existence of such
a franchise require formal incorporation. There are numerous
examples both of incorporations granted in this era without such
a franchise, and of boroughs exercising such a franchise without
incorporation. Nevertheless, the two were often linked, and when a
borough gained a franchise through incorporation in this era and
required, as almost all boroughs did, the services of a powerful

---

[54] A theme pursued in regard to Bristol, and by (sometimes questionable) implication in regard to other towns, in Sacks, *The Widening Gate*.

[55] e.g. David Loades, *The Mid-Tudor Crisis, 1545–1565* (1992), 43 and 49.

patron, the makings of a mutually beneficial patron–client relationship lay close at hand.

The availability of one or two parliamentary seats which could be bestowed upon, or at the request of, non-residents who might be influential in regional or national affairs could be particularly advantageous. This was especially so in boroughs of middling or smaller size, or in those whose political independence was of more recent vintage. Aside from parliamentary service went the quid pro quo of 'good lordship' in regional affairs or at court. Such 'service' replaced the seigneurial responsibility of an earlier age while accomplishing some of the same ends. It became increasingly vital to the tranquil operation of the corporate town.

Some examples suggest how this worked in practice, and what sorts of activities might be involved in such relationships.[56] One of the most successful patrons in the first half of the era at hand was Thomas Howard, fourth Duke of Norfolk. His grip on his titular shire and much of the rest of East Anglia has been well documented.[57] Aside from his extensive influence in selecting JPs, sewer commissioners, military officers, clergy, and incumbents for a host of lesser offices, Howard frequently controlled parliamentary seats in Norwich, King's Lynn, Great Yarmouth, Castle Rising, and Thetford between 1558 and 1571. This much is familiar. Yet it is less commonly appreciated what services he performed in return for that parliamentary patronage.

For Great Yarmouth, perpetually burdened by the costs of repairing a harbour rendered fragile by nature and essential by economic necessity,[58] the Duke frequently raised funds, lobbied at court, and mediated with other towns and various political officials. He supported Yarmouth's petition to gain a licence to export corn in the mid-1560s, 'supplied timber from his own estates [for building], secured a remission of subsidies, . . . [and] prevailed upon the Norwich aldermen to vote 200 marks toward the haven's repair'.[59]

---

[56] The following is based on Tittler, 'Elizabethan Towns and the "Points of Contact" ', 284–5.

[57] Neale, *Elizabethan House of Commons*, 193–6; Neville Williams, *Thomas Howard, Fourth Duke of Norfolk* (1964), *passim*; A. Hassell Smith, *County and Court: Government and Politics in Norfolk, 1558–1603* (1974), 32–41; Hasler (ed.), *House of Commons*, i. 206–13.

[58] Summarized in R. Tittler, 'The English Fishing Industry in the Sixteenth Century: The Case of Great Yarmouth', *Albion*, 9/1 (Spring 1977), 54–5. See also H. Swindon, *The History and Antiquities of the Ancient Borough of Great Yarmouth* (Norwich, 1772), 373–476.

[59] A. H. Smith, *County and Court*, 28–9.

For King's Lynn he mediated disputes over ownership of St James's Chapel and rights to the mussel-beds of the River Ouse. He used his influence on the Privy Council to gain a reduced contribution to military commitments, the settlement of foreign cloth workers to manufacture new draperies, and permission to export corn on the same terms as Great Yarmouth.[60] For Norwich he gave extensive charity for the poor, facilitated the settlement of Dutch and Walloon strangers, and mediated disputes between grand and petty juries.[61]

Though Norfolk's influence may have been greater than most, he was not the only patron of his stature to function at this level in the Elizabethan or early Stuart periods.[62] And even he, for that matter, had some competition for the exercise of patronal influence in the region from such figures as the Lord Keeper Sir Nicholas Bacon, the Earl of Leicester, and Bishop John Parkhurst of Norwich, who elbowed in as best they could.[63]

In some cases the strengthening and extension of borough–patron relationships which characterized this era actually emanated from a new-found need to acquire a charter of incorporation rather than from the application of such a document already in hand. Here the borough held out other resources at its disposal to secure the desired ends. The City of Worcester, for example, had enjoyed an extensive tradition of limited self-rule, in which the Trinity Guild and the Merchants' Guild combined to perform most of the functions of government.[64] Though it had long held a parliamentary franchise, and indeed had a long tradition of selecting its own members without outside intervention, it had not been incorporated. With the dissolution of the Trinity Guild, and the desire to hold securely a goodly share of dissolved guild and other lands in its midst, incorporation seemed imperative. Yet when it undertook the effort to gain such a status in the reign of Mary, it ran into difficulties at court. Apparently Worcester lacked sufficient clout with those who mattered around the Queen herself.

Whether in direct consequence of this or not we may only speculate, but in the election of October 1553, Worcester broke long precedent and for the first time offered one of its seats to an outsider. Sir John Bourne, scion of a local gentry family which regained its

[60] A. H. Smith, *County and Court*, 30.   [61] Ibid. 31.

[62] See e.g. Patterson, 'Leicester and Lord Huntingdon', 45–62; and Patterson, 'Urban Patronage in Early Modern England'.

[63] A. H. Smith, *County and Court*, 30–41; and Tittler, *Nicholas Bacon*, chap. 11.

[64] Dyer, *City of Worcester*, 189–93.

earlier prominence at Mary's accession, had been named a member
of the new Queen's Privy Council, and seemed anxious to extend his
power base in the shire of his family's chief holdings. Though it
remains unclear whether he accomplished much on behalf of the
City in the parliamentary session itself, we do know that in return
for his seat there, he secured the coveted incorporation. This is
acknowledged in the preface of the document itself.[65] A similar strategy seems to have been employed by Newtown, Isle of Wight, for
whom Sir George Carey secured a charter in return for patronal
influence.[66]

The tide of events in this era—the greater statutory empowerment of borough officials especially in social and economic affairs;
the more extensive lands, offices, and other resources at their disposal; and the greater authority wielded by such officials in newly
corporate boroughs—worked to break down the relative insularity
in which many boroughs, especially those under seigneurial jurisdiction, had long laboured. Many of the landed gentry, aristocracy, and
even court officials of the day worked towards the same end to
achieve this opening out.

This should not be taken to suggest that towns gave local magnates everything they asked for, or that magnates would do anything
asked of them. The experience of the Stanleys, Earls of Derby, in the
three towns with which they had closest relations throughout this
period—Liverpool, Chester, and Preston—suggests that at least
some towns could achieve a careful balance between welcome support and unwanted interference on the part of patronal families.[67]

Nevertheless the unfolding picture of relations between specific
towns and their landed patrons yielded by detailed case studies, a
picture made more vivid by the circumstances following the Dissolutions, differs substantially from an earlier perspective. The more
negative view of Neale and others in the context of parliamentary
patronage, which portrayed gentry activity in the towns as encroach-
ing, invasive, and threatening,[68] must yield to a picture of relationships which were often more equitable, cooperative, and mutually

---

[65] Discussed in Tittler, 'Elizabethan Towns and the "Points of Contact" ', 284–5,
drawing on Bindoff (ed.), *House of Commons*, i. 236–8; Hasler (ed.), *House of Commons*, i. 279–80; Dyer, *City of Worcester*, 213–14; and PRO, C. 66/884/m. 33.

[66] Michael Graves, *The Tudor Parliaments: Crown, Lords and Commons,
1485–1603* (1985), 133.

[67] Coward, *The Stanleys*, 127–41.

[68] Neale, *Elizabethan House of Commons*, esp. chap. 7; Tittler, 'Elizabethan
Towns and the "Points of Contact" ', 285–6.

beneficial. Far from being unwelcome, patronage links to powerful men did more to stabilize than to destabilize the internal affairs of borough governments and they enhanced the operation of individual towns within shire, region, and realm.

V

Two other forces external to individual towns must be considered in this same historiographic context: the role of neighbouring and potential rival towns, and the role of the Crown itself. It is probably premature to assess with confidence the impact of political activity by neighbouring towns on specific boroughs, and such impact will of course depend greatly on what sort of towns we may be considering. The case for the operation of an urban network in which large numbers of towns worked cooperatively towards mutually desirable ends[69] seems insufficiently proven for at least the first half of the century under consideration here, and less than watertight for many towns thereafter. Certainly in the early decades after the Dissolutions, and in the majority of the smaller and middling market towns as well as in many lesser ports, it still seems more likely that the aspirations of neighbouring towns may have been seen as more threatening than welcome by regional rivals. This was perhaps even more likely to be the case in towns which were still suffering from economic decay or deprivation.

Of course the challenge of effective competition from neighbouring communities long pre-dated the mid-sixteenth century. Yet the circumstances of the time, economic even more than political, seem to have intensified such frictions. The desire of Boston's merchants to avoid distraint of their goods by the Lord Mayor of London,[70] the spirited and even violent battles between the inhabitants of Old and New Carmarthen,[71] the challenges by the Tanners Company of Nottingham to the tolls imposed by the Bailiffs of Newark-upon-Trent,[72] and the loss of Leominster's Saturday Market at the hostile petition

---

[69] Suggested esp. in Sacks, *The Widening Gate.*

[70] *Huntwicke et al.* v. *Lord Mayor of London*, PRO, C. 1/1235/57.

[71] *Mayor and Bailiffs of Carmarthen* v. *Devereux, Awbrey, et al.*, PRO, STAC 2/17/271 and STAC 2/8/9–16; *L. & P. Henry VIII*, 15, no. 427; T. H. Lewis, 'Carmarthenshire under the Tudors', *West Wales Historical Records*, 8 (1919–20), 1–19; Glanmore Williams, 'Carmarthen and the Reformation, 1536–1558', *Carmarthenshire Studies* (Carmarthen, 1974), 136–57, esp. 144–5.

[72] *Crewe et al.* v. *Forster, Bailiff of Newark-upon-Trent*, PRO, STAC 2/11/40. Cf. also Christine J. Black, 'The Administration and Parliamentary Representation of Nottinghamshire and Derbyshire, 1529–1558', Ph.D. thesis (London, 1966), 35.

of the boroughs of Hereford and of Worcester,[73] all served to move the burgesses of those aggrieved communities to seek incorporation in the hope of defending their interests. All these towns, and others like them, sought and received incorporation shortly following such disputes.[74]

Once a town gained corporate status, its neighbours and rivals found it much more difficult to carry out such hostile acts. Not infrequently, they were then obliged to seek an incorporation of their own as a means of keeping pace. A map of towns chartered in the mid-Tudor era shows a remarkable incidence of imitative political behaviour deriving from the desire not to be outdone by regional rivals: in western Essex, Saffron Walden (1549) led the way for nearby Great Dunmow (1556) and Thaxted (1556); in northern Kent, Maidstone (1549) followed Faversham (1546); in northern Devon, Barnstaple (1557) strove to keep up with Torrington (1554); on opposite shores of the Wash, Boston (1545) vied with King's Lynn (1524 and 1537); and in the West Midlands, after Leominster and Droitwich received charters within weeks of each other (1554), Worcester felt pressed to do the same (1555). In this 'copy-cat' pattern within specific areas we may perceive incorporation rapidly becoming the normal and appropriate status for almost any borough of reasonable size and significance. Again, this rash of incorporations, and the pattern of regional rivalries in securing them, unfolds only after about 1540.

One might easily assume that the interference of the Crown or other institutions of central government provided an additional pressure on unincorporated towns in this era, and thus an additional cause for incorporation or similarly fortifying strategies. This is commonly taken to have been the case in the later seventeenth century, when the Crown brought *quo warranto* proceedings against a great many boroughs.[75] It certainly fits the classic Whiggish perspective on relations between the Crown and the periphery.

Yet though royal cooperation with the aims of incorporation

---

[73] L. T. Smith (ed.), *Itinerary of John Leland,* ii. 70–5.

[74] Boston in 1545 (PRO, C. 66/771/m. 32), Carmarthen in 1546 (C. 66/793/m. 50), Newark in 1549 (C. 66/825/m. 25), and Leominster in 1554 (C. 66/878/m. 26). The fact that all four derive from a single ten-year period reflects the author's preoccupation with this era, but it also indicates how common such factors were in the decision to seek incorporation. See Tittler, 'Incorporation of Boroughs', 24–42.

[75] Though this tradition has been questioned by John Miller for the reign of Charles II in 'The Crown and the Borough Charters in the Reign of Charles II', *English Historical Review,* 100/394 (Jan. 1985), 53–84.

seems everywhere apparent, Crown interference in borough affairs, including the effort to press a favoured candidate for high office in a particular borough, remained relatively uncommon (if not altogether unprecedented) at least until the early seventeenth century. A study of the relation between *quo warranto* and incorporation in the period at hand, for example, does not support the inference that challenges to borough status were often brought by *quo warranto*, and led to the issuance of new corporate charters. Though the use of *quo warranto* seems common enough throughout the period from *c.*1540–1640 there are but a few instances where this sequence may be found to apply.[76] Interestingly, it appears to be two or three times more common for *quo warranto* to have been brought within a few years following the attainment of incorporation than at other times.[77] It is difficult to tell from *quo warranto* proceedings themselves how a case came to be brought to the Attorney-General for prosecution in that manner. Yet it remains very likely that, as has been found for both earlier and later periods,[78] cases originated with local factional interests, hoping to enlist the Crown in challenges to the ruling clique, rather than with the Crown itself. In addition, though there were often suits in the central courts for writs of certiorari against the jurisdiction of borough courts, both before and after incorporation, these seem to have been brought and determined on points of law rather than politics.

Nor is there evidence that the Crown itself used the opportunity to trade off incorporation for support in Parliament: indeed, the whole

---

[76] The Borough of Worcester, for example, secured its 1555 charter of incorporation a little more than a year after having its liberties challenged by a *quo warranto*, and the charter does seem to respond to specific points raised in the court challenge (PRO, KB 29/187/m. 45ʳ; KB 27/1172/m. 26; and KB 27/1177/m. 2; *CPR, 1 and 2 Philip and Mary*, 80–1).

[77] Thus, for example, in the same decade as the Worcester sequence indicated in the previous note, three boroughs, St Albans, Maidstone, and Faversham, secured an incorporation and received a challenge by *quo warranto* to certain aspects of that document shortly thereafter. In a study of all incorporations between 1540 and 1640 and writs *quo warranto* issued in a sampling of every fifth year during the same interval, this pattern seems not to have changed except that the sequence experienced by Worcester is perhaps even less common than implied in the evidence of the mid-century. St Albans, *CPR, Edward VI*, v. 33–4 (1553), PRO, KB 29/188/m. 22ᵛ (1554), and KB 29/189/m. 56ʳ (1555); Maidstone, *CPR, Edward VI*, ii. 174–6 (1549), KB 29/187/m. 1ᵛ (1553); Faversham, *L. & P. Henry VIII*, 21/1, pp. 75–6 (1546), and KB 27/1157/m. 4 (1551–2).

[78] See Miller, 'The Crown and the Borough Charters', for the reign of Charles II, and, for the period 1508–47, Garrett-Goodyear, 'Tudor Revival of *Quo Warranto*', in Arnold, Green, Scully, and White (eds.), *On the Laws and Customs of England*, 231–95.

Whiggish framework of such speculation now seems antiquated and unsound. If anything, the Crown tended to use incorporation as a reward for loyalty for support in times of need. This is most evident at the accession of Mary, for example, when the loyalty of particular communities received one of its sternest tests. Here the charters of nine boroughs issued within a year or so of the event cite loyalty at the Queen's accession as a factor in the grant.[79] Yet even in these cases, the initiative for the move came from the towns, not the Crown. There were also in that reign several parliamentary enfranchisements of English boroughs (as opposed to Welsh, where the practice was normal) allowing but one borough seat instead of the customary two.[80] This could hardly be construed as an effort to 'pack' Parliament.

Other issues which undoubtedly did contribute to the desire to incorporate, and ones with which the Crown found itself in profound sympathy, had to do with social and economic regulation and with law and order. The former need followed readily enough from the great outpouring of regulatory legislation from the Tudor Parliaments, especially again from the mid-1530s on. In these statutory demands for local supervision local officials were singled out, through necessity, as those responsible for enforcement. The conventional wording of those statutes makes distinctions between towns and boroughs which were corporate and those which were not.

Law and order proved if anything an even more pressing concern. Threats of disruption to local government from within, whether motivated politically or criminally, had long been a concern of borough leaders. Given the economic and social stresses and the disruption in social services, these concerns undoubtedly grew in the mid-sixteenth century. It is in this light that we should approach the ordinance issued by the borough fathers of Abingdon, one of the first of the new corporations, that every household must 'have in redynes a good and sufficient clubbe for the conservacon of the peace'.[81] The spirit of the times was much more prominently reflected in the passage of the most severe anti-vagrancy act in the nation's history, 1 Edward VI, c. 3, in 1547.[82] Whether or not the

---

[79] These are, in order, Aylesbury, Banbury, Buckingham, Leominster, Maldon, and Sudbury (1554), Worcester (1555), Higham Ferrars (1556), and High Wycombe (1558).

[80] In Abingdon, Banbury, and Higham Ferrars.

[81] Abingdon Corporation Minute Book, Berkshire County Record Office, MS D/EP 7/84, p. 163.

[82] Cf. C. S. L. Davies, 'Slavery and Protector Somerset: The Vagrancy Act of

actual level of violence rose in this era remains problematical, though likely, and it often required greater local authority to put down. It can hardly be coincidental, for example, that the violent attacks on City officials by members of the Tailors' Guild of Exeter,[83] the several frays of Star Chamber proportion in pre-corporate Lichfield,[84] the tax riots in late Henrician Barnstaple,[85] or many other affrays like them came only shortly before the petition by leaders of those boroughs for incorporation. Certainly in its desire to have 'strong knots of reliable men'[86] present in the communities of the realm the Crown had a positive vested interest in incorporation in our period as well. It also tended to look with favour on initiatives for such an act taken on the part of townsmen themselves.

In this context, incorporation strengthened the hand of local authorities in a number of ways. It further legitimized the appointment of constables and other appropriate officials. It certified the right of local authority to maintain a lock-up or gaol cell. It could either move the judicature of first instance from the shire, hundred, or manorial courts to the borough itself, or it could provide sanction for such a move if previously made. This meant transferring responsibility for law and order from those who were more often than not non-resident in the community into the hands of those with most at stake in preserving peace and the political status quo within the borough.

Finally, of course, incorporation brought a town under the growing corpus of legislation devoted to keeping the peace throughout the realm. This legislation conveyed or strengthened authority for the mayors of corporate towns, for example to search gaming houses, to regulate unqualified users of firearms, to punish the unlawfully assembled and the spreaders of seditious words and rumours as well as beggars, rogues, and vagabonds.

1547', *Ec.HR*, 2nd ser., 19 (1966), 533–49; Lawrence Stone, 'State Control in Sixteenth Century England', *Ec.HR* 17 (1947), 116.

[83] *Mayor and Bailiffs of Exeter* v. *Stodden, et al.*, PRO, STAC 2/26/393. The City's earlier incorporation, of 1537, may also have been due in part to the spectre of unrest, in that case following the dissolutions of local ecclesiastical institutions. See Youings, 'Exeter and the Property of the Dissolved Monasteries', 128.

[84] *Worley, Bailiff of Lichfield* v. *Harding and Calloway*, PRO, STAC 2/31/91; *Rex* v. *Inhabitants of Lichfield*, STAC 2/2/197–203.

[85] *Mayor and Bailiffs of Barnstaple* v. *Golde, Hayne, Savell, et al.*, PRO, STAC 2/13/88–91.

[86] The phrase is from Clark and Slack (eds.), *Crisis and Order in English Towns*, 22.

vi

There are of course other motives aside from the political for seeking incorporation, and thus enhancing local governing authority, in
the years following *c*.1540. Many towns, as we have seen, sought the
powers and resources to improve their economic positions at a time
of particular stress, to re-found sorely needed educational or social
institutions in the community, or acted upon considerations in individual cases which are too disparate to permit ready summary. Yet
in a great many cases, incorporation and similar strategies for for-
malizing the powers of self-government proceeded apace in this era,
and brought with them important consequences for the political
structure and activity of English towns. It would of course be foolish
to consider these political changes as *sui generis*, isolated from the
dramatic political, social, and economic changes of the era. Yet
given the force and complexity of those factors, the role of the
Dissolutions and associated aspects of the early Reformation
proved powerful stimuli to change: stimuli which proved especially
consequential for the realm of urban politics.

9

The Triumph of Oligarchy

By about the 1570s or 1580s we begin to detect a subtle shift in the priorities of those who governed in most of the middling and more substantial boroughs of the realm. Though there is still a concern for gaining control of local resources, and also for acquiring jurisdiction over local government, these aims were often well on their way to attainment. The primacy of these issues began to give way to the consolidation of those attainments in the hands of a ruling elite. This has long been recognized as a prevalent tendency in agrarian society;[1] it was no less true for provincial urban society of the same era. It is from this time to the outbreak of the Civil War that we most commonly see the hardening of the political structure, the narrowing of the ruling circle, and the growing distance between government and governed. In short, the period from about the middle of Elizabeth's reign to the outbreak of the Civil War witnessed a crescendo in the pace and extent of oligarchic rule. (Once again, of course, the emphasis falls on the 'middling and more substantial boroughs'. We will not find an expansion of oligarchic tendencies in those towns which were still essentially seigneurial boroughs, where the offices of local government were still not run by the townsmen themselves in some form or other.)

In short, these decades witnessed, not the creation of oligarchic rule, which was not entirely new to the provincial scene by any means, but its consolidation as a prevalent governing format in the majority of England's more significant towns. They also saw the creation of supportive strategies for such rule which were often new, if not necessarily in form, then at least in substance. While the political use of such elements as ceremony, the built environment, and relgious doctrine remains important, we must first consider the bedrock of the political change which supported them. This chapter

[1] See esp. Keith Wrightson, *English Society, 1580–1680* (1982), chaps. 1, 2, and 6; and Wrightson and David Levine, *Poverty and Piety in an English Village: Terling, 1525–1700* (1979), esp. chaps. 5–7.

will take up the characteristics of local oligarchic rule as understood and practised at that time. We must ask further what 'oligarchy' meant in this context, how it came to be prevalent, who opposed it and how, and how it operated—both legitimately and illegitimately—in the governance of English towns during the period in question.

i

Odd as it may seem, it is probably inappropriate to condemn what we mean by 'oligarchy' as an evil thing in and of itself, and probably anachronistic to read into contemporary perceptions of it any resentment couched in terms of 'class interest'. In fact, as has been hinted at in Chapter 7 above, there seem to be two understandings of the term which applied in that time. One is familiar, because it is also ours: rule by the few, in itself a morally neutral state of affairs and, for that matter, close (as informed contemporaries knew) to what Aristotle called 'rule by aristocracy'. The other is the classic concept of oligarchy, so labelled by Aristotle and echoed in such sixteenth-century writers as, for example, Raleigh, who meant by that term the corruption of 'aristocratic' rule.[2] In this sense the rulers were not only few in number, but they placed their own interests before those of the community.

Yet if the general run of the freemanry met the latter usage with intolerance and concern, the former, neutral, usage elicited no great opposition. The interests of most of the better sort who came to power in these years coincided in most respects with the interests of the towns themselves. They were compatible—and seen to be compatible—with what most contemporaries saw as the common good.[3] This is not to say that a narrowing of rule to the domination of a few was absolutely unobjectionable. We will see evidence of some genuine pitched battles fought over questions of participation in or exclusion from local office-holding and political activity. At the same time, however, most contemporaries recognized at least in principle that only the wealthier and 'better' sort could undertake

[2] *OED*, *vide* 'oligarchy'.

[3] To a point, the argument would certainly apply to the strong boost for moral reform lent by the determined puritans who brought their strong concern for 'godly rule' to many a town hall in this era. See e.g. Underdown, *Fire from Heaven*. Yet similar concerns for socially responsible rule might well ensue without puritan convictions. Ian Archer, for example, emphasizes the strong sense of social responsibility amongst the London magistrates—an oligarchy of sorts but not necessarily puritan in tone—of the same era, while there are numerous examples of pre-Reformation townsmen working towards the same ends (Archer, *Pursuit of Stability*, 259).

the growing personal burdens of office, and that a number of factors worked to encourage oligarchic tendencies of this sort.

This continued general willingness to see the main offices of local government filled by a narrow slice of the population seems even more pronounced in hard times.[4] And as we must not forget, these were hard times for many English towns. Aside from the broad economic dislocations which are familiar for most of the latter half of the sixteenth and early seventeenth centuries, there were particular if short periods within this era which presented exceptional problems of local governance. The 1550s, fraught with harvest failures, higher prices, political instability, and epidemic disease, probably found most boroughs unprepared.[5] Legislation granting local officials much fuller authority to deal with social and economic issues had not quite caught up with the pace of social and economic change, as it would shortly do. Then, too, most borough governments had not yet consolidated their hegemony as they would also shortly do. The 1590s, marked by more harvest failures, price rises, and epidemics, and the stresses of war and rebellion, formed another such period. And the 1620s, when many of the same ills recurred along with one of the greatest economic slumps of the age, presents still another.[6]

In many such cases, the officials of England's provincial towns simply found their authority inadequate to the tasks before them. From the Crown's perspective, it had always been important to have trusted and authoritative officials at every level of administration. With the dissolution and resale of ecclesiastical and related properties creating a vast changeover in jurisdiction throughout the realm, the Crown had to find replacements for many local authorities displaced in the process. And, with the effort to interrupt local, often feudally based loyalties of long standing, that aim often led to a new interest in the potential for civic self-government under the royal aegis. Even many contemporaries attributed the social ills of the day in considerable measure to weak local authority.[7]

[4] See e.g. J. M. Martin, 'A Warwickshire Town in Adversity: Stratford-upon-Avon in the Sixteenth and Seventeenth Centuries', *Midland History*, 7 (1982), 26–41.

[5] These years form the heart of what some have and some have not called the 'Mid-Tudor Crisis'. But few would deny the social and economic problems of the decade. See esp. W. R. D. Jones, *The Mid-Tudor Crisis* (1973), esp. chap. 5; Jennifer Loach and Robert Tittler (eds.), *The Mid-Tudor Polity, c.1540–1560* (1980), and Loades, *Mid-Tudor Crisis,* esp. chaps. 3–4.

[6] See Peter Clark (ed.), *The European Crisis of the 1590s: Essays in Comparative History* (1985); Slack, *Poverty and Policy*, 48–53; D. M. Palliser, *The Age of Elizabeth: England under the Later Tudors, 1547–1603*, 2nd edn. (1992), 32.

[7] See e.g. Thomas Harmon's views in *A Caveat or Warning for Common Cursitors*

There were other considerations as well. The Crown was quick to recognize its own self-interest in empowering more local officials to carry out the dramatic profusion of regulatory legislation produced in this period. Finally, the constant and at times almost obsessive concern for order and tranquillity throughout the realm required ever greater authority in areas which were in other ways so distinct from the administrative apparatus of the countryside. All these factors pointed to the augmentation of local authority.

In most cases, as has been our theme all along, the recourse of central government was to respond positively to local demands for great powers in the hands of borough officials, and to identify mayors, aldermen, and other such officials as responsible for carrying out proclamations and legislation affecting the local community. But a word must also be said about the empowerment of parish government.

It is in these very years that the Crown, Parliament, and even the central ecclesiastical administration came to see the parish as an institution which could supplement the authority of secular officials in local government. In the event, Crown and Parliament now placed on the shoulders of parish officials some of the responsibility for poor relief, maintenance of roads and bridges, and a host of other, secular, functions. In the process, as is well known, parish government and parish life underwent a drastic, even revolutionary, change in these years. What had been an exclusively religious jurisdiction now became an integral part of the local governing structure, bringing relative isolation from external authorities, especially those of a secular nature, rapidly to an end. Governing structures which had drawn from an even broader spectrum of local society than that of the borough itself now became, especially with the advent of the 'select vestries' in the middle decades of the sixteenth century, miniature oligarchies of their own. Although the complete picture of relations between parish and borough authorities which pertained in the wake of these changes has yet to be drawn, a good deal more interaction came to ensue between the two. Some borough corporations had broad supervisory and even financial powers over local parishes, and the number of parish advowsons in the gift of borough corporations grew substantially in these years. It also seems likely that many a member of the select vestry wore aldermanic robes as well, bringing the structures of the two hierarchies

(1566), excerpted in A. V. Judges, *The Elizabethan Underworld* (1930 [1965]), 62, as cited by Manley, *Literature and Culture*, 80 n. 55.

into very close alignment.[8] In any event, this dramatic transition in the role of post-Reformation parishes in local government could only have enhanced the oligarchic nature of urban society from that time forward.

In discussing that acceleration of oligarchic tendencies, the line between the two concepts of oligarchy—one a natural, generally acceptable, and beneficial state rendered necessary by circumstances, the other a corruption of the first—may be difficult to draw. Popular response varied as well. Indeed, given the circumstances of the age, it is not surprising to find the frequent extension of oligarchy in ways which were considered corrupt as well as legitimate. The exclusion of the general freemanry from the governing process, the replacement of election by co-option, the circumvention of the traditional *cursus honorum*, the restriction of positions of authority to particular families, even the invitation of well-connected outsiders— allies to elite townsmen—to assume borough offices, could all be carried out with a semblance of due process. All these practices became much more common. Yet it seems safe to say that contemporary townsmen had a sense of what seemed right. They knew corruption when they saw it, and were often quick to protest it. While some processes of narrowing met with compliance, perhaps especially at hard times, other examples met with resistance and protest.

If the most salient feature of both types of oligarchy is rule by the few, we must begin our discussion by observing the narrowing of the political leadership in a representative selection of communities, again largely restricting ourselves to the more substantial and complex towns of the realm. Time and time again in this era we find in records of local elections the effort to exclude the multitude from the process, to replace election or at least a broad-based selection by co-option, and (allegedly) to conspire to restrict office-holding to particular families or factions. Obvious, too, especially where the means of such narrowing seemed illegitimate, are the frequent efforts by the freemanry or some form of political opposition to fight back: to work for by-laws limiting the right of mayors to succeed themselves in office, to demand greater scrutiny of official actions, to demand (often with the help of self-interested regional gentry) an expanded franchise in parliamentary elections,[9] and even to mount

---

[8] These themes are treated at length in Kumin, *Shaping of a Community*, esp. chaps. 5 and 6.

[9] Derek Hirst, *The Representatives of the People? Voters and Voting Behaviour under the Early Stuarts* (Cambridge, 1975), 62–3.

legal challenge to assertions of local governing authority. (This should not necessarily be taken as evidence of social conflict, for the opponents to such moves, insofar as they can be identified, were much more often than not men of roughly the same social and economic status as those whose rule they opposed.)

Earlier in our discussion two boroughs, Lichfield and Newcastle-under-Lyme, served to exemplify the operation of a communal ethos in pre-Reformation days. If we look at what became of these representative towns in the later period, we see very rapid developments in the opposite direction. By 1553 Lichfield gained a new and more extensive charter, granting it the status of a county, with its own sheriff and JPs. Although in this last of Lichfield's constitutional changes of the century the Bishop retained some rights, the government of the 'Town and County of Lichfield', as it had become, had already come to be dominated by a small number of families who would constitute the ruling elite even into the eighteenth century.[10] In Newcastle-under-Lyme, by the incorporation of 1590, all officials could for the first time be selected by co-option. The voice of the freemanry at large, having diminished from its former strength over a long period, now disappeared completely. It would not return again before the Municipal Corporation Act of 1835.[11]

The establishment of oligarchic rule in this era, both in the sense of 'rule by the few' and in the corruption of that form, frequently proceeded along these same lines elsewhere. Though the long view of the matter suggests a continuum over several centuries, it seems appropriate to suggest that this age saw only a few new wrinkles—including the transition in the role of the parish—but a marked acceleration of tendencies already in motion. For a great number of towns this era marked a formal and even legal and constitutional watershed, with a surviving emphasis on the 'commonalty' on one side of that divide and the predominance of an oligarchic ethos on the other. As with the acquisition of greater local control discussed above, these changes, too, more often than not came about through one of three legal devices which appear with particular frequency in this era: litigation over borough liberties, enfeoffment to uses, and charters of incorporation which gave the ultimate legal and constitutional powers to specific towns.

[10] *VCH, Staffordshire*, 14 (1990), 78.
[11] *VCH, Staffordshire*, 8 (1963), 26.

ii

An analysis of charters of incorporation in this later phase of our chosen century leaves little doubt about the intentional narrowing of the ruling circle along the lines of the examples from Lichfield and Newcastle offered above. Where a generation earlier incorporations most commonly served to recognize or create the autonomy of indigenous governing authorities, now they tended to ensure the consolidation of that authority in the hands of an elite few at the expense of the freemanry in general.

This pattern appears most vividly when we consider the striking number of boroughs which sought re-incorporation in the period from 1590 to 1640: sixty-five in all, thirty-six of them, more than half, in the reign of James I alone (see Table I). Far from supporting the view of a move away from oligarchy in this era, as has been suggested elsewhere at least with reference to parliamentary elections,[12] this evidence seems to identify the period from the late Elizabethan years to the Civil War as a particularly fertile patch for the incursion of oligarchic rule, a tendency encouraged by the Crown.

Beverley proved something of a harbinger of this trend. Here the burgesses at large had elected each year the governing Council of Twelve with retiring Governors rendered ineligible for re-election. But by the charter of 1573 the government came to consist of a Mayor and Twelve Governors as the Common Council, with the Governors serving for life and being replaced thereafter in a process of co-option. The surviving Governors simply selected one of the burgesses for that office. And where the charter gave the burgesses at least the theoretic right of consent in the selection of the mayor and the issue of orders by the Council, this ebbed very quickly in actual practice. By 1596 the Governors regularly appear to be issuing orders without consent, and the theoretic role of the burgesses in selecting MPs virtually disappeared. The 1573 charter, and abuses of the minimal rights granted therein to the burgesses at large (i.e. the freemanry), effectively established a narrow ruling oligarchy which remained in place until 1835.[13]

---

[12] Hirst, *Representatives of the People?*, 61–4.

[13] J. Dennett (ed.), *Beverley Borough Records, 1575–1821*, Yorkshire Archaeological Society Record Series, 84 (1933 for 1932), p. vii; Lamburn, 'Politics and Religion in Beverley', 55–88 *passim*. As the latter points out, this institutionalization of oligarchic rule ran counter to the long history of widely participatory government through the Middle Ages in which, under the governing authority of the Abbey and often as guildsmen, the freemanry functioned as a true 'commonalty' in deed as well

But if Beverley moved apace towards oligarchy from the early 1570s, the tendency became more apparent elsewhere in the 'difficult nineties'.[14] In Ludlow, where a relatively narrow base of self-governing authority had already been in force since an incorporation of 1461, a bitter and protracted dispute over governing authority arose in that decade. The dissidents in the struggle claimed that the freemanry had been excluded from a share of the electoral franchise in violation of the earlier charter, and that the ruling clique had been leasing corporate lands on favourable terms to their friends and even keeping some of the profits for themselves. Yet in 1596, even while the Court of Exchequer was hearing allegations of mismanagement of corporate leases brought against the ruling clique, the members of that clique fortified their position with a re-incorporation granting even greater authority.[15] Adding insult to the injury of the protesting freemen, the eventual Exchequer judgment not only upheld the new charter, but specified that every new member of the Inner Council, upon taking office, should present to the Corporation a silver spoon: a requirement which served effectively to bar from office any but the well-to-do.[16]

Such instances grew even more common after the turn of the century. In Stafford the charter of 1605 hardly served as a model of participatory government to begin with. Twenty-one chief burgesses were to sit for life and choose annually the two bailiffs to carry out the executive functions of the Corporation. But even this seemed too broadly based for the small ruling faction which came to the fore in subsequent years. Though opposed by a group of eighty petitioners, they were able to restrict the ruling group further by a new

---

as name. This is widely evident in the extensive records of this borough, including the specification of freemen's powers in the indenture made between the pre-corporate Mayor and Burgesses and the Archbishop of York who served as Lord of the Manor, 18 December 1554 (Beverley Borough Records, Humberside County Record Office, MS BC I/53). In contrast, Lamburn concludes, the charter created 'disunity, and enabled those who lacked concepts of mutual interest and common obligation to gain [and retain] power' (p. 176).

[14] See John Guy (ed.), *The Reign of Elizabeth I: Court and Culture in the Last Decade* (Cambridge, 1995), esp. the introduction and chap. 9; and Clark (ed.), *European Crisis of the 1590s*.

[15] Faraday, *Ludlow*, 25–36; Penry Williams, 'Government and Politics in Ludlow, 1590–1642', *Transactions of the Shropshire Archeological Society*, 56 (1957–60), 284–8.

[16] Williams, 'Government and Politics in Ludlow', 288. The same requirement applied in Exeter by 1581; Devon Record Office, Exeter Corporation Act Book No. 3, p. 13.

charter in 1614, providing for but a single mayor in place of two bailiffs, and an even smaller number to elect him. The oligarchic format continued unabated thereafter.[17]

In another example, the Borough Corporation of Rochester explained in petitioning for a new charter in 1629 that the town had changed since the grant of the existing (1461) charter in ways which rendered that document insufficient as a governing instrument. The town's physical boundaries had expanded considerably, as had its population. In addition, the incursion of large numbers of sailors, who were often disorderly, had become a very serious problem in that age of naval growth and activity. The authority of its officials had simply been overmatched by these circumstances. It wanted local governing authority strengthened overall and extended to cover unruly suburban areas which had emerged with population growth.[18]

And the Mayor and Aldermen of Newark-upon-Trent, operating under an incorporation of Edward VI and only slightly expanded by Elizabeth and James, petitioned for a new charter in 1626 for similar reasons. The port had become a much busier place, handling formerly unimaginable quantities of grain on the River Trent, hosting a considerable flow of travellers to and from Scotland, and expanding substantially in population. They, too, required more complete powers, more officials, another prison, and additional sources of revenue.[19] Petitions for re-incorporation by Exeter,[20] Colchester,[21] Derby,[22] Huntingdon,[23] and other boroughs tell of similar requirements.

The electoral provisions of many revised charters undoubtedly confirmed what had already become common practice. In this, amongst other ways, incorporation recognized and thus sanctioned a narrowing of popular participation which had already been brought about in practice, often by less legitimate or sanguine means. To by-laws of 1564 intended to preserve popular participation in the elections of Dartmouth, Devon, for example, the ruling elite of that town mounted strong challenges in subsequent years. In an effort to settle the matter for good, and—not coincidentally—in the interests of the ruling faction, the Mayor for the year 1577 simply

---

[17] Kenneth Raymond Adey, 'Aspects of the History of the Town of Stafford, 1590–1710', MA thesis (Keele, 1971), 39–42, 60.

[18] PRO, SP 16/131/4.   [19] PRO, SP 16/27/42.

[20] PRO, SP 16/14/41 (1627).   [21] PRO, SP 16/251/27 (1635).

[22] PRO, SP 16/378/64 (1638).   [23] PRO, SP 16/160/52 (1630).

ruled by fiat that he and the 'sworne council' of the borough should have the exclusive power to nominate two free burgesses for mayoral office, and then to choose thirty-six electors from amongst the freemanry to carry out the ultimate election. In both instances the mayor was to have two votes. This was confirmed in the Borough's eventual incorporation, in 1604, and then again in the Borough order book in 1625, which also stated the express purpose of preventing 'popular' elections.[24]

The 1638 petition for re-incorporation in the Borough of Derby called for the mayor and aldermen to be empowered to disenfranchise burgesses for misdemeanours. Yet it failed to specify what constituted a misdemeanour, and made no provision for appeal or redress.[25] The Borough of Cambridge successfully petitioned in 1632 for a new charter which would allow the mayor and bailiffs to appoint deputies to hold court and do all other things in their stead, such appointments to be entirely without public scrutiny or participation.[26] The Borough of Kingston-upon-Thames gained a re-incorporation in 1628 which extended the jurisdiction of its officers to the whole Hundred of Kingston, save for the King's own house at Richmond.[27]

As with the Ludlow example, the official nature of these charters of incorporation should not mask for us the frequent and intense opposition with which such moves were met by others in the community when they were seen to be narrowing the ruling elite. In Abingdon, for example, a Marian incorporation had designated a reasonably open governing structure. The inhabitants of the borough at large had a share in nominating two candidates for mayoral office, though not in choosing between the two, and they also nominated and elected one of the two bailiffs.[28] Yet in 1599 an allegedly corrupt ruling group, in office as the titular 'Mayor, Bailiffs and Principal Burgesses' by which the Corporation had been designated, attempted to eliminate that popular participation by seeking a new charter.

In response, a dissident faction, comprising freemen of similar background but who happened to be out of office at the time, petitioned the Privy Council with an objection to the proposed charter.

---

[24] Dartmouth 'Constitution Book', Devon County Record Office, North Devon Branch, MS SM 2003, fos. 22, 36–7.

[25] PRO, SP 16/378/64 (1638). The petition met with success and Derby, first incorporated as recently as 1612, gained re-incorporation with a much more stringently defined civic authority in 1638. Weinbaum, *British Borough Charters*, p. xxxvi.

[26] PRO, SP 16/194/50 (1632).   [27] PRO, SP 16/67/24 (1628).

[28] *CPR, 3 and 4 Philip and Mary*, iii. 381–3.

The petitioners claimed that the coveted powers would allow the governing clique to 'restrain' foreigners and 'do other things hurtful to the corporation'. For good measure they added that the present incumbents had already illicitly taken profits from Christ's Hospital and from the Corporation itself for their own use, and had greatly oppressed the inhabitants by rack renting corporate lands. In an effort to undermine this opposition, the Mayor suspended one of the protesters from office, but his ultimate victory seems at least to have been delayed. Abingdon's next charter was not forthcoming till 1610, though it does seem to have granted a much more restrictive form of government.[29]

In Totnes, where the townsmen had purchased the former ecclesiastical borough from the Crown in 1559, there had traditionally been a broad electoral franchise, as confirmed in the charter of 1505. In the 1590s, with much more at stake in the control of the Borough and its resources, a small clique led by the powerful Savery family sought a much more restrictive charter, which they succeeded in procuring in 1596. This allegedly undermined the governing role of the twenty-member Common Council in favour of the fourteen Burgesses and the Mayor, and removed the traditional role of the freemanry and the Common Council in electing the Mayor. Though townsmen had contributed to the costs of securing the charter, they later claimed, in a Star Chamber suit, not to have known how restrictive the new document would be. When it was first read out in a public meeting a great uproar ensued, from which the Star Chamber suit and even a *quo warranto* resulted. Yet by the end of the century the ruling clique, newly fortified, seem to have had matters well in hand.[30]

A similar campaign ensued in Warwick, where the restrictive charter of 1554 continued to be fought, sometimes with the help of powerful figures at court, right on into the 1580s, but with little success in the end.[31] In Stafford, as we have seen, the eighty petitioners failed to stop the eventual charter of 1614. In Dorchester the new charter of 1629 gave to the ruling oligarchy power of selection over the members of the governing council of the Company of Freemen,

---

[29] Abingdon Corporation Order Book, Berkshire County Record Office MS D/EP 7/84, fo. 20ᵈ.

[30] PRO, STAC 5/21/6; J. C. Roberts, 'The Parliamentary Representation of Devon and Dorset, 1559–1601', MA thesis (London, 1958), 217–30. The King's Bench proceedings, in the form of a *quo warranto*, are cited at several points in the Star Chamber case, but have not been found in the records of the King's Bench where they would have ensued.

[31] *VCH, Warwickshire*, 2 (1908), 492.

whereas, or so they claimed, the Company had enjoyed the right to elect their own Council. In addition, and in an increasingly common move, the Mayor and two of the fifteen Bailiffs were to enjoy the title and powers of Justices of the Peace even though no county status had been conferred.[32] The charter of incorporation of Newcastle-upon-Tyne, granted in 1589 and confirmed in 1600, allowed the ruling clique dominated by the Anderson, Selby, and Chapman families to legitimize their grip on the town.[33] The incorporation granted to the Cinque Port town of Hythe in 1575 had the same effect.[34] And in the Ludlow dispute, the opposition fought the ruling faction for nearly a decade, with a petition to the Council of the March of Wales, a *quo warranto* brought in Queen's Bench, and even an attempted coup which ended in a riot, before the re-incorporation of 1596.[35]

iii

The use of the writ of *quo warranto* by the dissident townsmen of Totnes and Ludlow brings us to one of the most important but least explored means of challenging the assertions of hegemony by ruling authorities in particular communities. It should not surprise us that a legal writ literally intended to ask 'by what warrant' a particular claim to authority had been held should have been used to challenge the assertion and exercise of local governing powers. Yet while most of the familiar scholarship on the use of this device pertains to the Restoration era, it was frequently employed in the sixteenth century as well. In fact, as a pioneering work by Harold Garrett-Goodyear has shown, *quo warranto* was employed with increasing frequency in the early years of that century.[36] Yet, as with incorporation, the use to which townsmen put this device changed with time.

In the years studied by Garrett-Goodyear (1512–47) only a minority of *quo warrantos* applied to towns. On those occasions, moreover, they were not employed, as they would be later on, as the Crown's way of challenging the exercise of local authority per se. In addition, in only a few of those cases did the Crown pursue litigation to a definitive, much less punitive, end. Instead, in these early years and insofar as *quo warranto* applied to towns at all, it seems largely

[32] PRO, SP 16/146/67 and 67 i; Underdown, *Fire from Heaven*, 151.

[33] Hasler (ed.), *House of Commons, 1558–1603*, i. 222.

[34] Ibid. 302.   [35] See p. 189.

[36] Garrett-Goodyear, 'Tudor Revival of *Quo Warranto*', in Arnold, Green, Scully, and White (eds.), *On the Laws and Customs of England*, 231–95.

to have been initiated either by a group of townsmen or their over-lord in the hope that the Crown might resolve jurisdictional disputes between rival claimants for local authority.

An important clue to the developing application of *quo warranto* to the problems of town government lies in the chronology of its appearance. Though only a small minority of all such cases documented in this study dealt with towns to begin with, most of those fell in the 1540s. Examining the records of *quo warranto* further we find that their use in regard to towns continued to be strikingly frequent in the mid-century years (e.g. thirty-eight cases between the death of Henry VIII in 1547 and the death of Mary in 1558), but that it came to an abrupt and almost complete halt in the early years of Elizabeth. Only one *quo warranto* may be found in the entire first decade of her reign. Finally, though the pace never again prior to 1640 reached the intensity of the 1540s and 1550s, we find a resumption of *quo warranto* in the latter decades of the century and the opening decades of the next.

This peculiar chronological incidence of the application of *quo warranto* to towns, plus an examination of a sampling of cases themselves over that entire span, does not yield as definitive an explanation as one would want. It is rarely possible to discover the origin of a particular case, and many were postponed a number of times and then prosecution dropped. Other cases were simply terminated at the death of the monarch, an especially frequent occurrence in the mid-century. Nevertheless, especially when court proceedings can be correlated with documentation surviving from the local scene, at least tentative conclusions may be suggested.

To begin with, the government continued to employ the device to resolve local disputes about political jurisdiction. It did so with particular intensity in the years immediately following the Dissolutions when such issues were especially pressing. Yet there was much less cause to do so in the period from about 1558. Most conflicts of jurisdiction between townsmen and external authorities had either been resolved or competing authorities had begun, as we have seen, to seek other strategies.

When *quo warranto* returned as a common feature of urban political life in the mid-Elizabethan years, it appears to have served a somewhat different function. Though the initiative still tended at least some of the time to derive locally rather than centrally, and the issues still of course concerned matters of local jurisdiction, *quo warranto* no longer seems very often to have been brought to bear

in contests between townsmen, on the one hand, and external authorities, on the other. Now both competing parties seem to have been townsmen, and the device came to focus on rival claims of authority within the same community. As we have seen in Totnes and Ludlow, it allowed one party to challenge the right of another to subvert the traditional political order to its own ends. *quo warranto* had become a useful weapon in the battle for and against the encroachment of oligarchy.

Though the use of *quo warranto* was by no means invariably successful in achieving these aims, it does suggest again that the use of incorporation to extend the powers of oligarchic rule in local communities remained vulnerable to legal challenge in this as well as other forms. The experience of Colchester in the reign of Charles I, when the Attorney-General issued not one but two such writs challenging the assertion of the Borough's liberties, seems not at all unique. Yet in the end an appeal to the Crown for re-incorporation in 1635 held out the only satisfactory response. The coveted charter came forth later in the same year.[37] Just as a challenge brought by *quo warranto* could result in a petition for a new charter, so could a new charter, especially one narrowing the base of government or newly extending the powers of the ruling elite, made a distinct target for *quo warranto*.

iv

Considering the cost and bother of seeking formal incorporation to begin with, it often proved more desirable to accomplish the aims of oligarchic rule by less formal means. It is thus entirely likely that the extension of oligarchy by incorporation represents but a modest proportion of all of those instances where leadership substantially narrowed and tightened in the period at hand. Even without resort to incorporation (or re-incorporation) several tactics could be employed to strengthen the grip of oligarchic rule in specific towns. Some may have been considered legitimate by most townsmen of the time. Others were not, and the frequent partnership of oligarchy and corruption, a partnership which gave oligarchy a bad name, remains familiar.

Restricted circles of government meant fewer eyes on those who ruled, fewer checks on their exercise of authority, and less chance of

---

[37] PRO, SP 16/251/27 (in which the petition for re-incorporation recites the saga of the two successive *quo warrantos*) and SP 16/252/8.

unseating unwelcome incumbents. With the vast increase in the scope and power of local jurisdiction wrought by the economic and social legislation, charters, and other devices of the age, those who ruled in the towns of the realm had much more opportunity for malpractice than ever. And, human nature being what it is, many took advantage accordingly. It seems entirely likely that the increased oligarchy of the latter decades became a self-perpetuating force, and that it brought with it a comparable tendency towards corruption in office. Power does indeed corrupt, and so, too, does it attract. The fact that corruption in office reached — or at least was widely perceived by contemporaries to have reached — unprecedented proportions in this era made such abuses both more likely and more readily detected.[38]

These practices were often intended to obtain or sustain incumbency as an end in itself. They were corrupt in the sense that they broke with established practice without consent of the community, and did so in a way which favoured personal interest over common interest. Such corruption extended to enhancing the authority or perquisites of incumbency by illegitimate means. They included the misappropriation of borough resources and the neglect of due process, both for personal gain, in ways which contemporaries often lumped together in the charge of violating the oath of office.

Of course there is little here which might not be found at other times, both earlier and later. Yet in borough government as in the sundry and expanding areas of central government, there appears a distinct crescendo at least in the allegation of these activities, suggesting something of a culture of corruption in these years.[39] Again we will best turn to the witness of local records and to cases brought to the central courts for a sampling of the nature and scope of such practices.

In some towns the ruling elite attempted to seize power, or to perpetuate its possession in friendly hands, by circumventing the customary route to office-holding known as the *cursus honorum*. This tradition-hallowed progression through the ranks of civic office preserved an emphasis on seniority and service as a criterion for high office, and on waiting one's turn to serve. Because the *cursus*

---

[38] The discussion which follows owes much to concepts developed in Linda Peck, *Court Patronage and Corruption in Early Stuart England* (Boston, 1990), and esp. to definitions offered on 7–8, 110–23, 161, and 183–4.

[39] As applied to the Jacobean era, the phrase is Peck's, in *Court Patronage and Corruption*, 110–12, 116–23.

virtually always entailed guild membership and some degree of pro-gression through that structure, it met wide approbation amongst the freemanry and provided an appropriate training for civic office.

The *cursus* could be circumvented when those in power simply co-opted into senior office those who had not come up through the ranks (sometimes including well-placed outsiders to the community and others who had not served in guild office), or by pointedly excluding from office—sometimes from the freemanry altogether—particular opponents of the incumbents who had so served. In Beverley, as we have seen, both these events transpired despite the provisions of the most recent charter.[40] Often such tactics were employed so brazenly as to provoke litigation, not to say violence, and these are the cases which tend most readily to be recorded and thus come to our attention.

The ruling clique in Much Wenlock moved in 1597 to circumvent the usual *cursus honorum* by allowing to be elected to the office of bailiff—tantamount to mayor in Wenlock—those who had not met the traditional and very lenient requirement of serving first as a burgess for at least a single year. The same by-law which permitted this also provided that any such person should hold within the town lands and tenements worth at least 100 marks: so long, as the order read, 'as for their good abilities in wealth and otherwise [they] have byn and are fytt and able men to take in hand and execute the saide office'. Though nothing like the £1,000 required of Elizabethan aldermen of London, this served in the same manner as the requisite silver spoon in Ludlow or Exeter to exclude the common run of the freemen from the Borough's highest office. Wealth had replaced seniority and length of residence as the prime criterion for office.[41] Another case of queue-jumping to high office is alleged to have occurred in Gloucester, in 1624,[42] and the same no doubt occurred elsewhere as well.

The tactic of bringing in an outsider from the regional gentry is well illustrated in Jacobean Chester, where one faction vying for power is alleged to have brought in its patron, Sir Robert Mainwar-ing, swearing him a freeman and an alderman at the same time. A landowner and something of a power in the shire politics of

[40] See above, p. 188.
[41] Order of September 1597, to take effect at the Feast of St Simon and St Jude, 1598. 'Borough Minute Book', Much Wenlock Borough Archives, MS B3/1/1, pp. 321–2. My thanks to Mr Vincent Deacon for facilitating use of the records in his care.
[42] *Jones* v. *Caple*, PRO, STAC 8/188/12, 21 James I.

Chester, Mainwaring was the father-in-law of the chief defendant in
the Star Chamber case noted above. He had not formerly been resident in the town, and had certainly not come up through the ranks of
office-holding as a freeman.[43]

Save for the offices of Steward and Recorder, in which the role of
outsiders remained a virtually necessity, this importation of shire
gentry remained uncommon. Yet we do find it in special circumstances from time to time. This may be especially evident in towns
where (*a*) pressure for influence from outside corporate authorities
(e.g. the Duchy of Lancaster) came on top of the more ordinary
efforts of individual families with regional influence; or (*b*) where, as
with Mainwaring, an outsider of particular abilities may have been
able to help the ruling factions out of specific difficulties. In all of
these instances, such involvement can only have come at the request
of the ruling clique of the day. It strengthened their hand on the tiller
and sacrificed for partisan advantage the normal sequence whereby
resident freemen came up through the ranks.

A study of the Stanley Earls of Derby, great magnates in Lancashire, Cheshire, and elsewhere and with considerable clout at
court, has shown their success in gaining political office in Liverpool
and Preston as well as Chester. At Liverpool, nominally within the
authority of the Duchy, Stanleys served as mayor five times between
1568 and 1640, including the Earl of the day himself in 1603 and
James, Lord Strange in 1625: both years in which the Borough
attempted to get charters from the Crown. In Preston three of the
Earls received 'foreign burgessships' in the same period, and at
Chester once again three of the family, including two of the Earls,
served as aldermen in the same span.[44]

In a similar vein, the ruling groups in some towns were accused of
conspiring to retain office for themselves and their associates by
illicit electoral practices. Some rigged elections. Others conspired to
overturn elections already held in favour of new ones which could be
made to bring more favourable results. Still others canvassed for
votes and thus attempted, illicitly in the eyes of most contemporaries, to influence the choice of those who were enfranchised.
(Though happily we still frown on most of these practices today, we
may well wonder what contemporaries might have found objectionable about the latter, as canvassing and other peaceful election-

---

[43] *Whitby and Whitby* v. *Brerewood et al.*, PRO, STAC 8/297/15 (18 James I).
[44] Coward, *The Stanleys*, table 6, p. 131.

eering practices have certainly become an accepted and integral part of our own political system. The answer seems to lie in the perception that canvassing violated the contemporary communal sense of fair play by the interjection of partisanship into local political behaviour. One would not be surprised to find a similar bias against open canvassing as ungentlemanly surviving in some gentlemen's clubs and other ancient institutions even today.) Again, none of these were entirely new under the sun in the period at hand, but they do seem to increase in frequency towards the latter decades of the sixteenth century.

Some of the possibilities of these efforts to monopolize power may be seen in a sampling of legal challenges from the period at hand, and something of their flavour may be retrieved by dipping into the rich language of contemporary deposition. Forms of election rigging and similar circumventions are well documented, as in, for example, Carmarthen in 1609. His opponents accused the Mayor, Martin Bynon, of improperly appointing his own candidate to the office of Town Clerk, having first forced the resignation of the popular incumbent. When dissident freemen challenged this appointment as not within the mayor's sole power to make, Bynon allegedly both denied the right of the burgesses and freeman to participate in the choice and packed the inner council (whose authority to ratify his choice he does appear to have accepted) so that it would support his selection. He also denied the role of the burgesses and freemen in choosing members of the council, doubly antagonizing his opponents.[45]

In Banbury, five members of the ruling elite were accused in a Star Chamber suit of 1603 of conspiring amongst themselves to monopolize the offices of bailiff and JP, the two commanding offices in the town, and of keeping others from attaining those posts. The defendants seem to have been related through marriage, forming a tight-knit clique of relatives and close friends. Their actions in removing two of the town's market crosses—the High Cross and the Bread Cross—against the wishes of many townsmen and market folk from the countryside suggests a religious dimension to the controversy as well. Although the plaintiff's bill stating the charges fully has not survived, the interrogatories and depositions of witnesses make clear the nature of the accusations. The defendants allegedly formed a clique through marriage and friendship, and had managed to

[45] PRO, STAC 8/20/14.

monopolize the offices in question by canvassing amongst the eligible voters. Worse, they had allegedly purchased some votes on their behalf and had offered a potential electoral rival forty marks not to stand.[46]

A similarly blatant effort at determining the outcome of elections comes from Doncaster, around the year 1618. Here the practice, as outlined in a Jacobean charter, was for the mayor, aldermen, and capital burgesses (the last two groups sitting as the inner and outer council of the borough) to nominate two of the aldermen each year to stand in a mayoral election held a fortnight later, though the franchise for such elections is not known.[47] But when two nominees, Clarke and Carver, had been chosen in 1618, Clarke's backers campaigned vigorously for him and against his opponent. Townsmen viewed this as unseemly behaviour. Worse still, Clarke's supporters allegedly turned up at the guildhall on election day in some numbers, and with arms, to intimidate the voters. They are said to have asked each voter how he would vote, and with 'great noyse, fearful clamours and showtes did then and there unlawfully publish the saide William Clarke to be their Maior', causing him to be chosen.[48]

Similar hijinks took place in a disputed 1604 election in the Borough of Lincoln where the defendants in a Star Chamber case were accused of considering 'howe and by what meanes they might wholie possesse themselves of the absolute government of the saide Cittie whereby they might have powre and opportunitie to oppresse and wronge the cittizens as they shold not like and favour'. The defendants allegedly violated due process in order to secure the election of John Becke. These allegations are unusual in that they suggest some social division between the rival factions. The custom in Lincoln had evidently been for the Mayor to select replacements for departed members of the common council, but Becke allegedly purged those of the council whom he did not favour, and replaced them with men who were considered to be 'mean and lesser'. Thus

---

[46] PRO, STAC 8/82/23.

[47] Ironically, this charter followed the charter of 1604 which had been sought as a means of eliminating the likelihood of election disputes implicit in the Elizabethan incorporation of 1559. A hotly contested election dispute ensued in the last years of Elizabeth's reign and, though mediated through the offices of the Privy Council, caused the Borough to seek a revised charter in 1598–9. It was finally sealed and delivered in 1604 (G. H. Martin, 'Doncaster Borough Charters', in the collection, *Doncaster, a Borough* (Doncaster, 1994), 20–1).

[48] *Carver, et al.* v. *Carleill et al.*, PRO, STAC 8/93/5.

fortified with a more compliant common (or outer) council, the larger of the town's two assemblies, and evidently already supported by most in the inner council, Becke and his allies allegedly 'then tooke theme selves to have an absolute powre and might to rule all things at their wills and pleasures'. They are said 'by false and synister cause . . . & conspiracie', and while some of the aldermen had absented themselves to go and see the King as he visited in York, to have purged more of their foes from office, replacing them with friends.[49] Though we do not have the outcome of this trial, it is worth noting that the defendants did not deny the accusations. Instead they claimed to have acted legally according to the powers vested in them by the City charter: an eloquent testimony to the close links between incorporation and oligarchy by the early seventeenth century.

Yet another case of a disputed and allegedly fraudulent election derives from Shrewsbury in 1587. Here the plaintiffs contrasted what they saw as heavy-handed tactics of the present with the view of the amicable and harmonious behaviour which they remembered in the recent past. They noted that traditionally all freemen had a free voice in elections, and all were welcome to use it as they wished, 'whereby love & amitie was norished, the peace and quiet government of the saide Towne p(re)served, and the good estate of the towne procured'. The dispute centred around the alleged efforts of twenty-five defendants to work through the night to secure the votes of certain candidates to fill an office of an alderman who had died hours before. By some accounts, in fact, the conspiring faction went to work even while he still drew breath. Those who would not be pressured to give their votes were allegedly threatened and intimidated in the hope of keeping them from the election meeting. Another alderman was allegedly bribed to quit his office and thus to create a second vacancy.

The election itself, held at the unusually early hour of seven in the morning in the guildhall, was restricted only to those whose votes could be counted upon. At the command of the defendants, the serjeant barred all others from the hall. Not surprisingly, the conspirators won the election, allegedly boasting after the event that 'in all thynges we comande, be it right or wrong, yea, though we were infidells'. In bringing suit against these alleged outrages, the plaintiffs wrapped themselves in what they saw as the cloak of tradition, being

---

[49] *Citizens of Lincoln* v. *Becke et al.*, PRO, STAC 8/121/12.

'bound by their burgesses othe to mayntayne & see mayntayned . . .
their aunrient composition'.[50] Disputes over allegedly corrupt elections were notably frequent in other towns as well in this era, consti-
tuting a virtual genre of court case all of its own.[51]

V

Returning for a moment to the wording of the Shrewsbury case
above, the reference to the burgesses' oath should neither be dismissed as a mere rhetorical flourish nor be allowed to pass without
comment. Allegations of oath violation are part and parcel of the
abuses which were seen to have been wreaked by the ruling elite on
townsmen of the day. The charge seems to have been used as a catch-
all for a wide variety of perceived transgressions, especially those
which subverted the common good for personal interest. The frequency of these allegations suggests both the seriousness with which
oaths of office were taken and the considerable variety of complaints
forthcoming at that time.

There can be little doubt about the gravity of the oath. Whether
sworn as part of the ceremony of becoming a freeman, or taken as an
essential element in the business of coming to office, oaths were
taken very seriously indeed. As Susan Brigden and Charles
Phythian-Adams have noted, the oath played a very vital role in
cementing the loyalty and identity of the individual to the larger
community of which, in traditional society, one thus became a part.[52]
It affirmed identity with the group or community—conjugal union,
household, guild, fraternity, freemanry, etc.—and signified the
moral and sacred obligation of loyalty and responsibility to its fellowship. Indeed, the passage from one stage of life, occupation, or
personal status to another had traditionally been marked by the
taking of oaths for this purpose. Its sacred character imposed a spiritual as well as moral and legal obligation to fulfil its terms. Failure to
honour it implied both sacrilege and perjury. And, though the ceremonial nature of the oath may have changed with the Reformation,
Reformers and Catholics alike viewed it with the same grave

---

[50] *Owen, et al., Aldermen of Shrewsbury* v. *Sherer, et al., Bailiffs of Shrewsbury*,
PRO, STAC 7/2/20.

[51] See e.g. the discussion in Hirst, *Representatives of the People?*, chap. 3.

[52] Phythian-Adams, 'Ceremony and the Citizen', in Clark and Slack (eds.), *Crisis
and Order in English Towns*, 57–85, esp. 59–62; and id., *Desolation of a City*, 138; Brigden, 'Religion and Social Obligation', 86–9; and id., *London and the Reformation*,
27, 141, 239.

regard. Not only, then, was it a salient feature of the traditional sense of community, but also one which survived without interruption or diminution into the Reformed era. To violate an oath was not only to commit a legal offence, but to violate a widely recognized and tradition-hallowed compact between an official and the community.

However legitimately an election may have been held, accession to office could not be considered complete or official until the oath had been administered. The rival faction of at least one town tried to block the accession to office of a duly elected candidate by preventing him from taking his oath.[53] Cases of compulsion to take oaths which were contrived or illegal are also recorded and were resisted by dissident townsmen. Two former mayors of Canterbury were accused in 1609 of adding onto the conventional burgesses' oath the promise not to bring suit against any other freeman. Their accuser saw this as precluding access to the King's courts.[54] A case embracing the same principle arose at Gloucester just a few years later.[55]

Allegations of oath-breaking, and thus violating trust to town and community, often came to the fore in local disputes. We see this allegation in the Shrewsbury dispute, and elsewhere as well. The Bristol Mayor of 1624, Abel Kitchen, was accused of granting a favourable loan of charitable funds to his own servant, against the spirit of two solemn oaths 'ministered to him upon the holy Evangelists according to the auncient & laudable customes'.[56] In a Hythe dispute of 1603 the jurat, magistrate, and former Mayor William Knight, having engaged in a long feud with the town Constable Richard Whyte, finally attacked Whyte physically. Whyte brought him to Star Chamber not only on charges of assault, but also on the charge that by his attack, Knight had violated his oath of office to keep the peace and observe the law.[57] Similar allegations come forth in the records from Newport (Isle of Wight),[58] Wallingford,[59] Doncaster,[60] Appleby,[61] Bridgwater,[62] and elsewhere in the same era. Given the frequency of its appearance, and the detailed explanation

---

[53] e.g. in Brecknock, 4 James I (PRO, STAC 8/304/25).
[54] *Denne* vs. *Paramore, et al.*, PRO, STAC 8/115/14.
[55] *Jones* v. *Caple*, 21 James I.
[56] *Attorney General* (Thomas Conventry) v. *Kitchen*, PRO, STAC 8/30/19.
[57] *Whyte* v. *Hooke, Hudson and Knight*, PRO, STAC 8/303/5, 2 James I.
[58] PRO, STAC 8/20/18 (1617).   [59] PRO, STAC 7/11/20 (35 Elizabeth).
[60] *Carver* v. *Carleill*, STAC 8/93/5, in the very opening statement of the plaintiff's bill.
[61] PRO, STAC 8/237/9 (temp. James I).   [62] PRO, STAC 8/161/2.

it often receives, allegations of oath-breaking must have had considerable significance for plaintiffs trying to impress those trying the case with the profundity and thoroughness of the alleged corruption.

If the allegation of oath-breaking served as a catch-all for a variety of perceived transgressions, perhaps the most common specific allegation made by dissident townsmen, aside from electoral abuses of one sort or another, concerned the misappropriation of funds and the corrupt management of corporate resources. It was also a charge more likely to be levied at a time when so many towns had come to control a much greater amount of rental and other properties, and at the time of such a wide-open market for lands and similar resources. Ironically, part of the tendency of local leaders to remain discreet about transactions involving corporate property stemmed from the frequency with which such lands had been concealed from the Crown following the Dissolutions.

As with Mayor Kitchen's alleged misappropriation of charitable funds in Bristol, it was frequently alleged, and no doubt often with good reason, that mayors and others in high borough office awarded leases on favourable terms to themselves or their associates, or dipped their own hands into the receipts for such properties. Ludlow provides a good example of a town where the accretion of corporate lands throughout the last two-thirds of the sixteenth century vastly improved the Corporation's fiscal position. Yet much of the very heated and prolonged troubles at Ludlow in the 1590s, presaged by a lawsuit in about 1577, revolved around allegations by those out of power that the ruling oligarchy had consistently let corporate lands on terms favourable to themselves and their associates.[63]

The ruling oligarchy of Wallingford even succeeded, in 1600, in issuing by-laws which restricted the lease or purchase of corporate lands to the mayor, aldermen, and burgesses (meaning, in this case, not the freemanry, but members of the outer council), though the rule did at least demand an open approval of these same officials in the Guildhall.[64] One of the grounds upon which the dissident freemen of Totnes sought to block the acquisition of a new charter by the oligarchic clique of the 1590s was that its members had shown

---

[63] Faraday, *Ludlow*, 36–7; P. Williams, 'Government and Politics in Ludlow', 282–94; PRO, E. 112/63/Eliz. 254, E. 134/39 & 40 Eliz./Mich. 37, E. 123/24/160, E. 123/25/10, E. 123/25/25, and E. 123/25/91.

[64] Berkshire County Record Office, MS W/AC 1/1, fo. 89ᵛ.

gross favouritism in the award of corporate leases and stock.[65] Dissident citizens of Lincoln[66] and of Beverley[67] echoed that allegation in the same era. Opponents of the ruling oligarchy in Abingdon accused its members, *inter alia*, of taking revenues and profits of the Corporation for their own uses, and of oppressing corporate tenants by rack-renting.[68] And in Gloucester, the Mayor was accused at the opening of James's reign of conspiring to obtain city lands which had been leased out as forfeit so that he himself could take them over.[69] Similar accusations were common in Winchester, especially in the decades from *c.*1590 to 1640.[70] They played a prominent part in the bitter controversies which plagued the boroughs of Warwick, Colchester, Chippenham, Malmesbury, and Newcastle-upon-Tyne in the same era.[71]

A somewhat oblique but telling indication of the extent of concern regarding such temptations may be found in the frequent efforts of borough councils to insist that all awarding of leases on corporate properties be done in the quasi-public scrutiny of full council meetings in the guildhall.[72] The Borough Assembly of Reading, for example, came to insist that all leases should be sealed openly in the Guildhall twice yearly. This was reaffirmed in 1554, with the proviso that the 'whole company' (i.e. the full council) should be present.[73] Even more complex by-laws governing the open award of leases on town lands were approved in Wallingford in 1600.[74] In yet a third Berkshire town a former Mayor of Windsor was accused in 1589 not only of concealing ecclesiastical lands from the

---

[65] PRO, STAC 5/21/6, Interrogatories to be administered to the deponents. (The plaintiff's bill itself has not survived.)

[66] *Citizens of Lincoln* v. *Becke, Hollingworth, et al.*, PRO, STAC 8/121/12, 2 James I.

[67] Lamburn, 'Politics and Religion in Beverley', 261.

[68] 'Corporation Minute Book', Abingdon, Berkshire County Record Office, MS D/EP 7/84, fo. 20ᵈ (20 July 1599).

[69] *Norton* v. *Machyn*, PRO, STAC 8/220/1, 1 and 2 James I.

[70] Rosen, 'Economic and Social Aspects of Winchester', 70.

[71] Hirst, *Representatives of the People?*, 52–6.

[72] e.g. in Reading as early as 36 Henry VIII and Beverley in 1610 as well as in the Wallingford example cited in n. 64 above. 'Black Book of Reading', Berkshire Record Office, MS R AC/1/1/1, 239 (and reaffirmed at regular intervals thereafter); Dennett (ed.), *Beverley Borough Records*, 46. (The earlier formulation in Beverley allowed the Mayor himself to have the collection of all rents and to be paid £5 for his pains: 1592 and 1596; ibid. 98.)

[73] The 'Black Book of Reading', Berkshire County Record Office, MS R AC/1/1/1, 239.

[74] 'Corporation Minute Book', Borough of Wallingford, Berkshire Record Office, MS W/AC 1/1, fo. 89ʳ ᵃⁿᵈ ᵛ.

Crown at Dissolution—at which fellow townsmen often winked—but of appropriating them to his own personal use: exactly the sort of abuse which both Crown and many freemen of individual boroughs tried to prevent.[75] A variation on this theme was to insist, as did the burgesses of Beverley in 1610, that the mayor should not receive rents himself, but rather this should be done openly in the Common Hall.[76]

Similar financial improprieties seem no less frequent even where the award of lands was not in question. In 1603 a former mayor of Banbury was accused in the Star Chamber of collecting the town's revenues, paying the fee farm out of them, and keeping the remainder for himself, all of course without accountability.[77] Mayor Kitchen of Bristol was alleged to have channelled £50 of charity funds to his servant in violation of the terms of the bequest, to have let corporate lands on the sly to his son-in-law at a rent below market value, and to have arranged for reduced subsidy assessments for himself and his friends.[78] Martin Bynon, Mayor of Carmarthen in 1609–10, found himself accused of taking waifs, strays, and estreats guaranteed by charter to the town for his own use instead. (Bynon was also accused of taking bribes in the same case.[79]) Others are alleged to have falsely arrested their political opponents and to have extorted money before letting them free,[80] or having allowed their friends to go free when arrested by authorities outside the town.[81]

vi

Abuses like these and objections to them might well have been forthcoming at any time in the history of English local government. Because we know of them largely through plaintiffs' bills in court cases, rather than by the decisions of those courts, they prove very difficult to quantify or evaluate in precise terms. Yet the frequency with which we do find them in the last decades of the sixteenth and

[75] This was William Simonds, former mayor of 'New Windsor', who allegedly took to his own use former lands of the Fraternity of the Holy Trinity in the same town; *Bagshawe* v. *Temple* (1589), PRO, E. 134/31 Eliz., Hil. 12.

[76] Dennett (ed.), *Beverley Borough Records*, 48.

[77] *Blynco* v. *Knight, et al.*, PRO, STAC 8/82/23.

[78] *Attorney General* v. *Kitchen*, PRO, STAC 8/30/19.

[79] PRO, STAC 8/20/14.

[80] Barnstaple, STAC 2/13/88–91; *Attorney General* v. *Marche, Mayor of Newport*, PRO, STAC 8/20/18 (1617).

[81] *Attorney General* v. *Willet, Mayor of Sudbury*, PRO, STAC 8/4/6 (1605); *Attorney General* v. *Marche*, STAC 8/20/18.

opening decades of the seventeenth centuries suggests that such corruption may have been particularly rife at this time and/or tolerance for it particularly low. In fact, both these explanations seem appropriate, and the frequency of such behaviour points up for us a turning point in the political values and outlook of English townspeople.

On the one hand stood those who appear to have held traditional civic virtues. They seem to have considered their officials as simply townsmen like themselves who came, as Cincinnatus from his plough and *primus inter pares* with themselves, to take their turn at civic responsibility. They recognized the virtues of steadily rising through the ranks of guild membership according to the *cursus honorum*. They expected their officials to recognize and serve the interests of the freemanry, if not necessarily the entire population, and certainly to be accountable for their actions. As a symbol of this solemn responsibility they held the oath of office as a sacred affirmation. When contemporary townsmen referred, as did, for example, some of those from Exeter in a Star Chamber suit of the sixteenth century, to 'the olde lib[er]ties customes and rules used and had for the welle peas and good gov[ern]mett of the same cities', these are the values they had in mind. Their outlook may perhaps have been coloured by a nostalgia for a past time which may or may not have existed, but it seemed vivid enough to those who shared it.[82]

On the other hand stood those who appear to have valued efficiency of administration over breadth of input; the preservation of office in the hands of those who were familiar, like-minded, and loyal; and the accretion of local governing authority as an end, at least partly, in itself. Despite what seems like a blossoming of 'a culture of corruption' in some boroughs as in some offices of central government at this time, at least some who espoused these newer values, after their own fashion, valued the common good every bit as dearly as their predecessors had done.

Many of those favouring a more oligarchic approach had a vision of civic government informed by a doctrinal rationale, one which they held sacred themselves and wished to enforce on their fellows. The quest for 'godly rule' was also part of the fall-out of the Reformation on the provincial urban scene. Though its nature and incidence is too familiar to warrant much reiteration here, it is well to keep in mind the disputes in such towns as Dorchester, where the

---

[82] *Mayor and Bailiffs of Exeter* v. *Stodder et al.*, PRO, STAC 2/26/393.

ascendancy of oligarchy rode on the shoulders of a zealous Puritanism.[83] To men of this persuasion, the John Whites of the day, only a firm grip on the mayor's mace and aldermanic bench by the chosen few could establish God's Kingdom on earth; only civic control of parish pulpits and endowed lectureships could point the way.[84] The fact that they seem often to have gone about establishing their campaigns of moral reform in ways which others considered illegitimate and corrupt, thus fatally dividing the very communities they wished to unite, forms one of the more fascinating paradoxes of the era.[85]

vii

The perceived division between these two approaches begs one more question. We must at least ask whether or to what extent it may have conformed to social cleavages in the contemporary urban milieu. Notwithstanding the evidence for the strong social fabric and broad civic involvement which has been noted for London,[86] there can be little doubt that social cleavages existed, and grew more pronounced, in most of the middling and larger provincial towns in these years. It also seems probable that the degree of this polarization and the rapidity of its attainment seems roughly coincident with the size of the population. In addition, the weight of evidence under consideration here underscores the notion that, as was also the case in London,[87] the demands placed upon them by the Crown and Parliament, and by the circumstances of the age (including the wealth required for holding local office), imparted a greater solidarity to the ruling elites of many of the more important towns than ever before.[88] But despite the obvious social divisions on hand by this time in most substantial urban communities, it has not yet been possible to establish that the most active proponents of the more aggressive oligarchic rule necessarily differed markedly in social or economic

---

[83] Underdown, *Fire from Heaven.*

[84] See esp. Seaver, *Puritan Lectureships*, esp. chap. 4; Collinson, *Birthpangs*, chap. 2; and id., *Religion of Protestants*, chap. 4.

[85] Assigning credit where credit is due, some have come to know this as 'Collinson's Paradox', from Collinson, *Birthpangs*, 31–2.

[86] See e.g. Valerie Pearl, 'Change and Stability in Seventeenth-Century London', *London Journal*, 5 (1979), 3–34; Rappaport, *Worlds Within Worlds*; J. P. Boulton, *Neighbourhood and Society: A London Suburb in the Seventeenth Century* (Cambridge, 1987).

[87] Archer, *Pursuit of Stability*, chaps. 1–4.

[88] See e.g. MacCaffrey, *Exeter,* chap. 6; Palliser, *Tudor York*, chap. 4 and esp. 92–3; Battley, 'Elite and Community', chaps. 5–6; Sacks, *The Widening Gate,* chap. 3.

terms from its most active opponents. In at least some of the cases where status and occupation can be determined, leading advocates of both positions seem to have come from the freemanry. Proponents of both sides seem to have shared a stake in the harmony and tranquillity of the community.[89]

[89] e.g. Underdown, *Fire from Heaven*, chaps. 1–4, where supporters both of Matthew Chubb and John White of Dorchester were of roughly the same social status; and Tittler, *Architecture and Power*, 58–9, where supporters of both the faction in power and the dissident followers of Nicholas Curie also shared the same approximate social and occupational status.

Oligarchic Rule

i

Now that we understand something about the origins and development of oligarchic tendencies in urban government in the context of the time, we must step back and examine their implications, both for local government as a whole and for the specific offices therein. Thus far oligarchy, at least in the benign, contemporary sense of 'rule by the few', has been presented as an increasingly characteristic governing format, especially in the middling and larger towns, between the Dissolutions and the Civil War. Yet the oligarchic ethos consists of more than a tendency towards a rule by the few. Without wishing to press the argument to the point of anachronism in the sixteenth and early seventeenth centuries, it implies a more regular, bureaucratic, and impersonal form of governance which smacks of something more modern and, to our eyes, more familiar. In the effort to observe these characteristics as salient features of this era, we need to examine this more closely. We must ask about the practical implications of oligarchic rule, and of the prevalent ethos of which it formed a part. What additional characteristics of government and administration may we associate with it and, thus, with the era at hand? In what ways does it depart from prevalent characteristics of earlier times?

Answers to these questions coalesce around two themes which will form the heart of this chapter. The first is the notion that the forms, procedures, and mechanisms of administration came now to be more formalized and standardized. This is especially clear in the way in which administrative activities and decisions came to be better supported by record-keeping than ever before. The second is the point that the offices of local government proliferated in number and (in some cases) grew in both stature and authority. This proliferation appears particularly in the low and middle ranking offices which remained accessible to a relatively wide spectrum of the free-

manry. At the same time, however, their incumbents remained far from the inner circle of local government. The offices which really counted became less accessible to the freemanry at large; those who held them sometimes moved closer politically to the regional gentry rather than to their fellow townsmen and women.

ii

The most obvious place to begin the first of these discussions is with the records themselves. They inform us not only in the conventional and literal sense, but also by the form and manner in which they were kept. It is striking how many important classes of borough records came to be kept in this era for the first time, or kept more regularly than before. A great many now moved in the language of their expression from Latin to English, and in their form from parchment to the more easily bound paper.

One may well be tempted to see this merely as an inevitable consequence of 'modernization' in the form and structure of town government. After all, some advances in record-keeping may be traced in at least some towns well back in time, and the sequence of such changes seems broadly similar from one town to the next.[1] Yet there is no compelling reason for us to accept these changes as natural, necessary, or inevitable: they came about for particular reasons and at particular times. Change in the nature of records always reflects change in those who kept them or in the circumstances of their keeping. As that is very central to our purpose, it pays to probe this more carefully. In fact, there seem to be several reasons for the frequency of these changes at this time.

The broadest explanation for this may lie in a recognition increasingly shared by the 'ruling sort' in the mid-century era: that government had to be carried out not so much in the expectation of providential intervention as in the context of cause and effect relationships observed accurately and over time. Changes in the prevailing religious belief which de-emphasized the value of the miraculous and intercessionary events in favour of a more rationalistic approach to causation certainly encouraged this view. The recognizably modern sense of History which emerged in consequence depended on an accurate and detailed comprehension of events, recorded in a faithful and methodical manner.

---

[1] See e.g. the list of important early borough record books in Ralph Flenley (ed.), *Six Town Chronicles of England* (Oxford, 1911), 11–14.

We see this new way of thinking in the increasing desires of country gentry and aristocracy to place a greater value on literacy and to
keep informed of current affairs. We see it in the proliferation of
offices in central government, especially from about the reign of
Henry VIII, and in the more prominent role of high government
officials with humanist training. The background of men like More,
Wolsey, and Cromwell in Henry's reign and Winchester, Cecil, and
Bacon later on, and of courtly intellectuals from Starkey and Morri-
son to Ascham, Cheke, and Sir Thomas Smith, brought a new sensi-
tivity to written communication and record-keeping in government.
The virtual 'renaissance of good record keeping' characteristic of
that time, to quote Smith Fussner, led very shortly to the point where
the 'argument from records' comprised the 'characteristic form of
English political debate'.[2]

The various courts and councils at the centre created models of
administrative practice which percolated down to the local level and
to the governing officials of individual towns. In its most advanced
form, the 'modernization' of record-keeping in central government
even extended to the introduction and use of printed forms for the
conduct of routine business in a number of administrative areas, a
development which has been traced to the 1530s.[3]

Though more difficult to document, there is also a sense in this era
that, metaphorically speaking, time began to move more quickly and
that contemporary events needed to be known more directly after
they occurred. This meant that events had to be recorded directly
and faithfully. Books and lesser publications treating contemporary
events grew more common. The readership which demanded and
read them grew steadily. News from abroad became more abundant
too, avidly received by a better-informed readership. Once common
only in London and the university towns at the beginning of the century, booksellers now became widespread, serving even middle-
rank provincial centres by the turn of the seventeenth century. By
that time, too, news itself, in the form of newsletters, personal correspondence, and reports from travellers, came to be disseminated
more widely and quickly to most parts of the realm, and especially to

---

[2] F. Smith Fussner, *The Historical Revolution: English Historical Writing and
Thought, 1580–1640* (1962), 83.

[3] See esp. e.g. Arthur J. Slavin, 'The Tudor Revolution and the Devil's Art:
Bishop Bonner's Printed Forms', in DeLloyd Guth and John W. McKenna (eds.),
Tudor Rule and Revolution: Essays for G. R. Elton from his American Friends (Cam-
bridge, 1982), 3–25.

and within urban areas. Foreign affairs (particularly wars involving England), great plagues, fires and other natural calamities, news of Parliament, and other current events made the rounds with increasing alacrity, until the great explosion of such dissemination after the outbreak of the Civil War itself.[4]

The political culture of English towns moved along in step with these developments. Urban officials came more than ever at this time to see the value of the written record both as a strong defence of local liberties and as an asset in the conduct of local affairs.[5] Much more prosaically, they also experienced the high cost of gaining access to records concerning their own rights and liberties which lay in central government archives. Both access to these records and transcription of them by paid clerks became more frequently necessary in this more litigious time, and more expensive with the years when they had to be obtained from elsewhere on an ad hoc basis.[6]

Though town governments rarely if ever went as far as to use standardized forms themselves, they could hardly have failed to notice these new and standardized means for record-keeping which were passed on down from Westminster. Writs of election or writs from the various central courts were of course well known by this time. They were soon joined by myriad new forms which came to be employed far more frequently and routinely at the borough or parish level. The required keeping of parish registers from 1538 and the replacement of enrolled customs accounts by the more regularly paradigmatic forms known as 'port books' in 1565 are but two examples of the record-keeping imperative being handed down from above. They are mirrored in London and some other provincial towns in, for example, bills of mortality by which local authorities could keep track of plague and other epidemic diseases,[7] and by many other forms of local records employed for purposes of

---

[4] In addition to the source in the previous note, my understanding of this issue has benefited greatly from conversations with Daniel Woolf about the spread of news in a general sense and from Stephen Porter about the spread of news concerning such events as fires and warfare. I am grateful to them both.

[5] These themes are developed more fully in a very extensive literature including e.g. Peter Burke, *The Renaissance Sense of the Past* (1969); F. J. Levy, *Tudor Historical Thought* (San Marino, Calif., 1967); Levy, 'How Information Spread among the Gentry, 1550–1640', *Journal of British Studies*, 21/2 (Spring 1982), 11–34; Levy, 'Hayward, Daniel, and the Beginnings of Public History in England', *Huntington Library Quarterly*, 50 (1987), 1–34; and D. R. Woolf, *The Idea of History in Early Stuart England* (Toronto, 1990).

[6] Fussner, *Historical Revolution*, 86–7.

[7] Paul Slack, *The Impact of Plague in Tudor and Stuart England* (1985), 113.

commerce, shipping and trade, freeman registration, apprenticeship, taxation, military musters, etc.

Where some of these sorts of records had previously been kept
together in the form of all-purpose court books or assembly minutes,
they came now increasingly to be kept as separate records, in books
of their own and sometimes as the result of a distinct administrative
activity. In this they closely approximated the manner in which, for
example, the various classes of state papers emerged after 1547
from that more general group of records eventually published as the
Letters and Papers of Henry VIII. At both local and national levels
of administration, the idea of recording information at regular intervals, and in standardized forms, grew stronger in the era at hand.

The contemporary emphasis on binding records in convenient
and accessible forms, and on storing them in a regular and secure
manner, provides important corollaries to this imperative. Records
needed to be close at hand so that they could conveniently be
employed in a multitude of ways: to establish and defend claims of
local authority, to verify transactions regarding such matters as registration of apprentices and freemen or the state of town lands and
leases, to verify local by-laws, and to perpetuate the record of
administrative acts and decisions covering the whole spectrum of
local administration.

Such concern for record-keeping did not always begin precisely
with the establishment of what we have called oligarchic rule. On the
one hand, of course, some records were well and regularly kept at
earlier times. On the other hand, constitutional milestones did not
always promptly produce better records, or greater care in their
keeping. In the first few years of incorporated government in Boston
(1545 ff.), for example, mayors simply took the minutes of council
proceedings home with them at the end of each session.[8] But on the
whole (and even, after a few years, in Boston) charters, assembly
minutes, leases, by-laws, apprenticeship indentures, freeman's
admissions, and the like came in this age to be kept with particular
care. Charters and analogous instruments of government especially
so: they were kept under lock and key[9] and often read ceremonially
on certain special days of the year.[10] And of course we see a parallel

---

[8] Bailey (ed.), *Minutes of Boston*, i. 7.

[9] Margaret Statham, 'The Guildhall, Bury St Edmunds', *Proceedings of the Suffolk Institute of Archeology*, 31 (1970), 131; Morpeth Borough Manuscripts, Historical Manuscripts Commission, *Sixth Report* (1877), appendix, 537.

[10] e.g. four times a year in Boston; Bailey (ed.), *Minutes of Boston*, i. 25.

development at the parish level, in which individual parishes were not only required to keep registers from 1538, but also to keep them safe in purpose-built chests.[11]

In general it may also be said that record-keeping became more formalized when borough government itself became more formalized, and this happened with particular emphasis at the point of incorporation. Some towns, including Boston, Tewkesbury, Abingdon, Kendal, Leominster, and Poole, had enjoyed very little self-government prior to incorporation, and thus they had little need for most classes of borough records. In communities like this, the essential civic records — e.g. the council minute book or borough assembly book, the treasurer's or chamberlains' accounts — really only began with incorporation.[12] (In some cases, with the process of acquiring a charter well under way, towns anticipated its receipt by initiating new institutions and, hence, new classes of town records, a year or so before a charter had formally been secured. The Borough of Marlborough, for example, began to keep formal chamberlains' accounts in 1574, and a mayor's court (and thus a court book) from 1575, though its incorporation did not come through till 1576.[13]) Needless to say, where there had been a substantial tradition of local governing institutions prior to incorporation we will find many classes of records already in progress, though even here new formulations of governing authority often led to marked changes in types and means of record-keeping.[14]

In other communities an earlier, less formal or efficient way of keeping records changed in the period at hand. In Hereford, this meant that the tradition of keeping the records of each year's mayoralty in a separate sheepskin bag, pulled shut with a leather-thong

---

[11] Kumin, *Shaping of a Community*, 243.

[12] e.g. 'The Minute Book of the Boston Town Assembly', uncatalogued, Boston Borough Archives; the 'Tewkesbury Minute and Order Book no. 1, 1575–1624', Gloucestershire County Record Office, MS TBR/A1/1; Abingdon 'Corporation Order Book' and Abingdon Borough Chamberlains' Accounts, Berkshire County Record Office, Reading, MSS D/EP 7/84 and D/EP 7/83; Ferguson (ed.), *A Boke off Recorde*, 22–39; Poole 'Old Record Book' ('The Great Boke') 1568–78, Poole Borough Archives, Poole Civic Centre, MS 26(4).

[13] Marlborough Borough Records, Wiltshire County Record Office, MS G22/1/205/2.

[14] The records of the Borough of Beverley, for example, make Beverley one of the most completely documented of all boroughs in the late medieval period, and many classes of records were already being kept prior to incorporation in 1575. Yet a new Order Book, known as 'The Small Order Book', began in that year to record Borough ordinances, monetary receipts, freemen's admissions, and the like; Humberside County Record Office, Beverley Borough Records, MS BC II/4.

drawstring, gave way to bound volumes.[15] In Boston it meant that the practice whereby 'Henry Ffox mayor . . . toke home with hym all his pamplets of Assemblies an so [they] ar lost and not registered'[16] came to be seen as counter-productive to the purposes of record-keeping in the first place.

In many towns it meant that the keeping of records in the form of rolls proved too cumbersome to store and retrieve, and led to keeping them in books instead. In some of these instances the form of records in rolls carried over from the days of manorial administration, whence they began as the conventional court roll. In Taunton, for example, the transition from manorial to borough jurisdiction of the local courts may be followed not only in the substance of what was recorded, but also in the manner in which such recording took place. Successive bishops of Winchester, former lords of Taunton, kept its borough records in the form of rolls to begin with, but by 1533 the accretion of some local governing powers enabled the townsmen to keep copies of registered transactions. This they did in books. When the Borough Court came under local jurisdiction (around 1564) its records were kept exclusively in book form, and by 1578 all the Borough's records were kept in books rather than rolls. Along with that change in format, the materials and language changed as well. Parchment often gave way to paper, which was less expensive, more easily cut to standard size, and more easily bound. Latin frequently yielded to English at the same time.[17]

This last point deserves some explanation. Any thorough familiarity with local records of this type makes clear the transition, especially from the mid-sixteenth century, from Latin to English as the principal and often the sole language of record-keeping. This mirrors changes apparent in the records of numerous courts and councils of the central government as well. By the end of the sixteenth century even some borough charters, which were of course issued in Latin, had begun to be translated into English for the ease of those who could not read Latin.

This should probably not be taken as a means of facilitating access to records by that increasingly broad swath of the freemanry who

---

[15] David Klausner (ed.), *REED: Herefordshire and Worcestershire* (Toronto, 1990), 22.

[16] J. F. Bailey (ed.), *Minutes of Boston*, i. 7 (entry for 1551).

[17] Exemplified by Taunton, where these trends are noted in R. G. H. Whitty, *The Court of Taunton in the Sixteenth and Seventeenth Centuries* (Taunton, 1934), 15–16.

could read English rather than Latin, though this could sometimes have been the effect. It seems instead to mark a changeover from administration by a manorial steward or bailiff, for whom Latin was a presumed accomplishment, to government by townsmen themselves, for whom it was not.

Though he was atypical in his own city of Chester, where he rose to be the most powerful and influential citizen of his day, Henry Gee typifies the sort of urban official of this age for whom record-keeping took on particular importance. Aside from serving as Mayor for two terms during the 1530s and steering a substantial amount of moral and other legislation through the City government, Gee took a sustained and avid interest in the City's record-keeping. He considered it necessary to keep regular record of the meetings of the City Assembly, which he caused to proceed in the form of Assembly Books during his first mayoralty in 1533. He did the same with the City's petitions to the various offices of the central government at Westminster, which he caused to be kept together systematically a few months later. The Assembly Books deal chiefly with recording the actions and decisions of the City council, including its orders in full, the resolution of disputes, and other such matters. But this was the first volume of Assembly Books to be kept, and Gee had the foresight to see such records as a central source of reference and authority for the future governance of the City. He thus had the clerk copy into the first several dozen pages such matters of record as the oaths of the mayor and other officials, a rental of City property, the City boundaries, and a record of all the mayors to have served in Chester so far as could be determined—a list which eventually extended back to the 1320s. In so doing, Gee obliged his clerk to draw on a considerable number of earlier documents. Perhaps these were in poor condition and needed to be copied for the preservation of their contents. It is doubtful if many of those survived into the modern era, making Gee's First Assembly Book especially valuable both in past times and our own.[18]

The tone having been thus set for the City in Gee's two terms as Mayor (1533–4 and 1539–40), the creation of new classes of records

---

[18] Chester City Archives, Assembly Books, MS AB/1 and Assembly Petitions (1533–), MS A/P/1– . See also *Archives and Records of the City of Chester: A Guide to the Collections in the Chester City Record Office* (1985); A. D. Mills, 'Chester Ceremonial: Re-creation and Recreation in an English "Medieval" Town', *Urban History Yearbook*, 18 (1991), 5; L. M. Clopper (ed.), *REED: Chester* (Toronto, 1979), pp. xi–xii and xiv.

followed at close intervals during the remainder of the century: Mayors' Letters from 1546, Mayors' Military Papers from 1550 (during the mayoralty of Henry's son Edmund, who died in office in that year), and the Corporation Lease Book from 1574.

Gee's influence on such concerns for record-keeping seems to have extended not only to his son Edmund, but also to his son-in-law, Henry Hardware, who served as Mayor in 1559–60 and 1575–6. Especially in his second term, Hardware caused the most important records of the City to be copied into a cartulary for purposes of preservation and easy reference.[19] With actions such as these, Chester rapidly became one of the best-documented urban corporations of its time. Thanks to the chance survival of most of its documents from this era, if not earlier, it remains one of the most thoroughly recorded to the present day. Though we rarely know their names, many contemporary borough leaders shared Gee's concern for records. Their accomplishments still serve us.

An integral part of this new emphasis on record-keeping concerns the question of storage. If Henry Fox of Boston and his successors were not to be permitted to take minutes of the Borough Assembly home with them, thence to carry them from their home to the council chamber of the Guildhall at each meeting, those minutes would have to have a place of their own. In many towns with older traditions of self-government this had long since ceased to be a problem, but as many more towns gained in self-governing powers in these years, the decision of where and how to keep such valued possessions came up in many towns anew or for the first time.

The contemporary formula 'in bag or box sealed or in chest locked' pretty well describes the answer to this quandary of the times, all the more so if we add the point that such bags, boxes, and especially chests came to lie in the town hall or guildhall. Many such buildings came now to have purpose-built muniment rooms which could be locked as further insurance against the sundry perils which could—and sometimes did—befall such important documents.[20] After all, if the charters and seals conveyed the legitimacy of local government, they were not only important to keep secure against

---

[19] Simon Harrison, Anette M. Kennett, Elizabeth J. Shepherd, and Eileen Willshaw, *Tudor Chester: A Study of Chester in the Reigns of the Tudor Monarchs, 1485–1603* (Chester, 1986), 14.

[20] *The Records of the Corporation of Leicester* (Leicester, 1956), 3; Tittler, *Architecture and Power*, 41–2, 89.

the prospect of legal challenge, but also important to keep from falling into the wrong hands.

Something of this may be observed in the conflict which ensued in the reign of James I between the Earl of Suffolk, Lord of the Town and Manor of Oswestry, and the inhabitants of that town. Apparently concerned that the Earl's steward meant to abrogate the townsmen's rights, the Earl's opponents placed a high priority on securing the safety of their charters and seals. These were customarily kept in the 'Election House' (not a house at all, but rather a chamber in the Town Hall) where they were stored in a stout chest with three locks and three keys. This conventional arrangement meant that the chest could only be unlocked if all three keys were available, each being held by a different high town official. To make the charters even more resistant to theft or tampering, local custom held that these three key-holders could only open the chest after all the freemen had been summoned by the ringing of a town bell to witness the event. Such precautions may strike us as excessive, but the fact that so many other towns did something similar suggests that perhaps it was not.

Despite these elaborate precautions, it was alleged that on 7 August 1610, the Earl's steward, a man named Lloyd, came to the Election House with a smith to break open the chest and tamper with the charters and seal or confiscate them altogether. The townsmen got wind of this, ran to the hall, and caught Lloyd in the act. They then sequestered the charters and seal elsewhere for safekeeping, and locked Lloyd and the smith in the room.[21] Concerns for the safekeeping of records were rarely reinforced in quite such a dramatic fashion as this, but in general terms at least the experience of Oswestry's burgesses was by no means unique.

Though these developments in the keeping and care of borough records offer a strong indication of contemporary administrative changes, it remains difficult to be precise about administrative procedures employed at this time. Town officials exhibited considerable and probably growing concern for procedural issues, with the emphasis again on regularity and efficiency. Some mayors and even members of town councils began to keep what amounted to regular office hours,[22] though the common injunction against mayors

---

[21] *Lloyd* v. *Morrys*, PRO, STAC 8/198/27 (7 James I).

[22] For example, in Bristol, 1560, Maureen Stanford (ed.), *The Ordinances of Bristol, 1506–1598*, Bristol Record Society, 41 (1990).

leaving the town, on business or otherwise,[23] during their year in office may not have been new.

One sign of the growing importance of proper procedures is the frequency with which we find oaths of office recorded in town assembly books like that begun by Chester's Mayor Gee. Another is the frequent recording of by-laws regarding the duties and conduct of borough officials, accompanied by notice of fines which were to be assessed in default of due performance. Still another lies in the often detailed and elaborate instructions for the changeover in personnel from one mayoral year to the next. These rites of succession entailed not only the intricate and ceremonial business of handing mayoral office from the incumbent to his successor, but also the year-end accounting of the town chamberlains or treasurers which often ensued at the same time. This included strict accountability for funds, of course, but also, especially by the early seventeenth century, it also entailed a handing over of and accounting for the corporate plate, armaments, leather fire buckets, and other important possessions.

iii

The second underlying theme to this discussion of the oligarchic town 'in action' concerns the manner in which the leading officers of the late Tudor and early Stuart town came to operate, at least in their official capacities, on a plane further removed from their fellows than ever before. That is not merely to say that important and powerful families rose to the pinnacle of local society, for in communities of any size or social complexity this had tended to be true for some time. It is also to say that such leading families now found the stakes of power very considerably enhanced, that the political distance between them and their fellow townsmen grew considerably, and that access to their ranks became more difficult. The earlier sense of working for the common good may often have remained, and the intricate weave of kinship and patronal ties no doubt remained as well. But the circumstances of this post-Reformation era frequently allowed officials of many towns to enjoy both greater hegemony and fewer restraints than their predecessors.

For this there are two essential and closely related explanations. First there was the vast social and economic legislation of the

[23] For example, the mayors of Abingdon, Berkshire Record Office, MS D/EP 7/84, fo. 6 (1559).

Tudors, and the necessity of placing responsibility for enforcement on the shoulders of those 'small knots of reliable men' who came to govern the towns of the realm. Secondly, a considerable number of functions which had been performed by other authorities prior to the Reformation—ecclesiastical authorities, guilds and fraternities, manorial lords, and the like—now came to rest on the shoulders of such officials as mayors and aldermen. Both phenomena caused the offices of borough government to grow in number and in force. (In a parallel development, of course, the obligations placed on the shoulders of parish officials expanded and grew much more secular in similar circumstances).

This proliferation extended to all levels. At the bottom of the scale we find a great many more posts which would fall today under the heading of municipal employees. Undoubtedly these men were residents, but not necessarily freemen; they would rarely have much education or social standing. Though their numbers increased, their authority or standing did not. The expansion of such posts merely reflected the growing breadth of civic jurisdiction as effected by parliamentary statute, occasionally by royal proclamation, and certainly by local by-law. A closer look at some of these offices will illustrate the point.

Positions of this sort fall roughly into several categories. One such group, occasionally embracing responsibilities accorded the parish as well, dealt with the maintenance of the market and other civic works: sweepers, scavengers, paviours, hall- and market-keepers, and similar jobs. The number of these positions increased with the addition of systems for street lighting and water supply, with schemes for paving, with the common proliferation in this era of town halls, market halls, gaol cells and prisons, work houses or bridewells, almshouses, schoolhouses, quays and customs houses, armouries, and animal pounds, all of which needed care and maintenance. Even by 1559 such a modest community as Boston found the need to add an official called the Town Husband, essentially a public works foreman, to supervise the care and feeding of its civic property.[24] It is impossible to comment further on the rate of growth amongst members of this group except to record the subjective impression, garnered from such documents as chamberlains' accounts which record stipendiary expenses, that it seems to have been considerable in the era at hand.

[24] J. F. Bailey (ed.), *Minutes of Boston*, i. 38a.

A step up from that lot would bring us to ale-conners and others concerned with the inspection of commercial goods and foodstuffs, constables, serjeants-at-mace, watchmen, waits, and toll gatherers. These were men of greater respectability: usually junior members of the freemanry or freemen of lesser occupational status and occasionally journeymen. They were remunerated by fees and/or annual payments from the borough itself. In contrast to members of the first group, most of them had the opportunity to climb at least part way up through the traditional sequence of offices—the *cursus honorum*—which could lead to major office later on.

Those involved in ceremonial events, including sword and mace-bearers, waits and other musicians, and especially the serjeant-at-mace, took on new importance and greater numbers as the civic ceremony of the town grew to replace the ceremony which had once revolved around the church. Though this begs a theme which has been reserved for the discussion of civic ceremonial in Part IV below, it seems reasonable here at least to look more closely at the growing role of the serjeant, which so closely paralleled that of the mayor whom he chiefly served.

Stripped to his most essential role, the serjeant was simply the mayor's personal aide, dressed up in ceremonial guise to add lustre to the mayoral presence. Yet he also had duties which would be performed in other times and places by the town crier, the gaoler, the court bailiff, the policeman, and the caretaker. The Serjeant of Reading had no cause to wonder about his job description. In the contemporary spirit of writing down the duties of officials of this era, his tasks were laid out in Edward's reign in the great minute book known as the 'Black Book of Reading'.[25] By these rules he was to attend the mayor at all times unless excused, bearing the mace before him on Sundays, holidays, and other public occasions. He was also to attend any meeting in the Guildhall, and to keep that building clean and ready for meetings at all times. He was to serve the Borough Court by summoning it to session, attaching suspects to come before it, proclaiming news of its decisions, and conducting the guilty to gaol. Many serjeants received a per annum stipend, though this could hardly be called a salary in the modern sense, but the bulk of their reward derived from the collection of fees for their work. In Reading this entitled the Serjeant to 6*d.* for everyone he conveyed to gaol, and 8*d.* for each person he attached for debt. There were

---

[25] Berkshire Record Office, MS R AC/1/1, pp. 278–9 (5–6 Edward VI).

probably a number of other fees which were not recorded at the time.[26]

Additional employees or minor officials were responsible for various aspects of security, including constables, waits, watchmen, gaolers, and the like. These posts grew too, as the concern for public order came to be reflected in legislation and by-laws throughout the period.

An increasing number of 'employees' were professionals like schoolmasters and clergymen. Though their social status was of course higher, they shared with the 'meaner sort' of civic employees a removal from the *cursus honorum* which led to more conventional civic office. They seem less likely to have been born in the town in which they served than others (though a great many freemen of any town in this era had also been born elsewhere), and in many respects they seem more in the town than of it.

Rounding out the governing structure of most provincial towns were those principal officials, including members of what was in almost all instances a two-council quasi-legislative or advisory structure, the (usually two) officials responsible for finances (variously styled chamberlains, treasurers, or bailiffs, depending on the derivation of the office and local tradition), both the town clerk and the recorder, and the mayor himself. Finally, if we wish to consider them town officials, we also have a proliferation of high stewards, who were non-resident and freemen only in an honorary sense. Selected by the ruling elite from the ranks of gentlemen, aristocrats, courtiers, and/or high government officials, the high steward represented the town's interests in the shire and at court.

Not until we arrive at these upper echelons of the governing structure can we see the clearest evidence for expansion in authority as well as in numbers. Here especially the tenor of the times placed new burdens, investing in such officials a degree of authority and responsibility which in most cases had rarely if ever been reached before. A closer look at some of these offices demonstrates this clearly.

The role of the town clerk, charged first and sometimes only with the keeping of records, grew in step with the growing concern for documentation and the proliferation of written records. The clerk's duties, authority, and social status varied widely with both time and place, though the office itself was not new on the scene in the sixteenth century. Officials bearing that title may be found even

---

[26] Ibid. 279.

in the early thirteenth century (clerks of guilds, a presumed antecedent, even earlier) and many towns had enjoyed the services of such an official long before the Reformation.[27] Colchester's office of the Town Clerk has been traced to an official who served the local reeve in the thirteenth century. The prestige of the office grew to the point where an incumbent sat in Parliament for the town by the fourteenth century.[28] Though still primarily under the authority of the Archbishop of York, Beverley's self-governing powers created need for a 'common clerk of the Guildhall', which sounds like a close ancestral form, by 1367.[29] Bridgwater employed a full-fledged town clerk from a few decades later,[30] and Hull considered its Common Clerk sufficiently important by the 1460s even to provide the incumbent a rent-free accommodation.[31] Yet Kendal, for example, like many towns first empowered and incorporated in the post-Reformation era, did not have a clerk until the year of its charter in 1575,[32] and Stafford did not have one in a formal sense until 1625.[33] Thus, while many pre-Reformation towns employed town clerks, some towns did not do so until the sixteenth or seventeenth century.

Whatever the antiquity of the office in a particular town, there can be little doubt that town clerks grew in number, authority, and social status in the period at hand. In the early years of the office, it appears that the clerk was simply a literate individual, not necessarily a freeman and not necessarily trained formally in the law.[34] His duties seem likely to have been construed very narrowly, consisting mainly in enrolling apprenticeships, leases, by-laws, and other pronouncements of local authorities, and of keeping the town records in an orderly and secure manner. As late as 1615 the small town of Melton Mowbray, governed largely by a trust rather than by a charter of incorporation, described the clerk's duties as nothing more than 'to keep the town book for the registering of accounts and other business'.[35]

[27] Reynolds, *English Medieval Towns*, 120–1.

[28] Stephen Alsford, 'The Town Clerks of Medieval Colchester', *Essex Archeology and History*, 24 (1993), 125.

[29] Historical Manuscripts Commission, 'Report on the Manuscripts of the Corporation of Beverley' (1900), 44.

[30] T. B. Dilks (ed.), *Bridgwater Borough Archives, 1377–1399*, Somerset Record Society, 53 (1938), items 383 and 476.

[31] Horrox (ed.), *Selected Rentals and Accounts of Hull*, 107 and 177 n. 89.

[32] Ferguson (ed.), *A Boke off Recorde*, 22–39.

[33] Adey, 'History of Stafford', 92.

[34] C. W. Brooks, *Pettyfoggers and Vipers of the Commonwealth: The 'Lower Branch' of the Legal Profession in Early Modern England* (Cambridge, 1986), 211–12.

[35] Pockley, 'Early History of Melton Mowbray', 134.

Yet well before that time in the more substantial (and, for the most part, more autonomous) towns, the town clerk was usually a local attorney, freeman ex officio, required to advise the mayor on legal matters. Colchester clerks were termed gentlemen in the fifteenth century, and usually had legal training by that time.[36] The Town Clerk of the City of Worcester even had an assistant clerk by 1595. Of the five town clerks of Worcester in the sixteenth century two came from prominent local families (three being born elsewhere and made freemen). All married well, and one went on to be a JP and a recognized member of the county gentry.[37]

Aside from the fact that the City of Oxford hosted a university, its population level, economic functions, and social complexity as a regional centre were roughly analogous to Worcester's. Its clerk's office also exhibited a similar pattern. The clerk's office in Oxford may be traced back well before the Reformation, and by the mid-sixteenth century he had become an official of considerable substance. Oxford City Clerks received the use of an office under the council chamber in the Guildhall, a wide variety of fees for their duties, and an annual stipend. Increasingly they were drawn from the ranks of the barristers. Though this was not the unexcepted rule for all town clerks by *c.*1600, it was increasingly common in towns of middling size or complexity and came to be the general rule in the greater provincial centres.[38] Oxford's clerks even travelled out of town on the business of the Corporation—which the Mayor was ordinarily enjoined from doing—while, by the end of the sixteenth century, deputies were employed to handle the more routine business of keeping records. By the early Stuart era the Oxford City Clerk had become a powerful local official. It seems reasonable to assume that at least in towns of this relative importance and self-governing authority this had become more common than not by that time.[39] In the largest provincial centres, as exemplified by Exeter, clerks were even busier and more powerful figures, even acting as

---

[36] Alsford, 'Town Clerks of Colchester', 125–30.

[37] Dyer, *City of Worcester*, 200–1.

[38] Prest identifies Dover, Plymouth, and Worcester, along with London and Bristol; Wilfred Prest, *The Rise of the Barristers: A Social History of the English Bar, 1590–1640* (Oxford, 1986), 241.

[39] *VCH, Oxfordshire*, 4 (1979), 149; Salter (ed.), *Oxford Council Acts, passim*; and Hobson and Salter (eds.), *Oxford Council Acts, passim* and appendix V, 452–67. Prest, *Rise of the Barristers*, 4, 20.

The practice of employing Town Clerks with legal training was considerably older in some other, particularly larger, towns. Bristol's Clerk, for example, was required to be an utter barrister by an ordinance of 1555, though the observation that this

clerks of the peace, supervising the night watches, and presiding over assizes of bread and ale.[40]

Such clerks had also become busy enough to make the clerkship a full-time occupation. By as early as 1572 the Borough of Ipswich felt obliged to insist that its clerk give up his own legal practice and devote his full energies to the Corporation's business, in return for a larger stipend.[41] Indeed, the Borough's legal business, including lawsuits in defence or assertion of local privileges, seems widely to have increased for such officials in these decades.[42] Without doubt, then, the town clerks of the realm had come a long way from their limited social status and professional expertise of earlier times.

In some cases, perhaps including Oxford and Bristol, the duties of the town clerk may somewhat have overlapped those of the recorder. In other cases, including towns like Colchester and Devizes, they shared the same status.[43] It is to this similar but yet more prestigious and powerful office which we must now turn.[44] Though the name itself would suggest a function much akin to that of the town clerk, the recorder had always been much more of a legal adviser than a keeper of records. In several respects, the office of the recorder offers much more dramatic evidence of the growing authority of borough governments, and the growing interchange between those governments and other authorities outside the bounds of the town, characteristic of the era at hand.

The recorder's office has been traced to the fourteenth century,[45] but remained rare in incidence and undeveloped in responsibility for

---

ordinance had to be reiterated in 1585 may suggest that it had come to be more honoured in the breach than in the performance (Stanford (ed.), *Ordinances of Bristol*, 23 and 87–8).

[40] Described in John Hooker's 'Commonplace Book', as cited in Brooks, *Pettyfoggers and Vipers*, 210–11.

[41] MacCulloch, *Suffolk and the Tudors*, 322. Brooks cites an annual stipend of £30 to the Coventry Town Clerk on condition that he worked full-time for that borough (Brooks, *Pettyfoggers and Vipers*, 212).

[42] MacCulloch notes, for example, that even the not especially large borough of Sudbury engaged in no less than seventeen separate suits concerning privileges in the reign of Elizabeth alone (*Suffolk and the Tudors*, 322). On this theme in general, see Brooks, *Pettyfoggers and Vipers*, chaps. 4–6.

[43] Salter (ed.), *Oxford Council Acts*; and Hobson and Salter (eds.), *Oxford Council Acts, passim*; Stanford, *Ordinances of Bristol, passim*; Prest, *Rise of the Barristers*, 241.

[44] Once again we must accept a wide variation in contemporary usage. In some instances the term 'recorder' served as a mere honorary title, in a few others the recorder's functions were described by a different title — as stewards, town clerks, etc. The usage here is the most conventional employment of the term at that time.

[45] Reynolds, *English Medieval Towns*, 120.

a long while thereafter. Plymouth, Bristol, Southampton, Winchester, Rochester, Norwich, Northampton, Stamford, and Coventry, nearly all of them relatively advanced in the development of self-governing institutions, seem to have had recorders in the fifteenth century.[46] Yet it is not until our period that recorders became common in towns with local self-governing institutions; not till then did their functions become more or less standardized and essential to those bodies. It has been stated that 'the number of recorderships sanctioned by royal charter jumped from fifteen to over fifty in the course of the sixteenth century, with the same number of posts being added in the seventeenth century prior to 1660'.[47] Yet there were also some recorders whose posts do not appear to have been sanctioned by charter, so that there were probably close to a hundred in place by c.1600. Their numbers continued to grow in the decades thereafter.[48]

Simply put, the recorder served the borough as the officer principally charged with knowing, interpreting, and applying the law of the land, and of advising borough officials of the same. At a time when the corporate borough and its officers came to be caught up in the great legislative outpouring of the Tudors, when it came to place greater emphasis than ever before on the regularization and formalization of local government and administration, and when it had a great many more resources to acquire, manage, and defend, the recorder's role became essential. It became all the more so with the greater value which contemporaries placed on the link between law and good government, a familiar theme amongst the educational reformers and other intellectuals of the day.

Virtually always a barrister, and thus almost always also engaged most of the time at the Inns of Court or elsewhere at the centre,[49] the recorder brought the town, or at least its ruling elite, in close touch with the political and intellectual currents of both the court and the metropolis of London and Westminster. His presence brought to an end the era of urban government run entirely—save for the odd town clerk with legal training—by amateurs, operating as *primi inter pares* with the commonalty at large, and by men whose scope of activity remained largely local and insular.

---

[46] Based on the constituency surveys provided in Bindoff (ed.), *House of Commons, 1509–1558*, for those towns, i. 71, 93, 101, 103, 117, 152, 167, and 211.

[47] Prest, *Rise of the Barristers*, 240.

[48] Some sixty-three towns are incidentally noted as having recorders during the Elizabethan era amongst parliamentary boroughs alone (Hasler (ed.), *The House of Commons, 1558–1603*, i, *passim*).

[49] Prest, *Rise of the Barristers*, 142–3, 240–52.

The rapidity with which this hitherto obscure office became essential to boroughs of any size or consequence may clearly be seen in Oxford. When Oxford's first recorder died in *c*.1511, it was not deemed necessary to replace him until 1554: surely a sign of the marginal value placed upon the office even into the mid-century. Yet Oxford seems not to have gone without one from that time forth, and the importance of the office grew to the point where, by century's end, some incumbents enjoyed the prominence and standing to earn them election as MPs.[50] King's Lynn first elected a recorder in 1525, a year after its first incorporation. Indeed, that charter permitted it to do so. By the time the first incumbent had to be replaced, fifteen years later, the Mayor and Council considered it necessary to secure the services of a serjeant-at-law for the post, and most of its recorders even in the sixteenth century served as MPs.[51]

In contrast to other town officials save for the high steward, the recorder did not necessarily live within the community and may only have been a freeman in an honorary capacity. Ironically, he was less likely to be a resident and freeman in larger and wealthier towns, because they would be able to employ the more prestigious sort of person who would have more on his plate elsewhere. In such cases deputies became quite common. But in the more modest-sized towns, recorders were somewhat lesser figures, and thus more likely to be native sons, connected by birth to the local elite, and more often both resident and actually present.[52] The fact that most recorders, and especially the more prominent, depended for the bulk of their careers on activity at Westminster or the Inns of Court led some towns to set aside a chamber in which they could stay when in town on business. In Leicester's Guildhall a reconstruction of the recorder's chamber may be seen today.

---

[50] *VCH, Oxfordshire*, 4 (1979), 148.

[51] The first Recorder of King's Lynn was William Conyngsby, elected Lent Reader at the Inner Temple in the same year of his election in Lynn. A Lynn native, he had already served as a JP in Hertfordshire for ten years and would represent Lynn in Parliament in 1536. Other 16th-cent. King's Lynn recorders who would also serve in Parliament include: Thomas Gawdy (Recorder, 1545–55; MP, Salisbury, 1545; Lynn, 1547; Norwich, Oct. 1553); John Walpole (Recorder, 1556–7; MP, Lynn, March and Oct. sessions, 1553); Ambrose Gilberd (Recorder, Lynn, 1557–8; MP, Liskeard, 1547; Bridgnorth, March 1553; W. Looe, Oct. 1554; Lynn, 1558); William Yelverton (Recorder, 1558–61; MP, Lynn, 1558); Robert Bell (Recorder, 1561–77; MP, Lynn, 1563, 1571, 1572); William Lewis (Recorder, 1589–93; MP, Lynn, 1593); and Thomas Oxborough (Recorder, 1597–1623; MP, Lynn, 1586, 1597, 1601, 1604, and 1614). Hamon LeStrange (ed.), *Norfolk Official Lists* (Norwich, 1890), *passim*; Bindoff (ed.), *House of Commons, passim*; and Hasler (ed.), *House of Commons, passim*.

[52] Prest, *Rise of the Barristers*, 244–5.

Yet recorders were by no means entirely absentee or ceremonial officials. Their presence must frequently have been required: certainly at borough court time, often when the borough council met, and always at such occasions as the swearing in of a new mayor (a task which, along with an edifying speech for the occasion, it was often the recorder's duty to perform). At least in the sixteenth century some towns kept their recorders on a particularly tight rein. A Gloucester ordinance of 1567–8 allowed the mayor to call the recorder to attend any meeting of the Common Council in which his advice might be required. The mayor enforced this at least once in ensuing years with a fine of £5: a sum which equalled the recorder's annual stipend (though far less than the sum of his lucrative fees) in many towns.[53]

Obviously, the growing demands placed on the technical expertise of the town recorder, the necessity of legal training, and the high desirability of political connections at court and elsewhere, made this a very powerful office. Though the governing elite of many towns chose their recorder annually, in almost all cases an incumbent could be assured of repeated re-selection and thus long-term service, often for life. From the incumbent's perspective, this permitted long-term financial stability, though based more on fees than on stipends as such. From the borough's perspective, it permitted continuity of policy and administrative direction in towns where the mayor and other senior officials were likely to change each year. By the end of the century towns vied to attract the best lawyers for the post. Even the great figures at court, often in their capacity as high stewards of particular towns, frequently asserted their influence in the choice of a recorder. The Borough of Doncaster successfully fought off the Earl of Shrewsbury's effort to choose the recorder of that town between 1588 and 1590, but the City of Gloucester's choice for a recorder in 1587 was determined at the suit of the Earl of Leicester. In Boston, William Cecil, Lord Burghley and Sir Henry Clinton, Steward to the Borough, vied for influence in the choice even of a deputy recorder in 1571.[54]

Though it may be stretching a point to consider high stewards as borough officials in the usual sense, they now came for the first time to enjoy an official status in most towns. Their appearance offers

---

[53] Gloucester Borough Records, Gloucestershire Record Office, MS GBR 3/1, fos. 22ʳ and 108ʳ.

[54] Brent (ed.), *Doncaster Borough Courtier*, 23; Gloucester Borough Records, MS GBR B3/1, fo. 108ʳ; J. F. Bailey (ed.), *Minutes of Boston*, i. 139–40.

another emphatic illustration of the expanding scope of town government, and of its progress beyond the traditional concept of governing officials rising from the ranks of the freemanry as *primi inter pares*. The high steward's chief role was to be a friend of the borough at court and in the country: to advocate its interests at Westminster and in the shire, and to exercise his 'good lordship' wherever he could. He should of course not be confused with the manorial steward who, in that and earlier times, served in a different capacity and at a level which was at the same time more literally authoritative but also less prestigious.

(The stewardship of such jurisdictions as an honour or even a duchy presents a variation on this theme, albeit with much more prestige. Thus for example members of the Hastings family served as Stewards of the Honour of Leicester from 1461 right through our period.[55] In both cases the incumbent held actual governing powers over the community and was chosen by the Crown or some other external authority rather than by the indigenous governing authority. To confuse matters further, the latter form of steward might well, as with the Hastingses, be a figure of wide notoriety, and serve as 'good lord' just as if he had been a high steward of the borough's own choice.)

Given the practical expense and difficulties which even the wealthiest and most important towns experienced in going to law or to Parliament with problems of major and long-standing significance (and given the increasing importance of so doing), the high steward's role became as essential as the recorder's.[56] We see this in Great Yarmouth. With a constant need to defend its herring fishery from interlopers, to prevent its haven from silting, and to attend to a number of other substantial concerns, Yarmouth first engaged a High Steward in the 1520s.[57] By Edward's reign Yarmouth's High Stewards were of the ilk of John Dudley, Duke of Northumberland. He was succeeded by the young Thomas Howard, Fourth Duke of Norfolk in 1554, and he, in turn, by Robert Dudley, Earl of Leicester in 1572.[58]

There are no doubt late fifteenth-century precedents for high

[55] Patterson, 'Leicester and Lord Huntingdon', 47.

[56] The readiness and ease with which towns took their most important concerns to Parliament has been overestimated. See Tittler, 'Elizabethan Towns and the "Points of Contact" ', 275–88.

[57] Paul Rutledge, *Guide to the Great Yarmouth Borough Records* (Norwich, 1972), 8.

[58] LeStrange (ed.), *Norfolk Official Lists*, 170.

stewardships. Yet they seem to appear with some regularity in the more highly developed towns only around the 1520s and 1530s, when we find high stewards for, for example, Cambridge and Bristol,[59] Exeter, Dorchester, Plymouth, and Oxford.[60] Yet many and perhaps even most important towns did not engage high stewards until mid-century or even after. Dr Catherine Patterson has counted forty-five corporate boroughs adding high stewards between 1580 and 1640,[61] though it would appear that quite a few had already emerged in the years just prior to the starting point of her study.[62] On the whole, a town required a considerable amount of independence, not to mention the resources to support such a venture, before it could name such an official. We less frequently find a high steward in the smaller or less consequential towns, and almost never in those still dominated by seigneurial authority.

In addition to providing a borough with a voice at court, which in itself proved a complex and diverse function, high stewards exerted their influence on their borough's behalf in the politics of the shire and region, and even in settling disputes or rendering advice within the borough itself. Of course these functions were not new in this era. They conformed to the traditional understanding implied in the provision of good lordship. It would not be far off the mark to think of the emergence of the high steward's office as essentially a formalization of that traditional role. But at a time when the more substantial English towns were more than ever being drawn into political and economic activities of a truly national scope, the high steward served to link particular urban communities with the realm as a whole in ways which towns could scarcely do for themselves to the same effect.

One might not guess as much on the basis of the paltry annual stipends they received from the town treasury (even as supplemented by the odd fat buck, fresh sturgeon, or barrel of sack), but high stewardships were also valuable to their incumbents. Of much greater value than tangible rewards were the honour, prestige, and influence which came with the post. The role of stewards in borough

---

[59] Patterson, 'Urban Patronage in Early Modern England', 40.

[60] Bindoff (ed.), *House of Commons*, i. 70, 71, 79, and 171.

[61] Patterson, 'Urban Patronage in Early Modern England', 41, building on the work of Vivienne J. Hodges, 'The Electoral Influence of the Aristocracy, 1604–1641', Ph.D. thesis (Columbia, 1977).

[62] Roughly thirty are cited in passing—which is to say that no methodical tally has been kept—as stemming from this era in Hasler (ed.), *House of Commons*, i, *passim*.

parliamentary elections has been familiar at least since the pioneering work on parliamentary patronage of Sir John Neale and Wallace Notestein, though we might now place a different interpretation on that phenomenon. We now see that this sort of interchange of prestige and honour between town and 'good lord' remained absolutely central to the patronage relationships of the time. It brought towns further into the sphere of regional and even national politics than ever before.

It stands to reason that the greatest figures in the land now became the most desirable candidates for high stewardships. Though coming at what seems the very beginning of the heyday of that office, Robert Dudley, the Earl of Leicester, furnishes a case in point. In addition to, also in part because of, his many roles at court and in the several towns under his own control as manorial lord, Leicester served at one time or another as High Steward for Abingdon (1566–74), Andover (1574–88?), Bristol, Great Yarmouth (1572–88), King's Lynn (also 1572–88), Reading (1562–88), St Albans (c.1579–88), Tewkesbury, Wallingford (1569–88), and Windsor (1563–88). In addition he served as the Honorary Recorder, an analogous post, at Maldon (1565–88).[63]

For these towns he might perform a variety of functions. He did so at all levels of political activity, from the internal operation of borough governments themselves, through the political intricacies of shire and region, and on to the highest circles of court and Parliament.[64] Though this role has often been neglected in biographical studies of Leicester and most comparable figures of state, in his formal patronal relationship with a multitude of boroughs Leicester typifies the Cecils, Howards, Walsinghams, and the Essexes of the sixteenth century and the Buckinghams, Bacons, and Northamptons of the early seventeenth.

Another figure of comparable stature was Thomas Howard, fourth Duke of Norfolk, whose activity as patron to several boroughs has been noted above. In his capacity as High Steward of Great Yarmouth, for example, we have seen how Howard sustained an active and beneficial concern for the Borough's valuable but notoriously fragile haven. He worked ceaselessly to raise funds for its repair, prompted the Privy Council to appoint a commission to investigate its decay, supplied timber from his own stock, and

---

[63] Hasler (ed.), *House of Commons*, i, *passim*.

[64] The most recent and detailed account of these functions is now Patterson, 'Urban Patronage in Early Modern England'.

secured a remission of subsidies for the Borough. Employing his vast influence elsewhere in the region he persuaded the City of Norwich, whose merchants depended on Yarmouth as their outlet to the sea, to contribute 200 marks to the project. And, employing his influence with the Crown, he supported the town's petition for a licence to export grain at a time when other towns were forbidden to do the same.[65]

No wonder, in the light of this record, that corporate towns scrambled to find the most powerful patrons they could afford, investing them with the title of 'high steward' to formalize the relationship. In the early decades of the period some high stewardships went to prominent gentry or to magnates of merely local influence. By the middle of Elizabeth's reign, if not before, the emphasis shifted to the aristocracy rather than the gentry, and to men of national rather than merely regional connections.[66] By that time chief officers of state could virtually be assured of multiple high stewardships, especially but by no means exclusively from towns in their own geographic area of residence and influence. And indeed, such patronage substantially enhanced their own stature at court.

The economically troubled City of Winchester recognized the importance of such a move only in 1582, when it first decided to engage a high steward. Though it allocated but £6. 13s. 4d. per annum for the office, its leaders well understood that this would be augmented with gifts, political influence, and honour, all of which they valued highly. They succeeded in attracting Sir Francis Walsingham to the post and expeditiously elected him for life, with the first year's payment in advance lest he should change his mind. Still on his way up in court circles, Walsingham thus garnered his second high stewardship, following a similar appointment at Ipswich. In subsequent years Winchester engaged the diplomat and courtier Thomas Sackville, Lord Buckhurst (1592–3), already High Steward at Ipswich and at Bristol; the Chancellor of the Duchy of Lancaster and Vice-Chamberlain of the Queen's Household Sir Thomas Heneage, already High Steward at Salisbury, from 1593; Charles Blount, Lord Montjoy, Earl of Devonshire, and High Steward of Portsmouth, from 1595; thence back to Sackville (1606–8) who, as Earl of Dorset, was by then also Lord High Steward and Lord Treasurer.[67]

---

[65] A. H. Smith, *County and Court*, 28–9.
[66] Patterson, 'Urban Patronage in Early Modern England', 45.
[67] Tom Atkinson, *Elizabethan Winchester* (1963), 92–3.

Although for most of the sixteenth century the selection of high stewards seems to have begun at the initiative of the boroughs concerned, it was not long before the magnates and would-be magnates of the realm saw the potential for enhancing their own careers in such an opportunity. One of the first to reach out and virtually solicit such offices, and amongst the most successful by far, was Robert Devereux, Earl of Essex, who may have learned the value of the office from his stepfather, the Earl of Leicester. Despite the brevity of his career, Essex eventually became high steward to Tamworth (1588), Leominster (1591), Dunwich (1593), Oxford (1593), Reading (1593), Andover (c.1597), Hereford (1597), Ipswich (1597), and Great Yarmouth (1597). His principal aim seems to have been the influence which such posts could, and in practice usually did, allow him in the selection of MPs. This would explain why Essex gained such posts in boroughs as modest in size and importance as Leominster, Andover, Dunwich, and Tamworth, as well as those more worth having on the strength of their other merits. Indeed, Essex's activity opened something of a new chapter in the quest for high stewardships amongst the politically ambitious.[68]

From the urban perspective, Essex's lust for stewardships as a means of boosting his parliamentary influence shows as well the increasingly close interaction between the borough and the centre. The traditional perspective on this issue derives from the Whig approach to History, and especially to the traditions of parliamentary history so greatly furthered by Sir John Neale, Wallace Notestein, and the History of Parliament Trust which they helped to create. In this view, boroughs enfranchised to send members to Parliament steadily lost their 'independence' in this period to an 'invasion' of landed gentry into those seats, or before an influx of gentry whom they were obliged, by even greater magnates who sat in the Lords, to accept in return for the favour of powerful patrons. Such towns were described as 'struggling to avoid', 'resisting', or 'fighting off' such 'encroachments' and 'incursions' on their liberties.

It cannot be denied that, even with the considerable increase in enfranchised boroughs to begin with, an increasingly greater number of MPs were non-resident in the towns for which they sat as the period wore on. Yet the idea that this represented a reluctant surrender to patronal influence can no longer be sustained. Clearly this derived much more from a mutually satisfactory patronage

---

[68] Hasler (ed.), *House of Commons*, i. 64.

relationship concluded between enfranchised boroughs and the landed classes, in which each party had something to offer the other. In this sort of equation the offer of parliamentary selection, along with other boons associated with high stewardship, proved a frequent commodity of patronal exchange. We may be sure that in most cases the borough in question received as good and as much as it gave. Equally important, such patrons as the Leicesters, Norfolks, and Essexes served not only to bring their personal influence to bear on behalf of these towns, but also to link the same communities with the Crown, the court, and the rest of the realm.

In this fact there is some degree of irony for, despite the importance and prominence of recorders and high stewards, neither of them played a part in the daily administration of the borough, and, save for some recorders, neither conventionally resided therein. (Indeed, in the high steward's case it would have been counterproductive to have done so!) To anyone 'on the inside', clearly the most central figure in the government of most towns in this period was the mayor himself: the highest-ranking official in the more ordinary sense of that term, always resident during his term of office, and both constantly and highly visible on a daily basis. His jurisdiction in borough affairs was easily the most comprehensive of all. His office had been most intimately linked to the community at large. We must therefore turn to the office of the mayor for the most revealing look at the development of urban government and administration in this era.

By the accession of the Tudors, the office of mayor was well into its third century at least, and some have even argued for pre-Norman origins.[69] Mayoral office emerged in several ways, and it would be misleading to suggest a uniformity of evolution from town to town. Yet it does seem safe to say that mayoral office always arose in response to the need for townspeople to have their own spokesman and representative to deal with the authority of, in most cases, the manorial lord and his court. Mayoral office seems often to have grown up in this regard within the aegis of such manorial jurisdiction, typically as the lord allowed a measure of self-government to his tenants.[70] Often it emerged from the leadership of the guild

[69] Reynolds, *English Medieval Towns*, 109; Henry Hartopp (ed.), *Roll of the Mayors of the Borough and Lord Mayors of the City of Leicester* (Leicester, [1935]), p. xi; R. Tweedy-Smith, *The History, Law, Practice and Procedure Relating to Mayors* (1935), chap. 1.

[70] Sidney Webb and Beatrice Webb, *English Local Government: The Manor and the Borough* (2 vols.; 1908), i. 264–5.

merchant or from the ranks of the communes which sprang up in some twelfth- and thirteenth-century communities.[71]

In these early stages of the office the terminology was far from fixed or uniform. Common synonyms for what we may recognize as mayoral office—i.e. the chief officer of the town and representative of its residents rather than of its lord—included 'portreeve', 'warden', or 'alderman', though all of these had alternative meanings as well. In addition, when the lord had two bailiffs, one often became 'the lord's bailiff', and the other the 'townsmen's bailiff', another mayoral analogue. In towns which were boroughs by prescription, mayoral office may have developed earlier and in a terminologically clearer fashion. In a manorial community like Sandwich or Liverpool, on the other hand, where there emerged both the lord's bailiff, who ran the lord's court, and the townsmen's bailiff, who came to preside over the townsmen's court, it took longer for the latter official to adopt the name of 'mayor'. Sometimes that new title does not even appear in the Early Modern period.[72]

The Webbs tell us that while most corporate towns by the sixteenth century had mayors called by that name, London and York alone had a 'lord mayor'. Kidderminster used the term 'high bailiff', while a swarm of others—including Andover, Bewdley, Blandford Forum, Brecon, Chippenham, Daventry, Leominster, Llandovery, Lydd, Pevensey, Romney Marsh, and Seaford—still used the term 'bailiff'. Some towns in Somerset (including Chard, Langport, and Yeovil) and elsewhere employed the term 'portreeve'. Yet all these usages denoted what we would call the 'mayor'.[73] This usage is more than occasionally confusing, for officers called bailiffs, aldermen, portreeves, and the like could as often be distinct from our sense of the term mayor as they could be, in specific cases, synonymous with it. The term 'mayor' will be used here as a generic label when it is clear that this will not betray the definition given above. That is to say that a bailiff will be called a mayor when he has the responsibilities associated with that office, but not when he is clearly the lord's administrative stand-in.

---

[71] James Tait, *The Medieval English Borough: Studies in its Origins and Constitutional History* (Manchester, 1936), 230–6 and 250.

[72] Ibid. 307–8.

[73] Ibid. 308–10. The tradition, repeated in D. M. Palliser, that the chief official of the City of York was known at this early stage as the 'Lord Mayor', remains open to question. The usage is not evident in Angelo Raine's editions of the City Assembly minutes covering this period. I am grateful to Mr Alasdair Hawkyard for raising this point. See Palliser, *Tudor York*, 65.

In effect, the mayor's office seems to have been shaped by the actions of three political forces in the medieval period, each acting in its own way. The first and chief of these was of course the needs of his fellow townsmen. They saw him as one of themselves, as *primus inter pares* with the leading merchants and other figures in the community, as arbiter of justice in his court, especially in such important matters as debt, trespass, breach of contract, and other unfair dealing. They relied on him to voice their concerns and stand up for them before higher authorities. They sometimes saw him as the guardian of their property or bequests and as executor of their estates, and they certainly saw him as the embodiment and defender of the rights and privileges of their community.

The second shaping force was at first permissive but eventually often unyielding in nature: this was the role of the lay or ecclesiastical landlord. Despite the fact that in many communities the mayor derived his official status with the lord's acquiescence, conflict between medieval townsmen and their lords is of course central to what we know of urban politics and political relations in earlier times. In those contests townsmen came to consider their mayors as champions of their communal interests and identity. At least from a local perspective, the standing of the mayor amongst his fellows depended considerably on his winning concessions from the lord of the town.

The third force at work in shaping the mayoralty consisted of the Crown and other institutions of the central government. This began chiefly as a force of recognition and enablement for burghal, and hence mayoral, aspirations. Beginning first with mayors in towns which were mesne boroughs or recognized as boroughs by prescription, and then extending to other towns which gained a significant degree of self-government with the passage of time, the Crown, Parliament, and courts recognized the mayor as the essential legal authority in such places. This is evident from at least the thirteenth century, though of course those were in many respects still early days for urban autonomy, mayoral authority, or even the force of central government.

These three forces—the townsmen, the lord, and the central government—helped shape mayoral responsibility well before the sixteenth century. By that time the mayor took responsibility for town finances and financial obligations to the Crown, for markets and fairs, for rogues, vagabonds, and other ne'er-do-wells, for writs from the Crown and central courts, and for the appointment of

subordinate officers in the community. He presided over the town's courts and he served as its spokesman to the outside world. He represented the Crown by serving as clerk of the market, coroner, and sometimes even JP. His rewards for all this came largely in non-pecuniary forms: honour, respect, and greatly enhanced stature in the eyes of his fellows, all of which were recognized in the richly ceremonial nature of late medieval town life.

It need hardly be said that there were a great many variations on the developmental pattern of mayoral office from town to town. One common story is exemplified by Reading, a seigneurial town under the aegis of the local abbot, where the mayoralty emerged in the form of the master of the merchant guild. The term 'mayor' was first employed in Reading in a royal writ of about the year 1300, though the descriptive term 'maior gildae mercatoriae' continued to be employed synonymously with 'maior villae Radinga' (except by the successive abbots of Reading, who refused to recognize the latter) right into the sixteenth century.[74] Not until the Reformation, and the incorporation which followed quickly on its heels, did the mayor come into his own as the undisputed authority in the community.[75] Totnes, King's Lynn, Leicester, and many other towns followed a similar pattern of mayoral emergence from guild origins.[76]

In Exeter, which typified many ancient boroughs by prescription, the mayoral office appeared around 1200: before the appearance of royal writs recognizing his jurisdiction, but after the emergence of a townsmen's court and certainly after the appearance of the King's bailiff for the city. For some time thereafter the mayor—still chiefly the representative of the townsmen—and the bailiff were rivals. Not until the early fourteenth century did the former triumph over the latter as the chief officer of the community and as the recognized

[74] *VCH, Berkshire*, 3 (1923), 346–53.
[75] The efforts of the townsmen to gain recognition for claims to self-government reached a milestone, if not a final resolution, in 1509. In that year a ruling in the Court of Common Pleas affirmed the corporate status of the 'mayor and burgesses of the gild merchant', though still placing them under the jurisdiction of the Abbot. By charter dated 18 Apr. 1542, these privileges were affirmed and extended to include incorporation as the 'Mayor and Burgesses of [the Borough of] Reading' (J. M. Guilding (ed.), *Reading Records* (4 vols.; 1892–6), i. 105; and PRO, C. 66/711, m. 1).
[76] H. R. Watkin, *The History of Totnes* (1914 and 1917), 909–20; Henry J. Hillen, *The History of the Borough of King's Lynn* (2 vols.; Norwich, 1907, repr. 1979), ii. 743; Hartopp (ed.), *Roll of the Mayors of Leicester*, pp. xi–xvi. The subject has been taken up anew by Rosser, whose preliminary studies are most instructive ('Town and Guild of Lichfield', 39–47; and 'Communities of the Parish and Guild', in Wright (ed.), *Parish, Church and People*, 29–55).

representative of royal authority therein. During that time of evolution, the mayor ruled as *primus inter pares* with twenty-four citizen-councillors sometimes known, as was also common elsewhere, as the Twenty-Four (though in an Exeter inquest of 1324 all twenty-four were known as *maiores*).[77] As Professor Bertie Wilkinson observed long ago, 'The earlier the period . . . the greater is the importance of the community, not that of its officers': an observation close to the heart of our principal theme![78] Even in the fourteenth and fifteenth centuries, the Council seems to have exercised authority equal to and sometimes even independent of the mayor's.[79] Yet with the passage of time the mayors of Exeter and of many other towns came gradually to gain power relative to their aldermen and councillors — indeed, often at their expense — and to distance themselves even further from the common run of townsmen as well. By 1608 the enhanced status of Exeter mayors came to be symbolized by the adoption of the honorific 'the right worshipfull the Maior'.[80]

This is not to say that the mayoral position was not without its severe challenges in the decades prior to the Reformation. The first hints of the statutory obligations which the Tudor Parliaments would place upon such officials may be discerned prior to *c.*1540, even in the so-called 'new monarchy' of the late fifteenth century.[81] The economic decay or stagnation of many towns placed great burdens on their chief administrative officer. They impinged on his

[77] B. Wilkinson and R. C. Easterling, *The Medieval Council of Exeter* (Manchester, 1931), pp. xvi–xxi. The sense of *maiores* here should merely be taken to denote citizen-jurors who possessed land in the City and were frequently listed as jurors in the more important inquests (ibid., p. xxi, n. 1).

[78] Ibid., p. xx.

[79] Ibid. 47–8. As Wilkinson points out, the Council also had substantial powers relative to the mayor in Winchester through the 15th cent., and this may indeed have been a common pattern elsewhere as well (see pp. 54–7). Tait established many years ago that the councils of many medieval towns were often considerably independent of mayoral jurisdiction (Tait, *Medieval English Borough*, 282–5).

[80] Devon Record Office, Exeter Corporation Act Book No. 5, 13.

[81] The concept of the 'new monarchy', first explored by such historians as J. R. Green and A. F. Pollard, has been revived in more recent studies by Alexander Grant, B. P. Wolff, J. R. Lander, and Anthony Goodman. See Green, *A Short History of the English People*, ii (1893); Pollard, *Factors in Modern History* (1910), 52–78; Grant, *Henry VII* (1985); Wolff, *The Crown Lands, 1461–1536* (1970); Wolff, *The Royal Demesne in English History* (1971); Lander, *Crown and Nobility, 1450–1509* (1976); Lander, *Conflict and Stability in Fifteenth Century England* (1977); Lander, *Government and Community: England, 1450–1509* (1980); and Goodman, *The New Monarchy, 1471–1534* (1988), the last of which provides a useful summary of the development of the concept on pp. 1–6. For relations between the Crown and the boroughs in this period, see esp. Wright, 'Relations between the King's Government and the English Cities and Boroughs'.

ability to govern effectively, and on his personal ability to give up his own business for the year of his mayoralty. Yet we still see a recovery in the strength and viability of mayoral office in the Reformation era, and a continued augmentation of his power and authority. In fact, the mayoralty expanded in its every dimension from about 1540 forwards, and probably at a faster rate than ever.

The striking growth in borough incorporation from about the 1540s proved an obvious boost for the mayoralty in towns of various types. In some, incorporation sanctioned the change whereby the mastership of many former town guilds became transformed into the mayoralty of the towns themselves, causing the number of towns with mayors to grow dramatically. In towns which had already had mayors, their powers grew greater and more specifically defined.

Of equal importance to the development of the mayoralty in this era lay the unprecedented, even staggering, outpouring of statutes, proclamations, and local by-laws which invested ever greater responsibility, and hence authority, in the government of corporate boroughs. Even excluding subsidy acts or acts in which only the Lord Mayor of London is mentioned, the Statute Book yields no fewer than 97 statutes between 1509 and 1603, the beginning of Henry VIII's reign to the end of Elizabeth's, which conferred powers specifically on the mayors of towns (along, in most cases, with other officials at other levels of administration).[82] Curiously, there are almost no statutes which serve to limit the powers of mayors or to protect townsmen against mayoral corruption, while one statute actually exempted mayors from an act against extortion which applied to other kinds of local officials.[83]

It could also be argued that the circumstances of English urban society and economic life enhanced the mayor's discretionary

---

[82] *Statutes of the Realm*, ed. A. Luders, T. E. Tomlins, and J. Raithby (11 vols.; 1810–28), *passim*. Broken down rather arbitrarily into categories, the purposes of these statutes may be counted as follows. As a few statutes have more than one purpose, the total exceeds 97.

Economic and social regulation (including poor relief, trade, industry, and related issues)	50
Judicial powers and/or the regulation of disorder (excluding poor laws)	22
Housing and public works	22
Military powers	5
Financial powers (exclusive of subsidies, which were not counted in the total)	5
Miscellaneous	3

[83] 29 Eliz. c. 4, 'An Act to Prevent Extortion in Sheriffs, Undersheriffs and Bailiffs or Franchises or Liberties . . .'. Numerous statutes do list mayors amongst officials

powers in purely local matters, again making the position more desirable to potential incumbents. His control of the increasing number of town lands, and his discretionary power to award leases, exemplify this well, as does his power (often recognized in statute) to appoint local officials.

This enhanced authority is reflected in a comparable increase in mayoral stipends, an increase which continued, in fits and starts, throughout these years. We should not confuse these with salary in the modern sense. Yet mayoral stipends were meant to cover rising expenses of office and to make it somewhat easier for mayoral incumbents to abandon their own businesses for a year while in office. Even allowing for inflation, these stipends may be taken as some barometric measure of the value placed locally on mayoral office (see Table VI).

In addition to these advances, we find mayors in this period dealing more and more with gentry and even aristocracy from the surrounding countryside and with figures of varying importance at court. Though they may have done so for the good of their towns, mayors nevertheless took more frequent initiatives in permitting such influential outsiders influence in town affairs—favourable leases on town lands, concessions on market rights, influence in selecting appointed officials, and even parliamentary patronage—in return for 'good lordship' to the town . . . and to themselves! Mayors, of course, conventionally lacked such genteel attributes as birth, title, or landed estate, and were usually considered socially subordinate to the landed classes. Yet these opportunities allowed the mayor to deal with those more privileged figures as a political (and eventually, in some cases, a social) equal: a very attractive prospect indeed in an age of intense social aspiration. It often followed from this both that the mayor looked upwards and outwards towards those coveted circles more than ever before, and also that, in consequence, he looked inwards and downwards towards his nominal fellows somewhat less than before. It suggests, too, that the converse of Wilkinson's statement about the importance of office in the medieval town was coming to be more accurate a description of the Early Modern town: the office was becoming more important than the community.

who may be fined for neglect of duty. Parliament and Crown did not seem to mind corruption as much as negligence of duty when that duty lay in the enforcement of statutory law.

iv

Closely related to the onset of oligarchy in town government at this time lie similar developments in the parish.[84] Like many a small urban community itself in earlier times, the parish had traditionally been run in a more or less consensual manner by the parishioners acting in the form of a vestry, aided only by a few (usually elected) officers like the churchwardens and the constable. In addition, and partly because it was so broadly based and widely participatory, the parish vestry had long served as a training ground for civic office in general. The 'cockpit of local government',[85] it served as an early step in the conventional *cursus honorum* towards more formal and higher office in the town itself.

But as with the government structure of towns, it, too, became markedly more complex and hierarchical in these years, and for many of the same reasons. For one, the traditionally broad-based 'open' vestry simply found it more difficult to operate once the parish came to share some responsibility for such things as the maintenance of roads and bridges, the registration of births, deaths, and marriages, the operation of schools and other social institutions, and the administration of the Poor Laws. By the early seventeenth century most urban parishes experienced a proliferation of offices just like towns themselves, with highway surveyors and overseers of the poor joining churchwardens as the dominant officials. The collection of local rates intended to support the poor or keep up certain local public works proved especially important in this process. This politically sensitive and difficult task required a degree of clout which only the leading members of the parish could bring to bear.[86] In addition, as is well known, such oligarchic tendencies were often driven forcefully along by puritan factions anxious to forge strong links between magistracy and ministry.

In consequence of these forces, parish government in many urban communities moved rapidly from the traditional 'open' vestry of pre-Reformation times to the 'select' vestry which came to predominate by the early seventeenth century. Members of this narrow body were drawn from the same elite which prevailed in civic offices, or were closely tied to it by kinship and common interests. They per-

---

[84] The following is based on Christopher Hill, *Society and Puritanism in Pre-Revolutionary England* (1969 edn.), 407–28; Archer, *Pursuit of Stability*, 69–74; Kumin, *Shaping of a Community*, 238–59.

[85] The phrase is Ian Archer's, in *Pursuit of Stability*, 69.

[86] Hill, *Society and Puritanism*, 417–19.

petuated their grip by similar means of co-option and patronage. What had once been a common early step in the *cursus honorum* of civic government now equated to much higher reaches of that ladder. Control of the parish became an important element in civic rule itself, and the tendency towards oligarchic rule seems as vivid in one as in the other.

V

What may we conclude from this discussion of office and authority? First, it becomes obvious that the field of vision taken by local government, which had traditionally been very largely inward to the town and its inhabitants, now extended much more readily to the region and the nation. Whereas the conduct of their offices formerly brought local officials in touch almost exclusively with their fellow townsmen, immediate seigneurial authorities, and perhaps a few neighbouring gentry, now they came to hobnob with a wider range of the county community, members of the legal profession, great figures of state, officials of the central government itself, and, in the case of some of the largest towns like Bristol, even with 'the wider world' beyond England's shores.[87] They did so for reasons of mutual concern and, at least in towns of substance, they did so in a manner which smacked more of political equality than of subordination.

At the same time, it appears that the elevated status and enhanced authority of these offices created a fundamental problem for their incumbents. Precisely because they still lacked the 'natural' or personal status of those who ruled at the level of the shire or of the realm, the mayor and other high urban officials had to find some means of eliciting deference and respect to their position from their fellow townsmen. They required this not merely as a sop to personal vanity, but as an essential support in the effort to govern. Without it, they would have had nothing more to facilitate their governance than the claims of their offices alone. These may have been sufficient to justify the exercise of authority in a legal sense, but insufficient to engender the sort of voluntary obedience and compliance essential to effective governance. Prior to the Dissolutions and other aspects of the early Reformation, such devices were supplied in many aspects of traditional belief and by the institutions associated with

[87] On this theme esp., see Sacks, *The Widening Gate*, though it is important not to assume that all but a handful of towns extended their vision as widely as this second city in the realm.

that belief. But after about the 1540s the civic officials of the realm operated without such props to their authority. At the same time their enhanced responsibilities, and the greater challenges of government characteristic of those years, made such devices more necessary than ever before. In response, as we will see in Part IV below, the ruling element of England's provincial towns strove earnestly and imaginatively in the post-Reformation years to compensate for those losses. In the end they created a revised vocabulary for the political culture of their milieu. At least until the advent of Puritanism as a dominant element in some towns, this revised vocabulary emphasized secular rather than doctrinal supports for urban governing authority. And in this effort they strengthened the urban identity of England's provincial towns as never before.

PART IV
Political Culture in the Post-Reformation Town

Introduction

'The difference between politics and political culture', it has recently been observed, 'is essentially the difference between political action and the codes of conduct, formal and informal, governing those actions.'[1] These codes of conduct, and the means by which they were expressed, seem universally directed towards making political systems work in their particular time and place. They are intended to establish and sustain harmonious interaction amongst those who govern, and between them and the governed. They usually engender loyalty to those cultural traditions, especially the religious and the historical, which most often legitimize contemporary authority. They are most often conveyed not only by institutions, but by such devices as physical structures and furnishings, symbolic artefacts, conventions of dress and speech, and certainly by ceremony and ritual. The manner in which those codes were exhibited, expressed, or conveyed in particular political societies allows us to see a particular political culture at work. If we want fully to comprehend the political and social implications of the Reformation in English provincial towns, we must examine their reflection in contemporary expressions of political culture.

This study began with a summary of some of the salient features of English urban society in the pre-Reformation era. It placed particular emphasis on traditional religion as a dominant force in both the governing systems and the prevailing culture of late medieval towns. That religion conveyed both the imperative of brotherhood and spiritual equality on the one hand and the reality of hierarchy and authority on the other, thus addressing both the egalitarian and hierarchical elements of the contemporary urban community. Ritual and ceremony, edifices and emblems, artefacts and behavioural conventions, all evolved to convey those central concerns. Institutions like chantries, guilds, fraternities, parishes, and town councils helped sustain them.

---

[1] Dale Hoak (ed.), *Tudor Political Culture* (Cambridge, 1995), 1.

We must now ask what happened to the complex and long-evolving political culture of that late medieval milieu, and to the society of English provincial towns in the wake of their destruction or transformation. How did urban communities accommodate? And when, as a more or less indirect result of those changes (along with coincident changes of a more social and economic nature), urban communities became narrower and more oligarchic, how did the virtues of harmony, order, and even deference continue to be affirmed and sustained?

For a number of reasons, of course, such problems of harmony, order, and deference tended to be more problematical in the urban rather than the rural environment. It is in the towns and cities of this era, after all, where population moved in and out most rapidly, where social and economic mobility tended to be most emphatic, where social and economic problems came often to be magnified by the factors of greater population and closer proximity. And it is in the town, rather than in the countryside, where the remnants of feudal structure least applied, and where social relations were always in a much greater state of flux. We must also consider an attribute of stability in an urban society which seems almost as important as the religious underpinning which has been discussed above. This the tradition which is sometimes called 'urbanism', a collective sense of the nature, behavioural expectations, and social conventions of urban life (and not to be confused with the French *urbanisme*, which connotes a concern for urban planning).[2]

In sharp contrast with some of the more urbanized areas of Western Europe at the time, especially Northern Italy and the Low Countries, England still lacked strong traditions of urbanism in the early sixteenth century. It was of course an overwhelmingly agrarian nation. Its political system and culture stemmed from a feudal and agrarian rather than burghal and urban context. Urban office holders of the day, in contrast to their agrarian counterparts, could rarely count on lineage, family, property, titles, or government service to help them establish the deference appropriate to successful governance. Mayors especially, almost never serving in office for more than a year at a time and sharing both their social origins and occupational identity with any number of fellow townsmen, no doubt found it particularly difficult to command deference and thus, when

---

[2] This and the following few paragraphs are inspired by the stimulating discussion of urbanism and its expression in London provided by Lawerence Manley, *Literature and Culture in Early Modern London* (Cambridge, 1995), 15–17, and *passim*.

push came to shove, to sustain order. Unlike their Dutch and many of their Italian and German counterparts, whose urban traditions were well entrenched and socially dominant, the burghers of England rarely had the personal standing in their own right, or the social or cultural confidence, which would allow them to participate as equals with the landed classes.

There was also the question of scale. Save for London, with about 50,000 residents in 1500 and about 200,000 in 1600, none of England's urban communities ranked in size, complexity, or significance with any of a hundred or so contemporary Continental cities. Even at the end of the century only London and (at a tenth its size or less) perhaps Bristol, Norwich, and York could truly be said to figure prominently in the urban structure of European commerce, or to represent examples of urbanism for other communities in England itself. In addition, the relative strength of the English Crown and/or aristocracy even in earlier times meant that its urban governing bodies (save in some respects for London) never attained the political autonomy of towns and cities in a number of Continental traditions.

The weakness of England's urban traditions extended as well to aspects of mind and intellect. Despite the philosophical model of Augustine's *Civitas Dei* and the pseudo-historical model of Geoffrey of Monmouth's city-building King Lud, both of which played a role in English thought, the dominant culture of medieval England remained agrarian and feudal (or neo-feudal) in almost every respect. This seems especially vivid when we compare it with that of Northern Italy, the Low Countries, or even some areas on the Baltic coast or along the trade routes of France or the Habsburg lands. And, despite the writing of Henrician Humanists such as Thomas More and Thomas Starkey, who saw the civilizing potential of urban society, urban life and its virtues became a central concern of English writing only during the course of subsequent decades, and even then almost exclusively with reference to London. Even by the century's end, the literary expression of urban themes remained far outweighed by forms and preoccupations which were neo-feudal, courtly, and aristocratic.

This may have been an era marked by substantial migration of newcomers from the countryside, by the assumption of much wider responsibilities on the part of borough corporations, and by the assertion of strong, even authoritarian, rule from the town halls of the land. Yet English towns and cities lacked the size, the historical experience, or the strength of urban identity which would allow

them confidently or easily to assimilate immigrants or to implement their newly gained authority. Following the destruction of late medieval Catholicism, the practical imperative of political stability required the replacement of doctrinally rooted values and institutions with alternative discursive strategies. Both the pressing social and economic condition of the age and the dramatically increased responsibilities imposed by Crown and Parliament upon local officials made such refashioning an urgent priority.

Numerous suggestions have been offered regarding the effects of the Reformation on these essential cultural aspects of urban life. Charles Phythian-Adams took the Reformation to mark a very sharp break with the cultural activity of pre-Reformation towns, one in which the abolition of the religious guilds, with their rich ceremonial, proved critical. In his view the destruction of such ritual and ceremony as he had described in Coventry promised certain discord, especially under what he saw as the crushing weight of contemporary economic and social conditions. He anticipated that social groups would have now to rub up against each other without the protective buffer of those traditions, producing a breakdown in civil harmony and concord.[3]

A quite different interpretation has been put forth in a number of studies of civic ceremony which carry over the Reformation divide. Several of these studies see neither the social discord which Phythian-Adams expected, nor the absolute cessation of traditional ceremonial which led him to that expectation. Though of course they acknowledge the cultural significance of the early Reformation, they emphasize the successful adaptation of traditional ceremonial forms to suit new purposes, thereby enabling many towns to maintain civic harmony after the Reformation as well as before.[4]

The last chapters of this study take up this broad issue of politics and political culture. Civic cultural activities did of course continue, though we must still ask in what ways and in what guises they did so, and to what extent traditional forms were refashioned to new requirements. We need to know how civic cultural activities were

[3] Phythian-Adams, 'Ceremony and the Citizen', in Clark and Slack (eds.), *Crisis and Order in English Towns*, 57–85.

[4] See e.g. Audrey Douglas, 'Midsummer in Salisbury: The Tailor's Guild and Confraternity, 1444–1642', *Renaissance and Reformation*, 25/1 (1989), 35–51; Mills, 'Chester Ceremonial', 1–19, both drawing heavily on evidence provided in the sundry volumes of *Records of Early English Drama*. See also Michael Berlin, 'Civic Ceremony in Early Modern London', *Urban History Yearbook* (1986), 15–27; Manley, *Literature and Culture*, chap. 5.

employed to legitimize the prevailing distribution of power, and to what extent and how successfully such cultural activities conveyed the essential civic virtues of harmony, order, and deference without the theological underpinnings of medieval Catholicism.

It may fairly be said at the outset that several themes underlie this effort. One, as noted above, is that, *pace* Professor Phythian-Adams's worst fears, most towns of any political autonomy or substance did succeed in constructing a revised civic culture more or less capable of doing its job. These purpose-built cultural renovations, well established in many places by the end of the sixteenth century, emphasized the importance of hierarchy and deference over an essentially (in a social sense) undifferentiated freemanry. If they sometimes permitted greater friction between governors and governed, this may merely be the inevitable concomitant of the greater distance opened between those two elements by the events described in the first three parts of this study.

A second theme is that the revised political ethos in view here was not necessarily the product of Protestant or even puritan efforts as much as their impetus. While the advent especially of Puritanism is most often explained in doctrinal terms, 'godly rule' may also be viewed in a more secular and prosaic light. It provided one answer to the problem of how to fill a doctrinal void, created by the overthrow of traditional Catholicism and largely sustained by the mainstream of Elizabethan belief, in the cultural ethos of a developing urban society. It provided as well a ready substitute for the extensive degree of lay voluntarism which had sustained the guilds, fraternities, and other aspects of lay religious life. And it provided a stern monitor of moral behaviour, much in the manner once performed by the guilds and fraternities of an earlier time. For the most part, these needs of the secular community, and of the individual layman and woman, may well have come first. The fact that 'godly rule' often proved innovative, powerful, and effective in fulfilling that role should not coax us to the view either that it arose out of thin air, or that it did so as part of some teleological necessity. When the Dorchester Puritan divine John White began his spiritual leadership in that town in the first decade of the seventeenth century, we must note that he was invited by the more disciplinarian sort of townsmen to come from elsewhere to do so.[5] Although it is not the task of this book to take up the role of Puritanism as such, it

---

[5] Underdown, *Fire from Heaven*, 24.

does seem worthwhile to note at least in passing the conditions which invited it.

A third theme is that neither the formation of this revised political ethos, nor the demise of its predecessor, were as sudden to come about or as decisive as one might imagine. It took several decades at least for one to be grafted onto the stock of the other. The appearance of a powerful town preacher at a particular time, or of a new and more restrictive charter, or of a great aristocrat given influence in town affairs, or of a ban on dramatic perform-ances, are merely signal events which give the illusion of precision to changes which had more often than not come about over a gener-ation or more.

And still a fourth theme concerns the timing and sources for the refashioning of a post-Reformation urban culture. The discussion here is framed by an implicit debate about sources and timing. On one side of the debate lies the work of Peter Clark and Peter Borsay, who date the emergence of a provincial urban culture from about 1660 and account for it largely in the appropriation of cultural mod-els established in the metropolis of London or by the landed aristo-cracy. On the other side we find the views of Jonathan Barry, who also dates the emergence of provincial urban culture to about the mid-seventeenth century, but who finds some of its roots in the provincial urban communities themselves.[6]

The argument which will be presented here accepts Barry's emphasis on indigenous sources for certain types of urban culture, and particularly political culture, but dates their formation to about a century earlier than 1660. It suggests that the emergence of such cultural forms followed from the need to compensate for the destruction wrought by the Reformation in its opening phases to *c*.1553, and not primarily from the consumer demands of landed society or the stylistic influence of the great metropolis.

How shall we proceed? Having already sketched out the processes which led to a revised political order in a great many Eng-lish towns, let us look in turn at some of the elements of the contem-porary political culture as they were refashioned to serve in this post-Reformation era. It is a well-supported assumption that human activities of significance are clearly reflected in the buildings

---

[6] The historiography of these positions is described in J. Barry, 'Provincial Town Culture, 1640–1780: Urbane or Civic?', in Joan H. Pittock and Andrew Wear (eds.), *Interpretation and Cultural History* (1991), 205–9, in which he cites specific works by Peter Borsay, Peter Clark, and others in notes 29–36.

designed for the purpose.[7] It follows, too, that a change in functions, or in the manner of carrying them out, will be reflected in a change in the use and perhaps design of buildings. Chapter 12 deals with the 'container' in which urban governments carried out most of their business: the civic building, and especially that seat and symbol of local governments, the town hall.

Secondly, in the belief that political societies of the past (as well, of course, as of the present) often turned to historical imagery and a sense of the indigenous heritage as a means of inculcating identity and loyalty in their own times, Chapter 13 takes up the invocation of the past as an element in the urban political culture of this age. Though one could approach this in many ways, the choice here has been to discuss several disparate but nevertheless highly indicative issues. First is the emphasis on the use of civic regalia, a means of inculcating a civic and secular ceremonial in place of the traditional, doctrinally associated ritual of the pre-Reformation era. Another is the appeal to historical mythology with particular associations of place, especially mythologies of foundation. Still a third is a more modern form of historical reference: the use of the written record and the changing attitudes towards its function and care. And finally we must consider the visual but non-written record as preserved in the rarely acknowledged genre of mayoral and aldermanic portraiture.

Because the refashioning of a new and more appropriate civic culture had necessarily to discourage some forms of culture just as it encouraged others, we must also look at the ways in which the town governments approached the free expression of ideas. Here we will emphasize efforts to censor the expression, in dramatic performances especially, of what came increasingly to be seen as subversive views. It would be foolish to pretend that these issues summarize in its entirety the urban political culture of late Elizabethan or early Stuart towns, but they do at least illustrate some dimensions of the subject.

[7] See e.g. Wolfgang Braunfels, *Urban Design in Western Architecture: Regime and Architecture, 900–1900* (Chicago, 1988).

Political Culture and the Built Environment

The developments in urban politics and political culture discussed above are often reflected in the civic buildings and building activities of the era. Schools and schoolrooms, prisons and workhouses, market places and granaries, church pews, and perhaps even almshouses as they were built anew or rebuilt after the Dissolutions all contribute to the story. Enhanced control of wells and conduits, gatehouses and walls, roads and bridges often plays its part as well. But if one were to try to invert the train of thought behind this study, and begin with a search for changes in elements of political culture in the effort to identify signs of change in politics as such, there could hardly be a more dramatic or visible example than in the construction, conversion, or acquisition of town halls.

Like many other issues discussed in these pages, town halls were by no means new to the urban scene in the period following the Dissolutions. Exeter's Guildhall is recorded as standing on its present site as early as 1160,[1] Gloucester's hall received its first surviving mention in 1192,[2] and several score others may be identified over the centuries between that time and the period under consideration here. But if we define a town hall as a civic-controlled building which served as the normal place of business for the governing authority of a town (and if we do not allow ourselves to be confused by the multitude of terms by which such buildings may have been known in different times and places, such as 'guildhall', 'tolsey', 'boothall', and so forth), it stands to reason that we will find a proliferation of this particular type of edifice when we find an increase in the number of towns running their own affairs, or running them to a greater extent than before.

---

[1] H. Lloyd Parry, *The History of the Exeter Guildhall and the Life Within* (Exeter, 1936), 1.

[2] M. D. Lobel (ed.), *Historic Towns*, i (Baltimore, n.d.), *vide* Gloucester, 5 and n. 62.

The sheer numbers alone are the first indication that our expectations will not go for naught. A systematic investigation of this proliferation has shown that between 1500 and 1640, 202 halls were either built anew, renovated, and converted from earlier uses, or substantially rebuilt, in a total of 178 towns, with some of those towns acquiring more than one hall in that span. In addition to this number, something like 150 additional halls seem likely to have been built or acquired in the same era, though documentation for this second list remains incomplete.[3] This means that, if we accept the conventional estimates of the number of towns per se in England at this time as around 650–700, close to half the towns in the realm probably acquired a town hall in this era. For those with any substantial powers of self-government, the proportion must surely have been much higher.

Very few of those acquisitions in our period came before 1540. In fact, there are two important points to make about the chronology of this picture. The first is that the few halls built or acquired between 1500 and 1540 seem to fit into the pattern extending back to the late fifteenth century, in which it was a rare event for a town to build a new hall. And the second is that a decade-by-decade tabulation of town hall acquisitions shows a sharp increase right from the period of the first Dissolutions. An average of less than four halls a decade for the first four decades of the sixteenth century (an average similar to that of the second half of the previous century as well) jumps to an average of more than fourteen new halls for each of the next four decades, and an average of almost twelve a decade from 1540 to 1640.[4]

In view of the foregoing discussion about the development of local autonomy in English towns from this time, this pattern should not surprise us. After all, many towns acquired former guildhalls, which had served the literal purpose implied in their name, and had converted them to the use of civic governing bodies which were either newly autonomous or substantially more authoritative. At least an equal number of other towns built new halls from scratch to accommodate the same purposes. The ratio of newly built halls to converted guildhalls becomes greater from about the early Elizabethan era as the supply of those older buildings dwindled.[5]

It stands to reason that some of these acquisitions came about

---

[3] Tittler, *Architecture and Power*, 11 and appendix, 160–8.
[4] Ibid., table I, p. 14.   [5] Ibid., table II, p. 16.

quite apart from any particular changes in the local political scene. After all, buildings do wear out and have to be replaced, and some simply prove inadequate in point of size, space, layout, or design to accommodate new requirements placed upon them. Blandford Forum built a new hall in 1593 to replace its predecessor which had burned down some years before.[6] The collapse of the large council chamber in the Norwich Guildhall in 1511 led eventually to the construction of an entire new wing for the building.[7] Peterborough's government took down its 'Old Mote Hall' in 1615 before it could collapse, and replaced it three years later. Similar experiences ensued in Hull, Liverpool, and Abingdon.[8]

On the model of swimming pools in modern suburbia, some towns seem to have needed to keep up appearances with a rival town in the same area by constructing a new, usually larger, hall. One cannot help but notice how the addition of halls comes in clusters on the map in several parts of the realm. The Dorset towns of Poole, Shaftesbury, and the newly united Borough of Weymouth-Melcombe Regis all built halls between 1568 and 1571. Bridport and Blandford Forum both opened new halls in 1593, and six Dorset towns (Lyme Regis, Cerne Abbas, Weymouth on its own, Beaminster, Eversholt, and Shaftesbury again) between 1612 and 1628. Similar evidence of rivalry in construction may be found in Cornwall (both Penzance and Truro in 1615), Westmorland (Kendal in 1592 and Appleby in 1596), Worcestershire (Evesham, c.1580 and Droitwich, 1581), and Yorkshire (Knaresborough, 1592; Leeds, 1598; and Ripon, 1599).[9]

Yet it is difficult to argue that either the simple need to replace obsolete structures or the desire to emulate fast-paced neighbours should have been particularly prevalent at one time more than another. In addition, and despite the very considerable costs of such projects, there seems surprisingly little correlation between hall building and moments of financial plenitude. Many towns seem to

---

[6] John Hutchins, *The History and Antiquities of the County of Dorset*, ed. W. Shipp and W. Hodson (4 vols.; 1861–70), i. 216; E. L. Jones, S. Porter, and M. Turner (eds.), *A Gazetteer of English Urban Fire Disasters, 1500–1900*, Historical Geography Research Series, 13 (Aug. 1984), tables 3 and 5.

[7] N. Pevsner, *Buildings of England: North-east Norfolk and Norwich* (Harmondsworth, 1962), 259.

[8] Mellows (ed.), *Peterborough Local Administration*, pp. xcvii–xcviii; E. Gillet and K. MacMahon, *A History of Hull* (Oxford, 1981), 108; Twemlow (ed.), *Liverpool Town Books*, i. 353 n. 3; *VCH, Berkshire*, 4 (1924), 433.

[9] Tittler, *Architecture and Power*, appendix, 160–8.

have built on borrowed funds even at times which were very difficult for them financially.[10] In our effort to account for this plethora of building after about 1540, we are thrown back to the more obvious factor of function: in this case function means the requirements of those civic authorities and institutions for whom such buildings were intended.

The connection between the acquisition of civic halls and the attainment of greater powers of self-government is particularly evident in the substantial number of towns which built or acquired a hall within just a few years of their incorporation. At least 31 towns receiving charters of incorporation between 1500 and 1649 built halls soon after that constitutional milestone.[11] Typical of these towns was Banbury, in Oxfordshire, whose freemen acquired their charter in 1556 and built their hall in the same year. The new charter gave the townsmen their autonomy from the lord of the manor, who had ruled from Banbury Castle. Very likely the townsmen could have arranged to continue using the Castle for their own administrative purposes, thereby maintaining a continuity of venue for their government. But in their view the fact of self-governing authority demanded the symbolism of a new building, and so the newly empowered officers of the Corporation of the Mayor and Burgesses of Banbury forsook the symbol of the feudal authority which had been exercised over them for the new hall of 1556.[12]

Many charters made direct mention of the right to hold a hall: these clauses imparted an enhanced status to the hall as the place of official business for the local governing authority. In some cases, just as other aspects of a charter could be descriptive rather than prescriptive, the towns in question either had a suitable hall already or, in a few cases, had begun to construct one in the anticipation of incorporation. But in either event the wording of the charter left no doubt as to the use and status of the building in question. This designation had such force that in a number of instances official activities, including elections and other such events, which were not carried out in the hall as prescribed came to be challenged on grounds that an inappropriate venue rendered them void.

The fact is that the governments of newly autonomous towns, or those which were at least more in control of their own destinies than before, had two related spatial requirements for the conduct of their affairs. One was an increased need for 'office space' in which

---

[10] Ibid., chap. 3.   [11] Ibid., table v, 90.
[12] W. Potts, *A History of Banbury* (Banbury, 1958), 103–6.

government could be carried out in all its parts, and in a manner which was secure, central, accessible, and not shared with other occupants. This led, as we will see, to the design of buildings which could accommodate the several offices of contemporary town governments. The second was the need for edifices which bore symbolic significance, and which were designed, decorated, and furnished with that purpose in mind. Let us look at each in turn.

In some uses of the term, and for good historical reasons, a 'hall' is often taken to mean nothing more than a single large room. Certainly this is implicit in the evolution of the baronial hall throughout the medieval period, and has survived in a number of usages even to the present. And, indeed, some of the 'town halls' of the pre-Reformation era especially had been little more than this. But just as the baronial hall evolved to suit the changing domestic requirements of aristocratic families, so did the civic hall come to take on more complex configurations as new demands came to be placed upon it. And at least before the advent of industrialization, no period placed so many new demands on those halls as the one under consideration here.

Halls of this era were either built in the fashion of the raised 'box on stilts' in a market space that we see in such places as Thaxted, Hereford, Leominster, Titchfield, or Ledbury, or in what is to us the more familiar building on the ground, and in line with other buildings. In either case, several spatial divisions emerged with particular frequency at this time according to need. If the lower floor were not open for the purposes of marketing we might well find there such features as a gaol or lock-up, a kitchen, a storeroom for the town chest and its records, and an armoury. In addition, either here or (in two-storey halls) in the floor above, we would have spaces demarcated for the main business of government. This meant combinations of council chambers (one or two, but almost never more) and court rooms (usually one). There were many variations in these features, often based on size, available resources, or, perhaps most obviously, the institutional configuration and requirements of a particular borough. Such variations might include a court chamber in addition to the two council chambers, a jury room, and perhaps a mayor's parlour.

Most of these features will have become much more prominent in the halls built in the post-Reformation era than in those constructed for an earlier and, administratively speaking, simpler age. And when we are able to learn something of the evolution of the interior space

of these buildings, or of the succession of one building by another in its place, we invariably find the specificity of spatial use growing with time. After all, as the authority of a town increased, so did its need for space, and so, too, did the forms of that need.

Perhaps the most striking example of the rapidity with which spatial requirements could evolve is provided by the Borough of Plymouth. The new hall which the townsmen built here in 1565 already proved inadequate forty years on. Despite the financial strains involved in constructing their Elizabethan hall, the town leaders undertook to replace it in 1606–7. The new hall contained more conciliar meeting space than the former, and, most important, a house of correction as required by the Elizabethan Poor Laws.[13]

The example of Plymouth also presents the possibility that much of the spatial evolution in contemporary town halls reflected the greater need to display the powers of government in a public manner, and even to associate its more coercive aspects—in this case the workhouse stipulated by the Elizabethan Poor Laws—with the symbol of the government itself. It is characteristic of this age as a whole that the political agendas of governing authorities never strayed far from the problem of order and deference. In consequence, we quite commonly see in Plymouth facilities for incarceration or punishment within, under, or in front of town halls. In the context of the times, it can hardly be coincidental to the symbolic purpose of the hall itself. This leads us from the realm of floor plans and the practical utilization of space on the one hand to the realm of imagery and the symbolic use of the same space on the other.

At a time when, as we have seen, the urban rulers of the day faced ever increasing responsibilities and wielded steadily growing authority, they had also more than ever to devise effective means of projecting that authority and commanding the necessary deference from their fellow inhabitants. In the construction or conversion of towns halls, and in their design and furnishing, civic officials found ample opportunity to trumpet their authority. This applies to urban governments as a whole, and it applies especially to the position of the mayor as chief officer. Several devices were commonly employed towards that end.

We have already noted in passing the appearance of the mayor's parlour. Like many characteristics of the built environment at this

---

[13] Edwin Welch (ed.), *Plymouth Building Accounts of the Sixteenth and Seventeenth Centuries*, Devon and Cornwall Record Society, NS, 12 (1967), 1–18, 19–61.

time, there are pre-Reformation precedents for such a space. Nottingham, for one, is recorded as having had a mayor's parlour by 1486.[14] Yet for the most part the examples we know of seem almost all to be post-Reformation, as indeed—if they are to be taken to reflect the course of political change—they probably should be. References to mayoral parlours in, for example, Southwark (*c.*1550), Leicester (1563 and again in 1637), and even such a modest community as Lostwithiel by the Caroline period illustrate the point.[15]

The origin of the parlour as a self-contained interior space may be found in the monastery and then in the aristocratic house. In both cases it was a room set aside for the purpose of speech, as is explicit in the French derivation of the term. In its civic adaptation, it provided the mayor with a private place in which to confer with his fellow officials, with suitors who came to see him, and with dignitaries who visited the town. Here, too, he could find his own privacy and personal comfort as befit his dignity.

The best example of a mayor's parlour on view today is undoubtedly that noted above in the Leicester Guildhall which was first constructed in 1563, refurbished in 1637, and restored to some extent in the modern era. It suggests how such a room may well have been used in the course of the Mayor's daily routine. It is furnished with a mayoral seat which is identified architecturally as a special place of dignity. It has an enormous and lavishly embellished fireplace to provide comfort and project a sense of grandeur. And it is strategically located so as to open off from the main council chamber cum courtroom in which the mayor presided. In this scheme he could make a quick and dignified entrance to or exit from his place of honour in the hall without having to proceed up the main aisle through the throng assembled. This has of course become a normal path of travel for presiding justices in the courtrooms of the modern era, a separate entrance providing the mystique appropriate to the office.

We must also take note of the mayor's seat, both literally and figuratively a seat of honour and of power. Because it illustrates the point at hand with particular force and because it largely evolved in the period at hand, we should trace its development as a form of civic furnishing. Such an exercise tells us that the mayor's seat in a

[14] W. H. Stevenson (ed.), *Records of the Borough of Nottingham* (3 vols.; Nottingham, 1885), iii. 253.

[15] D. J. Johnson, *Southwark and the City* (Oxford, 1969), 222–3; N. A. Pegden, *Leicester Guildhall: A Short History and Guide* (Leicester, 1981), 4; Historical Manuscripts Commission, 55, *Various Collections*, i (1901), 331.

council chamber conventionally began as the central place on a long bench or settle set along the front wall of the room. On this long piece of furniture the mayor and 'his brethren' sat in presumably fixed order, at the same height and on either side of the mayor himself.[16] The image perfectly captures the balance of hierarchy and community which formed the political ethos of so many pre-Reformation towns.

Though some mayors in wealthier or more politically precocious towns may have sat in special chairs in the pre-Reformation era, this seems likely to have been a rather rare event. The specialized development of mayoral seating appears almost exclusively to have been a post-Reformation development. Late to emerge as a furniture form in their own right, chairs (as opposed, for example, to benches, stools, settles, and similar forms) and especially armchairs of any sort seem not to have become common before the sixteenth or even the early seventeenth century.[17] At the outset of our period contemporaries still considered them seats of dignity and honour, worthy of the *paterfamilias* of the household, the bishop in his cathedral, the schoolmaster in his schoolroom, and the mayor in the council or court chambers.[18]

Yet there can be little doubt that the armed chair came into its own as a special form of mayoral seating in the Elizabethan and Jacobean periods. Sometimes this meant adapting an older piece of furniture to a new use, as we see in Coventry. Here at some time during the sixteenth century local authorities converted one-third of a former three-seat 'throne', thought to be built for the use of the masters of the City's three major guilds before Dissolution, into a

---

[16] A description as late as the 17th cent. from the Borough of Preston still refers to 'an elevated bench where at the three portmotes or the two leet days and the Grand Leet . . . sitts the Mayor, Aldermen, and such gentry as attend those meetings' (R. Kuerden, *A Brief Description of the Borough and Town of Preston*, ed. John Taylor (Preston, 1818), 4–5, as cited in G. H. Tupling, 'Lancashire Markets in the Sixteenth and Seventeenth Centuries', *Transactions of the Lancashire and Cheshire Antiquarian Society*, 58 (1947 for 1945–6), 11).

[17] The implicit debate about just how late they did appear may be reconstructed in Ralph Fastnedge, *English Furniture Styles, 1500–1830* (1969), 8; H. Cescinsky and E. R. Gribble, *Early English Furniture and Woodwork* (2 vols.; 1922), ii. 145; and Ursula Priestly and Penelope Corfield, 'Rooms and Room Use in Norwich Housing, 1580–1730', *Post-Medieval Archaeology*, 16 (1982), 108, on the one hand; and Penelope Eames, *Furniture in England, France and the Netherlands from the Twelfth to the Fifteenth Century* (1977), pp. xxi and 181, on the other.

[18] For commentary on all these forms, see Tittler, ' "Seats of Honour, Seats of Power": The Symbolism of Public Seating in the English Urban Community, c.1560–1620', *Albion*, 24/2 (Summer 1992), 205–23.

very impressive single mayor's chair. This truncated version retained all the ornate carvings of the original (or at least of one-third of the original), and was placed in St Mary's Hall where it may still be seen today.[19]

Coventry provides us with yet further evidence of the importance with which contemporaries took the business of seating their dignitaries. We have a particularly evocative description of the three grand seats provided for the mayor, in three different civic buildings, on the occasion of the visit of the Princess Elizabeth to that City in 1604. One was placed in the Mayor's Parlour where he no doubt conferred with her in private, one was in the form of a pew in St Michael's Church, and one was undoubtedly the same one noted above in St Mary's Hall.[20]

But if the St Mary's Hall mayoral seat seems almost certain to have been converted from an earlier piece, we have several kinds of provision made for mayoral seating which was purpose-built. Sometimes this was nothing more than a dais which was provided for the common bench on which he still sat with his fellow aldermen. In a famously contentious parliamentary election dispute in Chichester, in 1586, we read in two separate depositions of the mayor 'coming down from the bench' to intervene in the preliminaries to violence.[21] A similar form appears to have applied in Exeter, for the Elizabethan historian of that City referred to the serjeant carrying the City's oath book 'up to the benche where the mayor, Recorder and aldermen Do sytt', so that the oath of office could be administered to the newly elected incumbent.[22]

In a common sequence of the development of civic furnishings and the official dignity which was thereby signified, the bench holding the mayor and aldermen first became decorated or architecturally enhanced. Then the mayor's position grew distinct and eventually free-standing altogether in the form of a true armchair for his exclusive use. In Shrewsbury, for example, 'the seate for the

[19] Herbert Cescinsky, 'An Oak Chair in St Mary's Hall, Coventry', *Burlington Magazine*, 39/223 (1921), 170–7, summarized in Cescinsky and Gribble, *Early English Furniture*, ii. 154–63 and figs. 204 and 210; John Gloag, *The Englishman's Chair: Origins, Design and Social History of Seat Furniture in England* (1964), 33–4; Eames, *Furniture in England*, 196–7.

[20] R. Ingram (ed.), *REED: Coventry* (Toronto, 1981), 364–5.

[21] Deposition of James Cooke, PRO, STAC 5/C23/37.

[22] John Vowell, *alias* Hooker, *The Description of the Citie of Excester*, ed. W. J. Harte, J. W. Schopp, and H. Tapley-Soper (3 vols.; Devon and Cornwall Record Society, 1919–47), iii. 794.

baylyffs [an office which in Shrewsbury was tantamount to the mayoralty] and Aldermen in the Guyle hall . . . was waynskottid in more coomlyer and commendabler order than before', this in 1583/4. And a few months later we read in an early chronicle that the hall was 'sylyd within overhedd and newe garnyshyd to saye where baylyffs and Aldermen sytt . . . in bewtyfull and decent order'.[23] In York a dozen 'semely' cushions were brought to the Council Chamber for the mayor and his brethren to sit upon in 1562/3, which implies that they still sat together on the same bench. But fifteen years later the Council agreed that a 'mete and convenient chaire' be made for the mayor alone, presumably for the first time.[24] In Totnes, where mayoral authority had been in hot dispute a few years earlier, the mayor's seats in both Council Chamber and courtroom were covered with ornate canopies of carved oak in about 1624, an addition which may still be seen.[25]

And in Beverley, which had also experienced bitter factional divisions surrounding the office of the mayor,[26] we have an remarkable example of an intermediate developmental form of mayoral seating, constructed in 1604 and still surviving, which is almost certainly unique. It is a three-seat, box-like settle built with the middle seat raised up seven or eight inches above the level of the attached seats on each side. It is said in local tradition to have been built at the request of the mayor for that year, Henry Farrar. Both the date and the initials 'H F' may be seen carved into the piece. Of the same design and materials we have two lengthy benches meant to accommodate the town's aldermen, while we presume that the deputy mayor and the town clerk, or perhaps the recorder and clerk, sat on each side of the mayor. As the aldermanic benches look to be nearly contemporary or even earlier than the mayoral settle, it may well be that they represent the place where both aldermen and mayor sat before the construction of the smaller piece.

There are other examples of mayoral seating from this era as well, though none so intriguing as the arrangements in Beverley. In their

[23] Revd W. A. Leighton, 'Early Chronicles of Shrewsbury, 1372–1606', *Transactions of the Shropshire Archaeological and Natural History Society*, 3 (1880), 295 and 299.

[24] A. Raine (ed.), *York Civic Records* (8 vols.; Yorkshire Archaeological Society Record Series), 6 (1948 for 1946), 55; and 7 (1950 for 1949), 168.

[25] For the bitter dispute between political factions in Totnes, see above, p. 192. Information and photographs of the hall have been provided me by Mr Richard J. Butterfield, Town Clerk of Totnes, to whom I am grateful.

[26] See above, p. 188.

renovation of the Guildhall in 1637, Leicester's officials demarcated the mayor's place on the aldermanic bench by providing a classical architectural 'surround' attached to the wall behind the mayor's place on that bench, by adding cushions to his place alone, and by affixing the royal arms to the wall immediately behind it.[27] And in Salisbury we have two finely carved mayoral chairs of a *caqueteuse* style. One is dated 1585 (the date of the new town hall in which we presume it to have been placed) and built at the bequest of the standing mayor of that time, Robert Bower. The second, a replica of the first, was commissioned and presented by his eventual successor in that office, Maurice Green, who served in 1622. In addition to the fact that both chairs were presented by mayors, each bears the City's arms carved in the lower portion of the back panel. Having at least two council or court chambers in which the mayor presided, the new Salisbury Hall could accommodate both pieces.[28]

With frequent mention of the right to maintain town halls in charters of incorporation, and with the more common use of furnishings designed specifically to reflect the dignity and authority of those who held the reins of power over the towns themselves, halls seem well on their way to becoming highly emotive symbolic structures. In the vocabulary of the social anthropologists, the civic hall became in this era a 'tangible formulation of the notion of civic authority'.[29] As a semiotic form, it does indeed seem to have marked the centre as the centre. It was fashioned and furnished to legitimize the officials who ruled from its chambers, demonstrating a form of authority which, in considerable contrast to the authority of the contemporary and traditional landed orders, was 'made, not born'.

We can detect further evidence of this reality, not in evidence concerning structure itself, but in several indications of its use and of the perception which contemporary townsmen came to hold of it. The first of these indications comes in the form of court cases concerning local disputes in which the control and use of those buildings formed an important part of the controversy. One such case derives in the small but politically lively Borough of Evesham in Worcestershire.[30]

---

[27] Pegden, *Leicester Guildhall*, 4; T. H. Fosbrooke and S. H. Skillington, 'The Old Town Hall of Leicester', *Transactions of the Leicestershire Archeological Society*, 13 (1923–4), 1–72 and *passim*.

[28] Victor Chinnery, *Oak Furniture: The British Tradition* (1979), 448–9 and plate I; *VCH, Wiltshire*, 6 (1962), 87; H. Shortt (ed.), *The City of Salisbury* (Salisbury, 1957), 58 and 94; Wiltshire County Record Office, MS G23/1/3, fo. 61^r.

[29] Clifford Geertz, *The Interpretation of Cultures* (New York, 1973), 91.

[30] The following is drawn from G. May, *A Descriptive History of the Town of*

Evesham had technically been governed by the local Abbot as lord of the manor, though the townsmen had informally asserted a considerable amount of control in what (despite the absence of any charters which can be discovered) they declared to be the name of the Crown. Both the leet court and the three-week court of the town had long met in the building known variously as the 'Town Hall', the 'Old Booth Hall', and the 'Roundhouse'.

After Dissolution the Crown sold the Abbot's rights over the town to Sir Thomas Hoby, who built a new hall in which to collect tolls and hold his manorial court. But at the same time, the townsmen chose to assume that the Abbot's full jurisdiction had come instead to devolve upon them as a community. They assumed that their payment of the annual fee farm entitled them to choose their own bailiff and enjoy most of the perquisites of the three-week court. The ensuing dispute between Hoby as lord of the manor and the townsmen involved not only a conflicting interpretation of legal entitlement, but also a conflict involving the use of the two halls.

This contest wound up in the courts, but it came to be played out in town as well: a contest between buildings as well as between factions. We read in the ensuing testimony of deponents of the virtual guerrilla warfare whereby each side attempted to wrest control of the other's hall, and to defend its own, as if the two buildings had become the capital cities of warring states. The yeoman Henry Wylles described what seems to have been the first move in these campaigns, which saw Thomas Cesar, allied to the Hoby cause, securing the key to Hoby's hall and defending it at poignard's point against the attempted 'invasion' of the town's bailiffs. Shortly thereafter the bailiffs tried again, launching an assault against the newer hall while Hoby's steward held court. As described by a deponent, George Hawkins, the attackers seized a cucking-stool for use as a battering ram and drove it

through the face of the saide Courte . . . before the Steward and beneath the jury . . . and one Arnold Tickridge . . . in the Topp of the Same and a number of boyes hallinge the same makinge a Great Clamor and Voyce . . . and Cryinge a Steward a Steward a court a court a jury a jury and the foreman of the Jury shuld be sett by the heles.

And while these riotous events were transpiring, the two serjeants employed by Hoby's court stood at the door with great black staves

Evesham (1845); and PRO, E. 134/29 Eliz., East. 12, and E. 123/12/fo. 275ᵛ, *Hoby* v. *Kighley*.

and iron picks in their hands and 'being charged to serve the Quene [by the rioters, who claimed royal authority for their actions] they refused to do so'.

In the end, the Barons of the Exchequer worked out a compromise whereby the three-week court remained in the old hall under the aegis of the townsmen and the leet court came to be held in the new, under Hoby's jurisdiction. Eventually, in 1604, Evesham gained its full incorporation and assumed control over both courts . . . and both buildings.

Each side in this conflict had implicitly assumed that the appropriate building must be used for particular official functions, and that the use of the appropriate building legitimized the activities held within. This assumption became explicit in several other instances. When riotous townsmen in Waltham, Essex, wished to prevent the holding of the portreeve's court in the reign of Mary, they simply nailed shut the door to the Moothall and considered the issue settled. It seems never to have occurred to them that the same people might hold the same court elsewhere and in fact, according to the custom of the day, they probably would not have done so.[31] Similarly, when dissidents plotted to overthrow and replace the Mayor of Liskeard in 1611, they knew they would have to proclaim their own candidate in the Guildhall, and nowhere else but the Guildhall, if he were to have any chance at being recognized as a legitimate mayor.[32]

Like Evesham, Shaftesbury also had two civic halls, one of uncertain but ancient vintage, and a second built by the townsmen in 1568. Clearly the older building pertained to the manorial lord and the newer one, especially after the town's incorporation in 1604, to the townsmen. And perhaps inevitably, when a jurisdictional dispute broke out between the lord's steward and the townsmen in 1618, the symbolic role of both buildings figured heavily in the contest. It had long been the custom in Shaftesbury, both before and after incorporation, for the new mayor to be sworn into office by the lord's steward in the regular annual law-day after Michaelmas. But when the mayor-elect, John Sweetnam, presented himself before the steward, Robert Moore, in the new hall for that purpose, Moore refused to proceed. He considered that, if the authority of the lord over the townsmen were to be upheld, he could perform his role only in the

[31] PRO, STAC 4/Bundle 6/23.
[32] *Hodge* v. *Hunkyn et al.*, PRO, STAC 8/164/10.

old hall. When pressed to proceed, Moore stalked out of the building. The mayor-elect had to be sworn by the recorder, before the outgoing mayor and an assemblage of burgesses, and in the new hall. Preferring to stand on principle above getting on with the job, Moore then refused to hold any leet courts lest he be compelled to recognize Sweetnam as mayor. The principle of recognizing the old hall as the only appropriate place in which to swear in a new mayor had become more important to Moore, and to the Countess of Pembroke as Lord of the Manor, even than holding the annual law-day itself.[33]

Similar cases may be drawn from the archives concerning Hythe, Chesterfield, and no doubt other towns as well.[34] They all point to the widespread understanding of the hall not merely as a convenient place of business, but as an edifice irreplaceably symbolic of civic authority, power, and legitimacy.

A second indication of contemporary perceptions of the town hall as a symbol of governing authority may be found in the evidence of contemporary linguistic usage. In town after town, the language of local records uses the word 'hall' in this era as a shorthand reference to the governing authority within, much as one reads '10 Downing Street' or 'the White House' today. Thus, for example, an agreement of 1567 made by the Mayor and Assembly of the Borough of Boston that a new market cross 'shall . . . be mayntenyd and repayrede by the Towne Hall, as to them [*sic*!] shall seem goode'.[35]

And a third indication of the emerging perception of the hall as a place of authority may be found in the evidence that a number of town governments of this era, as part of the move to greater narrowness and exclusivity of the office holders, moved to restrict access by the general population to the building from which they governed. An early indication of this intent appears in 1550, when the ruling elite in the Borough of Southwark constructed a 'secret chamber' in which the mayor could confer in confidence with his brethren: in effect a form of the mayor's parlour.[36] But a few years later, in 1562, the mayor and burgesses of Bedford voted to exclude anyone from the entire premises of the hall, save for JPs and other officials of the

---

[33] *Mary, Countess Dowager of Pembroke and William, Earl of Pembroke* v. *Inhabitants of Shaftesbury*, PRO, E. 134/18 James I/East I.

[34] *Cramer* v. *Hudson et al.*, PRO, E. 134/19 James I/Mic. 25; D. F. Botham, 'A History of Chesterfield Marketplace', thesis presented to the Royal Institute of British Architects (Apr. 1974), 13.

[35] J. F. Bailey (ed.), *Minutes of Boston*, i. 90.

[36] D. J. Johnson, *Southwark and the City* (Oxford, 1969), 222–3.

town, unless they had official business to conduct therein. The freemanry eventually considered this so restrictive that, in the heady
iconoclastic days of the Interregnum, they repealed the decision.[37]
And in the same decade as the exclusion from the Bedford hall, the
senior officers of both Oxford and Bristol began to meet secretly in
a closed and separate chamber to prepare business for the council at
large, in both cases an employment of the hall to achieve greater
secrecy even amongst the members of the ruling element in the same
town.[38]

It was of course but a short step from this kind of exclusivity to the
narrowing of the franchise, not only in parliamentary elections, but
even in contests for the mayoralty. Here again the hall provided a
refuge from the public eye. By 1603 we have the mayor and
burgesses of Hastings objecting to mayoral elections being held
'abroad in the publick view of the wholl multitude not only of Inhabitants but also of many strangers assembling at such elecons in the
open Hundred place', and ruling that from henceforth such occasions would be held behind the closed doors of 'the Court Hall of this
towne, as a place more decent apt & secreat, . . . Any old custome
usage or decree to the contrary notwithstanding'.[39]

This use of the town hall was far from unique. In a similar manner
the ruling oligarchy of Winchester had grown so restrictive by the
1620s that even the members of the secondary council, the Twenty-
Four, complained that the mayor and the members of the Council of
Twelve, a more exclusive body made up of former mayors, failed to
let even them enter the council chamber and partake in deliberations. And in Chester, during a time of considerable duress on the
eve of Civil War (1640), participation in the traditional reconcilia-
tory ritual known as the 'Calveshead Breakfast' became severely
restricted to a small elite and moved behind the doors of the Guildhall. The occasion was now considered 'a more particular priuat
dynar for the Aldermen, gentlemen & Archers only [the archers
having contested for a shooting prize as part of the traditional festiv-
ities] *and no loose people to troble the hall*' (author's italics).[40]

These may well have been isolated examples of town elites mak-

---

[37] Bedford Town Hall Documents, Bedfordshire Record Office, MS B I, fo. 5ᵛ.

[38] Carl I. Hammer, Jr, 'Anatomy of Oligarchy: The Oxford Town Council in the
Fifteenth and Sixteenth Centuries', *Journal of British Studies*, 18/1 (Fall 1978), 7;
Stanford (ed.), *Ordinances of Bristol*, 29.

[39] 6 Apr. 1603, Hastings Town Record Book, as cited in J. M. Baines, *Historic
Hastings* (Hastings, 1955), 55.

[40] BL Harleian MS 2125, fo. 133, as cited in Clopper (ed.), *REED: Chester*, 451.

ing their halls secure from the general multitude: the evidence by which such instances have been discovered survives for only a small proportion of England's towns. Yet these instances do seem one of a piece with other indications to the same effect. As oligarchy grew apace in the wake of the Reformation process and as the governors grew further than ever apart from their putative fellows amongst the governed, doors did close both figuratively and literally.

Further occasions to note the use of the hall in the contemporary encouragement of political exclusivity will arise in due course as we discuss other issues. But this should suffice to suggest that by such force of symbolism, both in political practice and common parlance, did the town hall frequently mark two stages in the political evolution with which this study has been concerned. In the early decades of our chosen period, we see its service as a common symbol of greater self-determination in towns which only a short while before had emerged from the economic status of the village or (more commonly) the legal standing of a strictly manorial community. And with increasing frequency towards the latter decades of our study the hall reflects the growing force of a more vigorously oligarchic rule within the same sorts of towns.

13

Oligarchic Rule and the Civic Memory

i

In most political systems, and especially those faced with the challenge of change, successful governments have understood the benefits of inculcating civic pride and deference amongst the citizenry by an appeal to their common heritage. This was as true for the Emperors of Rome facing the barbarian incursions as for Churchill's Wartime Cabinet facing the Third Reich or the government of Lyndon Johnson facing both war and domestic protest. As Sir Keith Thomas has reminded us, 'the most common reason for invoking the past was to legitimize the prevailing distribution of power'.[1] For the pre-Reformation urban communities of provincial England, whose presiding townsmen could draw on few other contemporary devices even in normal times, this need had been fulfilled with considerable efficacy by the doctrines and institutions of traditional religion. While emphasizing a common fellowship in Christ as the foundation stone of a shared heritage, these doctrines and institutions also emphatically inculcated obedience, order, and deference.[2]

The first chapters of this study have suggested how both doctrines and institutions of the medieval urban community served these functions. One additional element of that traditional outlook had been the accretion of a collective memory for the local community. The concept of collective memory is of course well established by studies in a number of disciplines, and it has a variety of applications to European communities of this era.[3] But its connection with the practice of medieval Catholicism proved a particularly powerful force.

---

[1] Keith Thomas, 'The Perception of the Past in Early Modern England', Creighton Lecture, London University (1983), 2–4.

[2] See Duffy, *Stripping of the Altars*, esp. chap. 4.

[3] See e.g. Maurice Halbwachs, *On Collective Memory*, English translation (Chicago, 1992); Nora, 'Between Memory and History', 7–25; and Daniel Woolf,

If we think of medieval popular religion as dominated by a 'cult of the dead', as Eamon Duffy has recently suggested, then such a cult necessitated a collective memory.[4] The dead needed to be remembered because the fate of their souls depended in part on the prayers of the living; the living remembered the dead in part because they depended upon being remembered in turn. This imperative created all manner of occasions for remembrance, especially in the regular activities of family and parish worship. Families often recited the *De profundis* in memory of the dead before meals and the parish liturgy often invoked the name of the deceased.

Rich and poor not only shared some forms of remembrance but each had forms of their own. The rich were remembered by their benefactions, in the prayers of pensioners whom they endowed in their bequests, even by their names on church plate which they might bequeath. They might be remembered in visual imagery: funerary brasses, memorials, and even religious paintings which, as Duffy reminds us, 'however stylized, almost certainly reflected . . . a desire for a personal continuance amongst the living'.[5]

And for the poor and middling sorts there were more modest mnemonic devices: anniversaries, obits, lights, and finally, the bede-roll, 'the cheapest way of securing the perpetual recollection of one's name in the course of the worship of the parish'. This last device amounted to a virtual roll-call of deceased parishioners, read out regularly before the whole parish community as an invitation for prayer. It served both 'to present for imitation a pattern of piety, and to instill in the hearers a sense of the parish and its worship as a continuing reality'.[6]

These devices, and also the allegiance to a local patron saint as the spiritual guardian of the community, all helped in the vital task of 'conserving the parish's sense of a shared past' and thus the community's as well.[7] Much the same might even be said for other material accoutrements of parish worship which, if unconnected with particular people, at least imparted a shared sense of familiarity and local pride in such implements. These would have included stained glass

---

'Memory and Historical Culture in Early Modern England', *Journal of Canadian Historical Association*, NS, 2 (1991), 283–308. For an excellent example of the operation of collective memory in a contemporary Continental urban community, see D. V. and F. W. Kent, *Neighbors and Neighborhood in Renaissance Florence: The District of the Red Lion in the Fifteenth Century* (Locust Valley, NY, 1982), esp. 95.

[4] Duffy, *Stripping of the Altars*, 327. The following three paragraphs derive from Duffy (pp. 327–37), with quoted passages noted as appropriate.

[5] Ibid. 334.   [6] Ibid. 335–7.   [7] Ibid. 161–3 and 335.

windows, rood screens, reredoses, altar rails and screens, communion cups, chalices, and other church plate, sometimes reliquaries
and other such objects.

The loss of these mnemonic forms in the first stages of the English
Reformation has now been well and thoroughly documented. Yet as
a concept which transcends environment, the collective memory
provided by pre-Reformation religion has not been particularly well
considered in the urban context, nor has the importance of compen-
sating for its destruction been widely appreciated. Yet the striking
social and political changes of these years threatened the very stability which a viable collective memory had helped impart. The local
community faced a greater need than ever for a shared historical
identity: a fixed star from which to navigate the shoals of rapid
change. A collective memory could be made to inspire the harmonious interaction of the community's members, to sustain a common
purpose, to legitimize the contemporary political order. Though
they may not have understood the theory behind this effect, or
employed our vocabulary to describe it, urban leaders of the day
understood this concept rather well, and they strove to encourage
substitutes for these traditional mnemonic devices.

This chapter will concentrate on some of the elements of that
revised collective memory: strategies which form part of the political
culture of post-Reformation towns and which help to foster traditions of urbanism which were otherwise so feebly established in
English towns of this time. These include the design and use of civic
regalia, the use of secular mythology, a reinvigorated concern for the
historical record, the identification of the town with the nation
through a shared view of recent events, and the advent of civic
portraiture.

ii

The continued development and use of civic regalia provided continuity with the ceremonial aspects of civic traditions and with local
political institutions seen over time. Most regalia derived from an
essentially secular idiom. Yet because it also represented the collective purchases and contributions of local benefactors through the
years, it thereby consisted of valuable objects with very particular
local associations. In consequence, it served to bind the generations
in much the same way as the sight and use of church plate had done
(and in some cases continued to do). In fact, the destruction of a very

substantial amount of traditional church plate and other material accoutrements of traditional worship probably made the local possession of civic plate and regalia even more important than before. And as the attribute of antiquity—what contemporaries sometimes called 'auncienty'—conferred precedence, seniority, and virtue, it was considered very important to have regalia that dated, or could be made to date, a long way back. The townsmen of Faversham no doubt had precisely this in mind when, needing to replace their old ceremonial staff with a new one, they referred in their assembly book to the making of 'a new ancient staffe'.[8]

In addition, regalia had always had particular symbolic associations with the officers of the town in general and with the mayor in particular. In cycles of but a single year at a time, mayors came and mayors went. But the mace or chain or badge of office, even in due time the mayor's chair, continued in use and in view from year to year, symbolizing as they did so the continuation of mayoral authority over time.

In all these ways a town's civic plate and regalia could link the present to the past without risk of doctrinal infelicities. They encouraged an ever more pointed focus on the authority and prestige of the governing authorities, especially the mayor. Vestments and furniture aside, for they were not strictly speaking items of regalia at all, the civic regalia of most chartered boroughs might include seals, chains, badges, silver oars (especially in coastal towns), ceremonial cups, staffs, and both swords and hats of maintenance.[9] But perhaps the chief item was the mace, and many towns came in this era to boast of more than one.

Over the long run, the chief development in the mace's design was its evolution from an actual weapon of war, made to be held at the staff end, to a purely symbolic implement (now held at the butt end by a specifically designated official) and engraved with the town's arms. In that lengthy evolution the original iron or oak of the shaft often gave way to ornamented gold or silver. These developments began long before and continued throughout the period under consideration here.[10] The results may be seen in display cases and, more publicly, on civic occasions throughout the land today.

[8] Maidstone Borough Archives, Kent County Archives, MS FA FAc/9 Bundle 2.

[9] L. Jewitt and W. H. St John Hope, *The Corporate Plate and Insignia of Office of the Cities and Towns of England and Wales* (2 vols.; 1895), vol. i, pp. lxiii–lxxxix.

[10] This and the following paragraph are largely based on Jewitt and St John Hope, *Corporate Plate and Insignia of Office*, vol. i, pp. xviii–xl.

But in addition to this development, the sixteenth and early seventeenth centuries saw the relatively small 'serjeant's mace' give way to the larger and entirely ceremonial 'mayor's mace', and then, especially in the seventeenth century, to the form of a 'great mace'. These larger and more ceremonial models came to be carried not only on occasions of great ceremony, but often on more routine occasions. In some places the mace went before the mayor in the regular course of his perambulations around the town, as a daily and public reminder of his dignity and might. In Jacobean Shaftesbury, for example, the Mayor had the mace borne before him every day of the year save for the four days preceding Mid-Summer Fair.[11] Often it rested in public view during the course of official business in the Guildhall. In Macclesfield the mace was even replicated in a carving over the portal of the Elizabethan Guildhall.[12] With the addition of that image the building came to symbolize more than ever before not the fellowship of the guild which it once might have served, but the authority of the mayor over his fellows.

Given its own long history, the fact that it came so often to be inscribed with the town's arms (and occasionally with those of a particular mayor or with iconographical representations of local historical events),[13] the mace came more than ever to be seen as a symbol of the town's privileges and of both the authority and the dignity of its officers. Jurisdictional disputes between civic and ecclesiastical officials in cathedral cities, a common enough form of conflict in their time, sometimes revolved around the symbolic right of the mayor to have his mace carried before him when he entered the local cathedral. An example of this occurred in Winchester towards the end of our period. A similar dispute broke out in Chester, in 1606, regarding the mayor's right to enter with his ceremonial sword.[14] Like the regimental colours of conventional warfare, contemporaries considered the mace and its analogues as valuable symbolic trophies in the occasional political riot or skirmish.[15] And on those infrequent

---

[11] Deposition of Walter Hamon, Serjeant to the Mayor, in the case of *Countess and Earl of Pembroke* v. *Inhabitants of Shaftesbury*, PRO, E. 134/18, James I, East. I.

[12] C. S. Davies (ed.), *A History of Macclesfield* (Manchester, 1961), frontispiece.

[13] e.g. Arundel and St Ives (Cornwall); G. W. Eustace, *Arundel: Borough and Castle* (1922), 255; and J. H. Matthews, *A History of the Parishes of St Ives, Lelant, Towednack and Zennor in the County of Cornwall* (1892), 194.

[14] BL, Harleian MS 1944, fo. 92ʳ; Rosen, 'Economic and Social Aspects of Winchester', 229.

[15] *Mayor and Bailiffs of Carmarthan* v. *Devereux et al.*, PRO, STAC 2/Bundle 17/271, esp. the plaintiff's bill.

but grand occasions of a royal visit, the mace seems almost invariably to have been employed in two ceremonial ways. First, when the mayor led the town's officials to greet the monarch at the outskirts of the town, he gave the mace over to his lord and then received it back, much as a military regiment presents its colours to the commander-in-chief and receives them back today. And secondly, the mace was then carried before the monarch, often by the mayor himself, as a sign of welcome.[16] In both cases the action symbolized the community's obedience to the king or queen; the former symbolized as well the monarch's endorsement of the local government.

Maces and similar items of regalia often dated from a change in constitutional status. When, on the virtual eve of the Dissolutions, Henry VIII appropriated the lordship of what until that moment had been known as Bishop's Lynn, giving the townsmen greater independence from seigneurial control in the bargain, townsmen made a mayoral sword to mark the occasion. The commissioning of the new sword became so integral to this constitutional event that a local chronicler could imply that the sword itself lay at the heart of the change: 'and att that time that the maior gott the sword itt hath even since bene called Kinges Lynn and the sword hath been caried before the maior'.[17] As in Lynn, if a town did not have a sword or mace at its incorporation, it rapidly had one made. Upon its incorporation of 1614, the burgesses of Stafford spent virtually £50 on a gold and silver mace weighing 111.5 ounces.[18]

iii

The symbolic aspects of the local heritage did not all consist of material objects. To illustrate this quest for a redirected collective memory with a format to suit the times, we could hardly find better metaphors than the replacement in post-Reformation Canterbury of the pageant of the martyrdom of St Thomas Becket with a series of

[16] J. J. Anderson (ed.), *REED: Newcastle-upon-Tyne* (Toronto and Manchester, 1982), 10; A. Johnston and M. Rogerson (eds.), *REED: York* (1979), 155, 194–8, 554, 583, 586, 588–9, 599; David Galloway (ed.), *REED: Norwich, 1540–1642* (Toronto and London, 1984), 252. The infinitely grander and more complex ceremony surrounding a royal entry into London is recounted in R. Malcolm Smuts, 'Public Ceremony and Royal Charisma: The English Royal Entry into London, 1485–1642', in A. L. Beier, David Cannadine, and James Rosenheim (eds.), *The First Modern Society: Essays in History in Honour of Lawrence Stone* (Cambridge, 1989), 65–93; and Manley, *Literature and Culture*, chap. 5.

[17] BL, Add. MS 8937, fo. 1a.

[18] William Salt Library, MS D(W) 1721/1/4, fo. 90.

giants associated with the mythological foundations of the City,[19] or the replacement, in 1609, of the sculpted figure of Jesus on Coventry Cross with a figure of Lady Godiva.[20] The reference leads us to consider the reinvigorated use of local mythology as an integral element in the revised political culture of the age. The story of Godiva is well known at least in its broad outlines. The wife of the demanding lord of the town, Earl Leofric, Godiva was willing to sacrifice her modesty by riding naked through the streets of the town if her husband would rescind a harsh tax which he had levied on the townsmen. The story, for which there are elements of documentation, is set in the period before the Norman Conquest. It marked an important symbolic representation of the origins of the city's liberties. When those liberties seem to have been threatened on the eve of the sixteenth century the story underwent a revival. In seeking to remind the authorities of their ancient liberties, the townspeople posted a poem about Godiva on the door of their parish church in 1495, and again a year later.

This reminds us that, though (save for the reign of Mary) the images of late medieval popular theology faded steadily in the years after 1540, there remained an interest in figures drawn either from the Old Testament or either classical or earlier English mythology. The robust Tudor revival of Arthurian legends which, in the hands of Geoffrey of Monmouth and others, effectively linked Arthurian Britain to classical accounts of Troy, has been well established, especially in regard to the history of London.[21] The application which provincial town leaders made of this genre probably reflects in part a need to replace patron saints as guardians of the local community with similarly totemic images more appropriate to time and place. In any event, to return a moment to Coventry, we find in the year 1580 a visual reference to Godiva worked into Coventry's newly rebuilt market hall, and in 1586 we note the hanging of her portrait, astride a white horse and against the backdrop of an impressive Renaissance cityscape, in St Mary's Hall. It may still be seen today. And, as we have noted above, her image replaced that of Jesus on the Coventry market cross a few years later.[22]

[19] Cited in Hutton, *Merry England*, 74.

[20] Ingram (ed.), *REED: Coventry*, 577; F. Bliss Burbage, *Old Coventry and Lady Godiva* (Birmingham, n.d.), 53.

[21] This is well summarized in Manley, *Literature and Culture*, esp. 181–200, and notes therein. See also D. R. Woolf, 'Of Danes and Giants: Some Popular Beliefs about the Past in Early Modern England', *Dalhousie Review*, 71/2 (Summer 1991), 166–209.

[22] For this and the following, see I. N. Brewer, *A Topographical Historical*

In the City of York the analogous totem for citizens' rights and liberties, and one much more directly linked with Trojan and Arthurian associations, came in the form of King Ebrauk, said by Geoffrey of Monmouth to be a great-grandson of Brutus, founder of Britain.[23] The name no doubt derives from the Latin name for the city, Eboracum. The figure of Ebrauk appears at least twice in the fifteenth century. On the second occasion he is part of a tableau erected to greet Henry VII in his post-accession tour of Yorkshire in 1486. Ebrauk's role here seems not only to have been to welcome Henry to the City, but to let him know that York traced its origins to well before the line of the Tudors and their ancestors. But unlike many traditional religious images, Ebrauk's memory is sustained: we find him welcoming James I to the City in 1617 and Charles I in 1633, and we even find the City of Chester borrowing his image for a play in 1588.[24]

A similar example of an old myth flourishing after the Reformation derives from Lichfield. It is the myth of St Amphibalus and the nine hundred and ninety-nine Christian martyrs from St Albans in Hertfordshire.[25] The story is that Amphibalus, a Christian priest of the Roman town of Verulamiam, near what is now St Albans, gave shelter to the Christian missionary Albanus or Alban. When they were discovered, Albanus was taken out of the city and martyred for his faith on a nearby hill, almost certainly within the precincts of the present Cathedral of that eponymously named city. The Abbey which preceded it was built on what was thought to be the site of the martyrdom. But Amphibalus fled the scene, followed shortly by nine hundred and ninety-nine other Verulamiam residents who sought his blessing. They, in turn, were pursued by the authorities, captured, taken yet elsewhere, and slain to a man, save for

Description of the County of Warwick (1820), 139; Ingram (ed.), *REED: Coventry*, 577; Edwin S. Hartland, *The Science of Fairy Tales* (1891), 74; Burbage, *Old Coventry and Lady Godiva*, 51–3; J. C. Lancaster, *Godiva of Coventry* (1967), 50–1.

[23] Geoffrey traces Ebrauk's descent as from Brutus to his son Locrinus, to his son Madden, to his son Mempricious, and thence to Ebrauk, with Locrinus having gained from his father and passed down to his line the Kingdom of Leogria (Geoffrey of Monmouth, *The History of the Kings of Britain*, Penguin edn., trans. and ed. Lewis Thorpe (1966), 75, 78–9).

[24] Johnston and Rogerson (eds.), *REED: York*, 73, 140–1, 147–8, 552, and 583; Clopper (ed.), *REED: Chester*, 156.

[25] The following is drawn from Douglas Johnson, 'Lichfield and St Amphibalus: The Story of a Legend', *Transactions of the South Staffordshire Archeological and Historical Society*, 28 (1988 for 1986–8), 3–6. Geoffrey of Monmouth correctly identified Amphibalus as the confessor of Alban, but remained silent on the Lichfield connection (Geoffrey of Monmouth, *History of the Kings of Britain*, 131).

Amphibalus himself. As told by the St Albans monk Matthew Paris, the legend has this great slaughter of the nine hundred and ninety-nine taking place in what became Lichfield, Matthew deriving the name of Lichfield ('lich' meaning 'corpse' in Middle English) therefrom.

The account remained in the store of 'historical' knowledge throughout the medieval period, and was repeated or noted by a number of sixteenth- and early seventeenth-century writers, including Leland, Stowe, Camden, and Drayton. Yet curiously, and so far as can be discovered, none of the political institutions of medieval Lichfield itself made reference to it throughout the Middle Ages: not the dominant Guild of St Mary, whose seal pictured the Virgin and Child, or the community surrounding the cathedral, whose seal had the local patron saint St Chad. But when the City gained its incorporation in 1548 out popped the story of Amphibalus, employed in a representation of the martyrdoms on the new City seal struck for the occasion. Though the image itself had obvious religious associations, the source was secular, the event was considered to have been crucial to the founding and identity of the City, and the new image on the seal broke with the traditions of a guild which in many other respects seems the direct precursor of the City Corporation.[26] It served from then on throughout the remainder of our period as a reminder of Lichfield's putative ancient heritage and symbol of its new-found pride and independence.

We should not assume that the historic references invoked by the representation of such figures took place only in towns of the size or the administrative importance of diocesan centres like Coventry, York, Chester, and Lichfield. At quite the other end of the spectrum we find a similar usage in the small Dorset town of Bridport, and once again we find the representation of a mythical figure worked into a civic building. In this case the figure was King Lud, though unlike Coventry's Godiva there is no direct connection between Lud and Bridport. But there is an indirect connection, and therein lies the tale.

Thanks both to Welsh legend and to Geoffrey of Monmouth (who was very likely to have been Welsh himself[27]), Lud was known as a town planner and builder of cities. He had been credited in both sources as the rebuilder of London, where he is said to have been

---

[26] For the relationship between the pre-Reformation Guild and the post-Reformation City Corporation, see Rosser, 'Town and Guild of Lichfield', 39–47.

[27] Geoffrey of Monmouth, *History of the Kings of Britain*, introduction, 10–14.

buried, and for whom Ludgate, the putative place of his burial, was renamed by the Saxons.[28] This gets Lud slightly closer to Bridport, because Bridport sorely needed a rebuilding at the time. Its harbour, never much to begin with, had silted up beyond hope, and townsmen had just constructed a new market hall in the hope of encouraging additional overland marketing to replace the coastal trade once carried by sail. At the completion of the hall in 1593 the townsmen organized great festivities, in part to mark the hall's construction and perhaps partly to announce far and wide that this new marketing facility was now open for business. And along with funds for a great feast, the chamberlains' accounts refer to the expenditure for a 'King Lud', apparently an effigy to be carried through the streets in procession, much as a few decades earlier townsmen might well have carried the host or a figure of the local saint.[29] Having no obvious indigenous totem of their own, much less one which could invoke the building or rebuilding of a city, Bridportians appear simply to have borrowed one from elsewhere. The object of their choice symbolized the building of great cities, but it also linked little Bridport to the history of the nation, at least as contemporaries commonly understood that history.

iv

Not only did this period see a sustained interest in the folkloric aspects of the local heritage in the form of such mythological figures. It also sustained the role of what we ourselves would consider mythological events in efforts to construct a written historical record of the local community. As the responsibilities of borough government became more extensive and complex, it seems only logical that a paper trail of official records would grow in its wake, and we have already noted the increase in this activity (in Chapter 6). The urge to record current events—court proceedings, apprenticeship indentures, freeman's admissions, by-laws, property transactions, local licences, and similar official activities—in writing must also have stemmed from the imminent threat of their disappearance in those iconoclastic times. Then, too, this was also a notoriously litigious age. Lawsuits reached floodtide and remained there throughout the period at hand, and both legal and political argument began to be

[28] Ibid. 74, 106.
[29] 'Accounts . . . for the buyldinge of the MarKett House', Bridport Borough Archives, Dorset County Record Office, MS B3/M15, unpaginated.

grounded more than ever on the evidence of precedent.[30] Along with the increasing necessity of recording current events in the conduct of regular business, it also became increasingly important to retrieve and conserve a reliable record of the past. We now know that the great figures of state around the turn of the seventeenth century employed scholars to retrieve information for their use in the conduct of their affairs and the affairs of the nation.[31] Increasingly too, and notwithstanding the obvious continuing importance of oral testimony in, for example, law cases, one came to expect useful information to be written down.[32]

Of course this urge to retrieve and reconstruct the past of the nation as a whole is entirely familiar and well documented in modern scholarly literature.[33] It extends both before and beyond the sixteenth century in a rich corpus of annals and chronicles. Familiar, too, is the work of the early county historians who wrote in the Elizabethan and early Stuart years.[34] But we read far less of the work of town historians, to use the term 'historian' in its broadest sense, even though some of them wrote before or around the same time as Erdeswicke, Lambarde, Stow, and the rest.[35] The work of Robert Ricart, Henry Manship, or David Rogers, for example, passes without mention in several of our most authoritative monographs on Tudor and Stuart historical thought, while the even more justly famous John Vowell alias Hooker of Exeter receives but a bare nod.[36]

---

[30] On this trend generally, and on the role of lawyers themselves in sustaining it, see esp. Brooks, *Pettyfoggers and Vipers*, chaps. 3–6.

[31] Lisa Jardine and Anthony Grafton, ' "Studied for Action": How Gabriel Harvey Read His Livy', *Past and Present*, 129 (Nov. 1990), 30–78. I am grateful to Eyvind Ronquist for bringing this to my attention.

[32] See D. R. Woolf, ' " The Common Voice": History, Folklore and Oral Tradition in Early Modern England', *Past and Present*, 120 (Aug. 1988), 26–52.

[33] e.g. Fussner, *Historical Revolution*; Levy, *Tudor Historical Thought*; and Woolf, *Idea of History*.

[34] Some of the best of these include: William Lambarde, *Perambulation of Kent*, 2nd edn. (1596), *STC*, no. 15176; Sampson Erdeswicke, *Survey of Staffordshire* (*c*.1593, London, 1723); Richard Carew, *Survey of Cornwall* (1602), ed. F. E. Halliday (1953); Tristram Risdon, *The Chorographicall Description . . . of Devon* (*c*.1635, London, 1910); and Thomas Gerard, *The Particular Description of . . . Somerset* (*c*.1632), ed. E. H. Bates, Somerset Record Society, 15 (1900); and of course the most famous and perhaps best of them all, John Stow's *Survey of London* (1598 and 1603) of which the best modern edition is by C. L. Kingsford (1908).

[35] The best short treatment and listing is still the introduction to Flenley (ed.), *Six Town Chronicles of England*. Many of those which existed only in manuscript form in Flenley's time have been published since, but on the other hand, several more have come to light in the great flow of local records which came to county records offices since about 1945.

[36] Robert Ricart, *The Maire of Bristowe is Kalendar* (*c*.1484), ed. Lucy Toulmin

Any effort to discuss historical writing before at least the mid-seventeenth century runs up against problems of description. Despite the effort which contemporaries themselves made to distinguish amongst annals, chronicles, surveys, memorials, cosmographies, and a host of other terms, definitional precision is not an outstanding characteristic of these works.[37] Still, two points demand our attention. First, these writings taken together reflect a greater interest in local origins and in the local civic heritage than has generally been recognized. In so doing they fostered traditions of urbanism in a national culture which was still predominantly agrarian in tone. Such writings encouraged a sense of citizenship, for want of a better word, essential to social stability in an age of such large-scale immigration from the countryside. And secondly, they seem to undergo a distinct shift in both form and emphasis in the latter half of the sixteenth century.

Perhaps the oldest and best-established form of these endeavours consists chiefly of the compilation of records and information of a historical or constitutional sort. These works gathered and recorded, sometimes even codified, the various documents and even oral descriptions of how the borough should work. They included oath books, record books, order books, breviaries, Domesdays, custumals, and sundry combinations of the above. The titles of individual volumes might be taken from one of these or analogous terms[38] or simply allude to the colour of their original bindings, as with 'The Black Book of Bedford', 'The Black Book of Reading', the 'Red Book of King's Lynn' (said to be the first paper book produced in England), the 'Great White Book of Bristol', or the 'Black Book of Southampton'.[39] To a greater or lesser extent, such volumes most

Smith, Camden Society, NS, 5 (1872); Henry Manship, *The History of Great Yarmouth* (c.1612–1619), ed. Charles John Palmer (Great Yarmouth, 1854); David Rogers, 'The Breviary of Chester History', partly transcribed in Clopper (ed.), *REED: Chester*, 232–54; and John Vowell alias Hooker, *Citie of Excester* . . .

[37] A point reaffirmed in D. R. Woolf, 'Erudition and the Idea of History in Renaissance England', *Renaissance Quarterly*, 40/1 (Spring 1987), 11–47.

[38] e.g. the 'Small Order Book' of Beverley, Beverley Borough Archives, Humberside Record Office, MS BC II/4; 'Old Record Book', i–iii (the third volume known also as 'The Great Book'), Poole Borough Archives, Poole Civic Centre, MSS 23(1), 25(3), 26(4); John Hooker's 'Commonplace Book' of Exeter (not to be confused with his *Description of the Citie of Excester*, for which the former seems something of a dress rehearsal), Exeter City Records, Devon County Record Office, Book 51; Rogers's 'Breviary of Chester', Chester City Archives, Chester County Record Office; Ferguson (ed.), *A Boke off Recorde*; and the curiously named 'Courtiers' of Doncaster, compiled from 1565 (Brent (ed.), *Doncaster Borough Courtier*, i) .

[39] 'The Black Book of Bedford', Bedford Borough Records, Bedforshire Record

often included charters, oaths of office, local by-laws and regulations, precise descriptions of 'metes and bounds', and possibly the names of past officials.

As works of history these volumes are fairly primitive in form: uncritical transcriptions with little or no attempt at narrative, synthesis, or interpretation. Most of them lack the chronological arrangement and sequential listing of events which would allow us to consider them chronicles. But they are irreplaceable as raw materials for the more scholarly forms, and they succeeded in preserving a very great deal which would otherwise have been lost. Of even greater importance in their time, they enjoyed considerable success in establishing the antiquity of the liberties and institutions of many towns, which is of course one of their chief purposes. They no doubt did a great deal to inform contemporaries of a great many things essential to understand as preconditions to a stable civic order.

Thanks to the increasing administrative burdens placed by statute and proclamation on the shoulders of civic officials in the last two-thirds of the sixteenth century, this era witnessed a substantial stepping up of this sort of record-keeping. In consequence, a good many town clerks, recorders, and other officials, men such as Henry Gee of Chester and George Austen of Guildford,[40] played a more essential role than ever before in compiling and preserving the documentary foundations for local historical writing of a more narrative sort.

Many and perhaps most other historical writings fall into the broad category of the chronicle. This has been defined as a 'detailed and continuous register of events in order of time; a historical record, especially one in which the facts are narrated without philosophical treatment'.[41] The chronicle was of course a major form of writing the history of the nation, and had been so for a very long time. In most contexts it had begun to 'dissolve' into other forms by the end of the sixteenth century.[42] But for reasons which will become evident below, the town chronicle seems to have been of somewhat more recent

Office, MS B I; 'The Black Book of Reading', Berkshire Record Office, MS R AC/1/1/1; *The Great White Book of Bristol*, ed. E. Ralph, Bristol Record Society, 32 (1979); *The Black Book of Southampton*, ed. A. B. Wallis Chapman (3 vols.; Southampton Record Society, 1912–15).

[40] Mills, 'Chester Ceremonial', 5; G. H. Martin, 'The Origin of Borough Records', *Journal of the Society of Archivists*, 2 (1960–4), 152.

[41] *OED*, *vide* 'chronicle'. See the similar definition in D. R. Woolf, 'Genre into Artefact: The Decline of the English Chronicle in the Sixteenth Century', *Sixteenth Century Journal*, 19/3 (Fall 1988), 323.

[42] See esp. Woolf, 'Genre into Artefact', *passim*.

origin and remained a viable form of historical writing for a much longer duration than chronicles of the nation or the metropolis.[43]

Town chronicles usually drew heavily on the better-known chronicles of England or 'Britain', themselves judicious mixtures of mythology, tradition, and verifiable information, weaving local events into the story when, usually as the discussion reached the fourteenth or fifteenth century, available sources permitted. The use of national chronicles allowed local historians to identify their own communities with the very distant past, thereby invoking the authority of antiquity. By the late sixteenth century some local chroniclers may have suspected that, for example, Brutus did not found Britain following his departure from Troy. But the effort to identify their town as closely as possible with the events of antiquity created an understandable reluctance to abandon such claims. And as these chronicles approached the more recent past, a time at which local records, memory, and oral tradition came further into play, they could provide reconstructions of real events which were often finely detailed and reasonably accurate.

An early and most interesting example of this tendency, summarizing the form of pre-Reformation efforts and pointing towards the more sophisticated narrative syntheses of the sixteenth century, is Robert Ricart's *Maire of Bristowe is Kalendar*.[44] As Town Clerk of that city for many years Ricart had ample access to documents and he made extensive use of them. But in the first two parts of this six-part work Ricart gives a potted narrative of the history of Britain based closely on such uncritical authorities as Geoffrey of Monmouth and Matthew of Westminster. Here Ricart offers the obligatory story of Brutus's foundation of Britain. Not until the third book does he arrive at the era when he can employ local documents available to him, including mayoral lists from the earliest verifiable records. The second half of this large volume, comprising books three through six, records an extensive description of the rules, rituals, and forms of civic government in Bristol, transcripts of Bristol charters, and a useful selection of by-laws drawn from London as well as Bristol.

---

[43] Flenley notes but a few town chronicles in the 15th cent., with most appearing in the 16th to the 18th. Chronicles of London and of England, by contrast, may be traced to the 13th cent., and Woolf documents their decline in the late 16th cent. (Flenley (ed.), *Six Town Chronicles of England*, 7 and 27; Woolf, 'Genre into Artefact'). See also Alan Dyer, 'English Town Chronicles', *Local Historian*, 12/6 (May 1977), 285–6.

[44] Ricart, *Maire of Bristowe is Kalendar*. Dyer considers it 'the earliest clear provincial town chronicle' ('English Town Chronicles', 286).

But if Ricart appears to summarize the writing of local history up to the end of the fifteenth century and point it towards the future, we must remember that the Bristol of which he was writing was a larger, better-established, and more oligarchic place than almost any other city or town in England prior to the Reformation. Ricart's work was more a harbinger of the future than a representative of its time. Few were prepared to push this form of synthesis as far as Ricart before the latter part of the sixteenth century. In the interim the less sophisticated examples of historical writing multiplied at a greater rate than ever after the Henrician years, when the search for a legitimizing past became more acute. They also became slightly more sophisticated as the influence of such humanists as Polydore Vergil began to trickle down.[45] John Twyne, for example, who is reputed to have written a chronicle of Canterbury in the reign of Henry VIII, now lost, was a humanist in his own right and well connected with others of like mind and training.[46] Works of this type continued to be written right through and well beyond 1640.[47]

Prominent amongst these less sophisticated efforts are the substantial number of chronological lists of borough officials which came to be annotated, in annal fashion, with the notable events of particular years. Though these local lists closely paralleled annals of kings and even of lesser officials,[48] they may have derived quite independently, perhaps as extensions of the Easter tables which were kept by the Church and which would have been familiar to officials of the parish.[49] Whether or not we may justly refer to them as chronicles remains to an extent moot, though Dyer suggests, in effect, that we may do so when such lists come to have extensive annotation about events in particular mayoral years.[50] In any event, they seem especially common and perhaps even more important in the context of the urban community. They focus especially on the mayoralty, and are often referred to simply (and accurately) as 'mayoral lists'.

[45] Levy, *Tudor Historical Thought*, 170–4.

[46] Peter Clark, 'Visions of the Urban Community: Antiquarians and the English City before 1800', in Derek Fraser and Anthony Sutcliffe (eds.), *The Pursuit of Urban History* (1983), 112–13.

[47] A number are identified in Flenley (ed.), *Six Town Chronicles of England*, 27–37. See also David Underdown's description of the work of Dennis Bond and William Whiteway in Jacobean Dorchester, *Fire from Heaven*, 51–2.

[48] e.g. Francis Godwin, *Catalogue of the Bishops of England* (1601).

[49] This interesting suggestion has been put to me by Professor Daniel Woolf, to whom, once again, I am grateful.

[50] Dyer, 'English Town Chronicles', 285.

Most of them were undertaken between the mid-sixteenth and the mid-seventeenth century. Perhaps it was only at that time when local antiquaries had sufficient sources at their disposal methodically to reconstruct the desired information all at once. More likely it was only then that the mayoralty came into its prime as the possessor of such great authority, and only then when mayors faced at the same time the crisis of order and obedience which is so central to the age.

In their early pages most mayoral lists are little more than the name would imply but, as with local chronicles, annotations of local events which befell in each year become fuller and more frequent as the compiler worked his way closer to the present. In some cases these lists began and ended with the energies of a single chronicler, but many were kept up by his successors for some considerable time thereafter: some even into the nineteenth century. These lists satisfy the broad contemporary interest in the reconstruction of local traditions, but they also authenticate and celebrate the historic import-ance of the contemporary governing authority. Lineage conveyed authority. The farther back a line of mayors could be shown to have existed, the greater became the authority of the office. And if early mayors could be associated with other elements of antiquity, so much the better. Some lists also show mayoral arms, though a good many of these heraldic concoctions seem certainly to have been con-trived by the compiler.[51]

Mayoral lists survive from the period at hand for a number of the older and more established towns, including (in addition to Shrews-bury) Leicester, York, Grimsby, Southampton, Newcastle, Salis-bury, King's Lynn, and Lincoln.[52] But of these and others which may be found, no set better illustrates the popularity of this form in a single town than the mayoral lists of Chester. Beginning with what

---

[51] A particularly impressive list of mayors with their escutcheons painted in still-dazzling colour is the uncatalogued volume known as 'Escutcheons of the Bailiffs and Mayors of Shrewsbury' in the Library of Shrewsbury School. My thanks to Mr James Lawson for showing this to me.

[52] Hartopp (ed.), *Roll of the Mayors*; 'A List or Catalogue of all the Mayors of the City of York', BL, Harleian MS 6115; 'Majores Villae et Burgi de Grimesby Magna in Com. Lincoln', BL, Lansdowne MS 207(a), fos. 272–5; 'A Biographical List of the Mayors . . . of Southampton from 1498 . . .', BL, Egerton MS 868; W. H. D. Longstaff (ed.), *Heraldic Visitations of the Northern Counties in 1530 by Thomas Tonge*, Surtees Society, 41 (1863), pp. liv–lxxxvii; Salisbury Borough Archives, Wiltshire Record Office, MS G23/1/235; King's Lynn Mayoral List, untitled, BL, Add. MS 8937; and J. W. F. Hill, 'Three Lists of the Mayors, Bailiffs and Sheriffs of the City of Lincoln', *Associated Architectural Societies' Reports and Papers*, 39 (1928–9), 217ff., as cited in Clark, 'Visions of the Urban Community', 107 n. 7.

proved to be incomplete and sparsely annotated versions in the early Elizabethan era[53] and continuing on to the revised version put out by Robert Aldersey in the year of his mayoralty, 1594, at least twenty-seven of these were compiled or, in most cases, copied in the period at hand.[54] An acerbic contemporary like Thomas Nashe (who was himself a historian of Great Yarmouth) could disparage these 'lay chroniclers that wrote of nothing but of mayors and Sheriffs, and the dere yere, and the great frost'.[55] Still, they had their uses. One cannot help but suggest that official lists took so long to blossom as an urban form of historical record because the office which they most often celebrated came into its own so fully just at this time.

Serving, as he did, one of the very largest, most politically complex, and in many ways precocious provincial centres in England, it is understandable that Robert Ricart was one of the first to recognize the need for a written narrative which synthesized the sources of document and chronicle. Most all other communities, lagging behind Bristol in this as in so many other respects, came to that recognition only in the latter years of the sixteenth and early years of the seventeenth century. It is only then, after several decades of rapid changes in civic authority and in the nature of civic politics, that such local historical writing came more generally to be marked by some things already evident in Ricart. They became increasingly reluctant to accept divine or magical causation. They were more heavily chorographical, paying increased attention to the physical characteristics and setting of the particular locale.

They also situated the town in an appropriately wider context. By drawing heavily on the better-known and humanist-influenced national chronicles of England or 'Britain', certainly including the likes of Grafton and Camden, Holinshed and his collaborators, they tied the history of the local scene to that of England itself.[56] In addition, as the narratives which they conveyed approached the more recent past, when local records, memory, and oral tradition could be brought more usefully into play, they could provide more detailed reconstructions of real events. Though these reconstruc-

---

[53] e.g. Chester City Archives, MS AB/1, *c*.1567–8.

[54] Listed and described definitively by Clopper (ed.), *REED: Chester*, pp. xxxvi–xliii. Most are either in Chester or in various collections of the British Library.

[55] Nashe, *Pierce Penniless*, as cited in Stow's *Survey of London*, ed. C. L. Kingsford (1908), p. xxviii, n. 4.

[56] The point is made esp. well in Annabel Patterson, *Reading Holinshed's 'Chronicles'* (Chicago, 1994), chap. 12.

tions of course remained subjective in approach, they were often quite finely grained and reasonably accurate.

The construction of these histories naturally called for a more thorough use of records and a much more deliberate effort to retrieve them. The Town Clerk of Grantham, for example, was ordered to make a thorough search of local records in order to compile a summary of earlier by-laws in 1635.[57] An anonymous burgess of Wallingford, in compiling the history of his borough ('because we the Inhabitaunts could saye nothinge thereunto') in what his handwriting suggests may have been the reign of Elizabeth, could hardly have been unique in employing a gentleman of the Middle Temple to help him gather and translate Latin documents.[58] And when William Whiteway the Younger and his friend Denis Bond of Jacobean Dorchester undertook a history of their town in the opening years of the seventeenth century, they searched a wide variety of administrative records and written histories in the effort.[59]

Perhaps most impressively, Henry Manship the Younger describes for us the systematic effort to retrieve, sort, and calendar the records of his native Great Yarmouth, carried out by a committee of thirteen citizens in addition to himself, which met several times a week for two months.[60] This impressive task afforded Manship the archival basis for his monumental *History of Great Yarmouth*, completed in 1619.

Polished works of local history and topography are certainly announced by John Stow for London,[61] following in some respects the Kentish historian William Lambarde, but also by Manship for

[57] Cited in G. H. Martin, 'The Publication of Borough Records', *Archives*, 8/36 (1966), 200.

[58] Wallingford Borough Archives, Berkshire Record Office, MS W/AC 1/1.

[59] Underdown, *Fire from Heaven*, 51. Another, still unpublished but very full, effort of this type is known, from the name of its donor, as 'Dr. Taylor's History' of Shrewsbury, written between the late 1570s and 1603 and located in the Library of Shrewsbury School. Though its earlier sections derive from printed national histories (including Stow's *Annals*) which were well known at the time, those sections dealing with the author's lifetime are obviously drawn from personal recollections, oral testimony, and local records. My thanks to James Lawson, Librarian of Shrewsbury School, for his help with this volume.

[60] The process is described in the ultimate report of the committee, chaired by Manship. Consisting of six aldermen and seven Common Councillors, Manship's committee met twenty-three times between 22 June and 13 Aug. 1612, and for one final meeting (20 Jan. 1612/13) at which they subscribed their names to the document which Manship wrote up on behalf of his colleagues. A copy may be found in BL, Add. MS 23737, 'A Copy of a Catalogue of Charters of Great Yarmouth . . .'.

[61] Esp. in the most advanced of his works, the *Survey of London*. Here I have used Charles Kingsford's 1908 edition of Stow's second edition of 1603.

Great Yarmouth,[62] David Rogers for Chester,[63] Hooker for Exeter,[64] and William Somner for Canterbury,[65] all by 1640 and, to go just a few years further, Nathaniel Bacon for Ipswich.[66] Like Ricart they wrote in English, but they did a great deal more than attach the raw record of past officials and current processes and rules of governance to a potted narrative grounded in the works of medieval authorities.

And to introduce another great milestone, some of these were evidently written for publication and were duly put directly into print. The first published urban history has been identified as a London work of a slightly earlier time, Richard Arnold's *In This Booke is conteyned the names of ye baylifs custos mairs and sherefs of London* of 1503 (too early, it seems, for the author to have mastered the concept of the book title). And if John Hooker's publication of his *Orders Erected for Orphans . . . within the Citie of Exeter* in 1575 is not strictly speaking a work of history, his *Description of the Citie of Excester*, published in the same year, certainly is. Stow followed shortly with his *Survey*, first published in 1598, and Nashe with *Lenten Stuffe*, his history of Great Yarmouth, a year later.[67]

These works all display considerable sophistication as examples of historical writing. To take the little-known but nonetheless important work of Manship, for example, we find less in the way of a vademecum for local governing officials of the sort provided by Ricart

---

[62] Manship, *History of Great Yarmouth* (completed in 1619 but not published until 1854, when the local antiquary Charles James Palmer undertook this project, adding a volume of his own as a sequel). Oddly enough, for such a relatively small town, this was not the first but the third history of Yarmouth, being preceeded by the small work entitled *Greate Yermouthe: A Book of the Foundacion and Antiquitye of the Saide Towne . . .* (Great Yarmouth, 1847), once attributed to Manship's father but now known to have been written by Thomas Damet (*c.*1594–9) and the poet Thomas Nashe's interesting but literary and derivative *Lenten Stuff* of 1599, in *Harleian Miscellany*, ii (1809), 288–334. On the attribution of the former, see Paul Rutledge, 'Thomas Damet and the Historiography of Great Yarmouth', *Norfolk Archeology*, 33 (1965), 119–30; and Rutledge, 'Thomas Damet and the Historiography of Great Yarmouth', *Norfolk Archeology*, 34 (1969), 332–4.

[63] Rogers himself produced five different versions of this between about 1609 and about 1637, of which none have been published in their entirety. Chapter IV has been transcribed in Clopper (ed.), *REED: Chester*, 232–54. See also Mills, 'Chester Ceremonial', 3.

[64] Hooker, *Citie of Excester*.

[65] William Somner, *Antiquities of Canterbury* (1640).

[66] Nathaniel Bacon, *The Annalls of Ipswiche* (Ipswich, 1654 [1884]).

[67] The point is made by Martin, 'Publication of Borough Records', 199–200. The strange title of Nashe's work refers to the vital role of the herring fishery, herring being 'Lenten fare', in that town (Nashe, *Nashe's Lenten stuffe* (1599), *STC* 22918).

and even the more famous Hooker. Instead we have much more of a detailed and reasonably well-digested narrative description of institutions, geographic elements, and both economic and political issues, all placed in a historical context. Manship handles cause and effect with confidence, pushing anachronistic fallacies, miraculous interventions, and mythological figures largely off the page. He affords his readers ready access both to the town's origins and to the current state of its affairs. The work seems all the more significant for not having derived from a town which was either especially large or important by that time, or one as sophisticated as towns such as Norwich, Bristol, or Chester.

Like Ricart before him, Manship was also determined to situate the origins of his town in the distant past, and like Ricart he relied on chronicles of national history, even extending as far back as Bede. But he also tended to use the more recent and reliable works including Camden's *Britannia* and Contarini on the Venetian Republic, only made available in English in 1598.[68] Manship broke with the tradition of Brutus as the founder of Britain, and began instead with an entirely plausible derivation of Yarmouth itself in the Saxon period. Though we still do not find a firm chronological structure to the narrative, most of Manship's switchings back and forth in time stay at least close to his own age, in which he airs all manner of events and issues. Yet his use of primary sources and a critical eye to the published word remain hallmarks throughout, and even Camden comes in for criticism when he neglects or misreads the historical record.

And like all historians, Manship wrote with a purpose beyond the mere reconstruction of past events. Both in his selection of subjects and in his treatment of them he places the town's governing elite in the best possible light, thus to bolster their position. He gives us a full description of the several successive efforts to rebuild the haven, and of the virtues of so doing despite the cost involved to the citizens. He lays out in copious detail Yarmouth's eternal rivalries with both Lowestoft and the barons of the Cinque Ports for jurisdiction over the local herring fishery and fair upon which the fortunes of the town had long rested.[69] And he offers an equally detailed description of

[68] Contarini, *The Commonwealth and Government of Venice*, first published in English in 1598, *STC*, 2nd edn., no. 5642.

[69] Both the difficulties of maintaining the harbour from silting up and the disputes regarding jurisdiction over the fishery are treated in Tittler, 'English Fishing Industry', 40–60. Litigation between Yarmouth and members of the Cinque Ports seems to have been carried on almost continuously for generations, requiring a written record of events and documents which was accurate and readily available.

Kett's Rising, demonstrating the perils of revolt to all and sundry. This is but one of several chances for Manship to sing the borough's praises ('my most sweet beloved native town of Yarmouth', 'the very quintessence of England') and those of its government, and he misses none of them. We find him comparing his native place favourably, not only with Contarini's Venice, but even to ancient Athens.[70]

Though better known than Manship's *Great Yarmouth*, Hooker's *Description of Excester* proves a much less advanced work. Despite its eighty or so pages of historical narrative, the majority of its vast bulk is taken up with the reprinting of local records. In addition, though the author probably knew better, Hooker clung to Geoffrey of Monmouth's account of the founding of Britain by Brutus, giving ample play to the roles of kings Cadwallader and Briennus from the same source. Yet even though the documents take up the lion's share of Hooker's work, these are selected with a commemorative, or at least a polemical, view in mind. Published documents are offered to justify Exeter's position, for example, in jurisdictional disputes with the Bishop or with the Port of London over salvage rights on the south coast. Others are intended to fortify the role of local government by describing in considerable detail such matters as the rights and responsibilities of each and every governing official, the jurisdiction and operation of the City's Court of Orphans, the rules governing both the collection of customs and the administration of Sir Thomas White's bequest to enterprising journeymen, and the appropriate dress and demeanour of virtually everyone who had a hand in the business of government.

What may we infer about Hooker's intentions? Part of his interest no doubt lay in defending the position of the governing authorities by pre-empting challenges through the marshalling of documentation. Part rested, as it had in Ricart, with an obvious need to describe the operation of government, both for the benefit of those entrusted with its authority, and also, we must assume, for the large number of Exeter residents and freemen who were not native to the City and who would not otherwise have known much about its origin, rules, or regulations. Finally, as with Manship, Hooker seems determined to retell in considerable detail the story of historic revolts in the local area, especially the Western Rising of 1549, in order to demonstrate the consequences of flouting authority.

Though such forms as the 'pure' compilation, the chronicle, and

---

[70] Manship, *History of Great Yarmouth*, 118.

the mayoral list coexisted over a long time, there is a sequential chronological development to the subject. Clearly the compilation of lists and information emerged first, well before the Reformation. But it became more common and perhaps even more useful in the post-1540 period when the constitutional position of so many towns began rapidly to evolve. With readily accessible evidence of rights and privileges at hand, towns found it easier to seek confirmations or to petition for new charters. These transcriptions and compilations also served as 'how to' books for officials now faced with greater responsibilities than ever before but still armed with nothing in the way of formal training with which to carry them out. Even a substantial writer like Hooker reproduced and transmitted records which seemed to him especially significant to the political position of his city.

The failure to have such records at hand could greatly imperil towns seeking to have their powers confirmed or extended by charter, or trying to ward off challenges to accustomed rights and liberties from forces both internal and external. In an age when argument proceeded more than ever by the force of written precedent than by bluster or oral tradition, those precedents had to be ready at hand and well organized. And failure to have them that close could also entail considerable expense. Manship himself found in his inspection of local records that many were missing, 'whereof the Towne at their greate cost and chardge hath been enforced to take exemplifications, aswell out of His Majestys Records reymaininge at Westminster as also out of the Tower of London and other places. And . . . also, that those charters, Rolls, and Evidences, which doo remayne in the Vestry, Guildhall and other places doo lye not onely dispersedly, but also very disorderedly . . . to the no little damage of the whole Incorporacion'.[71]

A further and very important part of this greater imperative to keep and compile the historical record lay in the need to satisfy a need for 'auncienty'—the imperative represented in Faversham's 'new auncient staffe'—as an essential element in political legitimation. For most of the historical writings under consideration here the authority of the traditional chronicles of national history proved convenient starting places, upon which the local story could readily be grafted.

[71] BL, Add. MS 23737, fo. 4ʳ. On the expense of transcribing records from the offices of central government, see also Fussner, *Historical Revolution*, 86–7.

To one extent or another, all these factors help to account for the fact that the rise and fall of the chronicle form as it applied to towns followed a different chronological sequence than chronicles of nation or metropolis, remaining a viable form of historical writing well into the seventeenth century.[72] They served well as long as they maintained credibility. When some, like Manship, abandoned such accounts, they were able to replace them with other, perhaps more plausible, derivations to similar effect. And, to one extent or another, the chronicle and the other forms of local historical writing together helped re-create a common local history or memory following the destructive force of the Reformation. More than ever before, this common history took written form, not only in the Bristol of Ricart's day or the Exeter of Hooker's, but also in such smaller towns as Dorchester, Okehampton, Grantham, Wallingford, and of course Great Yarmouth.[73]

In this use of the past, of course, town governments were acting much as the Tudor monarchy itself. In their effort to strengthen their authority and remake the English state according to their own lights, the Tudor kings and queens relied heavily on legitimation by the historical record. Historians writing for the Crown tended, of course, to write their histories according to the needs of their masters. Thus we find an emphasis on the perils of disorder and the just rewards of obedience, on the origins of the Tudors in the farthest reaches of antiquity, and on the accomplishments of the current dynasty and ruler in contrast to their predecessors.

Town histories often worked towards similar ends, and they did so after the mid-sixteenth century with much less reliance on elements of traditional popular religious culture. Indeed they did so in a way which replaced many of the elements of the local collective memory which had been a feature of that culture. They, too, dwelt at great length on periods of local strife, taking great pains to demonstrate

[72] One more point should be added to account for this chronological pattern. That is to say that, while the growth of a reading public in both England as a whole and in the great metropolis of London created a market for published histories which pushed unpublished chronicles of those places to the side, the reading public of the much smaller provincial town had no such commercial effect. Without the competition of published histories of towns per se for a much longer time, the unpublished town chronicle remained viable in its place (see Woolf, 'Genre into Artefact', 321–54).

[73] Daniel Woolf's much more exhaustive study of the issue has yielded a map of the location of urban chronicles in the 16th and 17th cents., to be published in his forthcoming *The Origins of Modern Historical Culture*. No less than thirty locations are indicated. My thanks to him for sharing this information with me.

the perils of revolt against authority, as with Hooker's lengthy discussion of the Western Rising or Manship's equal emphasis on Kett's Rising in Norfolk. And in cases of contest between the town itself and its rivals, such as local bishops or rival towns, they offered copious documentation for the rectitude of their town's position.

It also seems clear that the period at hand saw a move to make these compilations more accessible. What seems to have begun as an effort to provide borough officials with accurate and convenient records to employ in the business of governing, moved towards a subjectively commemorative narrative history to serve the interests of those who governed. This could be made available to all who would purchase and read it, or have it read to them. Such dissemination seems also to reflect the need to assimilate newcomers to the ways of the community, an essential device at a time of accelerating migration from agrarian to urban areas of the realm. Certainly this widened accessibility to the history and traditions of the community had as much to do with creating a deferential citizenry, suitably impressed with the lineage of local government and the necessity of strong local rule, as with an informed one.

These developments came principally in the post-Reformation era; publication itself, in contrast to histories of nation and metropolis, came very late in that era indeed. Though Ricart's work served as a harbinger, it is only in the mid-sixteenth century that most records and compilations come to be in the English of common speech rather than the Latin of ecclesiastical and legal authority. It is then, too, that the cumbersome and expensive parchment rolls of earlier records came conventionally to be replaced with less expensive paper books which could more easily be bound, stored, and indexed for ready reference. And only in the last years of the sixteenth century did at least some such histories come to be written for publication, with the support of local authorities, so that they could be obtained and read by all who would acquire them. The more general fashion of publishing and reading local histories had of course still to wait until the latter half of the seventeenth century.

As men like Ricart, Manship, and Hooker had invariably held civic office, their histories remained closely tied to the outlook of town officials and certainly reflected the views of the ruling sort in general. Most such writings may virtually be taken to express an official view of events. They appealed to common but carefully selected historical experiences of the community, and they rested their sense of the civic heritage firmly on the shoulders of these elites. Of course

the social and cultural distance between that element and others varied widely from town to town, often roughly in step with the size and complexity of the local population. But for the most part such writings left no doubt that the responsibilities and authority of these governing officials set them clearly apart from other townsmen and women, laying claim to the deference and loyalty of the rest.

V

At the same time that these writings reflected the growing divisions between urban officials and their fellow townsmen, they also demonstrated a growing link between those officials and their towns on the one hand, and the Crown and the nation on the other. An early indication of this might be seen in the pages of town chronicles, in which the history of the nation formed the stem onto which local events could be grafted as the survival of written record, oral tradition, and human memory permitted. But the connection in those writings between town and nation remained oddly implicit, as if—save for the occasional royal visit—the two bodies grew side by side without much contact along the way.

It might be seen, too, in the gradual appearance of royal insignia, not only in parish churches throughout the land but also in spaces or on implements or furnishings associated with civic rule. The appearance of royal arms on the town mace seems to have occurred fairly early in our period. Guildhalls held the royal arms on their façade in several places including Norwich:[74] they may still be seen in King's Lynn. Their appearance over the mayor's chair came later in our period (as in Leicester *c.*1637) as an even more forceful and visible reminder of the royal authority exercised by that official.[75] The same could be said of the copies of portraits of contemporary kings and queens which came slowly to be acquired for display in some civic halls.

Yet perhaps the most distinctive symbolic linkage of the town with Crown and nation was the emergence in about the 1570s of a formalized contemporary history in which both shared. Central to this, metaphorically speaking, was the creation from that time of a new and national calendar, in which the bold type announced not the saints' days of old, but events in the recent history of the nation. Based on what David Cressy has called 'a mythic and patriotic sense

---

[74] Galloway (ed.), *REED: Norwich*, p. xxvi.
[75] Tittler, *Architecture and Power*, 109, 115.

of national identity', this calendar 'became an important instrument for declaring and disseminating a distinctly Protestant national culture'. If it did not often extend to commemorating the heroic deeds of local worthies in provincial towns as was done in London, its observance nevertheless served to bind the local community to the nation and thence to the ruling dynasty, 'securing it through an inspiring . . . interpretation of English History'.[76]

Of course this phenomenon was by no means distinctly urban. It revolved around the Tudor dynasty and the emerging Protestant Settlement of the Elizabethan age. It celebrated events which were implicitly national rather than local. It received literal expression in almanacs and other written forms which transcended local festive celebrations, and it may be observed at work both in all parts of the realm and in all manner of environment. But at a time when so many traditional festive activities had come under censure, in which civic governments had every need for ceremonial support, and in which mayoral office had become more than ever before a vehicle for statutory authority, it was certainly in the interest of borough officials to adopt this formulation and make it their own. They seem to have understood this very well.

Perhaps the first widely shared festive day in this new calendar was 17 November, the Accession Day of Queen Elizabeth, which in many parts of the realm became known as 'Crownation Day'.[77] Other events quickly gained a place in this new reckoning as well, including the celebrations following the 'miraculous deliverance' from the threat of the Spanish Armada in 1588, the Accession Day of James I in 1603, the anniversary of Gunpowder Plot in 1605, the safe return of Prince Charles from Spain in 1623, and so on.

But of all these landmarks in the new national mythology, none consistently garnered quite the enthusiasm of the first. The accession of Elizabeth, as John Foxe so vividly assured his readers just five years after the event, saved Protestant England from the Papal grip, and marked the liberation of English men and women from the clutches of Roman Catholicism. By the late 1560s it was marked by a wide variety of festive expressions: bonfires and bells to be sure, but

---

[76] David Cressy, *Bonfires and Bells: National Memory and the Protestant Calendar in the Elizabethan and Early Stuart Era* (1989), p. xi.

[77] John E. Neale, 'November 17th', in *Essays in Elizabethan History* (1958), 9–20; Sir Roy Strong, 'Popular Celebration of the Accession Day of Queen Elizabeth I', *Journal of the Warburg and Courtauld Institutes*, 21 (1958), 86–103; Cressy, *Bonfires and Bells*, 50–6; Hutton, *Merry England*, 148.

also sermons, feasts, pageants, dancing, drinking, games, and an infinite variety of merriment. In some areas the convenient coincidence of the date allowed the festival to be grafted onto the traditional feast day of St Hugh of Lincoln, thereby providing some continuity with the older festive tradition as well.[78]

The question of how this celebration came about remains problematical. Though an obviously powerful and convenient tool of royal propaganda, there is little indication of royal or parliamentary initiative in its inception. Yet it does seem to have appeared first in urban communities: in London in the late 1560s,[79] shortly thereafter in other, especially larger, provincial centres, and finally in rural parishes. By about 1580, it was virtually universal throughout the realm. In many forms of celebration the initiative of towns, and of the ruling element within them, seems especially prominent.[80] Bell ringing, often supported by town or parish coffers, proved a very common form of the Accession Day celebration, as documented in Worcester (from 1568), Salisbury and Ludlow (1571), Bath (1572), Cambridge (1573), Prescot (1579), and Sheffield (1585). In other celebrations the role of the mayor and his brethren was even more explicit and publicly visible. In 1578 Coventry erected a viewing stand from which the mayor, mayoress, and masters of the guilds could view plays performed for the occasion.[81] In Liverpool in 1576 the mayor organized a feast for his 'brethren', sanctioned a bonfire in the market square, and lit another bonfire in front of his own house. At York, City officials went in public procession to hear a sermon in praise of the Queen's government, with fines levied at the mayor's discretion for those officials who refused to attend. And at Leicester and elsewhere the mayor and his aldermen were enjoined to wear their robes of office.

These celebrations expressed several themes. One is certainly the idea of deliverance: of England from the Roman grip at the accession of Elizabeth and from the Spanish threat in 1588, of the King and Parliament from destruction in 1605, and of Prince Charles from the harm which might have come to him in Spain in 1623. Another is the triumph of the Nation over its enemies, and of the Protestant Settlement over Catholicism. A third is the emergence of an officially sanctioned form of civic and popular festivity to replace those

---

[78] Cressy, *Bonfires and Bells*, 50.   [79] Ibid. 52.

[80] Unless otherwise noted, the following is summarized and documented in Strong, 'Popular Celebration of Accession Day', 91–3.

[81] Ingram (ed.), *REED: Coventry*, 26.

which had been abandoned or disrupted in the mid-century: we shall have more to say about this in the next chapter.

A final theme is the connection, through the role of the mayor and his brethren, of the town with the nation, and with the national memory which had been forged by the middle years of Elizabeth's reign. This, too, is part of the opening out of urban society in this era which has hitherto been discussed chiefly in social and economic terms.[82] And this, too, marks a step in the association of mayoral authority with that of Crown and nation. It should be considered to mark another step away from that more insular notion of community which pertained to an earlier age.

vi

One final element in the refashioning of urban political culture, and of the collective memory integral to that culture, is the use of civic portraiture. It is but a modest imaginative leap from the mayoral list to the mayoral portrait, or from the mayor's pride of place in celebrating the monarchy to a celebration of the mayor himself. Yet so unfamiliar has this class of artistic expression remained that a definition seems more than usually appropriate. For purposes of this study then, 'civic portraiture' has been taken to mean portraits of civic officials or resident benefactors—as opposed to benefactors from amongst, for example, the landed gentry—known to have been purchased or commissioned by civic authorities and displayed in civic buildings. The parallels between the appearance of civic portraiture and the use of both mayoral lists and written narrative histories exploring the heritage of individual towns, all blossoming around the same time, seem very strong. In all three instances pre-Reformation practices gave way to analogous devices more in tune with contemporary requirements.

In the case of visual imagery, the precursors of civic portraits may be found most prominently in both funerary brasses and other memorials located in the parish church and perhaps in a few portraits which had been bequeathed for display in church settings. These had been designed to elicit prayers as much as to recall civic contributions. Commissioned by the family or by the figure himself through his will, and displayed in ecclesiastical rather than secular and civic surroundings, they do not at all conform to the definition of civic portraits offered above.

---

[82] See esp. Sacks, *The Widening Gate, passim.*

Civic portraits prove interesting in a number of respects, not the least of which is their neglect in the scholarly literature on English portraiture.[83] Part of this neglect may of course be due to their generally mediocre quality as works of art. It is useless to pretend that the history of portraiture between the work of Holbein in the early sixteenth century and that of Van Dyck a century later deserves anything close to centre stage in any history of the genre. Yet even given that lack of distinction in the whole type, scholarly attention has been paid almost exclusively to portraits of the monarchs, the aristocracy or landed gentry, or prominent court officials. The rest, including the civic portraits at issue here, have not often been considered worth the bother. Once again, with civic as opposed to royal regalia, or local as opposed to 'national' historical writing, one can hardly fail to note the neglect of things 'local' in mainstream historical scholarship. And, once again, one cannot simply assume that such local civic practices were familiar devices writ small.

We need not be concerned with aesthetic qualities (which, from the connoisseur's perspective may be just as well). To the historian of society or of political culture portraits serve as artefacts, and so they shall be considered here. They prove very interesting seen in this light, especially when we contrast them with the more familiar portraits of the aristocracy. To noblemen and gentlemen, the individual or family portrait served much as did the genealogical tables which were so popular at the same time, in the words of Lawrence Stone, 'as symbols of the frenzied status-seeking and ancestor worship of the age'. 'What patrons demanded', Stone continues, 'was evidence of the sitter's position and wealth by opulence of dress, ornament and background.'[84]

And so did they receive. The aristocratic portraits of this age may not be the most distinguished in the long history of that genre, but they certainly did show their subjects in opulent clothing and accoutrements. Sir Roy Strong has described the effect of many as exhibiting 'gorgeous gem-encrusted costumes, richly inlaid armour, and multicoloured plumes, wands of office and batons of command'.[85]

---

[83] See e.g. Lorne Campbell, *Renaissance Portraits* (New Haven and London, 1990); L. Gent and N. Llewellyn (eds.), *Renaissance Bodies: The Human Figure in English Culture, c.1540–1660* (1990); John Pope-Hennessy, *The Portrait in the Renaissance* (London and New York, 1966); Roy Strong, *Tudor and Stuart Portraits* (2 vols.; 1969); Strong, *The English Icon: Elizabethan and Jacobean Portraiture* (London and New York, 1969); and Strong, *The English Renaissance Miniature* (London, 1983).

[84] Lawrence Stone, *The Crisis of the Aristocracy, 1558–1641* (Oxford, 1965), 712.

[85] Strong, *English Icon*, 29.

Costumes not only tended towards the opulent, but they often suggested the virility or putative fecundity of the subjects, vital qualities in the aristocratic milieu in which they were commissioned. These are often marked by full-length views, tight clothing, and gestures or poses intended to emphasize those characteristics. And background views, of the sort so familiar in the 'Armada Portrait' of Elizabeth herself, tend again to summarize the achievements of the great and the wealthy, not of course necessarily with views of the Armada, but with country houses, battle scenes, fat cattle, or spouses and children. The objective was certainly to project personal fame, honour, and achievement. That intent was carried out in every way available to the skill of the artist or the pockets of the patron.

But civic portraits looked very different, as of course they had to, for they were commissioned by different sorts of people, were paintings of different sorts of people, and had very distinct purposes.[86] In a contrast which is often striking, the portraits with which we are concerned place little emphasis on personal fame, and virtually none on either virility or femininity, as the case may be (for some civic portraits are of female benefactors or mayoresses). Opulence of dress is restricted to the finery of the mayoral robe, iconography to the occasional scroll, glove, or skull in hand, or chain of mayoral office. Colours are limited in range and—save for the frequent scarlet robe—sombre in tone. Poses are uniform and the figure is most often only painted from the waist up. The body in these pictures does not so much portray virility or any other sensual image as much as it serves as a shapeless form on which to hang and display the livery and paraphernalia of office.

The impression conveyed in almost all of them which have been identified and viewed is one of weight and dignity. They seem visual reflections of that common wording of many a town's by-laws, that the mayor and aldermen should carry themselves 'in a sadd and wise manner'. Jaws are slack and sometimes hollow, mouths closed and grim, shoulders slightly stooped and brows frequently furrowed, eyes lined with age, care, and wisdom. Grey beards abound. Almost none of these paintings have background scenes or much in the way of architectural surroundings. Aside from the fact that in only a very few cases could a corporate town vie with a member of the

---

[86] The following draws upon my essay entitled 'Civic Portraiture and Political Culture in English Provincial Towns, c.1560–1640', soon to appear in *Journal of British Studies*, and on the census of English civic portraits from provincial towns to the year 1640 identified as appendix 1 in that study.

aristocracy for the services of the more skilled painters, these civic portraits stand in sharp contrast with the more familiar mainstream in almost every way.

Another distinctive feature of this peculiar sub-genre lies in the chronology of its production. Though aristocratic and certainly royal portraits continue to flow forth in fairly steady measure from the time of Holbein, civic portraits do not on the whole appear until the last few decades of the sixteenth century. After the 1549 portrait of the Norfolk benefactor Alan Percy, the next of this smallish group which can be dated with any certainty, four in number, date to the 1560s. Not a single civic portrait from a provincial town has been able to be dated confidently to the 1570s, though they follow in a steadier stream thereafter from the 1580s on through to 1640 and beyond.

And a third distinctive feature of this group is that, although many civic portraits seem to have been painted from life or but shortly after the sitter's demise, a surprising number were only painted some considerable time after death. Three of the impressive series of portraits from Norwich came forth in that manner. Robert Jannys, one of the wealthiest men in all of England in his time, last served as Mayor in 1517 and died in 1530.[87] John Marsham, who succeeded Jannys as Mayor in 1518, died in 1532.[88] Augustine Steward (d. 1572) served three times as mayor and was perhaps the most prominent Norwich citizen of his generation.[89] Yet all were painted (perhaps from earlier drawings) in the early seventeenth century.[90] In similar fashion there may have been a contemporary or near contemporary drawing of the fifteenth-century Bury St Edmunds benefactor Jankyn Smith, but the town did not acquire an oil portrait of him until 1616.[91] Nicholas Thorne, Mayor of Bristol in 1545, was first

---

[87] Cozens-Hardy and Kent (eds.), *Mayors of Norwich*, 42; Virginia Tillyard, 'Civic Portraits Painted for or Donated to the Council Chamber of Norwich Guildhall before 1687...', MA thesis (Courtauld Institute, 1978), 21 and 42.

[88] Cozens-Hardy and Kent (eds.), *Mayors of Norwich*, 43; Tillyard, 'Civic Portraits', 22 and 43.

[89] Cozens-Hardy and Kent (eds.), *Mayors of Norwich*, 48–9; Tillyard, 'Civic Portraits', 22 and 46. A biographical sketch of Steward appears in Bindoff (ed.), *House of Commons, 1509–1558*, iii. 383–5.

[90] Cozens-Hardy and Kent (eds.), *Mayors of Norwich,* 42, 48–9; Tillyard, 'Civic Portraits'; Andrew Moore and Charlotte Crawley (eds.), *Family and Friends: A Regional Survey of British Portraiture* (1992), 24, 26–8, 196–7.

[91] Statham, *Jankyn Smith and the Guildhall Feoffees*, 3. Smith, who died in 1481, is considered the founder of the Guildhall Trust which provided the townsmen the few elements of self-rule permitted under abbatial lordship. The Trust served as the only

painted in 1624.[92] The double portrait of John and Joan Cooke done around 1600 came as much as sixty years after their deaths.[93] Insofar as one can tell from surviving documentation, some of these portraits were purchased or donated from those—usually family members and sometimes guilds—who had presumably commissioned them privately. Perhaps the larger number were specifically commissioned by the town governments in question.

These apparent anomalies demand an explanation, though of course they are only anomalies if we consider the civic portraits as part and parcel of portraits in general during this era. In fact, the explanation for their generally sombre tone, their late appearance on the scene, and their tendency to include a considerable proportion of posthumous paintings, falls readily into place when we consider them in the context of the foregoing discussion. Along with the developments in regalia, in the use of secular mythology, and in the formation of the written historical record, the blossoming of civic portraits must also be seen as building a usefully legitimizing civic memory.

The object of the civic paintings is not the self-fashioning of the individual which was so central to the Renaissance style at this time, but the self-fashioning of the borough corporation. The paintings focus on the uniform of the civic official, the mayoral robe and gown, rather than on the gem-encrusted silks and satins, or the tight waist and stockinged legs, of the virile aristocrat. And they focus, too, not on the manly or feminine pose, all loin and limb, but on the head: the seat of wisdom, the governor of the bodily parts, as the mayor was the head of the body politic represented by the corporate borough. The props are not the battle sword (nor, more surprisingly, are they the ceremonial sword or mace) but rather the scrolled borough charter which some of the portrayed worthies, such as e.g. Giles Tooker of Salisbury,[94] may have helped obtain. In place of the jewelled pendant or the chain of the Garter we have the mayoral chain of office.

Gloves, which figure commonly in portraits of both types, may be a sign of gentility, attained without question by the aristocrat and at

essentially indigenous ruling body until the incorporation of the borough in the reign of James I, and it continued to exist on into the present century.

[92] Richard Quick (ed.), *Catalogue of the Second Loan Collection of Pictures . . . held in the Bristol Art Gallery . . . 1905* (Bristol, 1905), no. 202.

[93] John Cooke is deceased by 1538, and his wife lived on for some time thereafter (Stevenson (ed.), *Records of Gloucester*, 64–5, 431).

[94] C. Haskins, *Salisbury Corporation Pictures and Plate* (1888, 1910), 9–12.

least claimed by the merchant/mayor. They were also a sign of the protection afforded to market-goers by the lord of the market or, as time went on, by borough officials with authority over marketing activities.[95] But in the Borough of Wells, for example, gloves meant acceptance into the freemanry, so that when one was admitted to that body he gave gloves to his new fellows as a sign that he accepted their fellowship, and a drawing of a glove was placed in the margin of the town order book next to the admission registration.[96] Elsewhere gloves raised on a pole were the sign of the opening of the fair or market for the day's business.[97] It may well be that in civic, if not aristocratic, portraits, gloves connoted the traditions of the fellowship of freemen and the centrality of the market to the urban scene.

And, though both kinds of portrait include the armorial shield, we have in place of the personal motto of the aristocrat the inscribed exhortation to civic service and loyalty. Where the civic body itself had commissioned the portrait, as opposed to buying or being given it by a third party, such inscriptions seem likely to have been composed by the officials responsible and intended for the same didactic ends. The portrait of Philip Crew of Salisbury, a schoolmaster and benefactor rather than an office holder, has been made to emphasize 'brotherly love', always high on the list of civic virtues.[98] Other subjects are praised and thanked for civic bequests: John and Joan Cooke of Gloucester ('Esteemed myrrors . . . For Majestrats and Wives'),[99] Thomas Bell,[100] Thomas Poulton,[101] and John Thorne[102] of the same city.

---

[95] R. Stewart-Brown, 'Notes on the Chester Hand or Glove', *Journal of the Architectural, Archeological and Historic* [sic] *Society for Chester and North Wales*, NS 20 (1914), 122–47.

[96] Shaw, *Creation of a Community*, 157, 198–9.

[97] The use of a 'market glove' is documented for Barnstaple and Totnes, while in Wells, a new freeman presented gloves to his fellow freemen as a sign of accepting the authority of the whole freemanry (T. Wainwright (ed.), *Extracts from Barnstaple Records*, ii (1900), 117; Totnes Borough Records, Devon Record Office, MS 1579/A/7/3; Shaw, *Creation of a Community*, 157, 198–9). The usage may well be connected with the custom whereby the clergy used sometimes to wear gloves to show that their 'hands were clean and not open to bribes'; *Brewer's Dictionary of Phrase and Fable*, rev. and enlarged edn. (1952), 403.

[98] '*Haeredes isti quoties succeditis aulae fraternis mentibus adsit amor*': 'My successors, as often as you succeed to this hall, let brotherly love be present in your minds.' My thanks for help with this translation to my colleagues Dr Lionel Sanders and Dr Catherine Bolton.

[99] *Though death hath rested these life mates | Their memory survives | Esteemed myrrors may they be | For Majestrats and Wives | The School of Crist ye Bartholomews | The Cawseway in ye West | May wittness wch ye pious minde | This Worthy man possest. | This vertuous dame perform'd ye taske | Her husband did intend |*
[See opposite page for n. 99 cont. and nn. 100–2.]

This, then, seems the principal force behind the emergence of civic portraiture in English provincial towns at this time. Where the aristocratic portrait celebrated the personal fame of the sitter and of his family, a function of Professor Stone's 'frenzied ... ancestor worship', the civic portrait seems intended to contribute to the reconstruction and preservation of the collective memory of a particular community. Just as the periodic reading aloud of names on the bederoll had invited a recollection of departed townsmen and elicited prayers for their souls, so did the civic portrait—along with the civic mace, the town history, or the invocation of a founding mythology—invite a frequent recollection of public achievement and an exhortation to respect the heritage of wise and weighty governance. In so doing, it presented virtuous personifications of urbanism itself.

One might well note that, if these devices helped reconstruct a new collective memory, it was not quite the same memory as their grandparents might have shared. Out now were the props provided by the traditional and popular religious practices of the past, invoking the unity of the community as a whole in the fellowship of Christ. In their place emerged the mnemonic devices of a more secular and oligarchic age. Town maces now bore the arms of the mayor, the reconstruction of the past gave wide play to the accretion of self-governing powers and to the role of the mayoralty, the town hall became more a place for the ruling circle, and the memorial brass once intended to invite prayer and reverence gave way, after a hiatus of several decades, to the mayoral portrait, encouraging deference and emulation.

Taken together these devices certainly did work, in Keith Thomas's words, 'to legitimize the prevailing distribution of power'. In addition, they offer a useful contribution to the debate about the origins of provincial urban culture.[103] They make it difficult to

---

And after him in single life | Lived famous to her end. | Their bountye & benificence | On earth remaines allways | Let present past a future time | Still Celebrate yr praise (Brian Frith, *Twelve Portraits of Gloucester Benefactors* (Gloucester, 1972), 9).

[100] '... *He did wel for the poore Provide | his righteousnes shal still remaine | and his estate with praise abide | surpassinge gold & worldly gayne*' (Frith, *Gloucester Benefactors*, 11).

[101] An entirely prosaic '... *He gave vnto the same Citie of Glosester, 60, pownde forever*' (Frith, *Gloucester Benefactors*, 19).

[102] An entirely prosaic list of bequests, including a basin and ewer, presumably of silver and worth £30, to be part of the City's plate for ever; an annual payment for alms and a sermon to the parish church of St Nicholas; and land to support the latter (Frith, *Gloucester Benefactors*, 19).

[103] See above, p. 270.

sustain the view which derives provincial urban culture either from the tastes of the metropolis or of the affluent landed classes, and difficult to date such a culture merely to the Restoration. These are all forms of a refashioned political culture emerging in the decades following the Reformation, invoked by the political requirements of provincial town officials and others of the 'better sort', and with the Crown's compliance. They were well in place by the turn of the seventeenth century.

14

The Culture of Order and Deference

i

Over the portals of the present town hall of Ripon in the historic county of Yorkshire is inscribed the verse from Psalm 127, 'Except the Lord Keep the City the Watchman Waketh but in Vain'.[1] The sentiment could well describe the views of a great many of the ruling sort in the communities under consideration here. The response to this sentiment which has become most familiar to us is the encouragement of 'godly rule': the alliance of magistracy and ministry of the strenuously Protestant variety so well documented in recent scholarship.[2]

But even though a great many of the preaching moralists who served the civic parishes of the realm gained their posts at the appointment of these same magistrates, and although they certainly worked long and hard at moral discipline and reform, contemporary civic leaders were seldom willing to leave the business of watching entirely to the Lord or his clerical servants. They bent their own backs to the task, and in ways which might or might not invoke the helping hand of religion. After all, the fear of disrespect, of civic turmoil, or of political subversion knows no faith in particular. It remains universal amongst those who govern, and especially common amongst those who govern at difficult times. Waves of moral reform such as washed over the realm of England with particular force in the reigns of Elizabeth and James were not unknown in some periods of social and economic distress well before the advent of Protestantism.[3] And some known religious conservatives after

[1] It may also be found inscribed in some churches, as on a wall of St Benet's Church, Cambridge, but this is perhaps less worthy of remark.

[2] See esp. Collinson, *Birthpangs*, chap. 2; *Religion of Protestants*, chap. 4; and Underdown, *Fire from Heaven*.

[3] See e.g. Marjorie K. McIntosh, 'Local Change and Community Control in England, 1485–1500', *Huntington Library Quarterly*, 49 (1986), 219–42; Margaret Spufford, 'Puritanism and Social Control?', in A. Fletcher and John Stevenson (eds.), *Order and Disorder in Early Modern England* (Cambridge, 1985), chap. 1.

the break with Rome were as supportive of moral reform as many Puritans. One thinks, for example, of the merchant-philanthropist Sir Thomas White (1492–1567), founder of St John's College, Oxford, and sometime Lord Mayor of London. Almost certainly a Roman Catholic, White nevertheless issued a proclamation as Lord Mayor in 1554 against morris dancing and the playing of games and interludes.[4] One thinks, too, of the reformist ardour of numerous non-Puritan Elizabethan bishops in such sees as York, Chester, Chichester, Coventry, Lichfield, Hereford, and Lincoln who vigorously opposed morris dancing, sports, and other activities in the 1580s.[5]

The effort of the ruling sort to encourage a cultural perspective favourable to their interests, in which a new and selectively constructed civic memory formed a part, presents only one aspect of contemporary urban political culture. Another consisted of the suppression of beliefs and behaviour which those leaders found undesirable and even potentially subversive. And still another consisted of the reshaping of those undesirable forms so that they served rather than subverted the order of the day. In place of a comprehensive description of these strategies, this chapter will take up representative issues which convey the flavour of the whole: the regulation of dress and speech, especially in regard to civic officials; the restriction of both popular and high cultural forms; and the effort to replace such forms with analogues devoted to supporting the prevailing political structure. It should also be said at the outset that, once again, the tenor of urban political culture bears striking and obvious similarities to the political culture encouraged by the central government for the nation at large, but it also bears some differences peculiar to the urban context.

ii

Questions of appropriate dress and speech in the context of acceptable political behaviour are virtually ubiquitous in town by-laws and assembly minutes of the time. They applied both to the governors and the governed, and they relied on the time-honoured sense of what is appropriate relative to a particular time and place. The

---

[4] *DNB*, *vide* White, Thomas.
[5] Jeremy Goring, 'Godly Exercizes and the Devil's Dance? Puritanism and Popular Culture in Pre-Civil War England', *Friends of Dr Williams Library Lectures*, 37 (1983), 18.

impression that the period at hand saw an increased emphasis on such behavioural constraints may of course simply derive from its more abundant records. On the other hand such a tendency is also an entirely logical response to the political circumstances of the era. The assertion of ever broader authority on the part of civic leaders, and at times when not only towns but the nation as a whole felt the tensions of mounting insecurity, might well be expected to produce a reaction of this sort. And so it seems to have done.

The rules and regulations imposed by enfranchised townsmen in general on their mayors and aldermen worked towards several ends. One, which we see with perhaps greater emphasis than in earlier times, was to ensure that these officials functioned with certain minimum standards of propriety and responsibility. They included such practical considerations as the form and timing of mayoral elections, the requirement to attend council meetings, hold court, inspect the market, and carry out myriad other activities as part of the daily routine, and the common prohibition against mayors leaving the town during their term in office. We frequently find such rules and regulations in civic by-laws,[6] and they are codified with considerable clarity in the compilations of local antiquaries as discussed in the previous chapter.

These regulations regarding appropriate speech and dress seem obviously intended not only to uphold the honour and dignity of the borough, but to prevent the subversion of that honour and dignity by letting down the side with inappropriate behaviour on the part of its officials. Some towns recorded their dress regulations so well that one may follow the progress of their complexity over the course of several decades. From at least the opening years of Elizabeth's reign all aldermen of Chester had to 'come in decent and orderly sort' with their gowns and tippets to church every Sunday and Holy Day and to the council house on every council day. Towards the end of the reign these regulations extended to mandatory dress on mayoral election days and other occasions as well.[7] In 1563 the Mayor and aldermen of Bristol ordered, no doubt on the basis of various precedents, that the mayors and sheriffs must wear their scarlet gowns upon pain of fine on thirteen annual holidays and on fair days. By 1570 members of the Common Council were reminded to wear their black velvet

---

[6] e.g. 'The Charge & Dewtie of the Mayor' of Reading, 1552/3 as entered into the 'Black Book of Reading', Berkshire County Record Office, MS R AC/1/1, p. 276.

[7] Chester City Archives, Chester City Record Office, MS AB/1, for 19 Nov., 2 Elizabeth, and May, 36 Elizabeth.

tippets on special days, when on business in the Tolzey, Guildhall, or Council House, or when accompanying the mayor to burials, sermons, weddings, and other 'solemn' occasions. And in the same year it was ordered that wives even of former mayors and sheriffs must wear scarlet gowns when their husbands did so, 'pro honore et reverentia civitatis'. By 1594 both aldermen and councillors had to wear their 'gownes of the gravest sorte' to the Guildhall or Council House at all times, and by 1598 the Councillors attending the Mayor had to wear caps and not hats, unless specifically licensed to do so by the mayor himself.[8] Similar regulations applied in Boston,[9] Beverley,[10] Salisbury,[11] Hedon,[12] Hereford,[13] Coventry,[14] and probably the vast majority of those towns which had their own governing officials. In some towns, of which Newcastle-upon-Tyne is typical, appropriate dress even extended to the Town Clerk, the serjeants, and the waits as well as such employees (one may hardly call them officials) as plumbers and paviours.[15]

Breaches of such regulations could be met with more than the symbolic slap on the wrist. Fines and even expulsion awaited the forgetful. In Salisbury both the mayor and the mayoress could be fined £20, approximately twice the yearly stipend of many a schoolmaster or clergyman, for failing to wear their scarlet robes on appropriate occasions.[16]

Another aspect of the desire to keep up standards amongst those within the ruling circle was the increased emphasis on maintaining the secrecy of official proceedings. There is some irony in this, for we have noted the desire to make more accessible those elements of the civic heritage, especially the written histories of certain boroughs through the medium of print, to the urban population at large. But if borough leaders were anxious to disseminate some sorts of information outside their own circle, they were equally keen to keep others as closely guarded as possible. We have already noted part of this concern in the frequent restrictions on access to the town hall,

---

[8] Stanford (ed.), *Ordinances of Bristol*, 32–3, 44–5, 97, 105–6.

[9] J. F. Bailey (ed.), *Minutes of Boston*, i. 24.

[10] Beverley Borough Archives, Humberside Record Office, MS BC II/4 ('Small Order Book, 1575–1583'), fo. 3ʳ.

[11] Salisbury Borough Archives, Wiltshire County Record Office, MS G23/1/3, fo. 63ᵛ.

[12] Hedon Borough Archives, Humberside Record Office, MS DDHE/26, fo. 131ᵛ.

[13] 'The Great Black Book of Hereford', Hereford County Record Office, fo. 183ʳ.

[14] Ingram (ed.), *REED: Coventry*, 201.

[15] Anderson (ed.), *REED, Newcastle*, xvi. 68 and 138.

[16] Wiltshire County Record Office, MS G23/1/3, fo. 63ᵛ (16 Elizabeth).

whereby on most occasions only the officers of the town and those pursuing official business could gain entry to that sanctum.

But part also was reflected in the frequent concern for keeping the secrets of the government—often referred to as 'the secrets of the hall'—from anyone not directly concerned with their creation or application. The Mayor and Burgesses of Abingdon decreed in 1562 that anyone should be fined who 'shall reveale, declare or saye anye wordes being Spoken in the councelle howse'[17] and that, to prevent the temptation to spread news of proceedings while they were taking place, no one was to leave the council chamber until their conclusion.[18] In St Albans, by 1608, violations of this code of secrecy could result in deprivation of office.[19] And in a variation upon this theme, four townsmen of Bridport, where the town hall shared a common wall with a tenement, were found guilty of putting their ear to that wall and eavesdropping on the proceedings of the Borough Council in 1578.[20]

Sometimes secrets were kept by the inner circle of the ruling elite even from those of the outer circle of the same government. In Bristol, for example, members of the common council took an oath to 'secretlie keepe all thinges as shallbe secretlie comuned of, in the Counsell house and wch ought to be kept secret' from outsiders. And an ordinance of 1560 required the mayor to sit once weekly with the Aldermen alone, excluding the Common Councillors, 'in the Counsaile Chambre ouer the Tolzey secretely there to entreate and devise for the good order rule and gouernment of the said Citie and for the comon affaires thereof'.[21]

Concern for appropriate use of speech also extended to the enforcement of censorship in oral discourse to protect the dignity of civic officials, whether from attacks by other officials or from those outside the ruling circle altogether. The Borough of Abingdon punished the use of 'unseemly words' in the Council House with commitment to ward from 1561.[22] Hartlepool issued a whole schedule of

[17] B. Challoner (ed.), *Selections from the Municipal Chronicles of the Borough of Abingdon* (1898), 125.
[18] Abingdon Borough Records, Berkshire Record Office, MS D/EP 7/84, fo. 8. Similar rules applied in Hedon: Hedon Borough Archives, Humberside Record Office, MS DDHE/26, fo. 134ʳ.
[19] St Albans Borough Archives, St Albans Public Library, MS 152, fo. 94.
[20] Bridport Borough Archives, Dorset County Record Office, MS B3/C83, a 'Grand Inquest' of 21 Apr. 1578.
[21] City of Bristol, Common Council Proceedings, iv, Frontispiece, as cited in Stanford (ed.), *Ordinances of Bristol*, 29.
[22] Abingdon Borough Records, Berkshire Record Office, MS D/EP 7/84, fo. 7ᵛ.

fines to be paid for verbal abuse by or of the town's officials. In a sequence which tells us a lot about the social pecking order of contemporary urban society, they ranged downwards from 6s. 8d., for calling a chief burgess 'false', to 5s. for reproving a chief burgess in the presence of the mayor, and down to 2s. 6d. for calling a commoner a liar or 'false'. The most severe penalty was of course reserved for reproaching the mayor. This incurred a 20s. fine or punishment at that official's discretion.[23] Anyone rebuking an officer of the Corporation of Hedon, or calling him a vile name, faced a day and a night in prison and a fine of 3s. 4d. The fine doubled if the offender happened to be an officer of the Corporation itself.[24]

But as the ordinances of Hartlepool suggest, the most serious transgressions against the code of appropriate speech applied to abuses of the mayor. As early as 1535 any resident of Reading speaking opprobriously against the mayor or a former mayor could be expelled from the freemanry and fined 40s., and from 1544 the same offence could bring imprisonment as well.[25] The same punishment came to apply in both Boston and Hedon.[26] By those lights the prominent merchant and one-time mayor himself, John Mackanter of King's Lynn, got off lightly when he temporarily lost his burgessship for taunting the mayor in 1550, being readmitted only on payment of a £5 fine. The wages of this particular sin kept pace with inflation, for his fellow townsman Henry Violet had to pay £6. 13s. 4d. for a similar offence in 1586.[27] Henry Houghton of Chester paid a fine of £10 for slandering the mayor's wife in 1590, and, though we do not know the penalty incurred, we may be sure that when Thomas Benson, a Norwich cobbler, was hauled before the Mayor's Court in 1607 because, as it was alleged, he 'did yesterday . . . Bid a turd in Mr. mayor's tethe', he was served neither cakes nor ale.[28]

The direct attack of abusive or salacious speech is of course an obvious affront to any ruling authority. Though it seems likely to have been dealt with more harshly by borough officials in this period than in earlier times, its condemnation could hardly be seen as a

[23] Cuthbert Sharpe, *A History of Hartlepool* (Hartlepool, 1816), 66.

[24] Hedon Borough Archives, Humberside County Record Office, MS DDHE/26, fo. 132ᵛ.

[25] 'Black Book of Reading', Berkshire Record Office, MS R AC/1/1, p. 238; Guilding (ed.), *Reading Records*, i. 188.

[26] J. F. Bailey (ed.), *Minutes of Boston*, i. 80; Humberside Record Office, MS DDHE/26, fo. 132ʳ.

[27] Battley, 'Elite and Community', 267.

[28] Galloway (ed.), *REED: Norwich*, p. xxiv.

novelty. But a sharper break from past forms of expression appears when we consider the unfolding policy of both national and local authorities towards broader aspects of culture: the sundry expressions of what have come to be recognized (sometimes too distinctly) as popular culture on the one hand and the emergence of high culture on the other. These bear extended consideration.

iii

The term 'popular culture' has come to embrace a wide range of recreational and social activities in which members of all social groups commonly shared.[29] In England as in Europe generally these had become closely associated both with traditional entertainments and with the practice of medieval Catholicism, though they also contained elements of both pagan and purely secular activity. Much of popular culture under consideration here may simply be called, as it was at the time, 'merry-making', and the common literary reference to 'merry England' has been taken to refer to the time which drew to a close in the period at hand.[30] We have noted in the early chapters of this study the ways in which popular cultural forms had become incorporated, well before the Reformation, into a complex and effective support structure of beliefs, practices, and institutions for the prevailing values and authorities of that time, whether religious or secular.

Though a number of salient points remain open to debate, the broad outlines of the history of popular culture in this era, and of official attitudes towards it, are now familiar.[31] The eve of the

---

[29] The term and concept has been widely kicked about since the seminal discussion in Peter Burke's *Popular Culture in Early Modern Europe* (1978, 1994). Though many of the problems which have been raised about its use, including religion and ethnic identity, will apply more to the post-Reformation than the pre-Reformation era, one still wants to take particular care. In the present context it is taken to apply to traditional folk or vernacular activities in which a very large proportion of the population could share, though that sharing may not have been equal in either degree or kind by particular groups within the social milieu. For the state of the current debate, see Tim Harris (ed.), *Popular Culture in England, c.1500–1850* (1995), and esp. Harris's own contribution, 'Problematising Popular Culture', 1–27.

[30] As in Hutton, *Merry England*.

[31] Useful general treatments include: Burke, *Popular Culture in Early Modern Europe*; Michael D. Bristol, *Carnival and Theatre: Plebeian Culture and the Structure of Authority in Renaissance England* (1985); Cressy, *Bonfires and Bells*; Hutton, *Merry England*; and T. Harris, (ed.), *Popular Culture in England*. The most comprehensive collection of contemporary source material for these activities continues to be produced by the Records of Early English Drama Project in Toronto, whose volumes cover the period to 1642.

Henrician Reformation probably represents the high point of traditional popular cultural activities in England, followed of course by the great debacle of the ensuing decades. Yet even prior to the iconoclasm of the 1540s and beyond there were those who opposed popular excesses out of concern for disorder, expense, or transgressions against contemporary morality or religious doctrine. Opponents included individual writers and authorities as well as ecclesiastical officials and the governing bodies of a few borough corporations.[32] In Bishop's Stortford, for example, the local authorities banned the traditional parish ale from the church and churchyard (though not from the town itself) as early as 1451.[33] Exeter's ruling council restricted the performance of Robin Hood plays in 1510 because they were too rowdy,[34] and in Shrewsbury the traditional mayor's dinner which had been held between Matins and High Mass on Christmas Day had to be abandoned from 1524 on because of the disorder which had come to mark its celebration.[35] As we approach the 1540s these cases become somewhat more common. Hock Tuesday revels had to be abandoned in Wallingford in 1538 because they proved too expensive, and costs of official feasts had become too burdensome to continue in Coventry at about the same time.[36] Notwithstanding these isolated examples, festive celebrations remained in full flow up to that time. They were widely supported by the population at large, encouraged and even patronized by local officials. Many of them actually brought in a great deal more funds to the coffers of parish and town than they caused to be expended.

But with the iconoclasm of the early Reformation, especially in the reign of Edward VI, the great assault on traditional festivities moved into high gear. Most directly affected were the material implements and paraphernalia of traditional religion and religious celebration. In institutional terms, the abolition of the religious guilds hit especially hard, for they had supported a great deal of the traditional processions, pageants, and other forms of merry-making

---

[32] Hutton, *Merry England*, 70–1.   [33] Ibid. 33, 70.

[34] John Wasson (ed.), *REED: Devon* (Toronto, 1986); Ian Lancashire, *Dramatic Texts and Records of Britain* (Cambridge, 1984), 135.

[35] H. W. Adnitt (ed.), 'Orders of the Corporation of Shrewsbury, 1511–1735', *Transactions of the Shropshire Archeological and Natural History Society*, 11/2 (Feb. 1888), 158.

[36] *VCH, Berkshire*, 3 (1923), 535; and Ingram (ed.), *REED: Coventry*, 149. Dr Alexandra F. Johnston, Director of Records of Early English Drama, indicates in correspondence that the correct date of the former is 1538/9: I am grateful to her for pointing this out.

associated with traditional religion. By the end of Edward's reign most of the material ornaments and the vast majority of the seasonal festivities and liturgical rituals associated with popular religious practice had been abolished. Most of those which survived or which would be revived did so because their content could be transformed to reflect themes which were new, secular (or in some cases even Protestant), or benign to the government's aims.

The short reign of Mary offered official encouragement for the restoration of many popular festivities[37] (despite some concern for the subversive potential of contemporary theatre[38]), and some of them continued on in the relatively tolerant early years of Elizabeth's reign. This toleration took in stage plays and even some forms of traditional drama. It extended to those many forms of festivity and popular rite which held little religious connotation, what we might call the street culture of the times. Skimmington Rides, charivaris, games of chance, ritualized excuses for drinking and dancing, minstrelsy and 'false, fond ballads', and similar entertainments, some laced with symbolic social meaning and some not, were all part of this mélange. May games continued to be played, often (as in Rye) with mayoral support. The officers of Plymouth continued to fund morris dancing and various players, the erection of a maypole, and the performance of fools and mummers at the Yuletide. The mayor of Newcastle continued to support similar activities at both midsummer and Christmas.[39] In York the annual Nativity ritual, including the public Ride of Yule and his Wife, continued as well. York, Chester, Coventry, and possibly Wakefield are among those towns which still hosted their traditional cycle plays.[40] The 'Lord of Melton' continued to receive homage from his 'subjects' in Melton Mowbray, to the accompaniment of Robin Hood plays, maypole dancing, and feasting.[41] Bearwards and players continued to ply their craft even in firmly Protestant Bridgnorth.[42] And in Essex it has been reckoned that plays were performed in virtually four times as many towns in the first two decades of Elizabeth's reign as in the decade preceding them.[43]

---

[37] Summarized in Hutton, *Merry England*, 98–104.
[38] Brigden, *London and the Reformation*, 600.
[39] Summarized in Hutton, *Merry England*, 115.
[40] Collinson, *Birthpangs*, 100.
[41] Pockley, 'Origins and Early History of Melton Mowbray', 306–11.
[42] Alan Somerset (ed.), *REED: Shropshire* (Toronto, 1995), 381.
[43] John C. Coldeway, 'The Last Rise and Final Demise of Essex Town Drama', *Modern Language Quarterly*, 36 (1975), 249.

Sometimes, especially in the remote parts of the realm, activities of a traditional nature lasted even longer. Corpus Christi continued to be celebrated in the traditional manner in Kendal right up to the beginning of the seventeenth century,[44] and Shrewsbury's maypole analogue, the Shearman's Tree, only came into being after the abandonment of its predecessor around 1580. It was still being erected despite extreme controversy (as we will see below) as late as 1618.[45]

But by the latter 1570s or so the policy of the Elizabethan government, if not necessarily of the Queen herself, reverted to the sort of disciplined approach to popular culture, and particularly to its religious aspects, laid out under Edward. Those years saw the opening of Burbage's Theatre in London and stepped up attacks by the puritan zealots of the day, to whom Burbage and his ilk were the very devil. They saw, too, an increased wariness at court of the potential for civil subversion following such events as the Northern Rising of 1569, the excommunication of Elizabeth in 1570, and the Ridolfi Plot of 1571. And in addition, as is now commonly recognized, these years mark the point at which the majority of English men and women came to think of themselves as Protestants, and when enough of them were willing to support moves against traditional cultural expression to make a running battle of it.[46]

Under these conditions the full force of the campaign against 'merry-making' in general took broad effect. It amounted to a coordinated and methodical assault on those traditional forms and considerable support for their repression in many parts of the country. In their place, with a period of some chronological overlap, emerged two more recognizably modern modes of cultural expression. The first amounted to a greatly enhanced display of civic ceremony, preoccupied with the corporate and secular life of the civic body. This usually embraced a sanitized version of the traditional which turned accustomed forms more decisively towards the celebration of civic virtues. The second, applied especially to theatre, initiated an inventive, predominantly secular, and written dramatic tradition in which the performers were professionals on tour rather than local journeymen taking off a day's work to don angel's wings or Robin Hood green in the annual parish play.

---

[44] Audrey Douglas and Peter Greenfield (eds.), *REED: Cumberland, Westmorland and Gloucester* (Toronto, 1986), 17–19.

[45] Somerset (ed.), *REED: Shropshire*, 398–405.

[46] See e.g. Collinson, *Birthpangs*, p. ix; and Haigh (ed.), *English Reformations, passim*.

The prevailing historiographic tendency in considering the motivations for most of these developments has been to see a battle over cultural expression between Puritans and non-Puritans.[47] This rather simplistic picture has now been at least somewhat qualified by the fruits of closer research. Numerous examples have come forth both of non-Puritan reformers (like Sir Thomas White) and of Puritan non-reformers, and of opposition to such things as religious plays for reasons having both little and much to do with doctrine. We may now also question the putative homogeneity of Puritan thought itself, noting the many divisions amongst those often grouped under its heading.[48] Still, the battles over cultural expression and social behaviour at the time were real, frequent, and hard-fought. Even if Puritanism was only one (albeit prominent) cause, it is no exaggeration to see contention over behavioural reform as opening a vast crevice in English society and belief.[49]

iv

The concern here, of course, must be with the progress and significance of this battle in the urban communities of the realm, and this is by no means a contrived approach to the issue. Many of the skirmishes over reform were fought on urban soil. Many were fought between burgesses and their governing officials; others amongst burgesses themselves. Much of the political history of the English town in this era proves difficult to comprehend if we do not take these controversies into account. Parliament or the Crown might determine the rules; the general populace might influence the extent to which they were applied; the great aristocracy who patronized most of the professional troupes of players brought pressure to bear as well; and both laymen and clerics of the zealous sort pushed hard to achieve their aims. But as one might by now anticipate, both the effort to suppress popular cultural expressions or, alternatively, to sanitize them revolved both by law and circumstance (and probably

---

[47] V. Gildersleeve, *Government Regulation of Elizabethan Drama* (New York, 1908); Harold C. Gardiner, *Mysteries' End* (New Haven, 1946); R. W. Chambers, *The Elizabethan Stage* (4 vols.; Oxford, 1923). See also Jonah Barish, *The Antitheatrical Prejudice* (Berkeley, 1981), 82–104.

[48] See e.g. Margot Heinemann, *Puritanism and Theatre: Thomas Middleton and Opposition Drama under the Early Stuarts* (Cambridge, 1980); Paul Christianson, 'Reformers and the Church of England under Elizabeth I and the Early Stuarts', *Journal of Ecclesiastical History*, 31 (1980), 463–83; Barish, *Antitheatrical Prejudice*, 115; Peter Lake, *Moderate Puritans and the Elizabethan Church* (Cambridge, 1982).

[49] Well summarized in Collinson, *Birthpangs*, chap. 4.

the will of the Queen herself[50]) around the power of the urban magistracy.[51] Despite the tight corner in which they often found themselves, these ruling elites frequently realized the potential in such controversy to flex their own muscle and fortify their own position. For all but the most zealous the preferred course seems to have been to take the sting out of traditional festivities by regulating their content and turning them to celebrations of the contemporary leadership.

There was, of course, little uniformity in any of this, either from town to town, or even from one administration to the next within particular towns. Even the division of sentiment on these issues remained broad and imprecise. On the one hand, at least most of the time, lay the governing authorities of the nation, working from an agenda of both law and order and religious conformity, and the ruling sort of many (if by no means all) local communities, who often shared that agenda. On the other side lay a goodly, if indeterminate, share of the population at large, plus some local governing authorities and even occasional voices in the central government.[52] These people enjoyed a good time and saw no reason to curtail the activities which had hitherto provided it so long as they remained orderly. Over the course of time popular sentiment probably tended somewhat to sour on traditional festivities, thus making curtailment less objectionable. Still, victories in the battles over cultural expression tended to be short-lived and, to a point, reversible. But patterns of change do emerge and they allow us to see the direction of movement and draw some conclusions.

Those urban leaders of the sternest moral cast, like the notoriously zealous mayor of Chester, Henry Hardware, were unwilling

---

[50] Lancashire, *Dramatic Texts and Records*, p. xxx.

[51] For a similar dilemma faced by constables and jurymen in agrarian society who were also caught between the opinion of their fellows and neighbours and their responsibilities as royal officials, see Keith Wrightson, 'Two Concepts of Order: Constables and Jurymen in Seventeenth Century England', in J. Brewer and J. Styles (eds.), *An Ungovernable People* (New Brunswick, NJ, 1980), 21–46; and Joan Kent, *The English Village Constable, 1580–1642* (Oxford, 1986).

[52] Despite the evidence of statutes, proclamations, and numerous court decisions, we should not assume that the policy of the central government universally opposed popular festivities even well into the reign of Elizabeth. As the Privy Council wrote when asked to adjudicate a 1589 dispute over that issue in Banbury, 'we see no cause that those pastimes of recreation being not vsed at vnlawful tymes, as one the sabbath day in tyme of devine service & in disordered and riotous sorte should be forbidden the people'; cited in Somerset (ed.), *REED: Shropshire*, 402.

even to countenance the more benign versions of festivities which had survived to their time in office. They used their authority to quash what they could of these activities. They worked to bring to power others of like mind who might complete the task in subsequent mayoral terms. Hardware used his mayoral authority in 1599 to break up the giant which for many years had been paraded at Midsummer festivities, to take the bull ring from the high cross area, and to remove the dragon and the naked boys from the Midsummer show.[53]

Moralistic campaigns were rarely as forceful as that carried out by Hardware at the end of the century in Chester, but even well before the turn of the seventeenth century many other ruling elites worked to suppress various forms of popular festivity in their own communities. In York the work of a minority of religious zealots helped the ecclesiastical commissioners root out a number of festive rites against what seems the clear desire of the majority to maintain them.[54] In Coventry part of the cultural war surrounded the issue of the Hock Tuesday plays, which were suppressed around 1572 and revived at least for a time in 1575.[55] In Dorchester the censorious fulminations of the Reverend John White and his allies against popular celebrations and similar infelicities formed a continual cleavage point in community relations.[56] In both Canterbury and Leicester authorities took steady aim at maypoles and morris dances.[57] And under an earlier administration in Chester itself the Whitsun Plays came to an end in 1577.

But faced with the same political and moral imperatives to restrict cultural forms which had become offensive or potentially subversive in the eyes of many, outright suppression was not the only course of action open to town officials. In view of the extreme opposition which such suppressions could elicit, it was not even always the wisest plan. In some towns officials enjoyed considerable success well on into the Elizabethan era and beyond by encouraging the conversion of traditional popular festivities to strategies which were at least uncontroversial and at best emphatically celebratory of the contemporary civic regime. In most of these cases the idea was to acknowledge the popularity of merry-making and to sustain some degree of

[53] BL, Harleian MS 1944, fo. 90; and Clopper (ed.), *REED: Chester*, p. liii.
[54] Johnston and Rogerson (eds.), *REED: York*, 331–3.
[55] Cited in Hutton, *Merry England*, 137.
[56] Underdown, *Fire from Heaven*, esp. chap. 4.
[57] Hutton, *Merry England*, 138.

continuity with past practice by retaining traditional elements of form. Content could then be converted as necessary, from the potentially subversive to start with, through the neutral ground of the benign, and on over another notch to the usefully supportive.

Though practice varied widely from one region to another, the tradition of church ales illustrates this well. In that these often devolved into bouts of riotous drinking and disorder for as long as a week at a time, they were obvious targets for a reforming mayoralty. But they also brought in a pretty penny to the coffers of town and parish, which complicated the task at hand. In many areas they seem to have been allowed to flourish more or less in their traditional form right through the 1560s. Thereafter they often came to be abolished in name (though not statutorily until 1603), only to spring up in much the same form under the aegis of the civic oligarchy in such alternative forms as, for example, 'bailiff's ales', where they endured for at least a few decades more, or as formal rates, which were more enduring still.[58]

By the same token festivities which once surrounded the celebration of the Nativity of St John the Baptist came to be grafted onto the predominantly secular Midsummer's Eve celebrations which were held within a few days of the former. And those celebrations themselves became transformed to almost exclusively civic and secular rather than in any way liturgical occasions. In Barnstaple, a puritan bastion by the mid-Elizabethan era, traditionally disorderly Midsummer Eve celebrations came to consist chiefly of the mayor perambulating the bounds of the town accompanied by the town waits, effectively defining as he went the geographic limits of his authority.[59] In Carlisle, where Midsummer had also been a boisterous occasion in former times, it devolved in this period to a tame civic celebration featuring guild-sponsored wakes, music by the town waits, and a communal feast. To top off the day's conversion to positive and orderly purposes, a ritualized distribution of alms to the town's pensioners came to be appended by the 1620s.[60] And in Norwich, where the transition to post-Reformation forms has been

---

[58] David Underdown, *Revel, Riot and Rebellion: Popular Politics and Culture in England, 1603–1660* (Oxford, 1987), 60, 82–3, 92–3, 97–8; Alexandra F. Johnston, 'Folk Drama in Berkshire', in J. A. Raftis (ed.), *Pathways to Medieval Peasants* (Toronto, 1981), 1–2 and *passim*.

[59] Wasson (ed.), *REED: Devon*, p. xiii.

[60] Douglas and Greenfield (eds.), *REED: Cumberland, Westmorland and Gloucestershire*, 27.

seen as gentle and uneventful[61] and where Midsummer celebrations offered a prominent role for the mayoralty well before the Reformation, the suppression of other, especially liturgical, elements brought civic themes even further to the fore.[62] In such sanitized forms the Midsummer Eve celebrations, or Midsummer Watch, were often maintained in these towns and others (including e.g. Canterbury, Plymouth, Nottingham, York, and even Burford)[63] well into the period at hand, and sometimes even to 1640.

Even the much-heralded festivities performed at Corpus Christi, a red-letter day in the traditional liturgical calendar, came in most places by the mid-Elizabethan era to be abolished altogether or to be transformed into something much more secular and, by contemporary lights, innocuous. In London, Lincoln, and Norwich, Corpus Christi festivities disappeared in the reign of Edward VI. In York and Coventry they continued in watered-down versions, and elsewhere only the feast continued while the traditional celebrations ended.[64] Even in Shrewsbury Corpus Christi celebrations were moved to the following Monday and appended to the more innocuous Show Monday celebrations, where they continued in one form or another (save for during the Civil War and Interregnum) to 1878![65] And in Chester the Whitsun Play provides another excellent example of adaptability to new circumstances. Both the subject matter and the route of the procession were redesigned, not once but several times, to reflect the greater glory of the mayor and his brethren.[66]

As in the last-named city, the thrust of a good number of these transformations was to place the mayor and his brethren in the limelight once occupied by the pantheon of biblical and other religious figures: a transformation analogous to the replacement of Jesus Christ with Lady Godiva in the stained glass of St Mary's Hall, Coventry.[67] In remote Carlisle All Hallows Thursday came by the mid-Elizabethan period to consist chiefly of a mayoral perambulation

[61] Muriel McClendon, 'The Quiet Reformation: Norwich Magistrates and the Coming of Protestantism, 1520–1575', Ph.D. thesis (Stanford, 1990).

[62] Galloway (ed.), *REED: Norwich, passim*.

[63] Cressy, *Bonfires and Bells*, 27.

[64] Hutton, *Merry England*, 83. Hutton assumes that these festivities included Corpus Christi plays, but Records of Early English Drama has found little or no evidence of such performances.

[65] Somerset (ed.), *REED: Shropshire*, 397–8.

[66] Mills, 'Chester Ceremonial', 7–9; Clopper (ed.), *REED: Chester*, pp. lv–lviii.

[67] See above, p. 276.

of the bounds accompanied by the music of the waits and sundry fiddlers and jugglers. In Chester the traditional Shrove Tuesday celebrations came by the mid-sixteenth century to include a feast in the Mayor's honour sponsored by the wealthy Drapers' Company.[68] In Newcastle, Ludlow, and Coventry (the same Coventry whose mayor had complained so bitterly to Thomas Cromwell in 1539 about the costs of civic ceremony[69]) traditional drama gave way to such annual occasions as the productions put on by youths of the local grammar school for the mayor and his brethren. These often featured laudatory verses in the mayor's honour, as if the boys were poets declaiming at a royal coronation.[70] All these experiences point to the successful co-option of popular festivity by the ruling elites of English towns by the turn of the seventeenth century and after, albeit often against the wishes, as in Shrewsbury, of many fellow townsmen.

Along with the refashioning of traditional occasions, we often find the creation of new ones towards similarly justifying ends. The Mayor and Corporation of the Borough of Boston agreed in 1555 that the charter should be read publicly four times a year, to be followed each time by a dinner for the mayor, aldermen, and common councillors.[71] And in the following year Norwich began what became an annual celebration to mark the oath-taking of its mayor. In its first known form this consisted of no less than six pageants at the centre of a celebratory procession. One pageant wagon portrayed Time and consisted of music by the City waits. Others included a laudatory speech directed at the mayor by a local schoolmaster, and a second oration delivered from a castle.[72]

In this employment of festive forms for civic purposes there is both a firm parallel and a contiguity with events in the nation as a whole. On this larger scene, as David Cressy has shown, the traditional festive calendar gave way at the Reformation to a new sequence of annual festivities which were secular and patriotic, and which helped bind the nation in what he calls 'a mythic and patriotic

[68] Clopper (ed.), *REED: Chester*, 237.
[69] Ingram (ed.), *REED: Coventry*, 149.
[70] Anderson, *REED: Newcastle*, p. xvii; Somerset (ed.), *REED: Shropshire*, 380; Ingram (ed.), *REED: Coventry*, p. xx. In Ludlow, which did not yet have a mayoral form of government, these were directed to the bailiffs as the mayoral analogue.
[71] J. F. Bailey (ed.), *Minutes of Boston*, i. 24–5.
[72] Lancashire, *Dramatic Texts and Records*, 79 and 239.

sense of national identity'.[73] In that transition the void left by the abolition of traditional liturgical festivities came to be filled by such civic holidays as, for example, Accession Day (or, to use Cressy's term, 'Crownation Day') on 17 November to mark the accession of Elizabeth. Not only did the officials of many towns welcome these celebrations, but they frequently took the lead in developing them as annual civic rituals. At Liverpool in 1576 the mayor led the citizens in a banquet and bonfires, lighting a fire outside his own home to set the tone. The officials of Maidstone, Ipswich, Coventry, and Nottingham sponsored plays, those of Norwich fired guns and hosted a festive procession, and their counterparts in Kendal greeted the day with bells and music.[74] In subsequent years celebrations of victory over the Spanish Armada, the accession of James I, the revelation of the Gunpowder Plot, and the safe return of Prince Charles from his failed courtship of the Spanish Infanta in 1623 (an odd thing to celebrate, but still . . .), and his accession as Charles I joined the new seasonal round.

On these occasions concerns for expense, disorder, or physical damage, or even for the possibilities of licentious behaviour, seem to have been laid aside in the pursuit of more important civic aims. Opponents found it more difficult to attack bonfires and dancing when they honoured the Queen or the state; town officials found it easier to make exceptions for a cause so close to their hearts. By linking the town with the nation in the celebration of national events, civic leaders were also drawing attention to the greatly augmented links of their own authority with that of Crown and Parliament: a variation on the theme of placing the royal arms over the mayor's chair. It allowed them a means of showing their fellow townsmen how and where they and their community fit in with the larger scheme of things: a connection which would have been much more difficult to make a century or even a half century earlier. It was part of the widening out of the civic consciousness which also characterized this age, especially in such large and commercially successful towns as Bristol.[75] And, as with the focus of celebration on purely local institutions and offices in particular towns, such festivities became very useful substitutes for traditional celebrations which had come under a cloud.

---

[73] Cressy, *Bonfires and Bells*, p. xi.   [74] Ibid. 50–6.
[75] A theme pursued at greater length, and perhaps with excessive claims for towns not as large or complex as Bristol, in Sacks, *The Widening Gate*.

V

At the same time that such civic festivities evolved in this fashion, another alternative to the traditional celebrations made headway as well. This is the accelerated emergence of a professional element in public entertainment, and the simultaneous growth in civic authority for its regulation. Professional entertainers included the town waits, who were paid regularly for their performances at festive occasions as well as for their daily role in the town watch, who wore livery and who served full-time.

But even more importantly, the middle decades of the sixteenth century saw the blossoming of an important and increasingly high cultural tradition in the form of professional troupes of players and of theatrical conventions which are more familiar to the modern eye. The tendency towards full-time and peripatetic rather than occasional and stationary players, though long apparent, moved forth rapidly in these years. So did the tendency to augment and then often to replace the form and content of traditional drama, whether cycle plays or not, with plays of recent vintage. Though some openly anti-Catholic or Protestant drama emerged as well,[76] these newer plays took up secular and even contemporary themes in place of the annual repetitions of traditional plays on liturgical themes. They form another example of cultural transformation to suit the times. And in concert with these developments came new approaches to the regulation of theatrical performance. Civic officials became more than ever the front line of enforcement, thus further enhancing their regulatory authority over forms of cultural expression.

The history of dramatic performance in this era shared the same chronological sequence of ups and downs as other forms of festive expression, with the proclamation, in 1559, 'For Prohibiting Unlicensed Interludes and Plays', marking an important additional milestone. Once seen principally as the definitive prohibition of the theatrical treatment of religious and political subjects, it did at least place on the shoulders of the nation's mayors and similar officials a statutory responsibility for scrutinizing and licensing dramatic activities.[77] Armed with that authority, the civic officials were able to

---

[76] A point best made in Paul W. White, *Theatre and Reformation: Protestantism, Patronage and Playing in Tudor England* (Cambridge, 1993).

[77] P. Hughes and J. F. Larkin (eds.), *Tudor Royal Proclamations*, ii (New Haven and London, 1969), no. 458. The weight given its effectiveness in marking a definitive turning point in actual practice by e.g. E. K. Chambers can no longer be sustained (Chambers, *Elizabethan Stage*, i. 242).

respond with the full force of royal authority when a number of factors conspired to puff out the sails of moral reform for another two decades and more.

And though virtually all forms of popular festivity threatened certain developing notions of propriety and acceptability at this time, theatre conveyed a subversive potential which was both considerable and distinct. The professionalism and licensing of players and troupes meant that Elizabethan performers tended to move from one place to another to ply their craft. They were therefore almost always strangers, rarely belonging to the freemanry of the town in which they performed.[78] Save for the reputation of the great persons in whose names such troupes performed, they lacked the credit of personal reputation: a serious handicap at the time. Often they found themselves grouped with rogues, vagabonds, and other 'masterless men'.[79]

Then, too, players were seen as potentially subversive because of the nature of their craft itself. This, of course, was the art of delusion, and it was conveyed in several ways. Costume or disguise made actors appear as someone or something other than themselves. Gender inversion, in which men played women's roles as well as their own, reversed the normal order of things. Scenery and props transformed an audience out of the literal reality of their situation. Such conventions as the stage whisper and the soliloquy demanded both a further suspension of disbelief and a sense of shared conspiracy between actor and audience. And the conventions borne by the text, in which it was understood that many things could be said and done in performance which could not otherwise be assayed, surely involved a suspension of the normal rules of speech and behaviour.[80]

Concerns about this subversive potential grew in pace with other changes in the Reformation era. When traditional religious plays

[78] Jean-Christophe Agnew, *Worlds Apart: The Market and the Theatre in Anglo-American Thought* (Cambridge, 1986), 103; Muriel Bradbrook, *The Rise of the Common Player: A Study of the Actor and Society in Shakespeare's England* (1962), 40, 188; A. L. Beier, *Masterless Men: The Vagrancy Problem in England, 1560–1640* (1985), 95–6.

[79] For example in the Elizabethan Poor Law of 1597 (39 Elizabeth, c. 4).

[80] These themes are treated at much greater length in a substantial literature, of which the following are important examples: L. C. Knight, *Drama and Society in the Age of Jonson* (1937); Agnew, *Worlds Apart*, 109–14; Margot Heinemann, *Puritanism and Theatre: Thomas Middleton and Opposition Drama under the Early Stuarts* (Cambridge, 1980), 16 and chaps. 12–13; Bristol, *Carnival and Theatre*, 112–18; Peter Stallybrass and Allon White, *The Poetics and Politics of Transgression* (1986), *passim*; and Bradbrook, *Rise of the Common Player*, 23–9, 62–4.

and other dramatic forms had been largely abandoned or transformed, they were replaced by others which bore even greater potential for subversion. The older plays may have come to offend the prevailing beliefs of later Elizabethans, but they were at least known commodities. Their texts, plots, and even their costumes, props, and gestures varied little from year to year, and one knew exactly what would transpire before the play began. The dramatic traditions which grew in their wake involved plays newly written and acted in which neither the dialogue nor the message could necessarily be known beforehand. Furthermore, as the old subjects, many of them liturgical in derivation, were now considered inappropriate, new subjects, often with secular themes, emerged in their stead.[81] These could well be topical, political, and very sensitive in somewhat different respects.

Against these perceived dangers, and with the cooperation of the Crown and Parliament, local officials such as mayors worked out several strategies in the course of the Elizabethan era. To begin with, national and local officials alike recognized the importance of controlling content. Laws giving mayors and other officials responsibility for licensing plays were chiefly directed towards this end. In the context of the town, they allowed mayors a solution to a number of the problems raised by the issue of the theatre, amongst them the dilemma of having to serve both their fellow townsmen, their masters at Westminster, and a number of powerful aristocratic patrons whose troupes of players might come to perform. Under the emerging licensing laws of the day, visiting players came first to the mayor, presented their licence to perform, and awaited his pleasure in granting them permission to play. He then often requested that they put on their first performance in his presence, so that he could scrutinize the play itself, and so that they would know of that scrutiny.[82]

Another strategy came into more frequent effect here as well. That was for these plays to be put on not in the open air, the market place or church yard, as had more often been the case in earlier

---

[81] At least in the early days of the Reformation there were religious plays of a Protestant—or at least anti-Catholic—bent as well, though aside from the aggressively iconoclastic plays of John Bale, most of these have remained unfamiliar to us and many have not survived. For brief but incisive comments, see Collinson, *Birthpangs*, 102–6.

[82] Hughes and Larkin, *Tudor Royal Proclamations*, vol. ii, no. 115; Glynne Wickham, *Early English Stages, 1300–1600* (3 vols.; 1959–81), i. 269–70, ii. 178–9; Bradbrook, *Rise of the Common Player*, 115; Douglas and Greenfield, *REED: Cumberland, Westmorland and Gloucester*, 253.

times, but indoors. In the countryside, where members of the nobility had been invested with similar powers of scrutiny, this often meant theatre in the banqueting hall of the manor house, where in fact some performances had been held for generations. In the town this often meant the inn, the town hall, or even the grammar school. Here the elements of weather and at least some noise could be avoided, the players themselves could more effectively pass the hat, and the more formal and standardized playing space allowed the further development of theatrical convention. But the new indoor venues proved valuable for local authorities as well. The size of the spectacle could be controlled, the audience as well as the performance could be scrutinized, security could more effectively be maintained. The mayor's presence at the opening 'command' performance—especially where he could take a seat of honour—lent dignity to the occasion. His scrutiny of the whole proceedings enhanced his control over what his fellow townsmen saw performed. It lent dignity to his person and his office, for he acted in this capacity as the Queen at her court or the country magnate in his manor house or castle.

For a while performances under those circumstances were considered highly desirable. They brought money into the town by attracting audiences from the countryside. They provided entertainment for the townspeople and they allowed the local government to bask in the aura of conspicuous patronage. Especially in the mid-Elizabethan years the towns' authorities went to a lot of trouble to accommodate such performances. The conventional furnishings of town halls were often cleared out to permit the erection of a stage or the provision of seating.[83] A mid-sixteenth-century Norwich account describes wide poplar planks raised up on barrels to form a stage.[84] In Gloucester in 1559–60 the audience sat on benches and the players strode a raised platform built by a local carpenter paid for the task by the City government, while the mayor and aldermen of Stafford allowed players to erect stages in the Shirehall throughout the first four decades of the seventeenth century.[85] Shrewsbury allowed £5 a year for the expenses of erecting stages for players.[86]

---

[83] Richard Southern, *The Staging of Plays Before Shakespeare* (1973), 332–41.

[84] Nelson, *Medieval English Stage*, 136; Southern, *Staging of Plays*, 333; Wickham, *Early English Stages*, ii/1, 184.

[85] Douglas and Greenfield, *REED: Cumberland, Westmorland and Gloucestershire*, 253 and 298; Gloucestershire Record Office, MS GBR F/4/3, fos. 78, 79 and 107; Adey, 'History of Stafford', p. xiii.

[86] Southern, *Staging of Plays*, 338–9.

There were other concessions, too. The mayor of Cambridge not only granted permission for Iohannes Duke and Thomas Greene to put on a performance in the Town Hall in 1606, but he 'did also give them the key of the Towne Hall' so as to come and go as they pleased while preparing for the performance.[87] Norwich authorities employed the services of a doorkeeper during performances and permitted the use of candles and charcoal fires to illuminate and heat the hall.[88]

In the same vein, it had become common to pay or at least to reward players who gave approved performances, and this must be seen as well as a gesture of ingratiation to the sponsor of the troupe. In Exeter and no doubt elsewhere this had been the practice even in the fifteenth century, but it continued on well into the period at hand.[89] Similar payments were made by the mayor and aldermen of Plymouth in the 1530s and 1540s,[90] the mayors of Norwich in the 1540s and 1550s,[91] the mayors of Bristol throughout most of the century,[92] the Chamberlains of York through the 1580s and 1590s and as late as 1606,[93] and other towns as well.

But if such encouragement extended to players whose performances remained within the limits of acceptable behaviour, those limits varied from place to place and, even within the same places, from time to time. Towards the last years of the sixteenth century the broad acceptability of dramatic performance even in such controlled circumstances underwent something of a sea change in most of the towns whose dramatic traditions have been brought to light. Some of the motives for this volte-face simply amounted to the revival of old concerns. They included concerns for order and discipline, for the sheer cost which might be involved, for affronts to the dignity of the civic officials who nominally presided over such entertainments, and for the disorder which might be provoked.[94]

They included, too, the considerable damage which players and

[87] Alan H. Nelson (ed.), *REED: Cambridge* (2 vols.; Toronto, 1989), i. 403.

[88] Southern, *Staging of Plays*, 338.

[89] Wasson (ed.), *REED: Devon*, 92, 111, 115, 116, 146, 148, 150, 157.

[90] Ibid. 227, 228, 229, and 258.

[91] Galloway (ed.), *REED: Norwich*, 7 and 31.

[92] Information provided by Dr Mark Pilkinton, editor of the forthcoming Records of Early English Drama volume on Bristol, to whom I am indebted.

[93] Johnston and Rogerson (eds.), *REED: York*, i. 409, 419, 430, 435, 436, 441, 442, 471, 476, 488, 491, 501, and 521.

[94] An important treatment of non-religious factors in the late Elizabethan attack on theatre is Coldeway, 'The Last Rise and Final Demise of Essex Town Drama', 239–60.

especially their audiences sometimes wreaked on the buildings where performances were held. When those buildings were also towns halls, the seats and symbols of local authority, the damage added insult to injury. Such destruction included damage to the ceiling in the guildhall of Barnstaple by the boisterousness of 'Enterlude Players', damage to the hall stairs in Peterborough, and the destruction of part of the town armoury, adjacent to the main part of the Bath Guildhall, by the Earl of Pembroke's Players.[95] In York the doors, locks, keys, windows, boards, benches, and other furnishings of the Common Hall were found in 1591 to be 'greatly impaired and hurte, and diverse of the same broken, shaken loose and riven up by the people repairing there to see and hear plays',[96] and in Liverpool both dramatic activities and dancing had severely to be restricted in the 1570s for fear that the floor would fall in.[97]

And, most familiarly of all, dramatic performances and almost all other forms of popular entertainment, whether 'sanitized' and supervised or not, eventually slipped under the wheels of moral reform, most of it inspired by the strenuous Protestantism which had arisen by the middle years of Elizabeth's reign. The nature and extent of that offence can hardly be articulated more laconically than in the words of the Assembly Minute Book of the City of Chester, whose zealous Puritan Mayor Henry Hardware had already done so much to destroy the old, traditional form of dramatic entertainment by his destruction of pageant props and paraphernalia in 1599. Recording a meeting of 1614 in which the City Council banned the performance of plays in the Common Hall and elsewhere in its jurisdiction, the City Clerk captured the tenor of official sentiment as follows:

Moreover at the same Assemblie Consideracion was had of the common Brute and Scandall which this Citie hath of late incurred and sustained by admittinge of Stage Plaiers to Acte their obscene and vnlawful Plaies or tragedies in the Comon Hall of this Citie thereby Convertinge the same, beinge appointed and ordained for the Iudiciall hearinge and determininge of Criminall offences, and for the solempne meetinge and Concourse of this howse, into a Stage for Plaiers and a Receptacle for idle persons. And consideringe likewise the many disorders which by reason of Plaies acted in the night time doe often times happen and fall out to the discredit of this Citie and to the greate disturbance of quiet and well disposed People, and

[95] Summarized in Tittler, *Architecture and Power*, 146.
[96] Johnston and Rogerson (eds.), *REED: York*, i. 449.
[97] David George (ed.), *REED: Lancashire* (Toronto, 1991), 39.

beinge further informed that mens servantes and apprentices neglectinge their Masters busines doe Resorte to Innehouses to behold such plaies there manie times wastefullie spende thar Masters goodes, ffor avoidinge of all which inconveniences It is ordered that from henseforth noe Stage Plaiers vpon anie pretence or color Whatsoever shalbe admitted to set vp anye Stage in the said Common Hall or to acte anie tragedie or Commedie or anie other Plaie within this Citie or the Liberties therof in the night time or after vi of the clocke in the eveninge.[98]

These notions may well be attributed to a growing Puritan senti-ment amongst those who ruled in the towns and cities of the realm at this time. They may also be a part of that wider reformation of man-ners which appears in much of Western Europe at the same time and which operated as well in other religious traditions.[99] But they do clearly suggest that the members of that City Assembly on that par-ticular day were speaking for the 'quiet and well disposed People' of the community, those whom we now refer to as 'the better sort'.[100]

We find very similar sentiments in Norwich in the following decade. Having been much troubled by the excesses of professional entertainers of various sorts in 1623, the Mayor sought and received authority from the Privy Council to ban 'seuerall Companyes of Play-ers Tumblers dansers vpon the Roapes and the like' for drawing workers 'away from ther buisnes & labour by their occasions the sayd manufactors are in the mean tyme in such sort neglected as Causeth dayly very great & aparent Losses & damage to that Cyty'.[101] Taken together, these and other cases provide additional evidence that a more refined, literate, bourgeois, somewhat authoritarian, and recognizably 'polite' culture had begun to take hold by the turn of the seventeenth century. It tells us, too, that proponents of this view had come as often as not by that time to hold sway over the rest.

Applied to the activity of dramatic performance, this meant that authorities who had long been willing to encourage players to per-form under certain controlled circumstances, now considered even that degree of licence too risky or offensive. By that time players

[98] Chester City Assembly Books, MS AB/1, fos. 331ᵛ–332, as cited in Clopper (ed.), *REED: Chester*, 292–3.

[99] Burke, *Popular Culture in Early Modern Europe*, 207–33.

[100] Jonathan Barry and Christopher Brooks (eds.), *The Middling Sort of People: Culture, Society and Politics in England, 1550–1800* (1995), esp. the introduction; and Keith Wrightson, 'Sorts of People in Tudor and Stuart England', in Jonathan Barry and Christopher Brooks (eds.), *The Middling Sort of People: Culture, Society and Pol-itics in England, 1550–1800* (1995), 28–51.

[101] Letter from the Lords of the Privy Council to the Mayor and Justices of the City of Norwich, 27 May 1623, reprinted in Galloway (ed.), *REED: Norwich*, 177–8.

came, as in Chester, frequently to be banned altogether from performing within town limits. In Norwich this prohibition came earlier than in Chester, the City Assembly having forbidden freemen from attending plays as early as 1598. Its members argued that plays profaned the sabbath and encouraged vice, and also that they encouraged brawling and other forms of unrest. While it is likely that this particular ordinance may not have been enforced with the intended stringency, for there are certainly recorded performances in Norwich thereafter, it nevertheless remained on the books. And from time to time it clearly was enforced according to the views of a particular mayoral administration. In 1624, for example, the mayor of the day wrote to the Privy Council to encourage its members to take further measures against play performances at the national level. He emphasized especially that 'the maintenance of the Inhabitants here doth consist of worke & makinge of manufactures', and that these essential activities had been threatened by workers and apprentices who spent their time at plays.[102]

At roughly the same time plays were similarly forbidden in Great Yarmouth, a town which, in 1538, built what may well be the very first public playing space in England, almost forty years before Burbage's Theatre in London.[103] The cycle of Corpus Christi plays received their last performances in Newcastle in 1568,[104] York in 1569,[105] and Coventry in 1579,[106] though in each case a few individual religious plays came forth in subsequent years. Whitsun plays ended in Chester in 1575[107] and in Hadleigh in 1597.[108]

---

[102] Ibid., p. xxxiii.

[103] David Galloway, 'The "Game Place" and "House" at Great Yarmouth, 1493–1595', *Theatre Notebook*, 31 (1977), 6–9.

[104] Though in 1581 the Mercer's Company enjoined its members to participate whenever Corpus Christi plays were performed, 1568 marks the last recorded performance (Anderson (ed.), *REED: Newcastle-upon-Tyne*, pp. xi–xiv).

[105] The last recorded performance came in this year. In 1578 the commons of the City requested of the Mayor and City Assembly permission to put on a Corpus Christi performance, but he responded, in a phrase well worn by Queen Elizabeth to Parliament and (in general) by parents to children, merely that he 'would consider it'. No performance in that year or thereafter is recorded. Johnston and Rogerson (ed.), *REED: York*, 354–8 and 392–3.

[106] A few individual religious plays were put on for a few more years (Ingram (ed.), *REED: Coventry*, p. xix).

[107] This performance followed the strenuous efforts of the Archbishop of York to suppress the play just three years earlier (Clopper (ed.), *REED: Chester*, pp. liv–lv).

[108] Lancashire, *Dramatic Texts and Records*, 165, 108–9, and 148; additional information provided by Alexandra F. Johnston, Director of Records of Early English Drama, from REED research in progress.

And whereas for many years and in many towns the chamberlains laid out funds to support public performances, by the early seventeenth century they began commonly to pay players not to perform.[109] This seems to have become common policy in Plymouth by 1600.[110] Bristol offered players sums in 1631 'to send them out of the city' and in 1634 'to ridd them out of the towne'; Canterbury paid players in 1625 'to dep[ar]t the Cittie and not to play'; and Exeter laid out a sum in the same year 'for putting off a Companie of plaires'. Worcester paid a company in 1634 'to prevent their playing in the City', and Southampton did the same the year after.[111]

vi

With this shift in support even for such a readily controllable activity as the performance of plays, much less popular entertainments of more varied and spontaneous types, the authorities in many towns thus went beyond accommodation and transformation to outright censorship. But whether or not transformed festivities actually worked to re-create civic harmony or legitimize the contemporary civic leadership, and whether or not outright prohibition brought peace and harmony, are quite different questions. In the view of A. D. Mills and others the policies at least of accommodation and transformation seem assured. Yet even when we consider the difficulties provided by the survival of appropriate records to test the results, it is striking how many towns show both cultural preemption for civic purposes or outright banishment on the one hand, and continued (perhaps even augmented) civic disharmony on the other.

Ludlow's officers may have converted some forms of traditional festivities to occasions in which local schoolboys declaimed laudatory verses to its civic officials.[112] Yet the town was riven to its core by a fierce and prolonged dispute amongst the governing elite and between the freemanry and the oligarchy in the 1590s over allegations of illicit use of corporate funds, restricted entry to office,

---

[109] Wickham, *Early English Stages*, ii/2, 141–5; Bradbrook, *Rise of the Common Player*, 115; Galloway (ed.), *REED: Norwich*, p. xxxiv; Wasson (ed.), *REED: Devon*, 258; Wickham, *Early English Stages*, ii/1, 146–7; Historical Manuscripts Commission, *Tenth Report* (1894), 'Report on the MSS of Plymouth Corporation', Appendix, pt. 4, p. 540.

[110] Wasson (ed.), *REED: Devon*, 258; Historical Manuscripts Commission, *Tenth Report* (1894), Appendix 4, 'Reports of the Plymouth Corporation', 540.

[111] Summarized in Wickham, *Early English Stages*, ii/2, 145–7.

[112] See above, p. 320 n. 70.

and favouritism in awarding town lands to associates of those in power.[113] Dorchester's Puritan-led oligarchy of the early seventeenth century may well have lined up behind John White's sermons in the cause of moral reform, but its record of bitter factionalism of the early seventeenth century, featuring the acquisition of a new and much more restrictive charter in 1623, make it a textbook case of cultural warfare.[114] And Canterbury may have turned its Midsummer Watch into a celebration of civic harmony in the Elizabethan era[115] and paid players not to play in later years, but a bitter dispute broke out in 1608 in which two former mayors sued a number of freemen in the courts of Westminster.[116] In fact, of course, the effort to transform traditional festive activities, and especially the effort to ban them, often served as much to stir up local passions as to induce the desired harmony. Such efforts form chapters in the history of local conflicts far and wide.

An especially full and revealing case derives from Shrewsbury, and the hostilities which broke out both between freemen and the governing elite on the one hand and within that elite on the other. The case concerns the ritual known as the Shearman's Tree.[117] The Shearman's Tree was a tree which members of the Shearmen's Company took in from the countryside each June, erected in the forecourt of the Shearmen's Hall, and used as a focal point for boisterous celebrations marked by fireworks, dancing, and drinking. Ironically, it was not an old custom, springing up only after the accession of Elizabeth, as a substitute both for elements of Corpus Christi celebrations and for the traditional maypole which it so closely resembled.

Unfortunately for some in the community, the Shearman's Tree resembled a lightning rod as well as a maypole. The local preacher, John Tompkyns, railed against it with such effect that the town authorities (two bailiffs in Shrewsbury's mayorless structure at this time) banned the ritual in 1590. The bailiffs' resolve may have been further strengthened by their own membership in the Drapers' Company, which enjoyed a long and sharp rivalry with the Shearmen. Still, as was often the case in such contests, much of the

---

[113] Faraday, *Ludlow*, 25–36; P. Williams, 'Government and Politics in Ludlow', 284–8.

[114] PRO, SP 16/146/67 and 67 i; Underdown, *Fire from Heaven*, 151.

[115] Cressy, *Bonfires and Bells*, 27.

[116] *Denne* v. *Paramore, et al.*, PRO, STAC 8/115/14.

[117] The following is drawn from the description in Somerset (ed.), *REED: Shropshire*, 398–404, and accompanying documents.

populace supported the ritual against the authorities, and were by no means willing to let it go without a struggle.

In June of 1591 the bailiffs arrested six Shearmen who flouted the new prohibition, bringing in a tree in the usual manner and erecting it by night. Several score of the prisoners' supporters held a charivari in front of Tompkyns's house to protest the arrest. This went unpunished by the authorities—an early acknowledgement that they may have bitten off more than they could chew—but two of the prisoners submitted a confession and apology for their actions and were let off. The other four refused to give in. In fact they found sufficient support from within the town to hire two prominent lawyers and procure a writ of habeas corpus from Westminster. In the end, an Assize Justice acting as a mediator persuaded the bailiffs to back down and let the prisoners off. In exchange, they acknowledged what they had done, but refused to apologize and insisted that the ritual should be allowed to continue. To add insult to injury, the Borough's auditors snubbed the bailiffs by refusing claims for their legal expenses, and the Shearman's Tree continued to be celebrated until about 1618.

The episode suggests a number of points about these cultural battles in Shrewsbury and, by implication, elsewhere. First, it should be noted that the two sides to the dispute were not sharply divided along lines of social status. Both the Shearmen who protested and the Drapers who served as bailiffs were freemen, members of important guilds, and active at least to some extent in local affairs. Both the bailiffs who pressed the issue and the auditors who refused to commit borough funds to that effort were senior officials. But the Drapers were clearly the politically dominant group of the moment in the ruling oligarchy. They could well have felt threatened by the Shearmen, and certainly wished not to be shown up by Shearmen impudently flouting their ban on the ritual. Other evidence reveals their Puritan leanings. But even if they had not been sympathetic to Puritan ideas, the labours of Preacher Tompkyns offered a very attractive hook upon which to hang their judicial initiative. The Draper bailiffs thus acted out of mixed motives, of which the disposition of political factions within the borough appear as paramount.

The celebration itself, though newly reminted in the form of the Shearman's Tree, remained traditional in form and socially inclusive in content. It was exactly the sort of local festivity which had served to bind the traditional community in pre-Reformation days. It involved the festive participation of a goodly share of the local

population, probably of a wide social spectrum, in an annual and unchanging rite where everyone knew his or her part. And the pressure brought on the bailiffs by the external authority, in this case the Assize Justice Sir Francis Gawdy, seems to have come only after he ascertained that the erection of the tree had caused no disorder. Despite the bailiffs' claims, even the night watch had reported that no notice of the tree had been taken for several hours after its erection. In late Elizabethan Shrewsbury supporters of the traditional sense of community could still defend their values against the clumsy attempts of an emerging oligarchy to subvert them. Though this intriguing contest ensued over cultural expression, in a political sense it remains one of a piece with the contests we have seen in previous chapters over other assertions of oligarchic rule. Far from achieving harmony through conformity, the attempt to enforce a ban on a popular festivity, even one of fairly recent vintage and no obvious associations with traditional Catholic practice, utterly subverted that aim. Even worse, it deprived the townsmen of precisely the sort of festive event which had allowed them to bond with each other as members of the community in past times.

vii

In the effort to frame a conclusion it seems useful to return to the two perspectives on Reformation and civic culture with which we began. Charles Phythian-Adams's suggestion that the Reformation meant the obliteration of traditional ritual and ceremony in the urban context now seems hastily drawn in several respects. For one, his view too readily assumes an abrupt discontinuity of such forms. Thanks to the transforming instincts of the ruling sort, and however marked by sanitization and co-option they may have been, there does seem to be a substantial degree of continuity in ritual, dramatic activity, and similar forms for some time after the 1540s. His suggestion of an immediate breakdown in civic harmony, though only an afterthought at the end of an essay on the preceding period, now seems unduly blunt. Such breakdowns may be found to be sure, and they make for lively accounts. But they came later and may or may not have been as widespread as he anticipated. On the other hand, A. D. Mills's efforts to describe the manner in which, by encouraging a highly selective continuity of cultural forms, 'the authorities gave primacy to the promotion of a sense of community and civic dignity', also have their limitations. Though the statement seems incontrovertible in

itself, we should not assume that such efforts were always successful. In reality, the ruling elites of post-Reformation towns employed
several strategies towards those ends. Some of these strategies met
with more success than others; the success of some is more difficult
to assess than that of others. In towns like Chester even such a selective continuity sometimes failed to achieve the harmony and concord for which it was intended, while efforts at censorship and
prohibition of course had quite the opposite effect altogether. The
result of these strategies was not so much the re-creation of the community ethos of old, on the one hand, or of harmony through a
moralistic suppression, on the other, as the creation of an urban
political culture which was directed more to the interests of hierarchy and authority than ever before. In Chester and other
communities this set the stage for a battle not only between differing
cultural outlooks, but between different strategies of managing disorder. Some such strategies (including censorship) were short-term,
repressive, and rather blatant; they seem not to have succeeded
particularly well. Others (including the reconstruction of the local
collective memory in its sundry forms) were long-range, reconstruc-
tive, and more subtle. Though it is more difficult to observe their
results, they very likely proved more effective over the long haul,
and certainly elicited much less opposition in the event.

Conclusion

Amongst those who have set out to investigate the Reformation as matters primarily of church doctrine and popular belief, a healthy debate has emerged over the sharpness of discontinuity represented by the events of the 1530s and 1540s.[1] A similar, perhaps less explicit debate has emerged over the question of continuity in the politics and political culture of English provincial towns over the putative divide of the Reformation. While a few even of the most recent writers have surprisingly ignored the issue almost entirely,[2] some have argued for an essential continuity in the political function, if not the form, of such quasi-governing institutions as guilds and fraternities.[3] Continuities of such politically charged interpersonal relations as kinship, patronage, and clientage, especially of the sort discussed by Ian Archer for post-Reformation London, cannot be denied.[4] Examples of oligarchic governance were also well precedented, at least in some towns, well before the sixteenth century.[5] All these perspectives tend to minimize the significance of the Reformation, and particularly the events of the 1530s and 1540s, as a turning point in the history of English urban society. While not meaning to deny or overlook pre-Reformation precedents where they can be demonstrated, this book considers most such evidence as still somewhat exceptional for its time. It argues instead that the Reformation marks a distinct watershed, even a titular episode, in English urban history, and it views the urban scene as dynamic rather than static.

[1] Representative voices in this debate belong to Dickens, *English Reformation*, and numerous other works, on the one hand; and Haigh, *English Reformation Revised* and *English Reformations* (amongst other works); Scarisbrick, *Reformation and the English People*; and Duffy, *Stripping of the Altars*, on the other.

[2] See e.g. S. M. Jack, *Towns in Tudor and Stuart Britain* (1996).

[3] Esp. Rosser, 'Town and Guild of Lichfield', 39–47; and Faraday, *Ludlow*, 90–3.

[4] Archer, *Pursuit of Stability*, chaps. 1–3.

[5] Kowaleski, 'Commercial Dominance of a Medieval Provincial Oligarchy', 355–84; Carr, 'The Problem of Urban Patriciates', 118–35; Rigby, 'Urban "Oligarchy" in Late Medieval England', in Thompson (ed.), *Towns and Townspeople*, 62–86; Shaw, *Creation of a Community*, esp. chaps. 4–6.

In the words of Clark and Slack, these were indeed 'towns in transition'.[6]

To the student of urban politics and (perhaps especially) political culture in the Early Modern period, it is difficult to see how this could not be the case. So much of the political ethos of pre-Reformation towns depended on the doctrines, practices, material accoutrements, institutions, and even governing forms of the medieval church that—especially for towns of any size, substance, or complexity—its destruction could hardly but have been enormously consequential. In these towns especially the complex events comprising the Henrician and Edwardian phases of the Reformation had a profound impact on both the circumstances and the cultural context of local government. The wholesale redistribution of land and wealth in the wake of the Dissolutions first proved deleterious but eventually allowed many towns to achieve greater fiscal self-reliance and control of local resources. Amongst other effects, this fortified the position of those who governed, and afforded them greater latitude in carrying out their responsibilities. At the same time, the demise of the traditional, doctrinally informed urban political culture threatened the political stability of the local community. It necessitated the fashioning of an alternative political culture to fill that void: a culture which was secular and civic, and which effectively legitimized the prevailing distribution of governing authority.

Coupled with these phenomena, the intensified pressure of accelerating economic and social change, and the Crown's strategy of delegating authority to local officials, virtually necessitated a widespread expansion of the extant tendency towards oligarchic rule. The governments of a great many provincial towns thus became narrower, less participatory, more removed from the general run of townspeople, and more authoritative. Town officials became (and brought their communities) closer in several respects to neighbouring gentry, to the Crown, and to the nation itself. Partly in the hope of legitimizing such tendencies, those who came to rule encouraged their fellows to undertake a more informed appreciation of their own community, of its heritage, of its distinctiveness, and of the necessary authority of its governing elite.

In describing the general course of these developments it has been tempting to take up at greater length such key issues as the Tudor centralization of government and the economic and social tenor of

---

[6] Clark and Slack, *English Towns in Transition* (1976).

the times, as they came into play from about the 1530s and 1540s, and the role of Puritanism as it emerged by the end of the sixteenth century. Yet these are the more familiar elements in the broad picture at hand. Though they cannot be ignored, it seemed more important (in an already lengthy work) to focus on the urban scene itself, and to show how it served to bring some of these forces together. By the same token, it has been tempting to consider London as well, though cool reflection has reinforced the conviction that England's only true metropolis may well have turned out to be an apple in a study of oranges. As most historians of London have recognized by implicitly neglecting the provincial urban experience, the two milieux are sometimes best considered apart.

We have treated the centralizing policies of the Tudors as a catalyst in speeding up the tendency towards a more oligarchic rule. The demands of Crown and Parliament, statute and proclamation, necessitated a local governing authority which was both broader in scope and endowed with greater powers than before. In response, the 'better sort' of people in the middling and more complex provincial towns had no choice but to govern in a more vigorous and authoritative manner. It is tempting to think, in this age of extreme cynicism about government, that they did so primarily with their own interests in mind. Certainly this was often—perhaps increasingly often—alleged, and there does seem good evidence for an increase in corrupt practices. But one also detects in these mayors and magistrates a strong sense of necessity and civic responsibility.

We should not forget that the problems of maintaining order and stability in provincial towns were not solved by the mere delegation of greater authority, whether by royal charter, parliamentary statute, or local by-law. These devices may have defined the legal and political contours of local government, but they did not address the question of how governing authority could best be made to work. That question lies instead in the realm of political culture, and here the mayors and aldermen of the day found themselves challenged yet again.

In carrying out their augmented responsibilities, town officials of the post-Reformation years had to do without several advantages enjoyed by governing officials of other times and places. One was the possession of personal standing in the conventional, neo-feudal and agrarian, social structure of the day. Unlike those who wielded authority at the county or national level, mayors and aldermen of provincial towns held no hereditary status, family estates, personal

titles, or any of the other conventional claims to deference on their own account. In addition, and in contrast even to their predecessors in borough government, they had now lost many of the traditional supports to civic authority upon which earlier mayors and aldermen had been able to rely. Yet their responsibilities to serve both their neighbours and fellow townspeople, on the one hand, and the demands of Crown and Parliament, on the other, were greater by far than their predecessors had experienced. The same may be said for the pace and severity of economic and social change as it affected their own communities. In short, the ruling elites of provincial towns in this period faced more than ever before the problem of how to engender obedience and respect from those over whom they ruled.

Consciously or (as is less likely) unconsciously, they responded to that challenge by reconstructing a political ethos to suit their needs. In expanding the use of civic regalia, civic mythology, and civic buildings, in encouraging new traditions of civic portraiture and local historical writing, and in carefully adapting drama, ritual, and ceremony to appropriate uses (or banning it altogether), and in myriad other ways as well, they fashioned a civic political culture intended to encourage deference and to legitimize their authority.

Though many of these devices and strategies were purely secular in nature, they often came to include an alternative form of religious legitimation. Much like traditional Catholicism itself, this provided a doctrinal justification for civic authority, encouraged civic responsibility and charitable works, and held out appropriate strategies to obtain the desired ends. It is not the task of this book to discuss the significance of Puritanism to the urban milieu, nor would it have much to add beyond what a host of worthy scholars have already said on the same theme. Yet it may be well worth suggesting the possibility that, from about the 1570s, Puritanism may not always have prompted the demand for greater civic discipline as much as it was called into being to fill that need. It may, in other words, have been the egg (one of several!) and not the chicken.

Perhaps the final points to be raised concern the significance of these themes for the larger canvas of English Urban History. One wants at least some sense of whether these characteristic forms of politics and political culture succeeded in their purpose, of how long they endured, and of the extent to which they determined the nature of provincial urban society in years to come. These are of course broad and contentious issues, and issues for which definitive research—especially on urban politics and political culture during

the Civil War and Interregnum—lies well beyond the scope of this work. Yet if only to stimulate the further investigations of others, some tentative suggestions seem warranted.

For one, and notwithstanding short-term social and political upheavals on the London model in some towns during the Civil Wars, the pronounced tendencies towards oligarchic rule which came to dominate the urban political scene in this era seem to have been established here for a long time to come. In the years after the Restoration oligarchic rule more often than not grew tighter still, becoming more than ever the normative format of government in the vast majority of towns not still under effective seigneurial control. When, in preparation for the Municipal Corporation Act of 1835, a Parliamentary Commission set out to assess the governing structures and forms of the chartered boroughs of the realm, the majority could still be described as oligarchic in nature, and a surprising proportion still took as their operative instruments of government charters of incorporation obtained between 1540 and 1640.[7] This adds weight to the conclusion that these years proved decisive in establishing an oligarchic form of civic governance, firmly established in charter as well as in usage, as the norm rather than the exception, and that the governing format of most of the middling and more substantial English provincial towns between the Civil War and at least the Act of 1835 remained oligarchic in consequence.

Secondly, it has been argued, especially with regard to Puritanism, that the prevalent political culture of early Stuart urban communities had become severely divisive and fractious.[8] This is undoubtedly the case in many of those which have been investigated at length. But of course the question has almost always been asked with the thought of political divisions in the coming Civil War hovering in the middle distance, and rarely at all asked from the perspective of urban politics in its own regard. Here the evidence of this study remains somewhat less decisive.

There can be little doubt that the enhancement of oligarchic rule engendered bitter opposition in many communities. Some of the

---

[7] *Reports from the Commissioners Appointed to Inquire into Municipal Corporations of England and Wales, Report I* (1835), i. 102–32, and Appendix.

[8] Of the very substantial body of scholarship on provincial towns devoted to this point, see esp. Collinson, *The Religion of Protestants,* chap. 5; and id., *Birthpangs,* esp. chaps. 2, 4–5; David Underdown, *Revel, Riot and Rebellion: Politics and Culture in England, 1603–1660* (Oxford, 1987), and *Fire from Heaven*; Evans, *Seventeenth Century Norwich.*

evidence presented in these pages and elsewhere certainly points in that direction. Like Puritanism, which, as Patrick Collinson has shown with particular clarity, strove mightily for order and often paradoxically created just the opposite in so doing, some of the more blatant devices intended to engender order often resulted instead in its undoing. These included the examples of corruption and censorship which we have seen above. With or without the centrality of Puritanism to such conflicts, they were not uncommon and they undoubtedly fuelled the political divisions of some towns in the Civil War and Interregnum.

On the other hand, such conditions were far from universal. It may also be that in many post-Reformation towns the refashioning of the ambient political culture and especially by those more subtle devices included in the reconstruction of civic memory, succeeded, not only in sustaining oligarchic rule, but also in enhancing local loyalties, social stability, and a degree of political cohesion. By their very nature, the effect of these devices, which were long-term and subtle, and which did not provoke court cases and leave paper trails for our investigation, is obviously much more difficult to document. Yet we may perhaps attribute to their influence the strong local loyalties we also now know to have been exhibited in many towns during the Civil Wars, in which pride in locale and defence of the community took precedence over support for King or Parliament.[9] However we may rate their performance under conditions of exceptional duress, we may say with confidence that those cultural forms which emerged here—civic portraits and civic halls, the use of regalia, the writing of local histories and the rest—became established in these years as the essential vocabulary of the dominant civic political culture. To a degree, they remain so even in the present day.

Finally, against the implication brought by some scholars that the origins of provincial urban culture in the post-Restoration era derived principally from the cultural models of the London metropolis and the fashionable tastes of the landed classes,[10] the last four

---

[9] John Morrill, *The Revolt of the Provinces: Conservatives and Radicals in the English Civil War, 1630–1650* (1976, 1980), *passim*, and esp. 38–9, 45–6, 95–7. See also Roger Howell, Jr., *Newcastle upon Tyne and the Puritan Revolution* (Oxford, 1967); and Howell, 'Neutralism, Conservatism and Political Alignment in the English Revolution: The Case of the Towns, 1642–1649', in Morrill (ed.), *Reactions to the English Civil War, 1642–1649* (1982), 67–88.

[10] As described esp. by Jonathan Barry, 'Provincial Town Culture, 1640–1780: Urbane or Civic?', in Joan H. Pittock and Andrew Wear (eds.), *Interpretation and Cultural History* (1991), 206–9; and the following works which receive particular emphasis therein: J. H. Plumb, *The Growth of Political Stability in England,*

chapters of this study suggest an alternative approach. Without meaning to overlook the enormous influence of those external models and tastes, and their absorption by at least some of the more fashionable towns of that later day, we can no longer deny that the 'English Urban Renaissance' of the late seventeenth and eighteenth century also had roots which were indigenously urban, grounded in political necessity, and older than the Civil War. In fact, they extended back to what we may now perhaps call 'the Age of the Reformation in English Urban History'.

1675–1725 (London, 1967); Neil McKendrick, John Brewer, and J. H. Plumb (eds.), *The Birth of a Consumer Society: The Commercialization of Eighteenth-Century England* (1982); and the many works of Peter Borsay but esp. *English Urban Renaissance.*

Tables

TABLE I. Incorporation of English and Welsh Boroughs, 1485–1640

Reincorporations, which are understood to have substantially revised content, have been noted as (R); mere confirmations, which were very common, have not been listed. A few incorporations listed by Weinbaum (e.g. Romsey) prove not to have been real incorporations and have been omitted; a few errors in his list (especially to adopt new-style dating) have been corrected. Lines have been drawn to separate reigns.

Year	Town	Year	Town
1485	Llandovery		Sheffield
	Pembroke		Sudbury
	Scarborough		Torrington
1488	Guildford		Warwick
1489	Dunwich	1555	Maldon
1490	Southwold		Worcester
1505	Totnes	1556	Abingdon
1506	Chester		Brecon
1508	Ruthin		Dunheved
			Great Dunmow
1524	Bishop's Lynn		Higham Ferrars
1528	Sutton Coldfield		Ilchester
1537	Exeter		Thaxted
1539	Hemel Hempstead	1557	Axbridge
1542	Reading		Barnstaple
1543	Beccles	1558	High Wycombe
	Colnbrook		
1544	Seaford	1559	Lyme Regis
1545	Boston	(R)	Maidstone
	Warwick	1560	Tamworth
1546	Bridgnorth	1561	(R) Gloucester
	Faversham	1562	Beaumaris
	Carmarthen		Gravesend
			Radnor
1547	Aldeborough	1563	Bodmin
1548	Lichfield	1565	Durham
1549	Maidstone	1566	Preston
	Monmouth	1568	(R) Gravesend
	Newark-upon-Trent		Henley-upon-Thames
	Saffron Walden		Poole
	Wisbech	1571	Weymouth
1550	Stafford	1573	Beverley
	(R) Exeter		Bideford
1551	Louth		Bishop's Castle
1553	St Albans	1574	Eye
	Stratford-upon-Avon		Wells
	Lichfield		West Looe
1554	Aylesbury	1575	Godalming
	Banbury		Hythe
	Buckingham		Kendal
	Chippenham		Tewkesbury
	Droitwich	1576	Daventry
	Hertford		Marlborough
	Leominster	1577	Richmond
	Maldon	1579	Orford

Year	Town	Year	Town
1581	Tenby		(R) Maidenhead
	Thetford		(R) Maidstone
1582	Maidenhead		Ripon
1583	Cardigan		Shaftesbury
1584	Congleton		(R) Winchester
1585	Helston	1605	Blandford Forum
1586	Arundel		Cambridge
	Shrewsbury		Chipping Campden
1587	Liskeard		Devizes
	East Looe		(R) Evesham
1588	Winchester		(R) Gloucester
1589	Hastings		(R) Hertford
	(R) Hertford		Oxford
	Leicester	1606	(R) Aldeborough
	(R) Newcastle-upon-Tyne		Bury St Edmunds
	Truro	1607	Chipping Norton
	(R) Wells		Retford
1590	Bath		(R) York
	Newcastle-under-Lyme	1608	(R) Cambridge
	S. Molton		(R) Cardiff
1591	(R) Lyme Regis		Great Yarmouth
1593	Hartlepool		London
1594	Marazion		Lostwithiel
	Bodmin		(R) Louth
1595	Macclesfield		Newport (I. of W.)
1596	(R) Barnstaple		Whitchurch
	Newbury	1609	(R) Bideford
	(R) Ludlow		Yarmouth (I. of W.)
	(R) Totnes	1610	(R) Abingdon
1597	Hereford		Dorchester
1598	Chesterfield		Haverfordwest
	(R) High Wycombe		(R) Tewkesbury
	(R) Hull	1611	(R) Barnstaple
1599	Andover		(R) Wisbech
	(R) Leicester	1612	Derby
	(R) Northampton		Salisbury
1600	(R) Newcastle-upon-Tyne		Wokingham
	Portsmouth	1614	Penzance
	Tenterden		(R) Stafford
1602	(R) Durham	1615	Tiverton
	Plympton		Welshpool
1603	(R) Windsor	1616	Langport
			(R) Weymouth
1604	Berwick-upon-Tweed	1617	(R) Bishops Castle
	Bradninch		Oswestry
	(R) Carmarthen	1618	Berkhamsted
	Dartmouth		(R) Chichester
	(R) Doncaster		Hadleigh
	Evesham		(R) Kidwelly
	Godmanchester		Northampton
	Harwich	1619	Bridport
	Lancaster		(R) Hereford

Year	Town	Year	Town
	(R) Maidstone		Walsall
1621	(R) Coventry	1628	(R) Kingston-upon-Thames
	Penryn		(R) Lincoln
	Tregony	1629	(R) Dorchester
	(R) Worcester		(R) Rochester
1622	(R) Basingstoke	1630	(R) Huntingdon
	Southwell	1631	(R) Much Wenlock
1623	(R) Axbridge		(R) Tenby
	(R) E. Looe	1632	(R) Cambridge
	(R) Lichfield		(R) Gravesend
	Newport (Monmouthshire)	1634	Sunderland
	Okehampton	1635	(R) Colchester
1624	(R) Droitwich		(R) Colnbrook
			Malmesbury
1625	(R) Congleton	1636	(R) Kendal
1626	Leeds		Kidderminster
	Liverpool	1637	(R) Aldeborough
	(R) Newark-upon-Trent		Carlisle
	Queenborough		(R) Newport (I. of W.)
1627	(R) Exeter	1638	(R) Derby
	(R) Ludlow		(R) Devizes
	(R) Portsmouth		(R) Shrewsbury
	Taunton	1639	St Ives (Corn.)

Source: Martin Weinbaum, *British Borough Charters, 1307–1660* (Cambridge, 1943).

TABLE II. Incorporation and Landholding, 1540–1560

Borough	Date	Provisions for Holding Lands
Abingdon	1556	licence to acquire lands to 100 mks. p.a.; power to acquire lands to £40 p.a., w/out licence; grant lands of Hospital of St John
Axbridge	1557	licence to acquire lands to £40 p.a.
Aylesbury	1554	licence to acquire lands to £20 p.a.
Banbury	1554	licence to acquire lands to £20 p.a.
Beaumaris	1560	licence to acquire lands to £40 p.a.; grant lands in Llanvaes and chantry lands worth total £42. 12s. 9d. p.a.
Beccles	1543	Beccles Common and Fen
Boston	1545	grant lands of Augustinian, Gray, and White Friars; licence to acquire and hold in mortmain to £100 p.a.
Brecon	1556	licence to acquire lands to £20 p.a.
Buckingham	1554	licence to acquire lands to 20 mks. p.a.; Twelve Burgesses may hold lands to 13s. 4d. p.a., or goods to £20 p.a.
Chippenham	1554	licence to acquire lands to £20 p.a.
Exeter	1550	grant of lands worth £29. 18s. 10d.; licence to acquire lands in mortmain to £100 p.a.
Higham Ferrars	1556	licence to acquire lands to £10 p.a.
High Wycombe	1558	licence to acquire lands to £20 p.a.
Ilchester	1556	licence to acquire lands, no given limit
Launceston	1556	licence to acquire lands to £10 p.a.
Leominster	1554	grant of chantry lands worth £36. 17s. 3d. p.a.; licence to hold other lands to £10 p.a.
Lichfield	1548 and 1553	licence to hold or acquire lands to £20 p.a.
Louth	1551	licence to hold in mortmain to £40 p.a.; grant of diverse lands to be held in fee socage
Maidstone	1549	grant lands of Corpus Christi Gild and some of College of All Saints, worth £10. 7s. 4d. p.a.; licence to acquire lands to £10 p.a.
Maidstone	1559	additional licence to hold lands to £20 p.a.
Maldon	1554 and 1555	licence to acquire lands to £40 p.a.
Newark-upon-Trent	1549	licence to acquire to £40 p.a.
Reading	1542	grant of minor ecclesiastical lands
Reading	1560	licence to acquire lands to £100 p.a.; grant various ecclesiastical lands worth £41. 9s. 7d. p.a.
Saffron Walden	1549	licence to acquire lands to £40 p.a.; grants two mills, rent from a manor
St Albans	1553	licence to acquire lands to £40 p.a.; grants of some small lands
Seaford	1544	licence to purchase lands and tenements
Sheffield	1554	licence to acquire lands to £20 p.a.; grant of some lands in fee, worth £17. 9s. 4d. p.a.

Borough	Date	Provisions for Holding Lands
Stafford	1550	grant of chapel lands worth £20 p.a.; licence to acquire lands in mortmain to £20 p.a.
Stratford-upon-Avon	1550	grant former guild lands worth £46. 3s. 2½d.; licence to acquire lands to 200 mks. p.a.
Sudbury	1554	grant of rents from the manor of Sudbury; licence to acquire lands to £5 p.a. value
Tamworth	1560	licence to acquire lands to £40 p.a.
Thaxted	1556	licence to acquire lands to £40 p.a.
Warwick	1545	grant lands worth £58. 14s. 14d. p.a.; licence to acquire lands to 20 mks.
Warwick	1554	licence to acquire lands to £20 p.a.
Wisbech	1549	licence to acquire lands to £100; grant of former guild lands worth £28. 3s. 2½d. p.a.
Worcester	1555	licence to acquire lands to £40 p.a.

Note: Maidstone, Reading, and Warwick, incorporated twice each in this period, have been listed for each separate incorporation which had implications for landholding. Lichfield and Maldon, also incorporated twice in this period, are listed but once because the second incorporation held no additional implications for landholding.

TABLE III. Towns Bringing Particulars for Grants of Dissolved Lands

Town	Date	Estimated value, p.a.			Purchase price/term	E. 318
*Boston	36 Henry VIII	unclear			£1,646. 15s. 4d.	5/143
*Bridgwater	1 Mary	£ 8 17s. 8 d.			not given	46/2128
Bristol	36 Henry VIII	72	12	10	£399. 0s. 14d./ 11 years	5/172
Bristol	36 Henry VIII	105	2	6½	not given	5/173
*Canterbury	34 Henry VIII	25	4	10	£212/20 years	7/236
Chichester	6 Edward VI	3	3	7	not given	26/1496
*Colchester	4 Edward VI	15	18	7	£284. 5s. 0d./	27/1533
*Coventry	38 Henry VIII	68	18	6	£1,378. 10s. 0d./ 20 years	8/321
Coventry	6 Edward VI	169	9	3	£1,931. 0s. 0d./ 20 years	27/1548
*Crediton	6 Edward VI	29	5	4	not given	28/1555
Derby	7 Edward VI	30	2	4	not given	28/1575
*Dorchester	2 Edward VI	8	7	2	£83. 11s. 8d./	28/1583
*Faversham	37 Henry VIII	8	0	0	not given	10/433
*Gloucester	33 Henry VIII	24	13	8½	£493. 14s. 2d./ 20 years	11/486
*Lincoln	38 Henry VIII	27	17	9	£135. 14s. 3½d.	15/713
Ludlow	5 Edward VI	91	11	5½	not given	31/1766
*Newcastle	2 Edward VI	3	6	8	£80. 0s. 0d./ 24 years	32/1814
*Newcastle	2 Edward VI	27	0	8½	£27. 0s. 8½d.	32/1815
*Norwich	1 Edward VI	142	19	2½	not given	32/1827
*Shrewsbury	4 Edward VI	20	8	0	not given	35/1941
*Stamford	3 Edward VI	14	11	8	£145. 16s. 8d./ 10 years	36/1969
*Warwick	36 Henry VIII	58	14	4	not given	22/1187
*Winchester	7 Edward VI	21	18	1½	not given	39/2086
*Wisbech	3 Edward VI	28	9	2½	£260. 10s. 10d./ ? years	39/2098
*York	3 Edward VI	16	13	8	£212. 4s. 8d./ ? years	39/2116

* Towns eventually recorded in *Letters and Papers* or *Calendar of Patent Rolls* as having concluded the purchase on these or similar terms.

TABLE IV. Dissolved Lands Acquired by the City of Gloucester by the Early Seventeenth Century

Lands	Date (if known)	Value	Reference (GBR/)
Llanthony Priory, parts of	1542	£49. 4s. 4d. in 1547	J5/4 L & P, xvii. 488
Godstow Nunnery	deed of 1546		D 3269 # 3 St.
Bartholomew's Hospital	1564	£44. 7s. 2½d. in 1547 £53. 0s. 18d. in 1560 £100. 8s. 4d. in 1589 £116. 12s. 1d. in 1596	K1/4, p. 3 J5/8 J5/9 J5/10
Site and Parcels manor Abbots Barton	1542	£17. 15s. 1d. in 1544	J5/5 and L & P, xvii. 488
*Charnel House, St Catherine's Church	1543–1609		J1/1943A and J1/1277
*Chantry of Virgin Mary	1553		J1/1946b
Mary Magdalene Hospital	1598	£3. 6s. 8d. in 1546	VCH Glouc., iv. 353
Augmentation of St Oswald's Priory and St Catherine's Church	n.d.		J1/1781
*St Mary's Chantry in St Nicholas's Church	1549		J1/1243
St Mary's Chantry in St Michael's Church	n.d.		J1/1245
*St John Baptist Chantry in same church	n.d.		J1/1245
*St Mary's Chantry in St John's Church	n.d.		J1/1245
Site of Greyfriars Monastery	1542–4		J1/64 and 65
House of Greyfriars Monastery	1566		J1/1253–5
Parcels of St Peter's Abbey	1542		L & P, xvii. 488
Gloucester Abbey, parcels of	1542?		VCH, Glouc., iv. 56; L & P, xvii. 488
Aconbury Abbey, parcels of	1542?		VCH, Glouc., iv. 56; L & P, xvii. 488

* These were among properties acquired from Richard Pates.

Note: In addition to these post-Dissolution acquisitions, the City acquired St Margaret's Hospital by 1500, which was worth £8. 12s. in 1546 and £23. 16s. 8d. in 1596; *VCH, Gloucestershire*, iv. 353; J5/10.

TABLE V. Dissolved Lands Granted for the (Re)Founding of Town Schools

Year	Town	Value of Lands (p.a.)	CPR Reference
1545	Warwick	*	*L & P*, xx. i. 419
1547	Norwich	*	Edward VI, i. 17
	Crediton	£62. 5s. 4d.	i. 43–5
	Grimsby	£4. 5s. 6d. + licence to acquire to 40 mks.	i. 176
1549	Maidstone	*	ii. 176
	Saffron Walden	*	ii. 211
1550	Bruton	£11. 5s.	iii. 191–2
	Sherborne	£20. 13s. 4d.	iii. 192–3
	Marlborough	£14. 17s. 8d. with licence to acquire	iii. 226
	Bury St Edmunds	£21. 8s.	iii. 436–7
	Stafford	£20	iv. 21–2
1551	Birmingham	£21	iv. 40–1
	East Retford	£15	iv. 47–8
	Sedburgh	£20. 13s. 10d.	iv. 97–8
	Chelmsford	£20. 17s. 10d.	iv. 116
1552	Louth	£40	iv. 119–20
	Guildford	£13. 6s. 8d.	iv. 251
	Nuneaton	£10. 15s. 8d.	iv. 293
	Stourbridge	£17. 10s. 8d.	iv. 303–4
	Ludlow	*	iv. 345–6
	Macclesfield	£21. 5s.	iv. 361–2
	Morpeth	£20. 10s. 8d.	iv. 384
	Shrewsbury	£20. 8s.	iv. 387
	Bath	£25	iv. 439–40
1553	Grantham	£14. 3s. 3d.	v. 35–6
	Giggleswick	£23. 3s.	v. 68–9
	Totnes	guildhall site	v. 227–8
	Stratford-upon-Avon	£46. 3s. 2½d.	v. 279–80
1554	Walsall	£10	Mary, i. 204–5
	Leominster	£36. 17s. 3½d.	i. 395–8
	Clitheroe	£20. 1s. 8d.	ii. 192–3
1555	Boston	*	ii. 153–5
1556	Bromsgrove	£7	iii. 260–1
1559	Crediton	income from two vicarages	Elizabeth, i. 417–18
1560	Hoddesdon	*	i. 297–8
1561	Kingston-upon-Thames	* + licence to acquire to £30	ii. 186–7
1562	High Wycombe	£30	ii. 254
1563	Darlington	£5. 4s. 10d.	ii. 509
1564	Penrith	£6 + licence to acquire to £30	iii. 71
	Kingston-upon-Thames (re-endowed)	£18. 9s. 7d.	iii. 80
1566	Richmond, Yorks.	rent of several fairs	iv. 64–6
1571	Bridgwater	various lands to endow schoolmaster	v. 307
1574/5	Cheltenham	£19. 18s. 1½d.	vi. 262
1576	Faversham	unvalued monastery lands	vii. 202–3

* A general grant is indicated in which funds for the school are not distinguished from the whole amount.

Note: This does not list the numerous schools which were licensed merely with the authority to acquire funds to a stated limit rather than endowed with specific funds themselves. These were especially numerous under Elizabeth. Neither does it list the 30 of the 53 schools endowed in towns with formerly dissolved resources by the Augmentations not listed in the patent rolls.

This file, marked 'Particulars for Grants for the Refounding of Schools', is catalogued in the PRO as E. 319/File 1. It lists some institutions aside from schools as well, and it lists a number of schools not in towns as such; both categories being excluded from the count here. It is organized county by county, but only 23 counties are listed, plus one document each for all of North and South Wales. Clearly it represents but a minority of those schools which were refounded in Edward's reign with funds or resources even from the Augmentations. The 32 towns listed here but not in the Patent Rolls are: Alnwick, Basingstoke, Bodmin, Bradford, Brecknock, Bromyard, Chipping Norton, Coventry, Crewkerne, Derby, Durham, Evesham, Houghton, King's Norton, Ledbury, Northallerton, Nottingham, Oundle, Pembridge, Penryn, Rothwell, Saltash, Shenston, Sherbourne, Stamford, Thornton, Towcester, Trowbridge, Warwick, Wimbourne Minster, Wisbech, and Worcester.

TABLE VI. Typical Mayoral Stipends, *c.*1540–1640

Abingdon	£20 in 1582 for expenses, on annual account
Beverley	£30 *temp*. Eliz., for expenses only
Exeter	£26. 13*s*. 4*d*. in 1551
	£133. 6*s*. 8*d*. in 1590
	£120 in 1596
Hedon	20 marks, 1554, for expenses, on account
King's Lynn	£20 in 1541 'towards his howsekepyng'
	£40–£60 from late 1540s to late 1560s
	£100 *c.*1600
Oxford	£21 in 1583
	£40 in 1591
	£50 by 1626
Plymouth	£20 in 1560–1
	£30 in 1609–10
Reading	£10 in 1542
Winchester	£20 from 1555 to 1615

BIBLIOGRAPHY

UNPUBLISHED MANUSCRIPT SOURCES

British Library

Additional MS 8937, Re: King's Lynn
Additional MS 23737, 'Catalogue of Charters of Great Yarmouth', 1612/13
Egerton MS 868, 'A Biographical List of the Mayors of Southampton'
Harleian MS 1944, Re: City of Chester
Harleian MS 2125, Annals of the City of Chester
Harleian MS 6115, 'List of the Mayors of York'
Lansdowne MS 7
Lansdowne MS 43
Lansdowne MS 207(a), 'Majores Villae et Burgi de Grimesby Magna'

Public Record Office

Chancery
    C. 1 Early Chancery Proceedings
    C. 3 Chancery Proceedings, series II
    C. 66 Patent Rolls
    C. 93/1/11 (42 Elizabeth) Inquisitions and decrees for charitable uses
Duchy of Lancaster
    DL 44/1032
Exchequer
    E. 112 Bills and Answers
    E. 122 Customs Accounts
    E. 123 Decrees and Orders
    E. 133 Barons' Depositions
    E. 134 Depositions by Commission
    E. 178 Special Commissions
    E. 190 Port Books
    E. 302 Particulars for Concealments
    E. 318 Particulars for Grants of Crown Lands
    E. 319 Particulars for Grants, Refounding of Schools
King's Bench
    KB 9 Ancient Indictments
    KB 27 Coram Rege Rolls
    KB 29 Controlment Rolls

Probate
  PROB 11
Star Chamber
  STAC 2 Proceedings, Henry VIII
  STAC 3 Proceedings, Edward VI
  STAC 5 Proceedings, Elizabeth I
  STAC 7 Proceedings, Elizabeth I, Addenda
  STAC 8 Proceedings, James I
State Papers
  SP 10 State Papers Domestic, Edward VI
  SP 12 State Papers Domestic, Elizabeth I
  SP 16 State Papers Domestic, Charles I

Bedfordshire Record Office

'Black Book of Bedford', Bedford Borough Records MS B I

Berkshire County Record Office

Preston MSS D/EP 7/36
Abingdon Corporation Chamberlains' Accounts, MS D/EP 7/83
Abingdon 'Corporation Minute Book', MS D/EP 7/84
The 'Black Book of Reading', MS R AC/1/1
Wallingford 'Corporation Minute Book', MS W/AC 1/1

Chester City Record Office

Chester Borough Assembly Book, 1539 ff., MS AB/1
Chester Borough Assembly Petitions, 1533 ff., MS A/P/1
David Rogers's 'Breviary of Chester', MS CHB/3
Chester Treasurer's Account Rolls, MS TAC/1/14–16

Cumbria Record Office, Carlisle

Carlisle Chamberlains' Audit Book, MS Ca/4/1

Devon County Record Office, Exeter Branch

Exeter City Records, Book no. 51, John Hooker's 'Commonplace Book'
'Exeter Corporation Act Book No. 3'
'Exeter Corporation Act Book No. 5'

Devon County Record Office, North Devon Branch

Dartmouth Borough Records
  MSS 61296
       61303
       61306

Dartmouth 'Constitution Book', SM 2003
Totnes Borough Accounts, MS 1579/A/7/3

Dorset County Record Office

Blandford Forum, uncatalogued Chamberlains' Accounts
Bridport Borough Court Book, 1571–1602, MS B3/C83
Bridport Borough 'Red Book called Domesday', MS B3/H1
Bridport Borough Archives, 'Accounts . . . for the buyldinge of the MarKett
    House', MS B3/M15
Lyme Regis Mayor's Accounts, MS B7/G2/3a

Gloucestershire Record Office

Gloucester Borough Court Book, 1561–1604, MS GBR G 12/1
Gloucester Borough Corporation Minute Book, 1565–1632, MS GBR 3/1
Gloucester Stewards' and Chamberlains' Accounts, MS GBR F4/3
Tewkesbury Borough Archives, 'Minute and Order Book no. 1, 1575–1624',
    MS TBR/A1/1

Harvard University Library

The Letterbook of Robert Gregory, pf MS Eng 757

Hereford and Worcester County Record Office, Hereford Branch

Leominster Borough Records, MS B 56/12
'Great Black Book of Hereford'

Humberside County Record Office

Beverley Borough Records
    MS BC I/53 Indenture of 1533
        BC II/4 'Small Order Book 1575–83'
        BC II/7/2 BC II/7/3 'Minute Book 1558–67'
Hedon Borough Ordinances, c.1555, MS DDHE/26

Kent Archives Office, Maidstone

Maidstone Borough Archives, MS FA FAc/9 Bundle 2

King's Lynn Borough Records, King's Lynn

King's Lynn 'Hall Book, 1497–1544', MS KL/C7/5

Much Wenlock Borough Archives

Much Wenlock, 'Borough Minute Book', MS B3/1/1

Northamptonshire County Record Office

Letter to the Earl of Leicester, Daventry, MS YZ 9118

Poole Borough Archives, Civic Centre, Poole

Poole, 'Old Record Book no. 1', 1490–1553, MS 23(1)
Poole, 'Old Record Book no. 3', MS 25(3)
Poole, 'The Great Boke', 1568–76, MS 26(4)
Poole, 'A Benevolence', 1568, MS 63(18)
Poole, MS 92(48), a 'census' of the inhabitants, 5 May 1574
Poole, 'Answere of Christopher Ffarwell', MS 108(63)
Poole, 'Sir P. Thompson's Copy of an Ancient Paper', MS TDW 5

St Albans (Herts.) Old Public Library

St Albans, 'Mayor's Court Book, 1589–1633', MS 312
St Albans, 'Mayor's Accounts, 1609–', MS 152

Shrewsbury School Library

Anon., 'Escutcheons of the Bailiffs and Mayors of Shrewsbury' (uncatalogued)
'Dr Taylor's History of Shrewsbury' (uncatalogued)

Staffordshire Record Office

Stafford Borough Manuscript Book, MS D(W) 1721/1/4

Surrey Record Office

Kingston-upon-Thames Chamberlains' Accounts, 1567–1637, MS KD5/1/1

West Suffolk Record Office, Bury St Edmunds

Letter from Bacon to Clement Higham *et al.*, 29 Nov. 1562; MS C4/1
Bury St Edmunds, Guildhall Feoffees Minute Book, MS H2/6.2
Bury St Edmunds, Summary of Accounts, Bury St Edmunds, MS H2/3/1

Wiltshire County Records

Marlborough Borough Chamberlains' Accounts, MS G22/1/205/2
Salisbury Borough Ledger Book, 1571–1640, MS G23/1/3
Salisbury Calendars and Mayors' Lists, MS G23/1/235

UNPUBLISHED THESES

Adey, Kenneth Raymond, 'Aspects of the History of the Town of Stafford, 1590–1710', MA thesis (Keele, 1971).
Battley, Susan, 'Elite and Community: The Mayors of Sixteenth Century King's Lynn', Ph.D. thesis (SUNY, Stony Brook, 1981).
Black, Christine J., 'The Administration and Parliamentary Representation of Nottinghamshire and Derbyshire, 1529–1558', Ph.D. thesis (London, 1966).
Botham, D. F., 'A History of Chesterfield Marketplace', thesis presented to the Royal Institute of British Architects (Apr. 1974).

Cunich, P. A., 'The Administration and Alienation of Ex-Monastic Lands by the Crown, 1536–1547', Ph.D. thesis (Cambridge, 1990).

French, Katherine, 'Local Identity and the Late Medieval Parish: The Communities of Bath and Wells', Ph.D. thesis (Minnesota, 1993).

Hodges, Vivienne J., 'The Electoral Influence of the Aristocracy, 1604–1641', Ph.D. thesis (Columbia, 1977).

Housez, Janis C., 'The Property Market in Bury St Edmunds, 1540–1600', MA Original Essay (Concordia, 1988).

Jones, S. R. R., 'Property, Tenure and Rents: Some Aspects of the Topography and Economy of Medieval York', Ph.D. thesis (York, 1987).

Kennedy, Joseph, 'The Dissolution of the Monasteries in Hampshire and the Isle of Wight', MA thesis (London, 1953).

Kitching, C. J., 'Studies in the Redistribution of Collegiate and Chantry Property in the Diocese and County of York at the Dissolution', Ph.D. thesis (Durham, 1970).

Knight, Mark, 'Religious Life in Coventry, 1485–1558', Ph.D. thesis (Warwick, 1986).

Lamburn, D. J., 'Politics and Religion in Sixteenth Century Beverley', Ph.D. thesis (York, 1991).

McClendon, Muriel, 'The Quiet Reformation: Norwich Magistrates and the Coming of Protestantism, 1520–1575', Ph.D. thesis (Stanford, 1990).

Manterfield, John Bernard, 'The Topographical Development of the Pre-Industrial Town of Grantham, Lincolnshire, 1535–1835', Ph.D. thesis (Exeter, 1981).

Patterson, Catherine, 'Urban Patronage in Early Modern England: Corporate Boroughs, the Landed Elite and the Crown, 1580–1640', Ph.D. thesis (Chicago, 1994).

Pockley, Dorothy, 'The Origins and Early History of the Melton Mowbray Town Estate', Ph.D. thesis (Leicester, 1964).

Roberts, J. C., 'The Parliamentary Representation of Devon and Dorset, 1559–1601', MA thesis (London, 1958).

Rosen, Adrienne, 'Economic and Social Aspects of the History of Winchester, 1520–1670', D.Phil. thesis (Oxford, 1975).

Thomas, David, 'The Administration of the Crown Lands in Lincolnshire under Elizabeth I', Ph.D. thesis (London, 1979).

Tillyard, Virginia, 'Civic Portraits Painted for or Donated to the Council Chamber of Norwich Guildhall before 1687 . . .', MA thesis (Courtauld Institute, London, 1978).

Woodward, G. H., 'The Dissolution of the Chantries in the County of Somerset', M.Litt. thesis (Bristol, 1980).

Wright, A. P., 'The Relations between the King's Government and the English Cities and Boroughs in the Fifteenth Century', D.Phil. thesis (Oxford, 1965).

Wyndham, Katherine, 'The Redistribution of Crown Land in Somerset . . . 1536–1572', Ph.D. thesis (London, 1976).

OTHER SECONDARY SOURCES

The place of publication is London, unless otherwise stated.

Acts of the Privy Council, ed. J. R. Dasent (1890–1907).

Adnitt, H. W. (ed.), 'Orders of the Corporation of Shrewsbury, 1511–1735', *Transactions of the Shropshire Archeological and Natural History Society*, 11/2 (Feb. 1888), 153–210.

Agnew, Jean-Christophe, *Worlds Apart: The Market and the Theatre in Anglo-American Thought* (Cambridge, 1986).

Alsford, Stephen, 'The Town Clerks of Medieval Colchester', *Essex Archeology and History*, 24 (1993), 125–35.

Anderson, J. J. (ed.), *Records of Early English Drama: Newcastle-upon-Tyne* (Toronto and Manchester, 1982).

Anglin, J. P., 'Frustrated Ideals: The Case of Elizabethan Grammar School Foundations', *History of Education*, 11/4 (1982), 267–79.

Anon., 'A Discourse of Corporations' (*c.*1587), reprinted in R. H. Tawney and Eileen Power (eds.), *Tudor Economic Documents*, iii (3 vols.; 1924).

Archer, Ian W., *The Pursuit of Stability: Social Relations in Elizabethan London* (Cambridge, 1991).

Archives and Records of the City of Chester: A Guide to Collections in the Chester City Record Office (Chester, 1985).

Ashford, L. J., *History of the Borough of High Wycombe* (1960).

Aston, Margaret, 'English Ruins and English History: The Dissolution and the Sense of the Past', *Journal of the Warburg and Courtauld Institutes*, 36 (1973), 231–55.

Atkinson, Tom, *Elizabethan Winchester* (1963).

Attreed, Lorraine, 'Arbitration and the Growth of Urban Liberties in Late Medieval England', *Journal of British Studies*, 31 (1992), 205–35.

Bacon, Nathaniel, *The Annalls of Ipswiche* (Ipswich, 1654 [1884]).

Bailey, John F. (ed.), *Transcription of the Minutes of the Corporation of Boston* (3 vols.; Boston, 1980–3).

Bailey, M., 'A Tale of Two Towns: Buntingford and Standon in the Later Middle Ages', *Journal of Medieval History*, 19 (1993), 351–71.

Baines, H. M., *Historic Hastings* (Hastings, 1955).

Barish, Jonah, *The Antitheatrical Prejudice* (Berkeley, 1981).

Barry, J., 'Provincial Town Culture, 1640–1780: Urbane or Civic?', in Joan H. Pittock and Andrew Wear (eds.), *Interpretation and Cultural History* (New York, 1991), 198–234.

—— and Brooks, Christopher (eds.), *The Middling Sort of People: Culture, Society and Politics in England, 1550–1800* (1995).

Bateson, Mary (ed.), *Borough Customs* (2 vols.; Selden Society, 1904 and 1906).

—— (ed.), *Records of the Borough of Leicester*, iii (Leicester, 1905).

Bedos-Rezak, Brigitte, 'Towns and Seals: Representation and Signification in Medieval France', *Bulletin of the John Rylands Library*, 72 (Autumn 1990), 35–48.

Beier, A. L., *Masterless Men: The Vagrancy Problem in England, 1560–1640* (1985).

—— and Finlay, Roger (eds.), *The Making of the Metropolis: London, 1500–1700* (1986).

Bell, Arthur, *Tudor Foundations: A Sketch of Richard Pate's Foundation in Cheltenham* (Chalfont St Giles, Bucks., 1974).

Bell, C., and Newby, H. (eds.), *Community Studies* (1984).

Bennett, Judith M., 'Medieval Women, Modern Women: Across the Great Divide', in David Aers (ed.), *Culture and History, 1350–1600: Essays on English Communities, Identities and Writing* (1992), 147–75.

Berger, Ronald M., *The Most Necessary Luxuries: The Mercer's Company of Coventry, 1550–1680* (University Park, Penn., 1993).

Berlin, Michael, 'Civic Ceremony in Early Modern London', *Urban History Yearbook* (1986), 15–27.

Bettey, J. H., *The Suppression of the Monasteries in the West Country* (Gloucester, 1989).

Bindoff, S. T. (ed.), *The House of Commons, 1509–1558* (3 vols.; 1982).

—— 'Parliamentary History, 1529–1688', in *VCH, Wiltshire*, 5 (1957), 111–69.

Black, C. F., *Italian Confraternities in the Sixteenth Century* (1989).

Bond, Shelagh, and Evans, Norman, 'The Process of Granting Charters to English Boroughs, 1547–1649', *English Historical Review*, 91 (1976), 102–20.

Bonney, Margaret, *Lordship and the Urban Community: Durham and its Overlords, 1250–1540* (Cambridge, 1990).

Borsay, Peter, *The English Urban Renaissance: Culture and Society in the Provincial Town, 1660–1770* (Oxford, 1989).

Bossy, John, 'The Mass as a Social Institution, 1200–1700', *Past and Present*, 100 (Aug. 1983), 29–61.

Boulton, J. P., *Neighbourhood and Society: A London Suburb in the Seventeenth Century* (Cambridge, 1987).

Bradbrook, Muriel, *The Rise of the Common Player: A Study of the Actor and Society in Shakespeare's England* (1962).

Brady, Robert, *An Historical Treatise of Cities and Burghs or Boroughs*, 2nd edn. (1704).

Braudel, Fernand, *Civilisation matérielle, économie et capitalisme* (3 vols.; Paris, 1979).

Braunfels, Wolfgang, *Urban Design in Western Architecture: Regime and Architecture, 900–1900* (Chicago, 1988).

Brent, Andrew (ed.), *The Doncaster Borough Courtier*, i (Doncaster, 1994).

Brewer's Dictionary of Phrase and Fable, rev. and enlarged edn. (1952).

Brewer, I. N., *A Topographical Historical Description of the County of Warwick* (1820).

Bridbury, A. R., *Economic Growth: England in the Later Middle Ages* (1962).

Bridbury, A. R., 'English Provincial Towns in the Later Middle Ages', *Economic History Review*, 2nd ser., 34/1 (Feb. 1981), 1–24.

—— 'Late Medieval Urban Prosperity, a Rejoinder', *Economic History Review*, 2nd ser., 37/4 (Nov. 1984), 555–6.

Brigden, Susan, *London and the Reformation* (Oxford, 1989).

—— 'Religion and Social Obligation in Early Sixteenth Century London', *Past and Present*, 103 (May 1984), 67–112.

Bristol, Michael D., *Carnival and Theatre: Plebeian Culture and the Structure of Authority in Renaissance England* (1985).

Britnell, R. H., *Growth and Decline in Colchester, 1300–1525* (Cambridge, 1986).

Broadbent, R. J., *Annals of the Liverpool Stage* (Liverpool, 1908).

Brooks, C. W., *Pettyfoggers and Vipers of the Commonwealth: The 'Lower Branch' of the Legal Profession in Early Modern England* (Cambridge, 1986).

Browne, A. L., 'Richard Pates, MP for Gloucester', *Transactions of the Bristol and Gloucestershire Archeological Society*, 56 (1935 for 1934), 201–25.

Burbage, F. Bliss, *Old Coventry and Lady Godiva* (Birmingham, n.d.).

Burgess, Clive, 'A Service for the Dead: The Form and Function of the Anniversary in Late Medieval Bristol', *Transactions of the Bristol and Gloucestershire Archeological Society*, 105 (1987), 183–211.

—— ' "A Fond Thing Vainly Invented": An Essay on Purgatory and Pious Motive in Late Medieval England', in S. J. Wright (ed.), *Parish, Church and People: Local Studies in Lay Religion, 1350–1750* (1988), 56–84.

—— ' "For the Increase of Divine Service": Chantries in the Parish in Late Medieval Bristol', *Journal of Ecclesiastical History*, 36 (1985), 46–65.

—— and Kumin, B., 'Penitential Bequests and Parish Regimes in Late Medieval England', *Journal of Ecclesiastical History*, 44 (1993), 610–30.

Burke, Peter, *Popular Culture in Early Modern Europe* (1978, 1994).

—— *The Renaissance Sense of the Past* (1969).

Burne, R. V. H., *The Monks of Chester* (1962).

Butcher, A. F., 'English Urban Society and the Urban Revolt of 1381', in R. H. Hilton and T. S. Ashton (eds.), *The English Rising of 1381* (Cambridge, 1984), 84–111.

Calendar of Patent Rolls, Edward VI.

Calendar of Patent Rolls, Elizabeth.

Calendar of Patent Rolls, Mary I.

Caley, John, and Hunter, Joseph (eds.), *Valor Ecclesiasticus* (6 vols.; 1810–34).

Campbell, Lorne, *Renaissance Portraits* (New Haven and London, 1990).

Carew, Richard, *Survey of Cornwall* (1602), ed. F. E. Halliday (1953).

Carpenter, Christine, 'Gentry and Community in Medieval England', *Journal of British Studies*, 33/4 (Oct. 1994), 340–80.

Carr, David R., 'The Problem of Urban Patriciates: Office Holders in Fifteenth Century Salisbury', *Wiltshire Archeological and Natural History Magazine*, 83 (1990), 118–35.

Cescinsky, H., 'An Oak Chair in St. Mary's Hall, Coventry', *Burlington Magazine*, 39/223 (1921), 170–7.

—— and Gribble, E. R., *Early English Furniture and Woodwork* (2 vols.; 1922).

Challoner, B. (ed.), *Selections from the Municipal Chronicles of the Borough of Abingdon* (1898).

Chambers, R. W., *The Elizabethan Stage* (4 vols.; Oxford, 1923).

Chapman, A. B. Wallis (ed.), *The Black Book of Southampton* (3 vols.; Southampton Record Society, 1912–15).

Chinnery, Victor, *Oak Furniture: The British Tradition* (1979).

Christianson, Paul, 'Reformers and the Church of England under Elizabeth I and the Early Stuarts', *Journal of Ecclesiastical History*, 31 (1980), 463–83.

Clark, Peter, *English Provincial Society from the Reformation to the Revolution: Religion, Politics and Society in Kent, 1500–1640* (Hassocks, Sussex, 1977).

—— (ed.), *The European Crisis of the 1590s: Essays in Comparative History* (1985).

—— ' "The Ramoth Gilead of the Good": Urban Change and Political Radicalism in Gloucester, 1540–1640', in Peter Clark, A. G. R. Smith, and N. Tyacke (eds.), *The English Commonwealth, 1547–1640* (Leicester, 1979), 167–88.

—— 'Reformation and Radicalism in Kentish Towns', in W. J. Mommsen, P. Alter, and R. Scribner (eds.), *Urban Classes, the Nobility and the Reformation*, Publications of the German Historical Institute, 5 (1979), 102–27.

—— (ed.), *The Transformation of English Provincial Towns, 1600–1800* (1984).

—— 'Visions of the Urban Community: Antiquarians and the English City before 1800', in Derek Fraser and Anthony Sutcliffe (eds.), *The Pursuit of Urban History* (1983), 105–24.

—— and Hosking, Jean, *Population Estimates of English Small Towns, 1550–1851*, rev. edn. (Leicester, 1993).

—— and Slack, Paul (eds.), *Crisis and Order in English Towns, 1500–1700* (1972).

Clark, Peter, *English Towns in Transition, 1500–1700* (1976).

Clopper, L. M. (ed.), *Records of Early English Drama: Chester* (Toronto, 1979).

Coldeway, John C., 'The Last Rise and Final Demise of Essex Town Drama', *Modern Language Quarterly*, 36 (1975), 239–60.

College, Edmund, and Walsh, James (eds.), *A Book of Showings to the Anchoress Julian of Norwich* (1978).

Collinson, Patrick, *The Birthpangs of Protestant England: Religious and Cultural Change in the Sixteenth and Seventeenth Centuries* (London and Basingstoke, 1988).

—— *The Elizabethan Puritan Movement* (1967).

—— *The Religion of Protestants* (Oxford, 1982).

Constant, G., *The Reformation in England* (New York, 1940).

Corfield, Penelope J., *The Impact of English Towns, 1700–1800* (Oxford, 1982).

Coward, Barry, *The Stanleys, Lords Stanley and Earls of Derby, 1385–1672*, Chetham Society, 3rd ser., 30 (Manchester, 1983).

Cozens-Hardy, Basil, and Kent, E. A. (eds.), *The Mayors of Norwich, 1403–1835* (Norwich, 1938).

Craig, J. S., 'The "Godly" and the "Froward": Protestant Polemics in the Town of Thetford, 1560–1590', *Norfolk Archeology*, 41 (1992), 279–93.

Cressy, David, *Bonfires and Bells: National Memory and the Protestant Calendar in the Elizabethan and Early Stuart Era* (1989).

Cross, Claire, 'Communal Piety in Sixteenth Century Boston', *Lincolnshire History and Archaeology*, 25 (1990), 33–8.

—— *Urban Magistrates and Ministers*, Borthwick Papers, 67 (1985).

[Damet, Thomas], *Greate Yermouthe: A Book of the Foundacion and Antiquitye of the Saide Towne . . .* (Great Yarmouth, 1847).

Dance, E. M. (ed.), *Guildford Borough Records, 1514–1546*, Surrey Record Society, 24 (1952).

—— (ed.), *Guildford Borough Records* (1958).

Davies, C. S. (ed.), *A History of Macclesfield* (Manchester, 1961).

Davies, C. S. L., *Peace, Print and Protestantism, 1450–1558* (1976).

—— 'Slavery and Protector Somerset: The Vagrancy Act of 1547', *Economic History Review*, 2nd ser., 19 (1966), 533–49.

Dennett, J. (ed.), *Beverley Borough Records, 1575–1821*, Yorkshire Archaeological Society Record Series, 84 (1933 for 1932).

De Vries, Jan, 'Patterns of Urbanization in Preindustrial Europe, 1500–1800', in H. Schmal (ed.), *Patterns of European Urbanization since 1500* (1981), 77–109.

Dickens, A. G., 'A Municipal Dissolution of Chantries at York, 1536', *Yorkshire Archaeological Society Journal*, 36 (1944–7), 164–73.

—— *The English Reformation*, 2nd edn. (1989).

Dilks, T. B. (ed.), *Bridgwater Borough Archives, 1377–1399*, Somerset Record Society, 53 (1938).

Dinn, Robert, 'Death and Rebirth in Late Medieval Bury St Edmunds', in Steven Bassett (ed.), *Death in Towns: Urban Responses to the Dying and the Dead, 100–1600* (Leicester, 1992), 151–69.

Dobson, R. B., 'Cathedral Chapters and Cathedral Cities: York, Durham and Carlisle in the Fifteenth Century', *Northern History*, 19 (1983), 15–44.

—— 'Citizens and Chantries in Late Medieval York', in D. Abulafia, M. Franklin, and M. Rubin (eds.), *Church and City, 1000–1500* (Cambridge, 1992), 311–32.

—— 'The Risings in York, Beverley and Scarborough, 1380–81', in R. H. Hilton and T. S. Ashton (eds.), *The English Rising of 1381* (Cambridge, 1984), 112–42.

—— 'Urban Decline in Late Medieval England', *Transactions of the Royal Historical Society*, 5th ser., 27 (1977), 1–22.

Douglas, Audrey, 'Midsummer in Salisbury: The Tailor's Guild and Confraternity, 1444–1642', *Renaissance and Reformation*, 25/1 (1989), 35–51.

—— and Greenfield, Peter (eds.), *Records of Early English Drama: Cumberland, Westmorland and Gloucestershire* (Toronto, 1986).

Duffy, Eamon, *The Stripping of the Altars: Traditional Religion in England, c.1400–1580* (New Haven and London, 1992).

Dyer, Alan, *The City of Worcester in the Sixteenth Century* (Leicester, 1973).

—— *Decline and Growth in English Towns, 1400–1640* (Cambridge, 1995).

—— 'English Town Chronicles', *Local Historian*, 12/6 (May 1977), 285–91.

Dyer, Christopher, 'The English Medieval Community and its Decline', *Journal of British Studies*, 32/3 (July 1993), 195–225.

Eames, Penelope, *Furniture in England, France and the Netherlands from the Twelfth to the Fifteenth Century* (1977).

Elton, G. R., *Reform and Renewal: Thomas Cromwell and the Common Weal* (Cambridge, 1973).

Erdeswicke, Sampson, *Survey of Staffordshire* (c.1593, London, 1723).

Eustace, G. W., *Arundel: Borough and Castle* (1922).

Evans, John T., *Seventeenth Century Norwich: Politics, Religion and Government, 1620–1690* (Oxford, 1979).

—— 'The Decline of Oligarchy in Seventeenth-Century Norwich', *Journal of British Studies*, 14/1 (Nov. 1974), 46–76.

Everitt, Alan, 'The Marketing of Agricultural Produce', in J. Thirsk (ed.), *The Agrarian History of England and Wales*, iv. *1500–1640* (Cambridge, 1967), 502–6.

Faraday, Michael, *Ludlow, 1085–1660: A Social, Economic and Political History* (Chichester, 1991).

Fastnedge, Ralph, *English Furniture Styles, 1500–1830* (1969).

Ferguson, Richard S. (ed.), *A Boke off Recorde . . . of Kirkbie Kendall*, Cumberland and Westmorland Antiquarian and Archeological Society, 7 (1892).

Fleming, P. W., 'Charity, Faith and the Gentry of Kent, 1422–1529', in T. Pollard (ed.), *Property and Politics: Essays in Late Medieval English History* (Gloucester, 1984), 36–58.

Flenley, Ralph (ed.), *Six Town Chronicles of England* (Oxford, 1911).

Flynn, Maureen, *Sacred Charity, Confraternities and Social Welfare in Spain, 1400–1700* (1989).

Fosbrooke, T. H., and Skillington, S. H., 'The Old Town Hall of Leicester', *Transactions of the Leicestershire Archeological Society*, 13 (1923–4), 1–72.

Fox, F. F., 'On the Gilds of Sodbury and Dyrham', *Transactions of the Bristol and Gloucestershire Archeological Society*, 13 (1888–9), 6–9.

Fox, Levi, *The Borough Town of Stratford-upon-Avon* (Stratford-upon-Avon, 1953).

French, K. L., Gibbs, G. G., and Kumin, B. A. (eds.), *The Parish in English Life, 1400–1600* (Manchester, 1997).

Friedrichs, Christopher R., *The Early Modern City, 1450–1750* (1995).

Frith, Brian, *Twelve Portraits of Gloucester Benefactors* (Gloucester, 1972).

Fussner, F. Smith, *The Historical Revolution: English Historical Writing and Thought, 1580–1640* (1962).

Galloway, David, 'The "Game Place" and "House" at Great Yarmouth, 1493–1595', *Theatre Notebook*, 31 (1977), 6–9.

—— (ed.), *Records of Early English Drama: Norwich, 1540–1642* (Toronto and London, 1984).

Gardiner, Harold C., *Mysteries' End* (New Haven, 1946).

Garrett-Goodyear, Harold, 'The Tudor Revival of *Quo Warranto* and Local Contributions to State Building', in M. S. Arnold, T. A. Green, S. A. Scully, and S. D. White (eds.), *On the Laws and Customs of England: Essays in Honor of Samuel E. Thorne* (Chapel Hill, NC, 1981), 231–95.

Geertz, Clifford, *The Interpretation of Cultures* (New York, 1973).

Gent, L., and Llewellyn, N. (eds.), *Renaissance Bodies: The Human Figure in English Culture, c.1540–1660* (1990).

Geoffrey of Monmouth, *The History of the Kings of Britain*, trans. and ed. Lewis Thorpe (1966).

George, David (ed.), *REED: Lancashire* (Toronto, 1991).

Gerard, Thomas, *The Particular Description of . . . Somerset* (c.1632), ed. E. H. Bates, Somerset Record Society, 15 (1900).

Gibbs, R., *A History of Aylesbury . . .* (Aylesbury, 1885).

Gildersleeve, V., *Government Regulation of Elizabethan Drama* (New York, 1908).

Gillet, E., and MacMahon, K., *A History of Hull* (Oxford, 1981).

Gloag, John, *The Englishman's Chair: Origins, Design and Social History of Seat Furniture in England* (1964).

Godwin, Francis, *Catalogue of the Bishops of England* (1601).

Goodman, Anthony, *The New Monarchy, 1471–1534* (1988).

Goring, J. J., 'Godly Exercizes and the Devil's Dance? Puritanism and

Popular Culture in Pre-Civil War England', *Friends of Dr Williams Library Lectures*, 37 (1983).

Gottfried, Robert S., *Bury St Edmunds and the Urban Crisis: 1270–1539* (Princeton, 1982).

Grace, Mary (ed.), *Records of the Gild of St George in Norwich, 1389–1547*, Norfolk Record Society, 9 (1937).

Grady, Kevin, 'The Records of the Charity Commissioners: A Source for Urban History', *Urban History Yearbook* (1982), 31–7.

Grant, Alexander, *Henry VII* (1985).

Graves, Michael, *The Tudor Parliaments: Crown, Lords and Commons, 1485–1603* (1985).

Green, J. R., *A Short History of the English People* (1893).

Green, Mrs J. R., *Town Life in the Fifteenth Century* (2 vols.; 1894).

Guilding, J. M. (ed.), *Reading Records* (4 vols.; Reading, 1892–6).

Guy, John (ed.), *The Reign of Elizabeth I: Court and Culture in the Last Decade* (Cambridge, 1995).

Habakkuk, H. J., 'The Market for Monastic Property, 1539–1603', *Economic History Review*, 2nd ser., 10 (1958), 362–80.

Haigh, Christopher (ed.), *The English Reformation Revised* (1987).

—— *The English Reformations: Religion, Politics and Society under the Tudors* (Oxford, 1993).

Halbwachs, Maurice, *On Collective Memory*, English translation (Chicago, 1992).

Hammer, Carl I., Jr, 'Anatomy of an Oligarchy: The Oxford Town Council in the Fifteenth and Sixteenth Centuries', *Journal of British Studies*, 18/1 (Fall 1978), 1–27.

Hanawalt, Barbara, and McRee, Ben R., 'The Guilds of *Homo Prudens* in Late Medieval England', *Continuity and Change*, 7/2 (1992), 163–79.

Harris, Mary Dormer (ed.), *The Register of the Guild of the Holy Trinity . . . Coventry*, Dugdale Society, 13 (1935).

Harris, Tim (ed.), *Popular Culture in England, c.1500–1850* (1995).

Harrison, Simon, Kennett, Anette M., Shepherd, Elizabeth J., and Willshaw, Eileen, *Tudor Chester: A Study of Chester in the Reigns of the Tudor Monarchs, 1485–1603* (Chester, 1986).

Hartland, Edwin S., *The Science of Fairy Tales* (1891).

Hartopp, Henry (ed.), *Roll of the Mayors of the Borough and Lord Mayors of the City of Leicester* (Leicester, [1935]).

Harvey, Barbara, *Westminster Abbey and its Estates in the Late Middle Ages* (Oxford, 1977).

Haskins, Charles, *Salisbury Corporation Pictures and Plate* (1888, 1910).

Hasler, P. W. (ed.), *The House of Commons, 1558–1603* (3 vols.; 1981).

Heath, Peter, 'Staffordshire Towns and the Reformation', *North Staffordshire Journal of Field Studies*, 19 (1979), 1–21.

Heinemann, Margot, *Puritanism and Theatre: Thomas Middleton and Opposition Drama under the Early Stuarts* (Cambridge, 1980).

Hill, Christopher, *The Economic Problems of the Church from Archbishop Whitgift to the Long Parliament* (1956).

—— 'The Protestant Nation', in *Collected Essays II: Religion and Politics in Seventeenth Century England* (Brighton, 1986).

Hill, Christopher, *Society and Puritanism in Pre-Revolutionary England* (1969).

Hill, Francis, *Medieval Lincoln* (Cambridge, 1965).

Hillen, Henry J., *The History of the Borough of King's Lynn* (2 vols.; Norwich, 1907; repr. 1979).

Hilton, R. H., 'The Small Town as Part of Peasant Society', in id., *The English Peasantry in the Later Middle Ages* (Oxford, 1975), 76–94.

Hirst, Derek, *The Representatives of the People? Voters and Voting Behaviour under the Early Stuarts* (Cambridge, 1975).

Historical Manuscripts Commission, *Sixth Report*, 'Report on the Manuscripts of the Borough of Morpeth' (1877), Appendix.

—— 'Report on the MSS. of Plymouth Corporation' (1894), Appendix, pt. iv.

—— *Thirteenth Report, Appendix*, iv (1892), 'Report on the Manuscripts of the Corporation of Hereford'.

—— *Fifteenth Report, Appendix*, x (1899), 'Report on the Manuscripts of the Corporation of Shrewsbury'.

—— 'Report on the Manuscripts of the Corporation of Beverley' (1900).

—— 55, *Various Collections*, i (1901).

Hoak, Dale (ed.), *Tudor Political Culture* (Cambridge, 1995).

Hobson, M. G., and Salter, H. E. (eds.), *Oxford Council Acts, 1626–1665*, Oxford Historical Society, 92 (1933).

Hodgett, G. A. J., 'The Dissolution of the Religious Houses in Lincolnshire', *Lincolnshire Architectural and Archeological Society Transactions*, 4 (1951), 83–99.

Hohenberg, Paul M., and Lees, Lynn Hollen, *The Making of Urban Europe, 1000–1950* (Cambridge, Mass., 1985).

Hooker, John Vowell, *alias*, *The Description of the Citie of Excester . . .*, ed. W. J. Harte, J. W. Schopp, and H. Tapley-Soper (3 vols.; Devon and Cornwall Record Society, 1919–47).

Horrox, Rosemary (ed.), *Selected Rentals and Accounts of Medieval Hull, 1293–1528*, Yorkshire Archeological Society Record Series, 141 (1983 for 1981).

Hoskins, W. G., 'English Provincial Towns in the Early Sixteenth Century', *Transactions of the Royal Historical Society*, 5th ser., 6 (1956), 1–19.

Howell, Roger, Jr., 'Neutralism, Conservatism and Political Alignment in the English Revolution: The Case of the Towns, 1642–1649', in John Morrill (ed.), *Reactions to the English Civil War, 1642–1649* (1982), 67–88.

—— *Newcastle upon Tyne and the Puritan Revolution* (Oxford, 1967).

Hoyle, Richard (ed.), *The Estates of the English Crown 1558–1640* (Cambridge, 1992).

Hudson, William, and Tingey, J. C. (eds.), *Records of the City of Norwich* (2 vols.; Norwich, 1906 and 1910).

Hughes, Ann, *Politics, Society and Civil War in Warwickshire, 1620–1660* (Cambridge, 1987).

—— 'Warwickshire on the Eve of the Civil War: A County Community?', *Midland History*, 7 (1982), 42–72.

Hughes, Paul, and Larkin, J. F. (eds.), *Tudor Royal Proclamations*, ii (New Haven and London, 1969).

Hughes, Fr. Philip, *The Reformation in England*, i (1950).

Hurstfield, Joel, 'County Government, 1530–1688', in *VCH, Wiltshire*, 5 (1957), 80–110.

Hutchins, John, *The History and Antiquities of the County of Dorset*, ed. W. Shipp and W. Hodson (4 vols.; 1861–70).

Hutton, Ronald, *The Rise and Fall of Merry England* (Oxford, 1994).

Ingram, R. (ed.), *Records of Early English Drama: Coventry* (Toronto, 1981).

Jack, S. M., *Towns in Tudor and Stuart Britain* (1996).

James, F. R., 'Copy of a Deed by Richard Phelips, Dated 1535', *Transactions of the Woolhope Field Naturalists' Club* (1934), 100–4.

James, Mervyn, 'The Concept of Order and the Northern Rising of 1569', *Past and Present*, 60 (Aug. 1973), 49–83.

—— 'Ritual, Drama and Social Body in the Late Medieval English Town', *Past and Present*, 98 (Feb. 1983), 3–29.

Jardine, Lisa, and Grafton, Anthony, ' "Studied for Action": How Gabriel Harvey Read His Livy', *Past and Present*, 129 (Nov. 1990), 30–78.

Jewitt, L., and St John Hope, W. H., *The Corporate Plate and Insignia of Office of the Cities and Towns of England and Wales* (2 vols.; 1895).

Johnson, D. J., *Southwark and the City* (Oxford, 1969).

Johnson, Douglas, 'Lichfield and St Amphibalus: The Story of a Legend', *Transactions of the South Staffordshire Archeological and Historical Society*, 28 (1988 for 1986–8), 1–13.

Johnston, Alexandra F., 'Folk Drama in Berkshire', in J. A. Raftis (ed.), *Pathways to Medieval Peasants* (Toronto, 1981).

—— 'The Guild of Corpus Christi and the Procession of Corpus Christi in York', *Mediaeval Studies*, 38 (1976), 372–84.

—— and Rogerson, Margaret (eds.), *Records of Early English Drama: York* (1979).

Jones, E. L., Porter, S., and Turner, M. (eds.), *A Gazetteer of English Urban Fire Disasters, 1500–1900*, Historical Geography Research Series, 13 (Aug. 1984).

Jones, W. R. D., *The Mid-Tudor Crisis* (1973).

Kelly-Gadol, Joan, 'Did Women Have a Renaissance?', in Renate

Bridenthal, Claudia Koontz, and Susan Stuard (eds.), *Becoming Visible: Women in European History*, 2nd edn. (Boston, 1987), 175–202.

Kent, D. V., and Kent, F. W., *Neighbors and Neighborhood in Renaissance Florence: The District of the Red Lion in the Fifteenth Century* (Locust Valley, NY, 1982).

Kent, Joan, *The English Village Constable, 1580–1642* (Oxford, 1986).

Kermode, Jennifer, 'Obvious Observations about the Formation of Oligarchies in Late Medieval English Towns', in J. A. F. Thompson (ed.), *Towns and Townspeople in the Fifteenth Century* (1988), 87–106.

Kettle, Ann J., 'City and Close: Lichfield in the Century before the Reformation', in C. Harper-Bill and C. Barron (eds.), *The Church in Pre-Reformation Society: Essays in Honour of F. R. H. DuBoulay* (Woodbridge, Suffolk, 1985), 158–69.

King, A. J., and Watts, B. H. (eds.), *The Municipal Records of Bath, 1189–1604* (n.d.).

Kishlansky, Mark, *Parliamentary Selection: Social and Political Choice in Early Modern England* (Cambridge, 1986).

Kitching, C. J., 'The Disposal of Monastic and Chantry Lands', in F. Heal and R. O'Day (eds.), *Church and Society in England: Henry VIII to James I* (1977), 119–36.

—— 'The Search for Concealed Lands in the Reign of Elizabeth I', *Transactions of the Royal Historical Society*, 5th ser., 24 (1974), 63–78.

Klausner, David (ed.), *Records of Early English Drama: Herefordshire and Worcestershire* (Toronto, 1990).

Knight, L. C., *Drama and Society in the Age of Jonson* (1937).

Knowles, Dom David, *The Religious Orders in England* (3 vols.; Cambridge, 1950–9).

Kolve, V. A., *The Play Called Corpus Christi* (Stanford, Calif., 1966).

Kowaleski, Maryanne, 'The Commercial Dominance of a Medieval Provincial Oligarchy: Exeter in the Late Fourteenth Century', *Medieval Studies*, 46 (1984), 355–84.

Kreider, Alan, *English Chantries: The Road to Dissolution* (Cambridge, Mass., 1979).

Kuerden, R., *A Brief Description of the Borough and Town of Preston*, ed. John Taylor (Preston, 1818).

Kumin, Beat, *The Shaping of a Community: The Rise and Reformation of the English Parish* (Aldershot, 1996).

Lake, Peter, *Moderate Puritans and the Elizabethan Church* (Cambridge, 1982).

Lambarde, William, *Perambulation of Kent*, 2nd edn. (1596), *STC*, no. 15176.

Lancashire, Ian, *Dramatic Texts and Records of Britain* (Cambridge, 1984).

Lancaster, J. C., *Godiva of Coventry* (1967).

Lander, J. R., *Conflict and Stability in Fifteenth Century England* (1977).

—— *Crown and Nobility, 1450–1509* (1976).

—— *Government and Community: England, 1450–1509* (1980).

Latham, R. C. (ed.), *Bristol Charters, 1509–1899*, Bristol Record Society, 12 (1947).

Leach, A. F., *Beverley Town Documents*, Selden Society, 14 (1900).

—— *English Schools at the Reformation* (1896).

—— *Schools of Medieval England* (1915).

Leader, J. S., *Records of the Burgery of Sheffield, Commonly Called the Town Estate* (1897).

Lehmberg, Stanford, *The Reformation of the Cathedrals: Cathedrals in English Society, 1485–1603* (Princeton, 1988).

Leighton, Revd W. A., 'Early Chronicles of Shrewsbury, 1372–1606', *Transactions of the Shropshire Archaeological and Natural History Society*, 3 (1880), 239–352.

LeStrange, Hamon (ed.), *Norfolk Official Lists* (Norwich, 1890).

Letters and Papers of Henry VIII.

Levy, F. J., 'Hayward, Daniel, and the Beginnings of Public History in England', *Huntington Library Quarterly*, 50 (1987), 1–34.

—— 'How Information Spread among the Gentry, 1550–1640', *Journal of British Studies*, 21/2 (Spring 1982), 11–34.

—— *Tudor Historical Thought* (San Marino, Calif., 1967).

Lewis, T. H., 'Carmarthenshire under the Tudors', *West Wales Historical Records*, 8 (1919–20), 1–19.

Liljegren, S. B., *The Fall of the Monasteries and the Social Changes in England Leading up to the Great Revolution*, Lunds Universitets Årsskrift, N.F., Avd i, Bd. 19/10 (1924).

Lindenbaum, Sheila, 'Ceremony and Oligarchy: The London Midsummer Watch', in B. A. Hanawalt and K. L. Reyerson (eds.), *City and Spectacle in Medieval Europe* (Minneapolis, 1994), 171–88.

Livock, D. M. (ed.), *City Chamberlains' Accounts in the Sixteenth and Seventeenth Centuries*, Bristol Record Society, 24 (1966).

Loach, Jennifer, and Tittler, Robert (eds.), *The Mid-Tudor Polity, c.1540–1560* (1980).

Loades, David, *The Mid-Tudor Crisis, 1545–1565* (1992).

Lobel, M. D. (ed.), *Historic Towns*, i (Baltimore, n.d.).

Longstaff, W. H. D. (ed.), *Heraldic Visitations of the Northern Counties in 1530 by Thomas Tonge*, Surtees Society, 41 (1863).

MacCaffrey, Wallace T., *Exeter, 1540–1640* (1st edn. 1958; Cambridge, Mass., 1975).

MacCulloch, Diarmaid, *Suffolk and the Tudors: Politics and Religion in an English County, 1500–1600* (Oxford, 1986).

Macfarlane, Alan, with Harrison, Sarah, and Jardine, Charles (eds.), *Reconstructing Historical Communities* (Cambridge, 1977).

McIntosh, Marjorie K., 'Local Change and Community Control in England, 1485–1500', *Huntington Library Quarterly*, 49 (1986), 219–42.

McIntosh, Marjorie K., 'Local Responses to the Poor in Late Medieval and Tudor England', *Continuity and Change*, 3/2 (1988), 209–45.

McKendrik, Neil, Brewer, John, and Plumb, J. H. (eds.), *The Birth of a Consumer Society: The Commercialization of Eighteenth Century England* (1982).

MacKenzie, M. H., 'Records of the Feoffees of the Common Lands of Rotherham', unpublished typescript (Rotherham Public Library, 1960), copy in National Register of Archives.

McRee, Ben, 'Charity and Gild Solidarity in Late Medieval England', *Journal of British Studies*, 32/3 (July 1993), 195–225.

—— 'Peacemaking and its Limits in Late Medieval Norwich', *English Historical Review*, 109 (1994), 831–66.

—— 'Religious Gilds and Civic Order: The Case of Norwich in the Late Middle Ages', *Speculum*, 67 (1992), 69–97.

—— 'Religious Gilds and the Regulation of Behaviour in Late Medieval Towns', in J. Rosenthal and C. Richmond (eds.), *People, Politics and Community in the Late Middle Ages* (Gloucester, 1987), 108–22.

—— 'Unity or Division? The Social Meaning of Guild Ceremony in Urban Communities', in Barbara A. Hanawalt and Kathryn L. Reyerson (eds.), *City and Spectacle in Medieval Europe* (Minneapolis and London, 1995), 189–207.

Maitland, F. W., 'Trust and Corporation', in H. A. L. Fisher (ed.), *The Collected Papers of F. W. Maitland* (3 vols.; Cambridge, 1911).

Manley, Lawrence, *Literature and Culture in Early Modern London* (Cambridge, 1995).

Manship, Henry, *The History of Great Yarmouth* (c.1612–1619), ed. Charles John Palmer (Great Yarmouth, 1854).

Martin, G. H., 'Doncaster Borough Charters', in anon. (ed.), *Doncaster, a Borough* (Doncaster, 1994), 11–25.

—— 'The Origin of Borough Records', *Journal of the Society of Archivists*, 2 (1960–4), 147–53.

—— 'The Publication of Borough Records', *Archives*, 8/36 (1966), 199–216.

Martin, J. M., 'A Warwickshire Town in Adversity: Stratford-upon-Avon in the Sixteenth and Seventeenth Centuries', *Midland History*, 7 (1982), 26–41.

Martz, Linda, *Poverty and Welfare in Habsburg Spain: The Example of Toledo* (1983).

Matthews, J. H., *A History of the Parishes of St. Ives, Lelant, Towednack and Zennor in the County of Cornwall* (1892).

May, G., *A Descriptive History of the Town of Evesham* (1845).

Mellows, W. T. (ed.), *Peterborough Local Administration: Parochial Government from the Reformation to the Revolution, 1541–1689*, Northamptonshire Record Society, 9 and 10 (1937–9).

Merson, A. L. (ed.), *The Third Book of Remembrance of Southampton, 1514–1602*, i (1952), ii (1955).

Miller, John, 'The Crown and the Borough Charters in the Reign of Charles II', *English Historical Review*, 100/394 (Jan. 1985), 53–84.

Mills, A. D., 'Chester Ceremonial: Re-Creation and Recreation in an English "Medieval" Town', *Urban History Yearbook*, 18 (1991), 1–19.

Moore, Andrew, and Crawley, Charlotte (eds.), *Family and Friends: A Regional Survey of British Portraiture* (1992).

Moran, Joann Hoeppner, *Education and Learning in the Diocese of York, 1300–1500*, Borthwick Papers, 55 (York, 1979).

—— *The Growth of English Schooling, 1340–1548: Learning, Literacy and Laicization in Pre-Reformation York Diocese* (Princeton, 1985).

Morrill, John, *The Revolt of the Provinces: Conservatives and Radicals in the English Civil War, 1630–1650* (1976, 1980).

Morris, A. R., 'The Effect upon Schooling in Sussex of the Legislation Dissolving the Religious Houses and Chantries', *Sussex Archeological Collections*, 119 (1981), 149–56.

Muir, Edward, *Civic Ritual in Renaissance Venice* (Princeton, 1981).

Nash, T. R., *Collections for the History of Worcestershire* (2 vols.; 1781–2).

Nashe, Thomas, *Lenten Stuff* (1599), in *Harleian Miscellany*, ii (1809), 288–334.

Neale, John E., *Elizabeth and her Parliaments* (2 vols.; 1958).

—— *The Elizabethan House of Commons* (1949).

—— 'November 17th', in *Essays in Elizabethan History* (1958), 9–20.

Nelson, Alan H., *The Medieval English Stage: Corpus Christi Pageants and Plays* (Chicago, 1974).

—— (ed.), *Records of Early English Drama: Cambridge* (2 vols.; Toronto, 1989).

Nora, Pierre, 'Between Memory and History: Les Lieux de mémoire', *Representations*, 26 (Spring 1989), 7–25.

Norberg, Kathryn, *Rich and Poor in Grenoble, 1600–1814* (Berkeley, 1985).

Oliver, George, *History and Antiquities of the Town and Minster of Beverley* (1829).

Orme, Nicholas, *Education in the West of England, 1066–1548* (Exeter, 1976).

—— *English Schools in the Middle Ages* (1973).

—— 'The "Laicization" of English School Education', *History of Education*, 16/2 (June 1987), 81–9.

—— and Webster, Margaret, *The English Hospital, 1070–1570* (London and New York, 1995).

Outhwaite, R. B., 'Who Bought Crown Lands? The Pattern of Purchases, 1589–1603', *Bulletin of the Institute of Historical Research*, 44 (1971), 18–33.

Palliser, D. M., *The Age of Elizabeth: England under the Later Tudors, 1547–1603*, 2nd edn. (1992).

Palliser, D. M., 'A Crisis in English Towns? The Case of York, 1460–1640', *Northern History*, 14 (1978), 108–25.

—— *The Reformation in York, 1534–1553*, Borthwick Papers, 40 (1971).

—— *Tudor York* (Oxford, 1979).

—— 'The Union of Parishes at York, 1547–1586', *Yorkshire Archeological Journal*, 46 (1975), 87–102.

—— 'Urban Decay Revisited', in J. A. F. Thompson (ed.), *Towns and Townspeople in the Fifteenth Century* (1988), 1–21.

Parry, H. Lloyd, *The History of the Exeter Guildhall and the Life Within* (Exeter, 1936).

Parsloe, C. G., 'The Growth of a Borough Constitution, Newark-upon-Trent, 1549–1688', *Transactions of the Royal Historical Society*, 4th ser., 22 (1940), 171–98.

Patten, John, *English Towns, 1500–1700* (1978).

Patterson, Annabel, *Reading Holinshed's 'Chronicles'* (Chicago, 1994).

Patterson, Catherine F., 'Leicester and Lord Huntingdon: Urban Patronage in Early Modern England', *Midland History*, 16 (1991), 45–62.

Pearl, Valerie, 'Change and Stability in Seventeenth Century London', *London Journal*, 5 (1979), 3–34.

—— 'Social Policy in Early Modern London', in H. Lloyd-Jones, V. Pearl, and B. Worden (eds.), *History and Imagination: Essays in Honour of H. R. Trevor-Roper* (1981), 115–31.

Peck, Linda, *Court Patronage and Corruption in Early Stuart England* (Boston, 1990).

Pegden, N. A., *Leicester Guildhall: A Short History and Guide* (Leicester, 1981).

Pevsner, N., *Buildings of England: North-east Norfolk and Norwich* (Harmondsworth, 1962).

Phythian-Adams, Charles, 'Ceremony and the Citizen: The Communal Year at Coventry, 1450–1550', in P. Clark and P. Slack (eds.), *Crisis and Order in English Towns, 1500–1700* (1972), 57–85.

—— *Desolation of a City: Coventry and the Urban Crisis of the Late Middle Ages* (Cambridge, 1979).

—— 'Urban Decay in Late Medieval England', in P. Abrams and E. A. Wrigley (eds.), *Towns in Societies: Essays in Economic History and Historical Sociology* (Cambridge, 1978).

Platt, Colin, *The English Medieval Town* (1976).

—— *Medieval Southampton* (1973).

Plumb, J. H., *The Growth of Political Stability in England, 1675–1725* (1967).

Pockley, Dorothy, 'The Origins and Early Records of the Melton Mowbray Town Estate', *Transactions of the Leicestershire Archaeological Society*, 45 (1969–70), 20–38.

Pollard, A. F., *Factors in Modern History* (1910).

Pollard, A. J., *Northeast England During the Wars of the Roses* (Oxford, 1990).

Pope-Hennessy, John, *The Portrait in the Renaissance* (London and New York, 1966).

Postan, M. M., *The Medieval Economy and Society* (1972).

Potts, W., *A History of Banbury* (Banbury, 1958).

Poulson, G., *Beverlac, or the Antiquities and History of the Town of Beverley* (1829).

Pound, J. F. (ed.), *The Norwich Census of the Poor, 1570*, Norfolk Record Society, 40 (1971).

Powell, Edward, *Kinship, Law and Society: Criminal Justice in the Reign of Henry V* (Oxford, 1989).

Prest, Wilfred, *The Rise of the Barristers: A Social History of the English Bar, 1590–1640* (Oxford, 1986).

Priestly, Ursula, and Corfield, Penelope, 'Rooms and Room Use in Norwich Housing, 1580–1730', *Post-Medieval Archaeology*, 16 (1982), 93–123.

Pullan, Brian, *Rich and Poor in Renaissance Venice: The Social Institutions of a Catholic State to 1620* (1971).

Purvis, J. S. (ed.), *Bridlington Charters, Court Rolls and Papers* (no place of publication, 1926).

Quick, Richard (ed.), *Catalogue of the Second Loan Collection of Pictures . . . held in the Bristol Art Gallery . . . 1905* (Bristol, 1905).

Raine, A. (ed.), *York Civic Records* (8 vols.; Yorkshire Archaeological Society Record Series), 6 (1948 for 1946), and 7 (1950 for 1949).

Ralph, E. (ed.), *The Great White Book of Bristol*, Bristol Record Society, 32 (1979).

Rappaport, Steve, *Worlds Within Worlds: Structures of Life in Sixteenth Century London* (Cambridge, 1989).

Rathbone, M. (ed.), *List of Wiltshire Borough Records . . .* (Trowbridge, 1951).

Records of the Corporation of Leicester (Leicester, 1956).

Reports from the Commissioners Appointed to Enquire into the Municipal Corporations of England and Wales, Report I, Appendix (1835).

Returns Comprising Reports of the Charity Commissioners, Thirty-Second Report (1837).

Reynolds, Susan, 'The Forged Charters of Barnstaple', *English Historical Review*, 84 (1969), 699–720.

—— 'The History of the Idea of Incorporation or Legal Personality: A Case of Fallacious Teleology' (unpublished typescript provided by the author).

—— *An Introduction to the History of English Medieval Towns* (Oxford, 1977).

—— *Kingdoms and Communities in Western Europe 900–1300* (Oxford, 1984).

Reynolds, Susan, 'Medieval Urban History and the History of Political Thought', *Urban History Yearbook* (1982), 14–23.

Ricart, Robert, *The Maire of Bristowe is Kalendar* (c.1484), ed. Lucy Toulmin Smith, Camden Society, NS, 5 (1872).

Richardson, Walter C., *History of the Court of Augmentations* (Baton Rouge, La., 1961).

Rigby, S. H., 'Boston and Grimsby in the Middle Ages: An Administrative Contrast', *Journal of Medieval History*, 10 (1984), 51–66.

—— *English Society in the Later Middle Ages: Class, Status and Gender* (1995).

—— 'Urban Decline in the Later Middle Ages?', *Urban History Yearbook* (1979), 46–59.

—— 'Urban "Oligarchy" in Late Medieval England', in J. A. F. Thompson (ed.), *Towns and Townspeople in the Fifteenth Century* (1988), 62–86.

Risdon, Tristram, *The Chorographicall Description . . . of Devon* (c.1635, London, 1910).

Rogers, David, 'The Breviary of Chester History', partly transcribed in L. Clopper (ed.), *Records of Early English Drama: Chester* (1979), 232–54.

Rosser, Gervase [A. G.], 'Communities of Parish and Guild in the Late Middle Ages', in S. J. Wright (ed.), *Parish, Church and People: Local Studies in Lay Religion, 1350–1750* (1988), 29–55.

—— 'Going to the Fraternity Feast: Commensality and Social Relations in Late Medieval England', *Journal of British Studies*, 33/4 (Oct. 1994), 430–6.

—— *Medieval Westminster 1200–1540* (Oxford, 1989).

—— 'The Town and Guild of Lichfield in the Late Middle Ages', *Transactions of the South Staffordshire Archaeological and Historical Society*, 27 (1987 for 1985–6), 39–47.

—— and Holt, Richard (eds.), *The English Medieval Town* (1990).

Rubin, Miri, *Charity and Community in Medieval Cambridge* (Cambridge, 1987).

—— *Corpus Christi: The Eucharist in Late Medieval Culture* (Cambridge, 1991).

—— 'Religious Culture in Town and Country: Reflections on a Great Divide', in D. Abulafia, Michael Franklin, and M. Rubin (eds.), *Church and City, 1000–1500: Essays in Honour of Christopher Brooke* (Cambridge, 1992), 3–22.

—— 'Small Groups: Identity and Solidarity in the Late Middle Ages', in Jennifer Kermode (ed.), *Enterprise and Individuals in Fifteenth Century England* (Stroud, Glos., and Wolfeboro Falls, NH, 1991), 132–50.

Rutledge, Paul, *Guide to the Great Yarmouth Borough Records* (Norwich, 1972).

—— '"Thomas Damet and the Historiography of Great Yarmouth"', *Norfolk Archeology*, 33 (1965), 119–33.

—— '"Thomas Damet and the Historiography of Great Yarmouth"', *Norfolk Archeology*, 34 (1969), 332–4.

Sacks, David Harris, 'Celebrating Authority in Bristol, 1475–1640', in Susan Zimmerman and Ronald F. E. Weissman (eds.), *Urban Life in the Renaissance* (Dover, Del., 1989), 187–223.

—— *The Widening Gate: Bristol and the Atlantic Economy, 1450–1700* (Berkeley and Los Angeles, 1991).

Salter, H. E. (ed.), *Oxford Council Acts, 1583–1626*, Oxford Historical Society, 87 (1928).

Savage, Richard (ed.), *Minutes and Accounts of the Corporation of Stratford-upon-Avon, 1553–1620*, Dugdale Society, Oxford, 3 (1924); 4 (1926).

Scarisbrick, J. J., *The Reformation and the English People* (1984).

Scarse, A. J., *Wells: The Anatomy of a Medieval and Early Modern Property Market*, Faculty of the Built Environment, University of the West of England, Working Paper no. 30 (1993).

Seaver, Paul S., *The Puritan Lectureships: The Politics of Religious Dissent, 1560–1662* (Stanford, Calif., 1970).

Sharpe, Cuthbert, *A History of Hartlepool* (Hartlepool, 1816).

Shaw, David Gary, *The Creation of a Community: The City of Wells in the Middle Ages* (Oxford, 1993).

Sheils, W. J., 'Religion in Provincial Towns: Innovation and Tradition', in F. Heal and R. O'Day (eds.), *Church and Society in England: Henry VIII to James I* (1977), 156–76.

Shortt, H. (ed.), *The City of Salisbury* (Salisbury, 1957).

Simon, Joan, *Education and Society in Tudor England* (Cambridge, 1967).

Slack, Paul, *The Impact of Plague in Tudor and Stuart England* (1985).

—— *Poverty and Policy in Tudor and Stuart England* (1988).

Slavin, A. J., 'The Tudor Revolution and the Devil's Art: Bishop Bonner's Printed Forms', in DeLloyd Guth and John W. McKenna (eds.), *Tudor Rule and Revolution: Essays for G. R. Elton from his American Friends* (Cambridge, 1982), 3–25.

Smith, A. Hassell, *County and Court: Government and Politics in Norfolk, 1558–1603* (1974).

Smith, H. P., *The History of the Borough and County of the Town of Poole* (2 vols.; Poole, 1949–51).

Smith, Lucy Toulmin (ed.), *The Itinerary of John Leland in or about the Years 1535–1543* (5 vols.; 1906–8; repr. 1964).

Smith, Richard, ' "Modernization" and the Corporate Medieval Village Community in England: Some Sceptical Reflections', in A. H. R. Baker and D. Gregory (eds.), *Explorations in Historical Geography* (Cambridge, 1984), 140–79.

Smuts, R. Malcolm, 'Public Ceremony and Royal Charisma: The English Royal Entry into London, 1485–1642', in A. L. Beier, David Cannadine,

and James Rosenheim (eds.), *The First Modern Society: Essays in History in Honour of Lawrence Stone* (Cambridge, 1989), 65–93.

Somerset, Alan (ed.), *Records of Early English Drama: Shropshire* (Toronto, 1995).

Somner, William, *Antiquities of Canterbury* (1640).

Southern, Richard, *The Staging of Plays Before Shakespeare* (1973).

Spufford, Margaret, 'Puritanism and Social Control?', in A. Fletcher and John Stevenson (eds.), *Order and Disorder in Early Modern England* (Cambridge, 1985), 41–57.

Stallybrass, Peter, and White, Allon, *The Poetics and Politics of Transgression* (1986).

Stanford, Maureen (ed.), *The Ordinances of Bristol, 1506–1598*, Bristol Record Society, 41 (1990).

Statham, Margaret, 'The Guildhall, Bury St Edmunds', *Proceedings of the Suffolk Institute of Archeology*, 31 (1970), 117–57.

—— *Jankyn Smith and the Guildhall Feoffees* (Bury St Edmunds, 1981).

Statutes of the Realm, ed. A. Luders, T. E. Tomlins, and J. Raithby (11 vols.; 1810–28).

Stevenson, W. H. (ed.), *Calendar of the Records of the Corporation of Gloucester* (Gloucester, 1893).

—— (ed.), *Records of the Borough of Nottingham* (3 vols.; Nottingham, 1885).

Stewart-Brown, R., 'Notes on the Chester Hand or Glove', *Journal of the Architectural, Archeological and Historic* [sic] *Society for Chester and North Wales*, NS 20 (1914), 122–47.

Stocks, H., and Stevenson, W. H. (eds.), *Records of the Borough of Leicester* (Cambridge, 1923).

Stokes, Ethel, and Redstone, Lilian (eds.), 'Calendar of the Muniments of the Borough of Sudbury', *Proceedings of the Suffolk Institute of Archeology*, 13 (1909).

Stokes, James, and Alexander, Robert (eds.), *Records of Early English Drama: Somerset and Bath* (2 vols.; Toronto, 1996).

Stone, Lawrence, *The Crisis of the Aristocracy, 1558–1641* (Oxford, 1965).

—— 'The Educational Revolution in England, 1560–1640', *Past and Present*, 28 (July 1964), 41–80.

—— 'State Control in Sixteenth Century England', *Economic History Review*, 17 (1947), 103–20.

Stow, John, *Survey of London* (1598 and 1603), ed. C. L. Kingsford (1908).

Strong, Sir Roy, *The English Icon: Elizabethan and Jacobean Portraiture* (London and New York, 1969).

—— *The English Renaissance Miniature* (London, 1983).

—— 'Popular Celebration of the Accession Day of Queen Elizabeth I', *Journal of the Warburg and Courtauld Institutes*, 21 (1958), 86–103.

—— *Tudor and Stuart Portraits* (2 vols.; 1969).

Swindon, H., *The History and Antiquities of the Ancient Borough of Great Yarmouth* (Norwich, 1772).

Tait, James, *The Medieval English Borough: Studies in its Origins and Constitutional History* (Manchester, 1936).

Tawney, R. H., 'The Rise of the Gentry, 1558–1640', *Economic History Review*, 11 (1941), 1–38.

Templeman, Geoffrey (ed.), *The Records of the Guild of the Holy Trinity ... Coventry*, Dugdale Society, 19 (1944).

Terpstra, Nicholas, 'Apprenticeship in Social Welfare: From Confraternal Charity to Municipal Poor Relief in Early Modern Italy', *Sixteenth Century Journal*, 25 (1994), 101–20.

Thomas, David, 'The Elizabethan Crown Lands: Their Purposes and Problems', in Richard Hoyle (ed.), *The Estates of the English Crown, 1558–1640* (Cambridge, 1992), 58–87.

Thomas, Keith, 'The Perception of the Past in Early Modern England', Creighton Lecture, London University (1983).

Thompson, A. Hamilton, *The English Clergy and their Organization in the Later Middle Ages* (Oxford, 1947).

Thompson, Pishy, *The History and Antiquities of Boston* (Boston, 1856).

Thrupp, Sylvia, 'Social Control in the Medieval Town', reprinted in R. Grew and N. Steneck (eds.), *Society and History: Essays by Sylvia Thrupp* (Ann Arbor, 1977).

Tittler, Robert, *Architecture and Power: The Town Hall and the English Urban Community, 1500–1640* (Oxford, 1991).

—— 'Civic Portraiture and Political Culture in English Provincial Towns, *c.*1560–1640', unpublished essay under editorial consideration.

—— 'Elizabethan Towns and the "Points of Contact": Parliament', *Parliamentary History*, 8/2 (1989), 275–88.

—— 'The Emergence of Urban Policy, 1536–1558', in J. Loach and R. Tittler (eds.), *The Mid-Tudor Polity, c.1540–1560* (1980), 74–93.

—— 'The End of the Middle Ages in the English Country Town', *Sixteenth Century Journal*, 18/4 (Winter 1987), 471–87.

—— 'The English Fishing Industry in the Sixteenth Century: The Case of Great Yarmouth', *Albion*, 9/1 (Spring 1977), 40–60.

—— ' "For the Re-edification of Townes": The Rebuilding Statutes of Henry VIII', *Albion*, 22/4 (Winter 1990), 591–605.

—— 'Incorporation and Politics in Sixteenth Century Thaxted', *Essex Archeology and History*, 8 (1976), 224–32.

—— 'The Incorporation of Boroughs, 1540–1558', *History*, 62/204 (Feb. 1977), 24–42.

—— 'Late Medieval Urban Prosperity', *Economic History Review*, 2nd ser., 37/4 (Nov. 1984), 551–4.

—— *Nicholas Bacon: The Making of a Tudor Statesman* (1976).

Tittler, Robert, 'Political Culture and the Built Environment in the English Country Town, c.1540–1620', in D. C. Hoak (ed.), *Tudor Political Culture* (Cambridge, 1995), 133–56.

——— ' "Seats of Honor, Seats of Power": The Symbolism of Public Seating in the English Urban Community, c.1560–1620', *Albion*, 24/2 (Summer 1992), 205–23.

——— 'The Vitality of an Elizabethan Port: The Economy of Poole, c.1550–1600', *Southern History*, 7 (1985), 95–118.

Tupling, G. H., 'Lancashire Markets in the Sixteenth and Seventeenth Centuries', *Transactions of the Lancashire and Cheshire Antiquarian Society*, 58 (1947 for 1945–6), 1–34.

Tweedy-Smith, R., *The History, Law, Practice and Procedure Relating to Mayors* (1935).

Twemlow, J. A. (ed.), *Liverpool Town Books . . . 1550–1802* (2 vols.; Liverpool, 1918 and 1935).

Underdown, David, *Fire from Heaven: Life in an English Town in the Seventeenth Century* (London and New Haven, 1992).

——— *Revel, Riot and Rebellion: Politics and Culture in England, 1603–1660* (Oxford, 1987).

VCH, Bedfordshire, 1 (1904); 3 (1912).

VCH, Berkshire, 3 (1923); 4 (1924).

VCH, Buckinghamshire, 3 (1925).

VCH, Chester, 3 (1980).

VCH, Gloucestershire, 4 (1988).

VCH, Hampshire, 3 (1908); 4 (1911).

VCH, Leicestershire, 3 (1955); 4 (1958).

VCH, Northamptonshire, 2 (1906).

VCH, Oxfordshire, 4 (1979); 6 (1959).

VCH, Staffordshire, 8 (1963); 14 (1990).

VCH, Surrey, 3 (1911).

VCH, Sussex, 3 (1935).

VCH, Warwickshire, 2 (1908); 8 (1969).

VCH, Wiltshire, 5 (1957); 6 (1962); 10 (1975).

VCH, City of York (Oxford, 1961).

VCH, Yorkshire, East Riding, 2 (1974); 6 (1989).

Wainwright, T. (ed.), *Extracts from Barnstaple Records*, ii (repr. 1900).

Ward, Jennifer C., 'The Reformation in Colchester, 1528–1558', *Essex Archaeology and History*, 15 (1983), 84–95.

Wardle, F. D. (ed.), *The Accounts of the Chamberlains of the City of Bath, 1568–1602*, Somerset Record Society, 38 (1923).

Wasson, John (ed.), *Records of Early English Drama: Devon* (1986).

Watkin, H. R., *The History of Totnes* (1914 and 1917).

Webb, John (ed.), *Poor Relief in Elizabethan Suffolk*, Suffolk Record Society, 9 (1966).

Webb, Sidney, and Webb, Beatrice, *English Local Government: The Manor and the Borough* (2 vols.; 1908).

Weinbaum, Martin, *British Borough Charters, 1307–1660* (Cambridge, 1943).

—— *The Incorporation of Boroughs* (Manchester, 1936).

Welch, Edwin (ed.), *Plymouth Building Accounts of the Sixteenth and Seventeenth Centuries*, Devon and Cornwall Record Society, NS, 12 (1967).

Wenham, L. P., 'The Chantries, Guilds, Obits and Lights of Richmond, Yorkshire', *Yorkshire Archeological Society Journal*, 38 (1955), pt. 1, pp. 96–111; pt. 2, pp. 185–214; pt. 3, pp. 310–32.

White, Paul W., *Theatre and Reformation: Protestantism, Patronage and Playing in Tudor England* (Cambridge, 1993).

Whiting, Robert, *The Blind Devotion of the People: Popular Religion and the English Reformation* (Cambridge, 1989).

Whitty, R. G. H., *The Court of Taunton in the Sixteenth and Seventeenth Centuries* (Taunton, 1934).

Wickham, Glynne, *Early English Stages, 1300–1600* (3 vols.; 1959–81).

Wilkinson, B., and Easterling, R. C., *The Medieval Council of Exeter* (Manchester, 1931).

Williams, Glanmore, 'Carmarthen and the Reformation, 1536–1558', *Carmarthenshire Studies* (Carmarthen, 1974), 136–57.

Williams, L. F. R., *The History of St Albans Abbey* (1917).

Williams, Neville, *Thomas Howard, Fourth Duke of Norfolk* (1964).

Williams, Penry, 'Government and Politics in Ludlow, 1590–1642', *Transactions of the Shropshire Archeological Society*, 56 (1957–60), 282–94.

Wolff, B. P., *The Crown Lands, 1461–1536* (1970).

—— *The Royal Demesne in English History* (1971).

Wood-Legh, K. L., *Perpetual Chantries in Britain* (Cambridge, 1965).

Woodward, G. H., 'The Disposal of Chantry Lands in Somerset, 1548–1603', *Southern History*, 5 (1983), 95–114.

Woodward, G. W. O., 'A Speculation in Monastic Lands', *English Historical Review*, 79 (1964), 778–83.

Woolf, D. R., ' "The Common Voice": History, Folklore and Oral Tradition in Early Modern England', *Past and Present*, 120 (Aug. 1988), 26–52.

—— 'Erudition and the Idea of History in Renaissance England', *Renaissance Quarterly*, 40/1 (Spring 1987), 11–47.

—— 'Genre into Artefact: The Decline of the English Chronicle in the Sixteenth Century', *Sixteenth Century Journal*, 19/3 (Fall 1988), 321–54.

—— *The Idea of History in Early Stuart England* (Toronto, 1990).

—— 'Memory and Historical Culture in Early Modern England', *Journal of the Canadian Historical Association*, NS, 2 (1991) 283–308.

—— 'Of Danes and Giants: Some Popular Beliefs about the Past in Early Modern England', *Dalhousie Review*, 71/2 (Summer 1991), 166–209.

Wrightson, Keith, *English Society, 1580–1680* (1982).

—— 'Sorts of People in Tudor and Stuart England', in Jonathan Barry and Christopher Brooks (eds.), *The Middling Sort of People: Culture, Society and Politics in England, 1550–1800* (1995), 28–51.

—— 'Two Concepts of Order: Constables and Jurymen in Seventeenth Century England', in J. Brewer and J. Styles (eds.), *An Ungovernable People* (New Brunswick, NJ, 1980), 21–46.

—— and Levine, David, *Poverty and Piety in an English Village: Terling, 1525–1700* (1979).

Wunderli, Richard, and Broce, Gerald, 'The Final Moment before Death in Early Modern England', *Sixteenth Century Journal*, 20/2 (1989), 259–75.

Wyndham, Katherine, 'The Royal Estate in Mid-Sixteenth Century Somerset', *Bulletin of the Institute of Historical Research*, 52/126 (1979), 129–37.

Youings, Joyce, 'The City of Exeter and the Property of the Dissolved Monasteries', *Transactions of the Devonshire Association*, 84 (1952), 122–41.

—— *The Dissolution of the Monasteries* (1971).

—— 'The Terms of the Disposal of Devon Monastic Lands, 1536–1558', *English Historical Review*, 69 (Jan. 1954), 18–38.

—— 'Tudor Barnstable: A New Life for an Ancient Borough', *Report and Transactions of the Devon Association*, 121 (1989), 1–14.

Zell, Michael, 'The Mid-Tudor Market in Crown Lands in Kent', *Archaeologia Cantiana*, 97 (1982 for 1981), 53–70.

INDEX

Note: Whether indicated in specific instances or not, general headings listing categories of events, activities and characteristics shared by more than one town are listed under the names of specific towns as well as under the general heading.

DATE DUE

			Printed in USA